Lecture Notes in Computer Science

Edited by G. Goos and J. Hartmanis

207

The Analysis
of Concurrent Systems

Cambridge, September 12–16, 1983
Proceedings

Edited by
B.T. Denvir, W.T. Harwood, M.I. Jackson and M.J. Wray

Springer-Verlag
Berlin Heidelberg New York Tokyo

Editors

B. T. Denvir
M. J. Wray
ITT Standard Telecommunication Laboratories Ltd.
London Road, Harlow, Essex EM17 9NA, United Kingdom

W. T. Harwood
M. I. Jackson
Imperial Software Technology Ltd.
Fitzwilliam House, Trumpington Street
Cambridge, CB2 1QY, United Kingdom

CR Subject Classification (1985): D.1.3, D.2.1, D.2.4, F.1.2

ISBN 3-540-16047-7 Springer-Verlag Berlin Heidelberg New York Tokyo
ISBN 0-387-16047-7 Springer-Verlag New York Heidelberg Berlin Tokyo

Printing and binding: Beltz Offsetdruck, Hemsbach/Bergstr.
2145/3140-543210

<u>Erratum page II</u>

The affiliations of the editors should read as follows:

<u>Editors</u>

B.T. Denvir[1], W.T. Harwood[2], M.I. Jackson[1], M.J. Wray[2]
Standard Telecommunication Laboratories Ltd.,
London Road,
Harlow, Essex CM17 9NA
United Kingdom

[1] As from 1 January 1986 B.T. Denvir and M.I. Jackson will be at:
Praxis Systems plc.,
20 Manvers Street,
Bath, BA1 1PX,
United Kingdom

[2] W.T. Harwood and M.J. Wray are now at:
Imperial Software Technology Ltd.,
Fitzwilliam House,
Trumpington Street,
Cambridge, Cambs CB2 1QY,
United Kingdom

Lecture Notes in Computer Science, Vol. 207
The Analysis of Concurrent Systems. Edited by
B.T. Denvir, W.T. Harwood, M.I. Jackson and M.J. Wray
© Springer-Verlag Berlin Heidelberg 1985

FOREWORD

This volume contains the Proceedings of a Workshop on the Analysis of Concurrent Systems held at Clare College, Cambridge from 13th to 16th September 1983. It also contains papers presented at an associated Tutorial on the same topic, held on 12th September 1983. The events were organised by Standard Telecommunication Laboratories Limited (STL), the research centre of STC plc., with additional financial support from the UK Science and Engineering Research Council and the Department of Trade and Industry.

In organising the workshop, STL perceived the following objectives:-

> to improve the understanding of the relationships among the different theories of concurrency and, if possible, to attain a unifying view of them. This increased understanding is a prerequisite for the foundations of better engineering disciplines which will lead ultimately to more dependable products;

> to increase the awareness in industry of such theories in order to accelerate their acceptance and exploitation;

> to expose the (largely) academic researchers to the requirements of industrial software developers in order to focus future research efforts.

The event comprised three parts: A one-day Tutorial, open to industrial and academic delegates, at which the main types of concurrency theory were presented; a four day Workshop; and a half-day Debriefing on the Workshop presented to attendees of the Tutorial.

The workshop was cast in the format of a collection of ten problems which were circulated to the participants prior to the event. At the workshop the participants discussed and compared their solutions. These proceedings include the four Tutorial papers (section 2), a presentation of the problems (section 3), and the solutions provided by the participants (section 4). The editors have composed the Introduction (section 1) and their view of some Conclusions (section 5). It should be emphasised that the views expressed in the Conclusions are those of the STL organising committee, and are not necessarily shared by other participants and contributors.

The STL organising committee consisted of: B.T.Denvir, M.I.Jackson, P.M.Taylor (now at Brighton Polytechnic), W.T.Harwood and M.J.Wray (both now at Imperial Software Technology). They wish to acknowledge and thank Standard Telecommunication Laboratories Limited, the U.K. Science and Engineering Research Council, and the U.K. Department of Trade and Industry for making the workshop possible by their sponsorship, and most of all the participants for making it a success by their skill and efforts in addressing the workshop problems. The committee is also grateful to Messrs. B.S. Jackson and T.A. Cox of STL, Prof. B. Cohen of the University of Surrey, and Prof. C.B. Jones of the University of Manchester for their valuable assistance, to Mrs. M.P. Eden of STL for her efficient secretarial and administrative support, and finally to the staff of Clare College for their hospitality in surroundings of pleasant and historical ambience.

CONTENTS

1. INTRODUCTION

1.1 Background

This volume contains the Proceedings of a Workshop on the Analysis of Concurrent Systems held at Clare College, Cambridge from 13th to 16th September 1983. It also contains papers presented at an associated Tutorial on the same topic, held on 12th September 1983. The events were organised by Standard Telecommunication Laboratories Limited (STL), with additional financial support from the UK Science and Engineering Research Council and the Department of Trade and Industry.

The Workshop came about as a result of the continuing research pro- gramme into software engineering methods which has been in progress at STL since 1977. To focus work in this area, an international symposium on formal development methods was organised by STL and took place in Cambridge in 1979. At this symposium, the proponents of a number of proprietary methods (MASCOT, Wellmade, JSP, Hos, Gamma) presented their approaches and exposed them to comparative discussion. The event proved highly stimulating and influenced the STL group to concentrate on mathematically formal approaches as the basis of an engineering discipline for software development.

The advantages of formal approaches are considered to be:-

    improved specifications and designs for which behavioural proper- ties of systems can be precisely stated;

    support for reasoning about systems through formal analysis;

    a basis for (potentially) much more powerful support environments than exist today.

In the last few years the activities in STL have been directed at reviewing various approaches to formalism, trying out promising tech- niques in laboratory applications and transferring mature methods into development environments. For the latter purpose, the Vienna Develop- ment Method (VDM) has been chosen.

Currently mature methods, useful as they are, do not adequately address all aspects of concurrent systems - i.e. systems composed of separate sequential information processing systems (or 'processes') which need to synchronise or communicate in various ways.

Industry regularly designs and manufacturers engineering products which comprise concurrent processes. To design a product to produce success- ful results one must be assured that the component processes combine in adequate ways: for example, they must never reach a 'deadly embrace', they must not halt as a result of competing for an insufficient resource, and no individual process may be 'starved' by the continual execution of other processes. Indeed, one wishes to be assured that the behaviour of the individual processes will combine to give a desir- able behaviour of the whole. Trends such as the move to distributed systems, computer networks and exploitation of parallelism in system architecture, exacerbate the already difficult problems in this area.

The techniques used to date in industry for the specification and design of concurrent systems have been somewhat ad hoc, even if systematic. Techniques such as MASCOT or the CCITT SDL, for example, essentially consist of a standard kit of components out of which one may construct concurrent systems. No analytical technique is provided for demonstrating that a constructed design will exhibit a given stated behaviour (nor, for that matter, a means of stating such behaviour).

This imposes severe limitations on the confidence we can have in the reliability of the concurrent systems we are building. Since electronics and embedded computers are being deployed in an ever increasing range of critical applications (navigation, traffic control, on-board air and space vehicles, telecommunications), there is an urgent need to improve the confidence we can justifiably hold in these types of engineering product.

Sound engineering disciplines have to be based on tried and well-founded scientific theories, and such theories can take years to develop and refine. For sequential systems, a number of theories have matured and are starting to form the basis of development methods for actual products. However, there are a variety of emergent theories of the behaviour of concurrent systems. They do not compete, but rather are different perspectives of the phenomena of communicating processes. What is not yet achieved is a unifying view of these theories: how they relate to each other, and when it is best to use one formalism rather than another to describe a given system.

These considerations led STL to organise the Workshop on the Analysis of Concurrent Systems, with the following objectives:-

> to improve the understanding of the relationships among the different theories of concurrency and, if possible, to attain a unifying view of them. This increased understanding is a prerequisite for the foundations of better engineering disciplines which will lead ultimately to more dependable products;

> to increase the awareness in industry of such theories in order to accelerate their acceptance and exploitation;

> to expose the (largely) academic researchers to the requirements of industrial software developers in order to focus future research efforts.

1.2 Organisation

It was decided to organise an event with three parts: A one-day Tutorial, open to industrial and academic delegates, at which the main types of concurrency theory were presented; the four day Workshop; and a half-day Debriefing at which the outcome of the Workshop was presented to attendees of the Tutorial.

The participants of the Workshop were individually invited and included twenty-seven of the leading experts in theories of concurrent systems. Four of these participants made presentations during the Tutorial. A further twelve participants were from UK industrial organisations and helped to monitor and record the work done in the Workshop.

During the four-day Workshop the academic participants applied their various theories to the task of defining and analysing a number of problems which had been distributed in advance. The Workshop was divided into parallel sessions in which each problem was discussed, and participants presented their solutions. The STL organising committee and the other industrial participants acted as chairmen and rapporteurs for the sessions.

These problems had been carefully chosen to represent the essential characteristics of concurrency typical of systems which industrial engineering houses are called upon to design.

The final session of the three-part event was a half-day Debriefing of the Workshop to which all the attendees at the Tutorial were invited. The Debriefing was a preliminary and superficial assessment of the Workshop and is superseded by these proceedings and the work which led up to them. The Debriefing will therefore not be discussed further in this volume.

1.3   The Tutorial

The Tutorial was aimed at those analysts and computer scientists in either academia or industry who are concerned with concurrent systems, their specification, design and correctness. The objective of the Tutorial was to give attendees an insight into the trends of current theoretical development which may provide the underpinning of tomorrow's engineering design strategies for concurrent systems.

The Tutorial set the groundwork for the Workshop, by explaining to delegates the relevance of the event to the design and development of engineering systems, and by giving an exposition of four different approaches to the analysis and description of concurrent systems. The four main talks in the Tutorial elucidated samples of each of four of the different classes of approach to Concurrency, namely Algebraic, Net Theoretic, Temporal Logic and Axiomatic. There is some overlap between these classifications, and they are not exhaustive in that some of the approaches do not fall easily into any of these groups. However, they form a workable division of the approaches which are currently being investigated.

The speakers were:

   A.J.R.G. Milner (Edinburgh University)
   Dr. P.S. Thiagarajan (GMD Bonn, now at the
      University of Aarhus)
   Dr. L. Lamport (SRI International)
   Dr. J.R. Abrial (ex. Programming Research Group,
      Oxford University)

Their tutorial papers are reproduced in Section 2 of this volume (N.B. Dr.L.Lamport presented material published by his colleagues R.W.Schwartz & P.M.Melliar-Smith).

1.4   The Workshop

Prior to the event, a set of ten problems was devised and briefly documented. These were circulated to the participants in advance, and voting slips were distributed to try to determine which problems attracted the most interest. The answers to the voting slips indicated that a significant number of participants were interested in each of the problems, and so the whole set of ten was retained for the Workshop.

The following is a summary of the numbers of solutions finally received for each problem:-

		No. of Solutions
Problem 1	Two-way channel with disconnect	13
Problem 2	Simple Network service	5
Problem 3	Synchronising firing squad	3
Problem 4	Railway	6
Problem 5	Array Processor	0
Problem 6	Packet Network with re-routing	3
Problem 7	Parallel combinator reduction machine	4
Problem 8	Mixing Synchronous and Asynchronous input	11
Problem 9	'Cash-point' service	0
Problem 10	m x n matrix switch	3

The problems and their solutions are described in detail in Section 3 of this volume. The Workshop was centred around the presentation and comparative discussion of the various solutions. The Workshop discussions were recorded by rapporteurs drawn from the organising committee and other industrial representatives. Additional sessions were held which addressed the following topics:-

Describing the Notion of Delay in Hardware Systems.

A Unifying Framework for Theories of Concurrency.

Impressions from Industrial Participants.

Section 5 of this volume contains a summary of the conclusions arising from the Workshop.

2. TUTORIAL PAPERS

Using algebra for concurrency : some approaches

Robin Milner

Edinburgh University, September 1983

Introduction

A prominent feature of any algebra is that its expressions, by their
form, either exhibit the structure of the objects which they represent, or
exhibit the way in which those objects were built, or could be built, or
may be viewed.   Often indeed an object does not possess structure, but we
impose structure upon it by our view of it - and thereby understand it
better.   A rectangular array of numbers, for example, is not of itself a
row of columns, nor is it a column of rows;   these are views which we
impose upon it, and any linear expression of such an array will impose some
such biassed view.

So it is no accident that algebra is useful in understanding complex
distributed systems;   for such systems must have many parts (else they would
not be complex), and a structured view is essential in understanding something
with many parts.

In designing an algebra for distributed systems, we are first faced
with an inherent difficulty;   the connectivity of the components is not in
general tree-like, whereas the structure of an algebraic expression is
always tree-like.   It follows that the connectivity of a system is not
expressible merely by the form of an expression.   However, the analysis of
an expression into subexpressions will express the analysis of the system
into subsystems - and the expression will often be chosen in such a way that
the subsystems which are thus identified are physically meaningful, and
possess properties from which properties of the complete system follow
naturally.

A more detailed problem for the algebra is: what is the nature of the
connecting links between subsystems of a distributed system?   In a system
such as the following

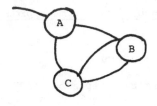

do the arcs represent directed channels carrying data from one node to another, in which case do they have any memory capacity?   Or do they represent simply the contiguity of the objects represented by the connected nodes - an interface across which they exchange an immediate interaction?   And in either case does the forked arc from B to A and C carry a communication between B and <u>both</u> A and C, or does it signify that a single communication occurs between <u>either</u> B and A <u>or</u> B and C but not both?

One modest purpose of this paper is to show that precise answers to these questions can indeed be given by choosing one algebra or another, and that the different choices differ markedly.   In section 2 we look at an algebra in which the arcs represent unbounded queues of data elements. In sections 3 - 6 we look at more primitive (but more general) models in which the arcs are immediate interfaces; in this case the queues of section 2 would themselves be represented by nodes of a particular nature. Another - not so modest - purpose is to illustrate in each case that algebraic proofs of system properties can indeed be carried out.   We have no space either to treat complex examples or to show the full richness of the algebraic theories concerned.   Instead, we hope that readers will find interest in the significance and importance of the fundamental choices in building an algebraic model - namely, fixing the nature of the <u>objects</u>, and fixing the basic <u>operators</u> by which a rich enough class of objects can be built.

In the final section 7, we comment very briefly upon the relation between algebra and other theoretical tools for analysing concurrent systems.

. Pipelining : Kahn networks

A particularly simple and attractive form of concurrency is provided
by the Data flow idea which arose first from the work of Jack Dennis at
MIT and his group, but was first put on an algebraic footing by Gilles Kahn -
first at Stanford and then at IRIA (now INRIA) near Paris.

Simple networks are considered in which each node receives a
(possibly infinite) sequence of values along each of zero or more input
lines, and delivers such a sequence along zero or more output lines.   If
an output line serves more than one succeeding node, then its values go to
all of them.   There may be loops in the network, and typically some lines
are designated as inputs and outputs of the entire network.   An example is
shown below, in which the nodes are uninterpreted

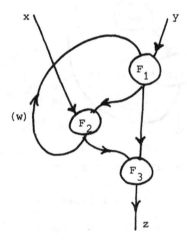

Now in this network, the node F_2 may be interpreted as a function of two
input sequences, yielding one output sequence; the other nodes similarly.

The question is: given the functions F_1, F_2 and F_3, how may we
express the function represented by the entire network, which takes input
sequences x and y and yields output sequence z ?   The answer is gained
simply by introducing an unknown w standing for the sequence of values
which travel along the single arc which loops back form F_2 to F_1.   For
then the output of F_1 is $F_1(w,y)$ - a sequence - and this is fed into F_2,
so that w satisfies the equation

$$w = F_2(x, F_1(w,y))$$

and it can be shown that under simple conditions there is a unique solution to this equation - though depending on F_1 and F_2 it may be an infinite, finite or even empty sequence. Finally, since F_3 receives as inputs w and $F_1(w,y)$, the output z is given by

$$z = F_3(w, F_1(w,y))$$

As a more concrete example, consider the following net S_1 (with no input lines and one output line). We can calculate that it generates the sequence $S_1 = 1.2.3. \cdots$ of all positive integers.

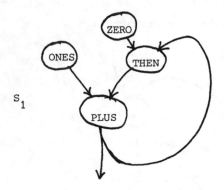

To do this, we must first interpret the four nodes:

ZERO = 0.ε   (a zero, followed by the empty sequence ε)

ONES = 1.ONES   (the infinite sequence of ones)

THEN(x,y) = first(x).y (the sequence y preceded by the first member of the sequence x)

PLUS(x,y) = (first(x) + first(y)).PLUS(rest(x),rest(y))
                        (adds the pairs of inputs, one by one)

Note that any sequence x can be split into its leading member first(x) and its remaining sequence rest(x). Now the sequence S_1 generated by the whole net clearly satisfies

$$S_1 = \text{PLUS(ONES, THEN(ZERO}, S_1))\tag{1}$$

Now we can begin computing S_1 as follows:

$$S_1 = \text{PLUS(ONES, THEN}(0.\varepsilon, S_1))$$

$$= \text{PLUS}(1.\text{ONES}, 0.S_1)$$

$$= 1.\text{PLUS(ONES}, S_1)\tag{2}$$

To go further, let's define inductively

$$S_{k+1} = \text{PLUS(ONES}, S_k) \quad (k = 1, 2, \ldots)\tag{3}$$

If we can show that for all $k \geq 1$

$$S_k = k.S_{k+1}\tag{4}$$

then we have what we want, for it will follow that

$$S_1 = 1.S_2 = 1.2.S_3 = 1.2.3.S_4 = \ldots$$

$$= 1.2.3. \ldots$$

So let us prove (4) by induction on k. It certainly holds for $k = 1$, since $S_1 = 1.S_2$ follows from (2) and (3); so now assume that (4) holds at k, and prove it at $k + 1$:

$$
\begin{aligned}
S_{k+1} &= \text{PLUS(ONES}, S_k) && \text{by definition of } S_{k+1}\\
&= \text{PLUS}(1.\text{ONES}, k.S_{k+1}) && \text{by assumption}\\
&= (k+1).\text{PLUS(ONES}, S_{k+1}) && \text{by PLUS}\\
&= (k+1).S_{k+2} && \text{by definition of } S_{k+2}
\end{aligned}
$$

which is what we wanted.

Nets of this kind can, in a very succinct manner, compute interesting and nontrivial functions. Wadge (in his work on LUCID) and others have given many examples, and the proofs can always be carried out in the above algebraic style - which is definitely a mathematical style rather than a specialised program-proof methodology.

Certainly the nets exhibit a form of concurrency and communication,
namely "pipelining" ; what are their limitations? First, the model
and the proof method become considerably more complex as soon as the
nodes are not assumed to be determinate - or at least not fully described
as functions; an example of a non-determinate node is the MERGE

in which it is known that z contains all members of x and of y
in the right order, but interleaved in an unspecified manner (e.g. according
to order of arrival, which is not specified in the model).   Such non-
determinism can be very useful.   Second, the model attains its simplicity
partly by omitting one feature of behaviour which we may sometimes wish
to take into account, namely the relative order in which the input elements
are received and the output elements delivered in a network.   For -
considering our first illustrated net with nodes F_1, F_2 and F_3 - the solution
which determines z as a function of x and y does not indicate how many
elements from x and y are absorbed before the first, second,... element
of z is generated.

A third limitation is that any realization or implementation of the
model will require unbounded memory capacity to represent the queues of values
which build up on internal arcs of a network.   It is important to be able to
ignore this detail at a high level of modelling, but if memory capacity is to
be modelled then the Kahn networks are not the appropriate tool.

To achieve a general model of communicating agents which removes these
limitations involves, apparently, a totally different approach.   We illustrate
one such approach - but emphasize that the purity of the Kahn model should
tempt us to use the latter whenever we can accept its limitations.

3. Interacting agents

We look now at an algebraic way of presenting agents which interact
with other agents linked to them.   A convenient simplification, to begin
with, is to treat interaction as neither input nor output of values, but
as a symmetric handshake between two (or perhaps more) agents;   its
occurrence carries no value from one agent to another, but merely means
that <u>something</u> (e.g. a high voltage pulse) rather than <u>nothing</u> has occurred.
Each agent - which may be realised by one or many processors - carries sites
or ports on its periphery at which such events may occur;   a Greek letter
may be conveniently used both to name a port and to stand for an event
occurring at that port.   Here is an agent with two ports:

If we wish P to be an agent which alternates between α and β events,
then it may be defined by the equation

$$P = \alpha.\beta.P$$

Of course, by expanding this, we can obtain

$$P = \alpha.\beta.\alpha.\beta.\alpha. \cdots$$

showing that the order of events (here, a strict alternation) at different
ports is indeed recorded.   A slightly more complex agent

which alternately performs <u>either</u> α_1 <u>or</u> α_2 , then β , may be defined
by the equation

$$Q = \alpha_1.\beta.Q + \alpha_2.\beta.Q$$

(which may be abbreviated by $Q = (\alpha_1 + \alpha_2).\beta.Q)$;   here the binary operator
"+" between agent expressions indicates that either arm may be entered,
but not both, during a computation.   Thus we already have two operations
on agent expressions;   summation - meaning disjunction - and the prefixing
$(\alpha.)$ of an atomic action at a particular port.

Typically, an agent P will have the form

$$P = \Sigma(\alpha_i.P_i)$$

where i ranges over some set, indicating the possible next actions of P.

We will not yet deal with how to stick agents together to form bigger agents; even with the slender resources introduced so far we can represent the handling of data values.   For suppose we wish an agent

to represent a buffer with capacity one, alternately receiving values in ℕ (non-negative integers) at port α and delivering them at β .   We may do this by taking α to stand not for a single port, but for a family $\{\alpha_i | i \in ℕ\}$ of ports, one for each value; likewise β .   Then our buffer can be defined

$$B = \sum_{i\in ℕ} (\alpha_i.\beta_i.B)$$

A convenient notation for this (avoiding writing Σ too often) is gained by introducing variables x,y,... over ℕ - or whatever data domain is appropriate - and taking the first occurrence of such a variable to imply summation over ℕ :

$$B = \alpha x.\beta x.B$$

A rather different - but equally simple - agent with two ports is a storage register which can be assigned a value at α and can deliver its current value at β :

The parameter v in R(v) indicates the current value stored in the register, and - using a variable as indicated above - we can define R(v) thus:

$$R(v) = \alpha x.R(x) + \beta v.R(v)$$

The importance of this example is that the formalism can treat both
passive agents — e.g. memory — and active agents on exactly the same
footing.   This is valuable in many applications;   if we consider the
systolic arrays discussed by Mead and Conway, for example, then we find
agents where memory capacity and processing power are united in the same
element, and it would be irksome to have these roles treated by different
notations.

It is often helpful to represent the possible "courses of action"
of an agent graphically.   For this purpose we can use a <u>derivation tree</u>.
If we expand the agent Q , given above, a little way, then we get

$$Q = \alpha_1 . \beta . (\alpha_1 . \beta . Q + \alpha_2 . \beta . Q) + \alpha_2 . \beta . (\alpha_1 . \beta . Q + \alpha_2 . \beta . Q)$$

and we can conceive the indefinite expansion by the tree

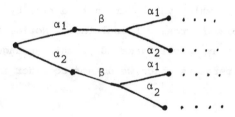

Such a tree represents both the action sequences which are possible
(these are the paths of the tree) and the possible alternatives at each
point in an execution (these are the branches from a node).

One final point before considering the composition of agents:
the treatment so far is ambiguous in the sense that it has not been
determined whether our agents are synchronous (forced to do something
at every tick of a universal clock) or asynchronous (able to wait indefinately
until an interaction is expected or demanded by the environment).   Operators
which <u>compose</u> agents cannot remain uncommitted in this sense;   from now on we
shall adopt the second (asynchronous) alternative, but here remark that a
synchronous calculus is equally possible.

4.   Product of agents

The focal point of an algebra of concurrent communicating agents, such as we are discussing, is undoubtedly the choice of an operator (a kind of product) which puts together two agents to make a single agent, whose behaviour reflects both the independent actions of each component and also their mutual interaction.

Let us consider two agents P and Q , which are buffer-like (as our very first example):

$$P = \alpha.\beta.P \qquad\qquad Q = \beta.\gamma.Q$$

We revert to the simple form in which values are not carried by handshakes, but the addition of values poses no real difficulties.   Notice that we have arranged P and Q to share a port name β ; this arrangement can be made by using "renaming" operators which we do not consider in this paper.

Now following the method of Hoare and his group, and also of George Milne, we wish to "multiply" P and Q together to form an agent which may be pictured

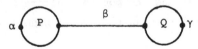

in which the actions α and γ may occur independently, but the action β may only occur (as "interaction") when both P and Q are capable of it. Let us denote this product operator by $\&_\beta$ — we may call it $\underline{\beta\text{-synchronization}}$. There will be such an operator $\&_\alpha$ for any action α , and in general we may wish to use $\&_A$, $\underline{A\text{-synchronization}}$, for any set A of actions.   Sticking to $\&_\beta$, and recalling that we wish to consider agents expressed in the form $\Sigma\alpha_i.P_i$, what equation should be satisfied by

$$(\Sigma\, \alpha_i.P_i) \ \&_\beta \ (\Sigma\,\gamma_j.Q_j) \qquad\qquad ?$$

The product agent should be able to do any α_i which is $\neq \beta$, <u>or</u> any γ_j which is $\neq \beta$, <u>or</u> β itself provided $\alpha_i = \beta = \gamma_j$ for some i and some j . So we propose :

If $P \equiv \Sigma(\alpha_i.P_i)$ and $Q \equiv \Sigma(\gamma_j.Q_j)$,

then $P \&_\beta Q =$

$$\sum_{\alpha_i \neq \beta} \alpha_i.(P_i \&_\beta Q) \quad + \quad \sum_{\gamma_j \neq \beta} \gamma_j.(P \&_\beta Q_j)$$

$$+ \quad \sum_{\alpha_i = \gamma_j = \beta} \beta.(P_i \&_\beta Q_j)$$

The first and second sums represent the independent actions of P and Q respectively, while the third represents their interactions for all pairs i,j such that $\alpha_i = \beta = \gamma_j$. Such a general equation may be less easy to understand than a particular case, so let us calculate $P \&_\beta Q$ for our particular case in which $P = \alpha.\beta.P$ and $Q = \beta.\gamma.Q$. We proceed as follows:

$$P \&_\beta Q = \alpha.(\beta.P) \&_\beta \beta.(\gamma.Q)$$

$$= \alpha.(\beta.P \&_\beta \beta.(\gamma.Q)) \tag{1}$$

Here we have used the product rule once, noting that the only possible first action is α performed by P , since P cannot yet allow Q to perform β . Now we shall be able to find some equations which determine the behaviour $P \&_\beta Q$, for we have

$$\beta.P \&_\beta \beta.(\gamma.Q) = \beta.(P \&_\beta \gamma.Q)$$

$$= \beta.(\alpha.\beta.P \&_\beta \gamma.Q)$$

$$= \beta.(\alpha.(\beta.P \&_\beta \gamma.Q) + \gamma.(\alpha.\beta.P \&_\beta Q)) \tag{2}$$

(this step reflects independent action by either component).

Also,

$$\beta.P \&_\beta \gamma.Q = \gamma.(\beta.P \&_\beta Q)$$

$$= \gamma.(\beta.P \&_\beta \beta.\gamma.Q) \tag{3}$$

while $\alpha.\beta.P \&_\beta Q$ is just the original $P \&_\beta Q$.

If we put (1), (2) and (3) together, and write R for $(P \&_\beta Q)$ and S for $(\beta.P \&_\beta \beta.\gamma.Q)$, we get the simple equations

$$R = \alpha.S$$

$$S = \beta.(\alpha.\gamma.S + \gamma.\alpha.S) \tag{4}$$

Apparently, then, our composite agent R first performs α, then
repeatedly performs β followed by α and γ in either order.   In
this simple case at least, we have been able to deduce a product-free
description of the product of two agents;   the equations (4) might have
been written down to describe the behaviour of a single agent R with
three ports:

Such transformations of description are the essence of the algebraic approach.
It may be compared with the algebra of regular expressions, which describe
the behaviour of finite automata in classical automata theory.   But automata
theory failed to provide a notion of product which was adequate to express
how two concurrent automata can interact.

    At this point, we should ask whether our product P &$_β$ Q has given us
what we want.   On the one hand, we note that it could again be   " β-synchronized
with yet another agent, T say, which is also capable of performing β   from
time to time.   The resulting agent P &$_β$ Q &$_β$ T could be pictured as follows

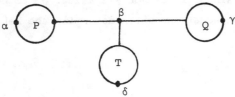

which reflects that the action β will only be performed when all three agents
are capable of it;   thus β-synchronization permits us to model multi-way
(not just two-way) handshakes.   In passing, we note that it is easy to show
that &$_β$ is both commutative and associative, that is:

$$P \,\&_β\, (Q \,\&_β\, T) \;=\; (P \,\&_β\, Q) \,\&_β\, T$$

$$P \,\&_β\, Q \;=\; Q \,\&_β\, P$$

and such algebraic laws are essential in a smooth calculus.

    On the other hand, we may have wished something different for the
product of P and Q.   For we may argue that the intermediate port β
sould serve only for interaction between P and Q, and that it should not

be visible or accessible outside the product.   In other words, we look
for a form of product in which the only remaining visible actions are
α   and γ .

Following Hoare and Milne, we choose to achieve this not by modifying
the product, but by introducing an operation called _hiding_ which may be
applied to any agent to conceal some of its actions.   Specifically, if
R   is some agent possibly capable of performing   β   from time to time,
then

$$R/\beta$$

will represent   R's   behaviour with all   β   actions omitted.   (Of course
we have operators   "/α"   for all actions   α , and operators   "/A"   for all
sets   A   of actions.)   Thus, instead of forming the product   R = P &   Q
of our two agents, we shall often prefer to form the _hidden_ product
R' = (P &$_\beta$ Q) /β ;   looking back at equations (4) above, we shall expect
R'   to satisfy instead the equations

$$R' = \alpha.S'$$
$$S' = \alpha.\gamma.S' + \gamma.\alpha.S' \tag{4'}$$

— i.e. the hidden product first performs   α , and thereafter repeatedly
performs   α   and   γ   in either order.   We shll not give the exact definition
of the hiding operators here;   it requires refinements which would take up
too much space.

There are variants of the product operators   &$_\alpha$ and   &$_A$.   Instead
of pursuing them further, we shall now look briefly at an alternative
originally introduced by the author;   it has an advantage over the above
in that just one product operator is required, in place of a family of
operators indexed by actions   α   or by sets   A   of actions, but a disadvantage
(in the form given here) that it models only two-way (not multi-way) handshakes.
Part of the purpose of describing two approaches in this paper is to dispel
the tempting impression that there is one clearly best algebra of concurrent
processes.

5.   An alternative agent product

To define an alternative product, we make a new assumption, namely that for every action α there exists an <u>inverse</u> action $\bar{\alpha}$, and that an interaction may occur between two agents whenever they may perform inverse actions.   Moreover, this interaction constitutes for the product agent a distinguished action — denoted by the symbol τ — which we may call the <u>silent</u> action.   By this means we can get away with just a single operator, called <u>composition</u> and denoted by "$|$", in place of the family $\&_\beta$ of operators — though (as here presented) we thereby sacrifice multi-way handshakes and retain only two-way handshakes.

Let us treat the same example as before:

$$P = \alpha.\beta.P \qquad\qquad Q = \bar{\beta}.\gamma.Q$$

(Note that we have named one of Q's ports inversely to one of P's ports, to make the product work).   Rather than writing down a general equation for the product $(\Sigma\alpha_i.P_i) \mid (\Sigma\gamma_j.Q_j)$, we shall state the rule informally: the next action of $P|Q$ can be <u>either</u> an action which is possible for P or Q independently, <u>or</u> a τ action if P and Q can perform inverse actions.

We now begin to compute $P|Q$:

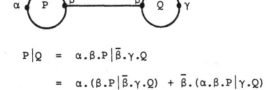

$$\begin{aligned}
P|Q &= \alpha.\beta.P|\bar{\beta}.\gamma.Q \\
&= \alpha.(\beta.P|\bar{\beta}.\gamma.Q) + \bar{\beta}.(\alpha.\beta.P|\gamma.Q)
\end{aligned}$$

No inverse actions were possible (hence no τ action results) on this first step.   But the second term, which was absent when we worked out $P \&_\beta Q$, represents the possibility that Q's $\bar{\beta}$ action may be complemented by a β-action performed not by P but by some further agent P' to be added later.   In other words, systems like

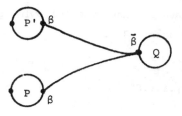

can be formed by this product operation, representing how Q may interact with <u>either</u> P <u>or</u> P' (but not both) through the same port. There is a disjunctive quality in " $|$ " which contrasts with the conjunctive quality of " $\&_\beta$ ".

If we were to proceed further in computing $P|Q$ we would get a rapid expansion; for example, for one of the terms we would get

$$\beta.P|\bar{\beta}.\gamma.Q \;=\; \beta.(P|\bar{\beta}.\gamma.Q) \;+\; \tau.(P|\gamma.Q) \;+\; \bar{\beta}.(\beta.P|\gamma.Q)$$

since the three possibilities of <u>independent</u> action by either component, and <u>interaction</u>, are all present.

But we can avoid so much expansion by using an analogue to the hiding operator. This time, we require something a little different; we use an operator $\diagdown\beta$ called <u>restriction</u>. The effect of $R\diagdown\beta$ is to discard from R all alternatives (appearing as summands of R) which begin with either β or $\bar{\beta}$. This means that the only use of these actions within R is to permit interaction between different components of R (yielding τ actions for R itself).

Let us now compute, not $P|Q$, but $R'' = (P|Q)\diagdown\beta$:

$$R'' = (\alpha.\beta.P|\bar{\beta}.\gamma.Q)\diagdown\beta$$

$$= \alpha.(\beta.P|\bar{\beta}.\gamma.Q)\diagdown\beta$$

$$= \alpha.\tau.(P|\gamma.Q)\diagdown\beta$$

At each step, alternatives involving uncomplemented actions β or $\bar{\beta}$ have been discarded. We now compute $S'' = (P|\gamma.Q)\diagdown\beta$:

$$S'' = (\alpha.\beta.P|\gamma.Q)\diagdown\beta$$

$$= \alpha.(\beta.P|\gamma.Q)\diagdown\beta + \gamma.R''$$

$$= \alpha.\gamma.(\beta.P\ Q)\diagdown\beta + \gamma.R''$$

$$= \alpha.\gamma.\tau.S'' + \gamma.\alpha.\tau.S''$$

Putting these together, we have obtained the following product-free
description of our composite agent R" :

$$R" = \alpha.\tau.S"$$

$$S" = \alpha.\gamma.\tau.S" + \gamma.\alpha.\tau.S" \tag{4"}$$

If we compare this with the equations (4') in the previous section, we
see that the only difference is in the presence of some τ actions, which
are so to speak traces of internal communications.   In fact, there is
mathematical justification for the algebraic law

$$\alpha.\tau.P = \alpha.P$$

(for arbitrary α and P), and this law removes all difference between
(4') and (4")!

There is a pleasant duality between the pair of operators $(\&_\beta , /\beta)$
on the one hand, and the pair $(\mid , \diagdown\beta)$ on the other:

$\&_\beta$ (β synchronization) <u>demands</u> certain interactions;

/β (β hiding) <u>releases</u> β from further synchronization demands;

while

$\mid$ (composition) <u>permits</u> both independent action and interaction;

$\diagdown\beta$ (β restriction) <u>inhibits</u> certain uncomplemented actions.

In both cases, the lesson learned is that a pleasant algebraic treatment
is obtained by separating the synthesis of concurrent agents into two phases:
a product operation which takes account of their interaction, and an
encapsulation operation which prevents external access to internal interfaces.
The importance of the separation is that a binary product operation can be
applied repeatedly - to link an arbitrary number of agents together — before
applying an encapsulation operation to "enclose" the composed system.

6. A bigger example

Consider the following system:

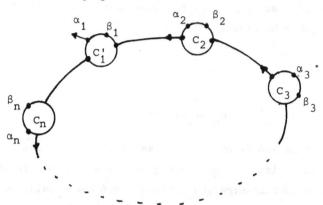

It consists of a ring of n identical agents, each waiting for a communication from its predecessor in the circular order (as indicated by the little arrows). except for C_1' which is waiting for a communication on its a_1 port. It is intended to act as a distributed scheduler for n independent agents $P_1, \ldots, P_n$ (not shown). P_i will be connected to C_i at both ports α_i and β_i; P_i requests (at α_i) to initiate a certain activity, and indicates (at β_i) when it has completed the activity. The scheduling discipline is as follows:

    (1) Requests are treated in cyclic order, starting with P_1;

    (2) Each P_i must alternate between α_i and β_i — i.e.
         it cannot be running more than one instance of the activity
         at any time.

It is quite easy to define the agents C_i, and then to put them all together, using either product operator; moreover, the algebraic proof that the resulting system has the two desired properties is not hard. If we are going to use the second form of agent product, then we will define C_i as follows:

$$C_i = \bar{\gamma}_i \cdot C_i'$$

$$C_i' = \alpha_i \cdot (\gamma_{i+1} \cdot \beta_i \cdot C_i + \beta_i \cdot \gamma_{i+1} \cdot C_i)$$

(where subscript addition is modulo n)

Intuitively, c_i first learns (at $\bar{\gamma}_i$) from his predecessor that he may now grant a request (at α_i) ; after that request he then transmits request permission (at γ_{i+1}) and receives termination signal (at β_i) in either order; then he repeats.

It is not hard to see that this system works. In fact, the scheduler is expressed as

$$S = (c_1^{\cdot}|c_2| \cdots |c_n)\diagdown\gamma_1\diagdown\gamma_2 \cdots \diagdown\gamma_n$$

and the formulation and proof that S satisfies properties like (1) and (2) above is not difficult. It has been given as an example in the author's book "A Calculus of Communicating Systems", and can equally well be treated using the operators $(\&_\beta, /\beta)$ instead of $(|, \diagdown\beta)$.

Conclusion

This short introduction to an algebraic approach to concurrency has necessarily omitted some intricate details, as well as paying no attention to other algebraic approaches (for example, Vaughan Pratt has suggested an approach which generalises the Kahn networks in a different manner). What we hope to have shown is that four kinds of operator - namely atomic action $(\alpha.)$, summation $(+)$, product $(\&_\beta$ or $|$) and encapsulation $(/\beta$ or $\diagdown\beta)$ - together give great expressive power, and moreover satisfy interesting algebraic identities.

In a methodology for proof about particular systems, we almost certainly need more than "just" algebra. With algebra, we can typically prove equations between agent expressions; we often wish also to prove that an agent possesses some property which is not expressible by an equation. It is therefore important to look at the relation between such algebras and logics - Temporal or Modal logics - designed to express interesting properties of processes.

Another important relationship to study is between the algebraic approach and Net Theory. The emphases of these models are different; communication is the cornerstone of the algebra (in the present approach), while Net Theory emphasizes causal independence, provides a totally different graphical aid to intuition, and provides different tools for abstraction.

Finally, synchronous systems demand some form of treatment.   The
author has found one way of integrating the above asynchronous algebra
with an algebra of synchronous (clocked) systems; this method has some
mathematical simplicity - for example, the algebra becomes more conventional,
being at least a semi-ring (with agent sum and product as the semi-ring
operations) - but is by no means obviously the best integration possible.

Some Aspects of Net Theory

P.S. Thiagarajan[*]
GMD, Schloß Birlinghoven
5205 St. Augustin
W. Germany

0. Introduction

Net theory deals with distributed systems and processes. The essential tool
employed by the theory to study systems is called a marked net. A process
can be viewed as a special kind of a system. Hence in what follows we discuss
just systems in terms of marked nets.

A marked net is a (directed) net together with a marking of the net. The
net part represents the structure of the system under study. The marking
represents a state - often the initial state - of the system.

A net may be viewed as a directed bipartite graph composed out of two kinds
of nodes called S-elements and T-elements. S-elements are used to denote
local atomic states. T-elements are used to denote local changes-of-states-
(i.e. transitions). The directed arcs capture the neighbourhood relationship between the S-elements and T-elements.

A marking of a net is a distribution of objects called tokens over the
S-elements of the net. In this sense, a state of the system is a distributed entity. Wherein the tokens do not have any internal structure and
hence can not be distinguished from each other, the resulting marked nets
are ofen called Petri nets. As the name suggests, Petri nets were first
proposed by C.A. Petri as a model of concurrent systems in his dissertation [27]. In general though the tokens can have internal structure.
This leads to a variety of powerful system models based on nets [10, 19, 35].

The dynamics of a marked net is specified by a firing rule. It states when
and how the transitions associated with the T-elements can transform the
marking. In general the marking can be transformed by a number of transi-

tions proceeding independently. In this sense a change of state is also a distributed entity.

A sizable part of net theory is devoted to the study of Petri nets. The chief advantage of Petri nets is they provide a simple, abstract and general setting for investigating distributed systems. In particular they provide the means for clearly separating the three fundamental relationships that can exist between the occurrences of two transitions t_1 and t_2 at a state of a system.

(1) t_1 followed by t_2. (sequence, causality)

(2) t_1 or t_2 but not both. (choice, non-determinism)

(3) t_1 and t_2 but with no order (concurrency, non-sequentiality).

The chief disadvantage of Petri nets is a practical one. They yield vast and unstructed descriptions of "real life" systems. To get around this difficulty one must employ marked nets in which the tokens can have internal structure. We shall call such nets - without any present justification - first-order marked nets. As a matter of preference, we shall from now on call Petri nets (where the tokens do not have any structure) just marked nets. A major aim of net theory is to transfer the insights, tools and results developed in the domain of marked nets to first-order marked nets.

We now have touched upon the topics to be adressed in the paper. In the next section we discuss how states and transitions are viewed in net theory. In section 2, we sketch selected parts of the theory of marked nets. The emphasis here is on basic concepts such as choice and concurrency. We point to sub-classes of marked nets obtained through restricted combinations of choice and concurrency. Section 3 presents mainly with the aid of examples, first-order marked nets. We indicate how the transition from marked nets to first-order marked nets can be understood in terms of the transition from propositional logic to first-order logic. In the concluding part of the paper we briefly mention what we have failed to mention in this account of net theory.

1. States and Transitions.

Two ideas determine our view of states and transitions.

(1) Both states and transitions are distributed entities.

(2) States and transitions are two orthogonal concepts that deserve an even-handed treatment.

Set theory can be used to formalise this pair of ideas. We start with a set of local states called <u>conditions</u>. A (distributed) state is a sub-set of conditions; the conditions that hold concurrently at the state. We also postulate a set of local changes-of-states called <u>events</u>. A (distributed) transition is a sub-set of events that can occur concurrently at a state. We demand that conditions and events be disjoint.

In standard terminology the states are called <u>cases</u> and the transitions are called <u>steps</u>. Let $\emptyset \neq B$ be a set of conditions. $C \subseteq \mathcal{P}(B)$ is the set of cases denoting the state space. ($\mathcal{P}(X)$ is the set of sub-sets of the set X). Let c be a case and b a condition. Then b is said to hold at c iff $b \in c$. $\emptyset \neq E$ is the set of events with $B \cap E = \emptyset$. For the cases c and c' and the event e, c [e> c' will denote that e can occur at c to lead to c'.

Suppose c [e> c'. Then the extent of change caused by the occurrence of e at c can be represented as the pair $(c \smallsetminus c', c' \smallsetminus c)$. The conditions in $c \smallsetminus c'$ cease to hold and the conditions in $c' \smallsetminus c$ begin to hold when e occurs at c to lead to c'. A basic assumption of net theory is:

(A1). The extent of change caused by an event occurrence is solely determined by the identity of the event (and not by the state at which it occurs).

Suppose we have c_1[e> c_2 and c_3[e> c_4. Then (A1) demands that $c_1 \smallsetminus c_2 = c_3 \smallsetminus c_4$ and $c_2 \smallsetminus c_1 = c_4 \smallsetminus c_3$. As a result we can associate with each event e, the set of conditions $\dot{}e$ that cease to hold and the set of conditions $e\dot{}$ that begin to hold whenever e occurs. $\dot{}e$ is called the set of <u>pre-conditions</u> and $e\dot{}$ the set of <u>post-conditions</u> of e. Note that $\dot{}e \cap e\dot{} = \emptyset$.

When can e occur c? We write Concess (e,c) to denote that e can occur at c. More precisely,

$$\text{Concess (e,c)} \overset{\text{def}}{\Longleftrightarrow} \exists c' \in C. \ c \ [e> c'.$$

Suppose that Concess (e,c). Then for some c' we must have c[e>c'. This implies that $c \smallsetminus c' = {}^\cdot e$ and $c' \smallsetminus c = e^\cdot$. This in turn implies that ${}^\cdot e \subseteq c$ and $e^\cdot \cap c = \emptyset$. Thus,

$$\text{Concess (e,c)} \rightarrow {}^\cdot e \subseteq c \wedge e^\cdot \cap c = \emptyset.$$

In other words, if e is to occur at c then each pre-condition must hold at c and no post-condition may hold at c. Net theory is devoted to the study of systems in which the above necessary criterion is also sufficient.

(A2) $\qquad$ $\text{Concess (e,c)} \longleftrightarrow {}^\cdot e \subseteq c \wedge e^\cdot \cap c = \emptyset.$

The question we now pose is: When can a set of events u occur concurrently at a case c to lead to the case c'? Extending the notation we already have, the question becomes: When is c[u>c' possible? Intutively, two events can occur concurrently at a case iff the extent of changes caused by the two events involve disjoint sets of conditions. Formally,

(A3) $\quad$ Let c, c' $\in$ C and $\emptyset \neq u \subseteq E$.

$\qquad$ c [u>c' $\leftrightarrow$ (1) $\forall e \in u. \ \text{Concess (e,c)}$.

$\qquad\qquad$ (2) $\forall e_1, e_2 \in u. \ e_1 \neq e_2 \rightarrow ({}^\cdot e_1 \cup e_1^\cdot) \cap ({}^\cdot e_2 \cup e_2^\cdot) = \emptyset$

$\qquad\qquad$ (3) $c \smallsetminus c' = \cup\{{}^\cdot e | e \in u\}$ and $c' \smallsetminus c = \cup\{e^\cdot | e \in u\}$.

(1) States that each event in u can occur individually at c. (2) states that no two events in u "interfere" with each other while carrying out the changes attributed to them. (3) demands that the global change in the state should be the sum of the local changes. The step u is said to occur at c to lead to c' if c[u>c'.

These are the major assumptions made in net theory concerning states and transitions. Some additional assumptions in informal terms are:

(A4) Each event can occur at least at one case.

(A5) C, the state space is connected and closed (forwards and backwards) w.r.t. event occurrences.

(A6) Two events have the same extent of change off they are identical.

A detailed list of such assumptions can be found in [12]. The ideas discussed above originate from [29]. To conclude this section we propose an informal graphical representation of systems that satisfy our requirements.

Structure

Condition b –   (b)

Event   e –   [e]

b ∈ ˙e –   (b)→[e]

b ∈ e˙ –   [e]→(b)

State.

Let c ∈ C.

b ∈ c –   (•)b

b ∉ c –   ( )b

State Transformation (caused by an event occurrence).

Let c[e>c'.

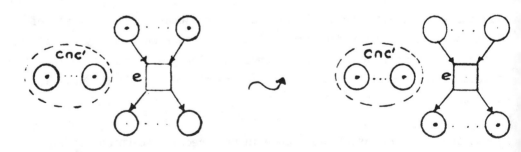

Fig. 1

2. Marked Nets

We shall first introduce marked nets. A restricted version of marked nets calles <u>safe</u> <u>marked</u> <u>nets</u> will reflect our view of states and transitions. Using safe marked nets we shall discuss some of the basic concepts of net theory. Finally we shall point to some sub-classes of marked nets which have a well developed theory.

2.1 Nets

A (directed) net is a triple $N = (S;T;F)$ where

      1) $S \cup T \neq \emptyset$ and $S \cap T = \emptyset$

      2) $F \subseteq (S \times T) \cup (T \times S)$; $\mathrm{dom}(F) \cup \mathrm{range}(F) = S \cup T$.

S is the set of S-elements, T is the set of T-elements and $X = S \cup T$ is the set of <u>elements</u> of N. F is the <u>flow</u> <u>relation</u>. As might be guessed, in diagrams S-elements will be drawn as circles and the T-elements as boxes. The flow relation will be indicated through directed arcs.

For the element x, $\dot{}x = \{y \in X | (y,x) \in F\}$ is the <u>pre-set</u> of x and $x\dot{} = \{y \in X | (x,y) \in F\}$ is the <u>post-set</u> of x. This notation is extended to a sub-set of X in the obvious way. Depending on the application, various interpretations can be attached to S,T and F (see [30]). In this paper we shall use the S-elements to denote local states, the T-elements to denote local transitions and the flow relation to denote the extent of change caused by the local transitions of a system.

Different sub-classes of nets can be obtained by placing suitable restrictions on the flow relation. For example, the net $N = (S,T;F)$ is said to be <u>pure</u> iff for each $x \in X$, $\dot{}x \cap x\dot{} = \emptyset$. Thus in the graphical representation of a pure net, there will be no directed cycles of length 2. The net $N = (S,T;F)$ is said to be <u>simple</u> iff for every two elements x and y, $(\dot{}x = \dot{}y \wedge x\dot{} = y\dot{}) \Rightarrow x = y$. In this section every net we encounter is assumed to be finite (i.e. the set of elements is finite), pure, simple and connected (in the graph theoretic sense). In the latter parts of this section we shall define a few other sub-classes of nets.

2.2 Markings, the Firing Rule and Related Notions.

A state of the system whose structure is given by the net N = (S,T;F) is denoted by a marking of N. A marking of N is a function $M:S \to \{0,1,2,...,\}$. In diagrams M is shown by placing M(S) tokens (small dots) on each s.

A marked net is a quadruple $\Sigma = (S,T;,F,M^O)$ where $N_\Sigma = (S,T;F)$ is a net called the underlying net of Σ. M^O is a marking of N_Σ called the initial marking of Σ. An example of a marked net is shown in fig. 2.

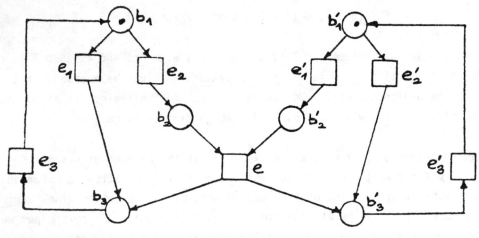

Fig. 2

Let M be a marking of the net N = (S,T;F). The T-element t is enabled at M iff for each $s \in {}^\cdot t$, M(s) > 0. If t is enabled, it may fire. When t fires at M, a new marking M' is obtained where,

$$\forall s \in S. \ M'(s) = \begin{cases} M(s)-1, & \text{if } s \in {}^\cdot t \smallsetminus t^\cdot \\ M(s)+1, & \text{if } s \in t^\cdot \smallsetminus {}^\cdot t \\ M(s), & \text{otherwise.} \end{cases}$$

The transformation of M into M' through the firing of t is denoted as M[t>M'. The state space generated by the marking M of the net N = (S,T;F) is called the forward marking class defined by M. It is represented as

[M>, and is the smallest class of markings of N given by:

1) M ∈ [M>

2) If M' ∈ [M> , t ∈ T and M" is a marking of N with M' [t> M",
   then M" ∈ [M'> .

Liveness and safety are two important behavioural properties of marked nets. Let $\Sigma = (S,T;F,M^0)$ be a marked net.

Σ is <u>live</u> iff for each M ∈ [M^0> and each t ∈ T there exists a M' ∈ [M> such that t is enabled at M'.

Σ is <u>safe</u> iff for each M ∈ [M^0> and each s ∈ S, $M(s) \leq 1$.

In a live marked net no T-element permanently loses the possibility of occuring. In a safe marked net no S-element will ever carry more than one token. Fig. 2 is an example of live and safe marked net.

2.3 Fundamental situations

A safe marked net viewed as a system model reflects our approach to states and transitions outlined in section 1. To see this, consider the safe marked net $\Sigma = (B,E;F,M^0)$. Then every M ∈ [M^0> can be viewed as a sub-set of the set of conditions B; {b ∈ B|M(b) = 1}. In other words [M^0> corresponds to the set of cases. E is the set of events. F may be taken to be a specification of pre-conditions and post-conditions of the events. The firing rule captures (A2). The notion of a step for a safe marked net, guided by (A3) is defined in the obvious way.

Causality, conflict, concurrency and confusion are four basic notions of net theory. They can be brought out with the help of safe marked nets.

<u>Causality</u>

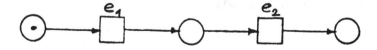

The occurrence of e_2 must be preceded by the occurrence of e_1.

conflict

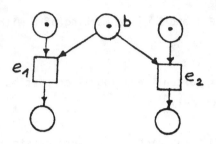

At the marking shown e_1 and e_2 can occur individually. But $\{e_1, e_2\}$ is not a step (due to the shared condition b). Thus either e_1 or e_2 but not both can occur. This is called a _conflict_ situation. Non-determinism enters the picture at this stage because the choice as to whether e_1 occurs or e_2 occurs, is left unspecified.

Concurrency.

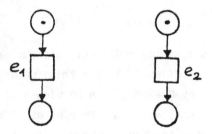

e_1 and e_2 can both occur at the marking shown. Note that no order is specified over the occurrences of the two events. Thus in general, the occurrences of events (and the resulting holdings of conditions) will be _partially ordered_; our systems can also exhibit non-sequential behaviour. We also note that $\{e_1, e_2\}$ and $\{e_2, e_3\}$ being steps at a marking does not necessarily imply that $\{e_1, e_3\}$ is a step at the marking. In the jargon, one says that concurrency is not a transitive relation.

Confusion.

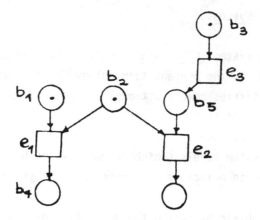

Let $M^0 = \{b_1, b_2, b_3\}$, $M^1 = \{b_4, b_5\}$ so that $M^0[\{e_1, e_3\}> M^1$. Here there could be disagreement (among sequential observes) over whether or not a conflict was resolved in going from M^0 to M^1. Two honest sequential observes O_1 and O_2 could report:

$\underline{O_1}$ e_1 occurred first without being in conflict with any other event. And then e_3 occurred.

$\underline{O_2}$ e_3 occurred first. e_1 and e_2 got into conflict. This conflict was resolved in favour of e_1 which then occurred.

This is a <u>confused</u> situation. Confusion arises whenever conflict and concurrency "overlap". This pheomenon appears to be basic in nature and can not be defined away through temporal assumptions. It we do so, the problem will appear at a lower level of description. In hardware systems the problem is called the glitch problem or more appropriately, the synchronisation failure problem [43]. Below we show a symmetric form of confusion.

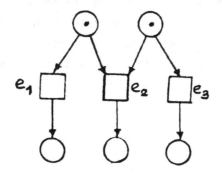

2.4 Condition/Event Systems.

The Condition/Event system (C/E system) model is the elementary system
model of net theory. In the present terminology, a C/E system is a safe
marked net which satisfies some additional axioms. This model is elementary in that it is meant to provide the "semantics" of every other system
model considered in net theory. Stated differently, net theory is concerned with those system models (which do not have to be necessarily based
on nets) that can be in principle, expressed as C/E systems.

Several advantages obtain by basing the net theory of systems and processes on C/E systems. Firstly they can be used to clearly distinguish between phenomena such as causality, conflict, concurrency and confusion.
Here we have instead used the weaker formalism of safe marked nets to keep
the presentation short. Secondly, the language of C/E systems can be augmented in a number of ways without leaving the domain of net theory. Through
these extensions, we can express one class of system invariants with the
aid of propositional logic. A second class of system invariants can be expressed in terms of a metric defined over the event occurrences. We can
also introduce and explain the concepts of information and information flow
with the help of conflict and conflict-resolution. The details can be
found in [11]. (see also [28,33] for motivations). Finally, the non-sequential processes generated by a distributed system can be elegantly defined
using C/E systems. This is the subject of the next sub-section. Once again
for convenience we shall stick to safe marked nets to illustrate the main
ideas.

2.5 Processes.

A process of a system is a record of a run of the system. The non-sequential runs of a safe marked net are best represented by a special kind of
marked nets called marked occurrence nets. To bring this out, consider the
safe marked net of fig. 2. One possible run of this system is shown below.

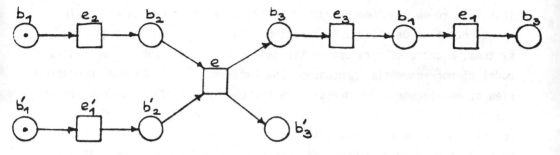

Fig. 3

The idea is to run the system, resolving conflicts (in any arbitrary fashion) as and when they arise while preserving concurrency. If we record the occurrences of events and conditions during such a run a labelled net of the type shown in fig. 3 will be obtained.

In this net each S-element has at most one T-element at the input side. This is because the <u>safe</u> marked net of fig. 2 was exercised. Each S-element has at most one T-element at the output side. This is because all conflicts were resolved one way or the other to obtain this stretch of behaviour. The net is also acyclic. This is due to individually recording each <u>occurrence</u> of the events and conditions. Nets which satisfy these requirements are called occurrence nets. Formally,

An occurrence net is a net $N = (B,E;F)$ in which

1) $\forall b \in B.$ $|{}^{\cdot}b|, |b^{\cdot}| \leq 1.$

2) F^{*}, the relexive transitive closure of F, is a partial ordering relation.

A process of a safe marked net $\Sigma = (B,E;F,M^{0})$ can now be viewed as a mapping pr from the elements $\hat{B} \cup \hat{E}$ of the marked occurrence net $\hat{\Sigma} = (\hat{B},\hat{E};\hat{F},\hat{M}^{0})$ into the elements $B \cup E$ of N_{Σ}. (pr: $\hat{B} \cup \hat{E} \rightarrow B \cup E$). pr must be such that the token game that can be played on $\hat{\Sigma}$ can also be played under the image of pr on Σ.

This is a rough and "non-standard" sketch of what processes of a safe marked net are. Detailed definitions can be found in [11]. Forgetting systems, occurrence nets can be studied in their own right as an abstract model of non-sequential processes. The fundamentals of the net theoretic view of non-sequential processes are set out in [31,32]. A sample of results on occurrence nets can be found in [1, 2, 7]. The study of the relationship between marked nets and their processes has been initiated in [15]. A more general model of processes called event structures have been studied and used in a (denotational) semantic setting [26 , 39 , 40].

2.6 ls S-graphs

We shall now consider three sub-classes of live and safe marked nets. We shall write ls instead of live and safe. Since liveness and safety does not make sense in the absense of markings we will say ls nets instead of ls marked nets. The three sub-classes of ls nets we wish to consider are determined by the type of the underlying nets. Recall that we have agreed to look at only those nets that are finite and connected.

A S-graph is a net $N = (S,T;F)$ in which $\forall t \in T$. $|{}^{\cdot}t|$, $|t^{\cdot}| \leq 1$. A ls S-graph is a ls net $\Sigma = (B,E;F,M^O)$ in which N_Σ is a S-graph. It is easy to verify that the marked S-graph $\Sigma = (B,E;F,M^O)$ (i.e. Σ is a marked net and N_Σ is a S-graph) is live and safe iff N_Σ is strongly connected and $\sum_{s \in S} M^O(s) = 1$. Below we show an example of a ls S-graph.

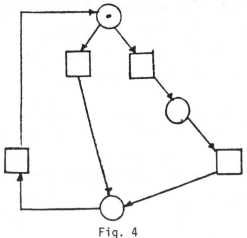

Fig. 4

A 1s S-graph in general can get into conflict situations; it can exhibit non-deterministic behaviour. However no two events can ever occur con-currently. In this sense 1s S-graphs model sequential non-deterministic systems. Automata thery has a good deal to say about these systems. We note that due to the absence of concurrency, 1s S-graphs are free of confusion.

2.7 1s T-graphs

A T-graph is a net $N = (S,T;F)$ in which $\forall s \in S. \ |^{\cdot}s|, \ |s^{\cdot}| \leq 1$. A 1s T-graph is a 1s net $\Sigma = (B,E;F,M^0)$ is which N_Σ is a T-graph. Marked T-graphs (i.e. marked nets based on T-graphs) are often called marked graphs and sometimes synchronisation graphs. Below we show an example of a 1s T-graph.

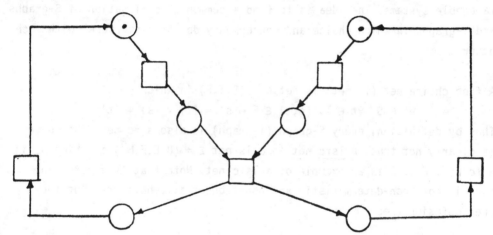

The theory of marked T-graphs is well-understood [5 , 8 , 20]. In parti-cular, 1s T-graphs can be charecterised as follows.

The marked T-graph $\Sigma = (S,T;F,M^0)$ is live iff every elementary circuit of N_Σ passes through some S-element which is marked (i.e. carries at least one token) at M^0.

The live marked T-graph $\Sigma = (S,T;F,M^0)$ is safe iff every S-element is con tained in an elementary circuit π which carries exactly one token under M^0. In other words letting S' be the set of S-elements that π passes though,

$$\sum_{s \in S'} M^0(s) = 1.$$

In a 1s T-graph in general two events may occur concurrently. But no two events can ever be in conflict. In this sense 1s T-graphs model non-sequential deterministic systems. Due to the absense of conflicts, 1s T-graphs are also confusion-free.

2.8 1sfc nets

Systems that are both non-deterministic and non-sequential are difficult to analyse. Where confusion is present, they are also difficult to implement in practice. One of the virtues of net theory is that it enables one to control the dosage of choice and concurrency to obtain increasingly complicated mixtures. Free choice nets (fc nets) represent one particular mix of choice and concurrency which leads to a class of non-trivial but manageble systems. The idea is to find a common generalisation of S-graphs and T-graphs in which choice and concurrency do not "interfere" with each other.

A free choice net (fc net) is net $N = (S,T;F)$ in which
$$\forall s \in S \;\; \forall t \in T. \; (s,t) \in F \Rightarrow s^{\cdot} = \{t\} \vee \{s\} = {}^{\cdot}t.$$
Thus by definition, every S-graph (T-graph) is also a fc net. The converse is clearly not true. A 1sfc net is a 1s net $\Sigma = (B,E;F,M^0)$ in which N_Σ is a fc net. Fig. 2 is an example of a 1sfc net. Note that 1sfc nets can exhibit both non-deterministic and non-sequential behaviours. But they are confusion-free.

The theory of 1sfc nets is also quite well understood. We shall mention a characterisation of 1sfc nets. Let $N = (S,T;F)$ be a net and $S' \subseteq S$. Then S' is a deadlock iff ${}^{\cdot}(S') \subseteq (S')^{\cdot}$. The point is every T-element which could increase the token count on S' must, for doing so, remove at least one token from S'. The "opposite" notion is called a trap. S' is a trap iff $(S')^{\cdot} \subseteq {}^{\cdot}(S')$. Every T-element which could decrease the token count on S' must, for doing so, put back at least one token into S'. A deadlock which is free of tokens can never acquire a token again. A trap which has acquried a token can never again become free of tokens. Live fc nets admit the following characterisation [6].

A marked fc net $\Sigma = (S,T;F,M^o)$ is live iff every deadlock $S' \subsetneq S$ contains a marked trap S''. In other words, $S'' \subseteq S'$ and $\sum_{s \in S''} M^o(s) > 0$.

For characterising satefy we need the notion of a SM-componet. The net $N' = (S',T';F')$ is a SM-component of the market net $\Sigma = (S,T;F,M^o)$ iff

    1) N' is a strongly connected S-graph.
    2) N' is a sub.net of N_Σ
    3) $\forall s \in S'$. $\cdot s \cup s \cdot$ (in N') = $\cdot s \cup s \cdot$ (in N_Σ).
    4) $\sum_{s \in S'} M^o(s) = 1$.

The live marked fc net $\Sigma = (S,T;F,M^o)$ is safe iff for every $s \in S$ (and hence every $t \in T$) there is a SM-component $N' = (S',T';F')$ of Σ such that $s \in S'$ [16].

It might be instructive to verify that the above results when specialised to marked S-graphs and T-graphs yield the results mentioned in the two provious sub-sections. In his classic work [16], Hack has also constructed a decomposition theory of lsfc nets. This theory shows that lsfc nets are, in a behavioural sense, a common generalisation of ls S-graphs and ls T-graphs. As a beautiful side-effect it turns out that in lsfc nets conflict and concurrency are in a strong sense, dual notions.

A modest supplement to Hack's theory of lsfc nets can be found in [37]. Additional results appear is [3 , 4]. What is lacking at present is a synthesis theory for this class. There is however a synthesis theory for a sub-class of lsfc nets called well behaved bipolar schemes [13] which properly include the class of ls s-graphs and ls T-graphs. These schemes admit a computational interpretation which then leads to a class of "well formed" concurrent programs [14]. At present not much is known about larger classes of ls marked nets (in comparion to lsfc nets). We can not however rest satisfied with lsfc nets as the following example shows.

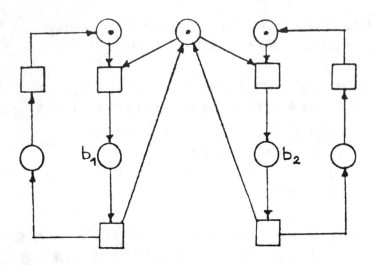

Fig. 5

3. First-order Marked Nets

As mentioned earlier, safe marked nets yield unwieldy descriptions of large
systems. One way to obtain a more flexible modelling tool is to provide the
tokens with internal structure. This can be done in a number of different ways.
Here we propose a generalisation of marked nets called first-order marked
nets. Our model is basically a streamlined version of Predicate/Transition
nets [10]. What is perhaps novel in our approach is the attempt to use
standard notions in logic to illuminate the main idea. In doing so we shall
borrow hearily from Smullyan [36].

As a first step we argue that a safe marked net can be interpreted as a
fragment of propositional logic. Using this as a stepping stone we shall
obtain a system model which can be viewed as a fragment of first-order logic.
In what follows we assume our nets to be composed out of denumerable sets
of elements. We start with three kinds of symbols.

1) $\hat{B}$ = {$b_1, b_2, \ldots$}, a denumerable set of <u>propositional</u>
   <u>variables</u>.
2) The logical connectives $\sim$, $\wedge$, $\vee$.
3) The left paranthesis (, the right paranthesis).

Let $B \subseteq \hat{B}$ be a non-empty set of propositional variables. Then WF_B, the set
of <u>formulas</u> over B is given by the inductive scheme:

1) $B \subseteq WF_B$

2) If $A \in WF_B$ then $\sim A \in WF_B$.

3) If $A, D \in WF_B$ then $(A \wedge D)$, $(A \vee D) \in WF_B$.

For convenience we assume B to be fixed and write WF instead of WF_B. By a formula we shall means a formula in WF. We take in addition a set of truth values {t,f} composed out of two distinct elements. A boolean val-uation of WF is a function v : WF $\rightarrow$ {t,f} which satisfies:

1) The formula $\sim A$ receives the value t iff the formula A receives the value f.
2) The formula $(A \wedge D)$ receives the value t iff both A,D receive the value t.
3) The formula $(A \vee D)$ receives the value t iff at least one of A,D receives the value t.

Let V be the set of all boolean valuations of WF and V' $\subseteq$ V. A formula is said to be V'-valid iff it is true (i.e. receives the value t) under every boolean valuation in V'. Thus a tautology is a V-valid formula.

An atomic boolean valuation (also called an interpretation) of WF is a function c : B $\rightarrow$ {t,f}. It is a fact of propositional logic that every atomic boolean valuation can be extended (using the inductive definition of formulas) to exactly one boolean valuation of WF. The unique boolean valuation which is the extension of the atomic boolean valuation c of WF will be denoted as v_c. Let C be a set of atomic boolean valuations of WF. A formula is said to be C-valid iff it is {$v_c | c \in C$}-valid.

Let $\Sigma = (B,E;F,c^o)$ be a safe marked net and $C = [c^o>$. Then each element c of C can be viewed as an atomic boolean valuation of WF. (Replace 1 by t, and 0 by f in the range of c). Consequently Σ may be looked upon as a (peculiar) representation of C, a set of atomic boolean valuations of WF.

The occurrence of an event in Σ transforms one atomic boolean valuation into another. Using steps, such transformations can be carried out in a

distributed fashion. In the net jargon, the C-valid formulas are called
facts. For example, for the safe marked net shown in Fig. 5, $\sim (b_1 \wedge b_2)$
is a fact. Wherein the safe marked net model a system, the facts of the
safe marked net denote a class of invariants of the system. In net theory
facts are represented by dead transitions. Details concerning the net representation and calculus of facts can be found in [9,11].

We now wish to construct a net model that plays a similar role from the
standpoint of first-order logic. We start with.

1) The symbols of propositional logic other than the
   propositional variables.
2) The two quantifier symbols $\forall$, $\exists$.
3) A denumerable set $\hat{X}$ of symbols called individual variables;
   henceforth called just variables and not to be confused
   with the propositional variables used earlier.
4) For each positive integer n, a denumerable list of symbols
   called n-ary predicates or predicates of degree n; the
   collection of all such predicates will be denoted as $\hat{\Pi}$
5) $\hat{U}$, a non-empty set of individuals.

Let $X \subseteq \hat{X}$, $\Pi_S \subseteq \hat{\Pi}$, $U \subseteq \hat{U}$ be three non-empty sets. In what follows we keep
X , Π_S and U fixed. Every variable (predicate, individual) we encounter is
assumed to be a member of X (Π_S,U). We shall use x,y,z with or without
subscripts to denote variables. We shall use a,b,c with or without subscripts
to denote individuals. We shall use P,Q,R with or without subscripts to denote predicates; their degree will be clear from the context.

By an atomic formula we mean a (n+1)-tuple $P d_1 d_2 \ldots d_n$ where P is a predicate
of degree n and $d_1, d_2, \ldots d_n$ are variables or individuals. A pure atomic formula is a (n+1)-tuple $P x_1 x_2 \ldots x_n$ where P is a predicate of degree n.

Starting with the atomic formulas the set of all formulas is built up by the
formation rules of propositional logic (used to contruct WF_B) together with
the rule:
If A is a formula then both $(\forall x)A$ and $(\exists x)A$ are formulas.

In order to define (first-order) valuations we need the notion of closed formulas which in turn requires the notion of substitution. For every formula A, variable x, individual a, the formula A_a^x is defined by the following inductive scheme:

1) It A is atomic then A_a^x is the result of substituting a for every occurrence of x in A.

2) $[\sim A]_a^x = \sim [A_a^x]$. (For convenience we use in addition to
(,) the symbols [,]).
$[A \wedge B]_a^x = A_a^x \wedge B_a^x$
$[A \vee B]_a^x = A_a^x \vee B_a^x$.

3) $[(\forall x)A]_a^x = (\forall x)A$
$[(\exists x)A]_a^x = (\exists x)A$
But for variable y distinct from x,
$[(\forall x)A]_a^y = (\forall x) [A_a^y]$
$[(\exists x)A]_a^y = (\exists x) [A_a^y]$.

By a <u>closed</u> <u>formula</u> we mean a formula A such that for every variable x and every individual a, $A_a^x = A$. (i.e. no variable has a free occurrence in A). We let CF denote the set of all closed formulas.

A <u>first-order</u> <u>valuation</u> of CF is a function $v : CF \to \{t,f\}$ which for every formula in CF and every variable x satisfies:

1) v is a boolean valuation.
2a) $(\forall x)A$ is true under v iff for every individual a, A_a^x is true under v.
2b) $(\exists x)A$ is true under v iff for at least one individual a, A_a^x is true under v.

On the other hand, an <u>atomic</u> <u>valuation</u> of CF is a function M which assigns a truth-value to every <u>atomic</u> element of CF. A fact of first-order-logic is that every atomic valuation can be extended to exactly one first-order valuation. For the n-ary predicate P and the atomic valuation M of CF, we define $P_M^* = \{(a_1, a_2, \ldots a_n) \mid Pa_1 a_2 \ldots a_n$ is true under M$\}$.

We can now obtain a net representation of a set of atomic valuations of CF. Start with the net $N = (\pi_S, E; F)$. Denote the atomic valuation M of CF as follows. Place on each <u>S-element</u> $P \in \pi_S$, the set of n-tuples (the <u>predicate</u> P is assumed to be of degree n) of individuals P_M^*. (Since P_M^* might be in-finite the verb "place" in the previous sentence should be interpreted ge-nerously). Now M can be viewed as a (first-order) marking of N. The event $e \in E$ then represents a transformation of one atomic valuation into another. Whenver e occurs a fixed set tuple of individuals is removed from each S-element in ·e and a fixed tuple of individuals is added to each S-element in e·. In diagrams, the change associated with e is indicated on the directed arcs of the net. Consider the example shown below.

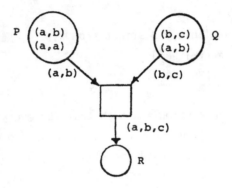

For the marking M shown, $P_M^* = \{(a,b), (a,a)\}$, $Q_M^* = \{(b,c),(a,b)\}$ $R_M^* = \emptyset$. The event e can occur at M because Pab and Qbc are true under M while Rabc is false. Following (A2) in Section 1, this is the necessary <u>and</u> <u>sufficient</u> condition for e to occur at M. When e occurs a new marking (atomic valuation) M' is obtained where $P_{M'}^* = \{(a,a)\}$, $Q_{M'}^* = \{(a,b)\}$ and $R_{M'}^* = \{(a,b,c)\}$.

Based on this simple idea, we can (but we shall not do so here) derive the system model called a <u>safe</u> <u>first-order</u> marked net. Suppose Σ is a safe first-order marked net with the <u>initial marking</u> M^O. Then $[M^O>$, the forward marking class defined by M^O, denotes a (potentially large) set of atomic valuations of CF. In this sense, Σ is a succinct and structured presentation of a set of atomic valuations.

We could in principle stop here with our model building. This would however
amount to throwing away a good deal of descriptive power offered by first-
order logic. The point is, our informal description of safe marked nets
does not make any use of variables and substitution. By bringing these into
play a group of events can be often collapsed together to form a single event
scheme. The diagram shown below gives a flavour of the main idea.

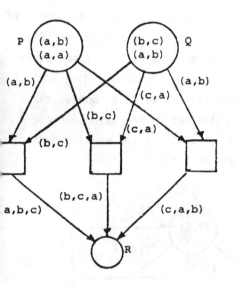
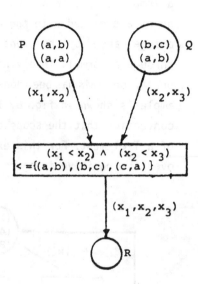

We augment π_S by the set of predicates π_T (disjoint from π_S). CF, the set
of closed formulas is now assumed to be defined over $\pi_S \cup \pi_T$ (instead of
just π_S), X,U. We wish to use a predicate in π_T to denote a __constant__ set
of events. Consequently we demand that each such predicate have a fixed
interpretation.

More precisely, we demand that for each predicate R of degree n in π_T, there
be a fixed non-empty set of R^* of n-tuples of individuals such that:
For every atomic valuation M of CF, $R_M^* = R^*$.

We then form the net N = $(\pi_S, \pi_T; F)$ where attached each __T-element__ R in π_T is
a specifications of R^*. To identify the events denoted by the n-ary predicate R in π_T, we associate a __pure__ formula $Rx_1x_2...x_n$ with the __T-element__
R in N. Suppose that P $\in$ 'R (in N) and the degree of the predicate P is m.

Then with the arc (P,R) (in N) we associate a m-tuple of variables where the variables are taken from the set $\{x_1,\ldots x_n\}$. (i.e. the variables that occur in the pure formula associated with the T-element R). We do this for every arc that comes in or goes out of R. An event denoted by R is then obtained by a proper substitution of individuals for the variables occurring in $Rx_1,x_2,\ldots x_n$. By a proper substitution we mean a substitution which yields a member of R^*. This substitution, when carried over to the tuples of variables associated with the arcs around the T-element R will reveal the extent of change caused by the event. Through suitable conventions R^* can be specified through a formula involving just $x_1,\ldots x_n$ and predicates with a fixed interpretation. This has been done in the toy example shown above. A less trivial example is shown in fig. 6. In drawing this labelled net we have adopted the convention that the scope of a variable is restricted to the neighbourhood of a T-element. For this example, $U = \{1,2,3\ldots\}$ and < is the usual ordering over the positive integers (viewed as a binary predicate).

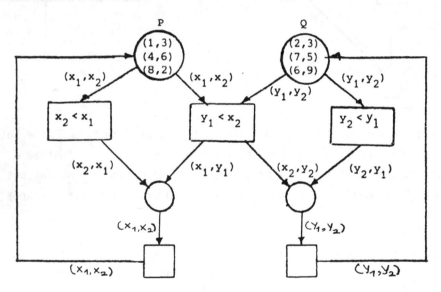

The goal of the system is to "shuffle" the ordered pairs initially on P and Q so that eventually ordered pairs with low components end up on P and those with high components end up on Q. This systems has <u>terminal</u> markings reachable from the initial marking. (i.e. markings at which no event can occur). At each such terminal marking P and Q will be marked and no other S-elements will be marked. One such terminal marking M is given

by: $P_M^* = \{(1,2), (2,3), (3,4)\}$, $Q_M^* = \{(5,6), (6,7), (8,9)\}$. A second terminal marking M' is given by: $P_{M'}^* = \{(1,2), (2,3), (3,4),\}$
$Q_{M'}^* = \{(5,7), (6,8), (6,9)\}$. Consequently the computation carried out by
the system is both non-deterministic and non-sequential.

First-order facts can be used to describe certain invariants of systems
modelled by safe first-order marked nets. For the formalisms considered
in [10, 19 , 35], linear algebraic techniques can be used to used to compute
invariants called S-invariants. Apart from this, very little theory is
available for these "high level" net models.

The trouble with first-order nets is they are too powerful in some sense.
A great deal of taste and care is required for their effective use. On
the theoretical side one way to proceed would be to study restricted sub-
classes. A start has been made along this direction in [24].

4. Conclusions.

In this paper we have discussed some aspects of net theory. Our aim has
been to expose the major concepts of net theory. Not all the concepts of
net theory have been dealt with here. We have not mentioned a number of
lines of research concerning marked nets. No detailed examples have been
presented. We have not made any attempt to indicate the applications of
net theory. Finally, we have ignored other approaches to the study of
distributed systems.

A number of tools and techniques are needed to apply net theory. S-invariants
(and T-invariants) [11] are a tool rooted in lineare algebra that turns out
to be very useful. Indeed at present, S-invariantes are the work horses of
net theory when it comes to the analysis of net models [10,19,35].

The ability to perform "meaning-preserving" transformations of system descriptions is crucial from the practical standpoint. The tool proposed by
net theory to perform such transformations are net morphisms. As the name
suggests, a net morphism is a mapping between a pair of nets which respects

the flow relation and the nature of S-elements and T-elements [11]. At present, the theory of net morphism is an underdeveloped area; they are mostly used for definitional and descriptive purposes. What we need are sub-theories concerning restricted morphisms where the restrictions reflect the needs of the chosen applications. One such theory, based on a net morphisms which preserves the token-game has been recently developed in [41].

A number of workers have viewed and studied marked nets as special (token-crunching) automata. A variety of decidability, complixity and language theoretic results have been obtained through this line of research. The interested reader may consult [17, 34, 44, 22].

A number of contributions in [42] present applications of net theory. [21, 24,38] are also examples of applications. This list is highly selective and hardly exhaustive. Unfortunately we do not have the competence to give more helpful pointers to literature on this important topic. (Perhaps someone more experienced in the applications area will take up the challenge).

We have not discussed other approaches to the study of distributed systems. Path expressions [23], Calculus of Communicating Systems [25] and Communicating Sequential Processes [18] are some of the formalisms that come readily to mind. Once again, lack of competence and not lack of respect is the reason for this gap. We felt that a superficial "stock taking" in the absence of a serious discussion would be pointless. So instead the paper has been devoted to a few selected topics within net theory that the author is familiar with.

Acknowledgements

Carl Adam Petri is the founder of what I consider to be the heart of net theory. I have been fortunate to have had him as a teacher for several years. The inspiration to anchor first-order marked nets in (first-order) logic came from Hartmann Genrich. The contents of section 3 have been strongly influenced by my discussions with him.

References

(LNCS is an abbreviation for:
Lecture Notes in Computer Science,
Springer Verlag, Berlin, Heidelberg, New York.)

1. E. Best: The Relative Strength of K-density.
    LNCS 84 (1980)

2. E. Best, A. Merceron: Discreteness, K-density and D-continuity of
    Occurrence Nets.
    LNCS 145 (1982)

3. E. Best, M.W. Shields: Some Equivalence Results on Free Choice Nets
    and Simple Nets and on the Periodicity of Live Free Choice Nets.
    Proc. CAAP (1983)

4. E. Best, K. Voss: Free Choice Systems have Home States.
    Arbeitspapiere der GMD 46, GMD, St. Augustin, W. Germany (1983)

5. F. Commoner, A.W. Holt, S. Evens, A. Pnueli:
    Marked Directed Graphs. TCSS 5 (1971)

6. F. Commoner: Deadlocks in Petri Nets.
    Applied Data Research Inc., CA-7206-2311,
    Wakefield, Mass., U.S.A (1972)

7. C. Fernandez, P.S. Thiagarajan: D-continuous Causal Nets: A Model
    onf Non-sequential Processes.
    ISF Report 82.05, GMD, St. Augustin, W. Germany. (to Appear in TCS.)
    (1982)

8. H.J. Genrich, K. Lautenbach: Synchronisationsgraphen.
    Acta Informatica 2 (1973)

9. H.J. Genrich, G. Thieler-Mevisson:
    The Calculus of Facts. LNCS 45 (1976)

10. H.J. Genrich, K. Lautenbach: System Modelling with High-level
    Petri Nets. TCS 13 (1981)

11. H.J. Genrich, K. Lautenbach, P.S. Thiagarajan:
    Elements of General Net Theory. LNCS 84 (1980)

12. H.J. Genrich, K. Lautenbach, P.S. Thiagarajan:
     Substitution Systems: A Family of System Models based on Concurrency.
     LNCS 88 (1980)

13. H.J. Genrich, P.S. Thiagarajan: A Theory of Bipolar Synchronisation
     Schemes. Report DAIMI PB-158, Aarhus University, Aarhus, Denmark.
     (to. Appear in TCS). (1983)

14. H.J. Genrich, P.S. Thiagarajan: Well-formed Flow Charts for Concurrent
     Programming. In: Formal Description of Programming Concepts-II,
     Ed. D. Bjørner, North-Holland Publishing Company, Amsterdam, New York,
     Oxford (1983)

15. U. Goltz, W. Reisig: Processes in Place/Transition Nets.
     Proc. ICALP'83, LNCS (1983).

16. M.H. Hack: Analysis of Production Schemata by Petri Nets. M.S. Thesis,
     TR-94, Project MAC, MIT, Cambridge, Mass., U.S.A. (1972).

17. M.H. Hack: Decidability Questions for Petri Nets.
     Ph.D. Thesis, TR 161, Project MAC, MIT, Cambridge, Mass., U.S.A. (1976)

18. C.A.R. Hoare: Communicating Sequential Processes.
     CACM 21, 8 (1978)

19. K. Jensen: Coloured Petri Nets and the Invariant Method.
     TCS 14 (1981)

20. J.R. Jump, P.S. Thiagarajan: On the Equivalence of Asynchronous
     Control Structures. SIAM J. on Computing, 2, 2 (1973)

21. W. Kluge, K. Lautenbach: The Orderely Resolution of Memory Access
     Conflicts among Competing Channel Processes. IEEE Transactions
     on Computers, C-31, 3 (1982)

22. S.R. Kosaraju: Decidability of Reachability in Vector Addition
     Systems. Proc. 14th Annual ACM Symp. on Theory of Computing. (1982)

23. P.E. Lauer, P.R. Torrigiani, M.W. Shields:
     COSY- A System Specification Language Based on Paths and Processes.
     Acta Informatica 12 (1979)

24. K. Lautenbach: Simple Marked-graph-like Predicate Transition Nets. Arbeitspapiere der GMD 41, GMD, St. Augustin, W. Germany (1983)

25. R. Milner: A Calculus of Communicating Systems. LNCS 92 (1980)

26. N. Nielson, G. Plotkin, G. Winskel: Petri Nets, Event Structures and Domains, Part I. TCS 13 (1981)

27. C.A. Petri: Kommunikation mit Automaten. Schriften des IIM 2, Institute für Instrumentelle Mathematik, Bonn, W. Germany (1962)

28. C.A. Petri: Fundamentals of the Representation of Discrete Processes. English Translation of a paper (in german) Presented at 3. Colloquium über Automatentheorie 1965, ISF-Report 82-04, GMD, St. Augustin, W. Germany (1982)

29. C.A. Petri: Concepts of Net Theory. Proc. of MFCS'73

30. C.A. Petri: Interpretations of Net Theory. Interner Bericht ISF-75-07, GMD, St. Augustin, W. Germany (1975)

31. C.A. Petri: Non-sequential Processes. Interner Bericht ISF-77-5, GMD, St. Augustin, W. Germany (1977)

32. C.A. Petri: Concurrency. LNCS 84 (1980)

33. C.A. Petri: State-Transition Structures in Physics and in Computation. International J. of. Theor. Physics, 21, 12 (1982)

34. J.L. Peterson: Petri Nets and the Modelling of Systems. Prentice-Hall, Englewood Cliffs, N.J., U.S.A. (1981)

35. W. Reisig: Petri Nets with Individual Tokens. Informatik-Fachberichte 66, Springer Verlag (1983)

36. R.M. Smullyan: First-order Logic. Ergebnisse der Mathematik und ihrer Grenzgebiete, 43, Springer Verlag (1968)

37. P.S. Thiagarajan, K. Voss: A Fresh Look at Free Choice Nets. To Appear as Arbeitspapiere der GMD, St. Augustin, W. Germany.

38.   K. Voss: Using Predicate/Transition Nets to Model and Analyse
      Distributed Data Base Systems. IEEE Transactions on Software
      Engineering, SE-6, 6. (1980)

39.   G. Winskel: Events in Computation. Ph.D. Thesis, Dept. of Computer
      Science, University of Edinburgh, Edinburgh, G.B. (1980)

40.   G. Winskel: Event Structure Semantics for CCS and Related Languages.
      LNCS 140 (1982)

41.   G. Winskel: A new Definition of Morphism on Petri Nets.
      Unpublished Manuscript. (1983)

42.   Net Theory and Applications. LNCS 84 (1980)

43.   C.L. Seitz: System Timing. In: Introduction to VLSI Systems,
      (Mead, Conway), Addison-Wesley Publishing Company (1980).

44.   M. Jantzen, R. Valk: Formal Properties of Place/Transition Nets.
      LNCS 84 (1980).

From State Machines to Temporal Logic: Specification Methods for Protocol Standards

RICHARD L. SCHWARTZ AND P. MICHAEL MELLIAR-SMITH

Abstract—This paper attempts to lend perspective to several different methods that have been employed for specifying computer communication protocols by comparing a spectrum of specification techniques. The paper characterizes specification languages such as state transition diagrams, variants of temporal logic approaches, and sequence expressions by the extent to which information is encoded as properties of a single state versus properties of a history of the entire computation state sequence. Taking the prototypical alternating bit protocol as an example, each method is used to specify the requirements for the send process of the distributed system.

I. INTRODUCTION

IN its classical meaning, a "protocol" is a formal code of etiquette for dealings between communicating parties. A *protocol standard* specifies required etiquette to be followed by all parties wishing to communicate.

Computer network protocols form a system of hierarchical support. Each protocol provides service operations to the next higher layer in the hierarchy, by using services of the next lower layer. Fig. 1 illustrates the usual components [1] in the specification of a protocol layer. A hierarchical structure, such as this, is necessarily present in any protocol specification, even if only by implication. A *service specification* defines the services provided by the layer, describing only that behavior visible to the user at the next layer. There should be no description of how the service is actually realized; this is a system-wide view of the layer as a single unit. The *protocol specification* refines the service specification to define requirements on how each (possibly physically distributed) entity supports the service through interaction with the services of the next lower layer. This is a specification of how multiple entities interface to provide the specified services.

In this paper we take the view that a protocol standard should specify the *minimum required externally visible behavior* of each entity. Ideally, the protocol standard should be sufficiently constraining to ensure that *any* implementation that satisfies the standard will uphold continued communication between entities. The standard should also be sufficiently liberal to allow any implementation that would uphold continued communication with other implementations satisfying the standard. The protocol specification should serve as a formal contract between the overall protocol layer and

Manuscript received March 10, 1982; revised July 16, 1982. This work was supported by the National Science Foundation under Grant MCS-8104459 and by the Defense Communications Agency under Contract DCA100-80-C-0044. This paper was presented at the Second International Workshop on Protocol Specification, Testing, and Verification, Idlewild, CA, May 1982.

The authors are with the Computer Science Laboratory, SRI International, Menlo Park, CA 94025.

each distributed component: any component satisfying its local specification should be capable of successfully joining the network. Requirements imposed beyond this point simply constrain possible implementation solutions and might preclude otherwise valid implementations. A protocol standard should define *requirement* rather than *expedient*, leaving the implementor the maximum flexibility to take advantage of his particular context. Of course, the onus for deciding what constitutes "minimum" required behavior falls on the designers of the protocol; the requirements should both ensure that the protocol guarantees communication between any conforming implementation and is flexible enough to allow the desired class of realizations.

After describing the nature of the alternating bit protocol, the spectrum used to classify specification methods is introduced in Section III. Section IV then briefly reviews temporal logic. Having completed the background material, Section V illustrates how five specification methods across the spectrum deal with the behavior required by the protocol.

II. THE AB PROTOCOL USED FOR ILLUSTRATION

The alternating bit (AB) protocol is used to coordinate the flow of messages between two nodes in a distributed network. The protocol provides reliable communication over an unreliable transmission line by repeated transmission. The protocol considers messages one at a time, and cannot proceed to the next message until it receives acknowledgment that its current message has been received correctly. The message is placed in a packet with a one-bit sequence number (whence the name) and an acknowledgment is assumed to consist of the return of the same packet (though only the sequence number is really required). Several packets may be in transit simultaneously. The protocol recovers successfully from packets lost, duplicated, or delayed by the transmission line as long as no packets arrive out of order. Assuming perfect detection, corrupted packets are also handled successfully. We consider only the half-duplex protocol providing unidirectional message transfer.

Fig. 2 illustrates the structure of the network interfaces. Shown in dotted outline are the two entities comprising the protocol layer; they communicate with each other via the lower layer transmission services shown at the bottom of the figure. At the sender's end, the user at the next higher layer is provided an $Enq(m)$ service to request that message m be enqueued for transmission. This message will be later handled by a sender process S, that calls $Dq(m)$ to obtain the next message to be sent. The interface between process S and the transmission line T consists of two operations

0090-6778/82/1200-2486$00.75 © 1982 IEEE

Fig. 1. Specification of protocol layer i.

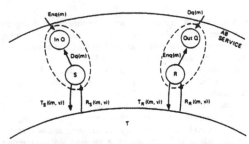

Fig. 2. Structure of network interface for AB protocol.

$T_s(\langle m, v \rangle)$ and $R_s(\langle m, v \rangle)$, used by the S to transmit a packet $\langle m, v \rangle$ to T and by T to transmit a packet to S, respectively. The receiver's end is analogous. When transmission is successful, a call $T_s(\langle m, v \rangle)$ by the sender results in a later $R_r(\langle m, v \rangle)$ to the receiver. In the other direction, a $T_r(\langle m, v \rangle)$ call by the receiver should later result in an $R_s(\langle m, v \rangle)$ call to the sender. In this view of the transmission line service, the receipt of a packet is passive, since the R_s and R_r operations are defined within the transmission service. This allows us to define actual buffer behavior associated with asynchronous packet delivery.

The following description describes *one* operational procedure that satisfies the AB protocol standard. When the process S is ready to send a message, a packet containing the next message m from the input message queue and the sender's current sequence number v is formed, and is transmitted by calling $T_s(\langle m, v \rangle)$. The sender then awaits an acknowledgment packet from the receiver indicating that the message was received.

When the receiver notices a packet delivered by the transmission line by means of $R_r(\langle m, v \rangle)$, an acknowledgment packet is transmitted back to the sender. In our model, the receiver acknowledges a packet by transmitting it back to the sender by calling $T_r(\langle m, v \rangle)$. If the transmission line properly delivers the acknowledgment packet to the sender, an $R_s(\langle m, v \rangle)$ occurs. In addition, if the packet $\langle m, v \rangle$, noticed by the receiver, contains the sequence number v currently awaited by the receiver, the message m is added to an output queue via the operation $Enq(m)$, and the receiver increments (modulo 2) the currently expected sequence number.

At the sender's end, when an uncorrupted acknowledgment packet for the currently pending message is received, the sender takes note by incrementing its current sequence number and is free to transmit the next message in the input queue. If an acknowledgment is not received for a pending message within a timeout period, the sender is required to retransmit the packet, and to continue retransmitting intermittently until an acknowledgment is received.

The service supported by the AB protocol is to deliver messages enqueued at the sender's service interface in a first-in first-out order at the receiver's service interface. Given certain properties of the lower-level transmission services such as

- at least occasionally delivering to the receiver in uncorrupted form the packet transmitted by the sender, or
- possibly losing, duplicating, or corrupting, but not *reordering* packets,

one can show that the sender, receiver, and transmission line working together can provide the required queue-like network service.

For the remainder of the paper we focus on the process S with $Dq(m)$, $T_s(\langle m, v \rangle)$, and $R_s(\langle m, v \rangle)$ interfaces. This portion of the layer is sufficiently interesting to illustrate the major differences between specification methods while still remaining manageable. The specification of S must be combined with that for an asynchronous queue to form the specification of the sender entity as a whole.

Consider what requirements one would like to impose on the visible behavior of the process S as part of a protocol standard. In this paper, we will assume the following requirements are desired.

1) Successive messages must be transmitted in packets having alternating sequence numbers.

2) The sequence of distinct packets transmitted must follow the sequence of messages dequeued.

3) Having initiated transmission of (a packet containing) a new message, until the first uncorrupted acknowledgment with the transmitted sequence number is received, only that message may be retransmitted.

4) Having initiated transmission of a message, continued retransmission must occur (at least) until an acknowledgment is received and noticed.

5) If acknowledgments for the last transmitted packet are repeatedly received, they must eventually be noticed.

6) An uncorrupted acknowledgment that is noticed must cause eventual transmission of the next message in sequence, if any.

These are the only requirements placed on the sender. Of the above requirements, 1)–3) reflect *safety* properties, i.e., that "nothing bad will happen," and 4)–6) reflect *liveness* properties, i.e., that "something good will happen."

Notice that the sender is not required to respond immediately to an awaited acknowledgment by ceasing transmission of the packet. One cannot guarantee either that a given acknowledgment will be noticed or that the sender can immediately take heed of it and initiate transmission of the next message. Requirements 5) and 6) state that if acknowledg-

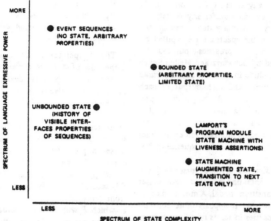

Fig. 3. A spectrum of specification methods.

ments continue to arrive, eventually the sender must notice and take action. However, what constitutes "notice" is not, and need not be, defined. Requirement 4) allows the sender to cease transmitting the packet any time after an acknowledgment is noticed, or to continue to transmit a packet until the packet containing the next message is ready.

In addition, the sender may dequeue messages in advance of its need of them for transmission, as long as the order is preserved. The various specifications below are designed to be used in conjunction with the specification of a queue and, thus, where more convenient, limit advance dequeuing to at most one message. All the methods are, of course, capable of describing a finite, asynchronously accessed queue.

III. A SPECTRUM OF SPECIFICATION METHODS

Formal specification techniques are intended to express requirements on system behavior. For the range of specification techniques we consider in this paper, the same basic model can be used to define computations of the system. A model for system execution is the set of (possibly infinite) state sequences that can result from execution. Each state assigns an interpretation for each program variable and for the locus of control. Concurrent execution of a multiprocess (possibly distributed) system is modeled by arbitrary interleaving of enabled atomic actions from each process. One normally assumes some form of *fair* scheduling criteria [2] to ensure that no enabled action can be indefinitely delayed. A formal treatment of appropriate underlying models can be found in [3], [4].

Specification techniques have two mechanisms available to encode meaning:

- information encoded within the state
- information encoded as requirements on the sequence (history) of states.

A spectrum of specification approaches can be identified based upon this state versus history encoding. Specification methods can be characterized by how extensive the state component of the underlying model is, and how much expressive power the language provides to define allowable sequences of states. Fig. 3 illustrates this spectrum.

At one end of the spectrum is the state machine specification; the only description of history allowed is the set of possible successor states from a given state. For this technique to be successful, the state component of the underlying model must be sufficiently rich to fully characterize a computation by the domain of states and a (possibly nondeterministic) transition relation. State machine specifications [5], Petri-net specifications [6], and programming language descriptions all lie at this extreme. Further down the spectrum is Lamport's concurrent module approach [7]. Lamport's method introduces both a set of program variables comprising a state and a set of state functions to define transition between states. A derived temporal logic specification language is used to specify allowable behavior of the state functions.

At the other end of the spectrum are event specifications, where the state component of the underlying model simply defines whether a given event, possibly parameterized, occurs. To highlight this lack of dependence on any further state component, the model is sometimes defined as a set of event sequences rather than state sequences. At this extremity are event languages in which specifications may be arbitrary predicates on the event history (e.g., [8], [9]). Somewhat removed from the extreme are *sequence expression* languages that require generative (constructive) definitions of allowable event sequences (e.g. [10]-[12]). In either case, the meaning of an event is given purely in terms of constraints on earlier events that must have occurred and future events that will occur.

A duality exists between information encoded in terms of state and in terms of previous history. A state records some portion of previous history. Given a set of (possibly infinite) sequences of finite states as an underlying model and a language capable of expressing arbitrary first-order properties of sequences, one can eliminate any state information in favor of properties of the history, or can transfer any finitely expressible portion of the history to auxiliary state components.

Two intermediate points in the spectrum are typified by the state-based temporal logic approaches pursued by Hailpern and Owicki [4] and by Schwartz and Melliar-Smith [13]. Hailpern and Owicki include in the state an *unbounded* auxiliary variable for each input and each output of each process module. This variable records the sequence of previous parameter or return values that have occurred at that point. In this approach one has available, in the current state, the complete prior history of module interface values. Modules are specified in terms of properties that the sequence of history variables must satisfy.

The temporal logic specification method pursued by the authors [13] uses a model containing *bounded* state, closer in spirit to that of a state transition model. A modicum of internal state is introduced wherever it appears more convenient to express temporal properties in terms of a finite history of the past rather than to resort to temporal formulas. A more operational flavor is thus given to the specification, mirroring more closely the cause–effect relationship between module interfaces. Unlike both the state machine approach and Lamport's module approach, no specification of state transition functions is given.

IV. BRIEF REVIEW OF TEMPORAL LOGIC

Before illustrating specifications for the sender process, a brief review of temporal logic is presented. Recall that the underlying model we employ consists of a set of possibly infinite state sequences, each of the form $s_0, s_1, \cdots$. For a sequence $s = s_0, s_1, \cdots, s_n, \cdots$, we introduce the notation

$$s^+ \equiv s_1, \cdots$$
$$s^{+n} \equiv s_n, \cdots.$$

Using these auxiliary operations we can define the meaning of formulas in temporal logic. A temporal formula is an assertion about state sequences. A temporal logic specification, consisting of a set of temporal axioms, specifies properties that must be true of all state sequences resulting from system execution.

Given a temporal formula A and sequence s, the interpretation for A on s, denoted A_s, is defined (recursively) by the following.

For A being an atomic predicate: $A_s = s_0(A)$
i.e., A is evaluated in the first ("current") state of the sequence s.
For $A = B \wedge C$: $B_s \wedge C_s$
$B \vee C$: $B_s \vee C_s$
$\sim B$: $\sim B_s$
i.e., using the standard model for the logical connectives.
For $A = \Box B$: $A_s = \forall n \geqslant 0 \, (B_{s+n})$
i.e. B must be true in the current state and all future states.
For $A = \Diamond B$: $A_s = \exists n \geqslant 0 \, (B_{s+n})$
i.e., either B is true in the current state or there exists a future state in which B is true.

For $A = B$ Until C:
$A_s = \forall n \geqslant 0 \, [\forall i \; 0 \leqslant i \leqslant n \sim C_{s+i}] \supset B_{s+n}$
i.e., B must be true in every state until the first state in which C is true.

The $\Diamond$ operator in our *linear time* temporal logic [14] is the dual of $\Box$. From the above definition, one can see that $\Diamond P \equiv \sim \Box \sim P$. Strictly speaking, the Until operator is really the only primitive temporal operator needed, since $\Box P$ is expressible as P Until *false*.

Using only the unary $\Box$ and $\Diamond$ operators, many properties of systems can be stated. That I is invariant throughout system execution is stated $\Box I$. To state that a property P always causes a property Q to subsequently occur (a liveness requirement), one writes $\Box(P \supset \Diamond Q)$. (Notice that this allows P and Q to occur simultaneously.) To assert that a property P is satisfied infinitely often, one writes $\Box \Diamond P$. This says that, from every point in the computation, there is a future point at which P will be true. Similarly, the formula $\Diamond \Box P$ asserts that at some point in the future the property P will become true and remain true for the remainder of the computation.

To express more complicated relationships between two points in a computation, the binary Until operator is used. A common use of the Until operator is in an assertion of the form $P \supset (P$ Until $Q)$, stating that if P is true in the current state, it will remain true until Q becomes true (if ever). Composing the Until, the formula P Until $(Q$ Until $R)$ expresses the requirement that P must hold until Q becomes true, which in turn, must hold until R becomes true. Two valid formulas that are very useful when reasoning about Until intervals are P Until $Q \supset \Box P \vee \Diamond Q$ and $(P$ Until $Q) \wedge (\sim Q$ Until $R) \supset P$ Until R.

To augment these primitive operators, we define several derived operators that will be useful in our specifications. To express that P must remain true until *after* Q has become true, we define

$$P \text{ Until-After } Q \equiv P \text{ Until } (P \wedge Q).$$

In order to specify a property which, when becoming true, remains true (i.e., "latches") until some future point, we define

$$P \text{ Latches-Until } Q \equiv (P \supset (P \text{ Until } Q)) \text{ Until } Q$$

which states that, until Q becomes true (establishing the scope of the implication), if P is true, it will remain true until Q becomes true. Based on this predicate, we define Latches-Until-After by

$$P \text{ Latches-Until-After } Q \equiv P \text{ Latches-Until } (P \wedge Q).$$

The Latches-Until and Latches-Until-After operators have logical properties similar to the Until and Until-After operators. Two valid formulas useful in reasoning about Latches-Until (and analogously, Latches-Until-After) intervals are P Latches-Until $Q \supset \Diamond Q \vee \Box \sim P \vee \Diamond \Box P$ and $(P$ Until $Q) \wedge (Q$ Latches-Until $R) \supset (P \vee Q)$ Latches-Until R.

A component of the state concerns the point at which

control resides within each concurrent process. To reason about the currently active control point within each process, we use predicates at, in, and after. At S is true if control is just at the beginning of the execution of operation S; in S is true if control is currently within the statement S; and after S is true if control is just after the end of S. We assume that control resides at the beginning and ending points of each operation only once per call.

Apart from our assumptions of the temporal ordering of at S, in S, and after S, for any operation S, the specification method makes no assumptions about the implementation of operations. Any degree of simultaneity or concurrency not specifically precluded by the specification is acceptable. The operation may have an arbitrary *atomicity*—any number of internal control points and corresponding state changes. Any restrictions on state changes must be expressed within the temporal logic specification. The requirement $x = a$ Latches-Until $x = a + 1$, for example, constrains the value of x to monotonically increase by 1 with no intermediate values (a is a free logical variable). As part of the definition of a programming language for concurrent systems, the granularity would be specified. Any granularity that does not violate the constraints on allowable execution state sequences is acceptable.

We see these low-level operators as a first step in temporal abstraction, almost as "assembly-language level" operators. We are currently working on higher level temporal operators and systems to improve the clarity of specification.

V. SPECIFICATIONS FOR THE AB SENDER PROCESS

Having discussed in general terms how *state* in the underlying model and *properties of the sequence of states* expressed in the language are combined to specify behavior, we now give examples of the spectrum of approaches we have discussed. Using as an example the requirements of the AB sender introduced in the previous section, we illustrate

- the use of a state transition diagram specification
- temporal logic used
  - with a complete, but bounded, state and state transitions
  - with bounded state, including some internal state
  - with unbounded auxiliary state variables and no internal state
  - with parameterized events and no other state component.

In employing temporal logic language primitives for each of the three approaches, we highlight the effect of transforming state-based information into temporal properties of the sequence of states.

A. State Transition Specification

In giving a state transition specification, we use the graphic representation described in [5]. Nodes in the diagram are represented as circles, tagged arcs as transitions possible when the tagged state predicate is true, and boxes as actions on the state. State transition diagrams need not be deterministic: a nondeterministic choice of transitions is made if more than

one transition is possible. Each action is defined to have some effect on the state; a transition diagram has as a model the set of state sequences corresponding to all possible traversals through the diagram. Any sequence of states that can be generated from the state diagram satisfies the specification and is valid behavior.

Fig. 4 illustrates a state transition specification corresponding to the six English-language requirements given in Section II. The specification consists of two state machines communicating via shared state components. The state components used are

- S_o—used to record the last packet value transmitted using T_s.
- *packet*—a temporary variable used to prepare the next packet value to be sent following acknowledgment of the current message
- *packetready*—a Boolean flag used to loosely synchronize preparation and use of *packet*
- S_l—used to record the last acknowledgment packet value received by the transmitter using R_s.

Careful analysis should convince the reader that safety requirements 1)-3) given in Section II are expressed by the specification. The use of two communicating, asynchronous machines expresses the flexibility to decouple transmission of the current packet and to prepare that of the packet containing the next message from the queue, allowing the sender to dequeue one message ahead. It is not possible, given only a finite state, to express the flexibility to dequeue an unbounded number of messages in advance of transmission while preserving the first-dequeued first-transmitted requirement. Analysis of the permitted behavior becomes increasingly difficult as the number of interacting machines increases, possibly limiting the complexity expressible or forcing simplification and loss of liberality by the merging of state machines.

Liveness requirements 4)-6) are not expressed in the diagram. Each arc indicates possible transitions from a given state, but the specification cannot require that any particular transition ever occur. Bochmann has suggested a "hybrid" specification method that augments arcs by an operator indicating that the arc must eventually be taken if the enabling condition ever becomes true.[1] This method would allow single-transition liveness to be specified—any more global requirements on eventual behavior would have to be proven on the basis of the composition of single-transition eventualities. Without such a hybrid solution, one must resort to asserting fair scheduling and to proving, in the *metatheory*, that a given transition eventually occur using the method of well-founded sets. To achieve this, one defines an additional counter state variable and introduces an action to each relevant arc which reduces the value of the counter each time the transition is taken. By appropriate enabling conditions on the arcs, one can demonstrate that eventually a given arc must be taken. This method

[1] In adopting such an interpretation, one must carefully specify whether one intends the requirement to be based on the enabling condition being true in even a single state, infinitely often, or continually. See [2] for a discussion.

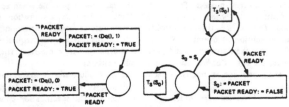

Fig. 4. State transition specification for AB sender.

has been used by Berthomieu [15] to prove liveness properties of protocols using Affirm [16].

B. State Function Temporal Logic Specification

Strongly related to the state transition specification method presented in the previous section is Lamport's *program module* approach [7]. Like the state transition approach, one specifies a collection of state components and possible atomic state transitions (called *actions*). Unlike the state transition approach, one can express safety properties for individual program states and liveness properties for sequences of states. Temporal logic is used both to express the required liveness properties and to provide an underlying logical foundation. Lamport's approach thus preserves the basic style of state machine specification, but allows greater generality in defining required properties of state sequences.

Safety properties have one of three forms:

1) P

2) α leaves unchanged f when Q

3) allowed changes to g_1 when Q_1,

$$\cdots$$

$$g_n \text{ when } Q_n$$

$$\alpha_1 : R_1 \to S_1,$$

$$\cdots$$

$$\alpha_m : R_m \to S_m.$$

The first form consists of a predicate P which defines required properties for each program state. Form 2) specifies that a set of state transition actions α may not modify state variable f when condition Q is true. For a given module m, $\alpha[m]$ denotes the set of atomic actions within m. Form 3) constrains changes to each named state variable g_i, when condition Q_i is true, to be modified *only* by the m specified atomic transitions. Each transition $\alpha_j : R_j \to S_j$ specifies that an action in the set α_j may, in the case that the current state satisfies R_j, cause an atomic transition to a state satisfying S_j. This fully characterizes allowed state changes to variables $g_1 \cdots g_n$ under conditions $Q_1 \cdots Q_n$, respectively.

Liveness properties are stated in temporal logic using only unary $\Box$ and $\Diamond$ operators.

Fig. 5 illustrates the sender specification using the program

safety properties

A1. at Dq ⊃ ~packetready

A2. after Dq ⊃ packetready

A3. allowed changes to S_o

    waiting,

    packetready when ~in Dq

  a. $\alpha[S]$: ~waiting ∧ packetready ∧ ~in Dq

    → ~packetready' ∧ S_o' =< nxtmsg, $\overline{S_o.seq}$ > ∧ waiting'

  b. $\alpha[S]$: $S_o = S_i$ ∧ ~corrupted(S_i) → ~waiting'

A4. allowed changes to S_i when ~in Dq

    nxtmsg when ~in Dq ∨ in Dq ∧ $\alpha[S]$

liveness properties

A5. ~waiting ⊃ ◇~packetready

A6. □◇$S_i = S_o$ ∧ ~corrupted(S_i) ⊃ ◇~waiting

A7. □waiting ⊃ □◇in T_s

A8. ~packetready ⊃ ◇in Dq

Fig. 5. Lamport's program module specification for the AB protocol.

module approach. We omit the structural components of the specification, illustrating only the axioms defining allowable behavior. One additional internal state component appears in the specification: the flag *waiting* is used to indicate the sender is awaiting acknowledgment of an outstanding message. One other departure in the composition of the state: rather than include a temporary *packet* state variable, as was done in the previous section, a *nxtmsg* variable is used to record the next message which has been dequeued and is ready to be transmitted. Structurally, the S module consists of a set of atomic actions, denoted $\alpha[S]$. Subroutine Dq and T_s are assumed to be provided within external modules.

The specification for S is partitioned into safety and liveness sections. The first two safety axioms A1 and A2 define the semantics of the auxiliary *packetready* variable: it must be false upon entry to Dq and true upon exit. Parts a and b of axiom A3 define the two allowable state transitions concerning S_o, *waiting* and *packetready*. Part a expresses the transition taking the next message at a time when no acknowledgment is pending. Each primed variable in the output assertion refers to the value *after* the transition. The transition expressed in part b corresponds to noticing any uncorrupted acknowledgment and ceasing to wait further for an acknowledgment. Together these define all allowable transitions—from which one can deduce safety requirements 1)-3).

Safety axiom A4 contains an empty set of allowed transitions. This prevents S_i from being modified by an S action and $nxtmsg$ from being modified by a transition of S during a call on dequeue. Because no safety constraints on calls to T_s are present within the axioms, transmission of the output packet S_o may occur at any time.

Liveness axioms A5–A8 express liveness requirements 4)–6) of Section II. Axioms A5, A2, and A3a together express requirement 6). A5 contributes the requirement that a non-waiting state eventually lead to an observable state in which the next packet has been taken. Safety axiom A3a guarantees that the only way the next packet could have been taken is to have placed it in S_o. A8 then requires that, the next packet having been taken, there must eventually be an attempt to dequeue the next message. This, together with A2 and the specification of dequeue (not given here), guarantees the message will be available for the next packet. Axiom A6 provides liveness requirement 5). Axiom A7 is a bit subtle: if one will never reach a nonwaiting state, because an acknowledgment is never received or never noticed, retransmission must occur infinitely often. Together with axioms A5 and A6, this ensures liveness requirement 4).

The similarity between the program module specification and the graphical state machine specification of the previous section should be apparent. Both have rather complete sets of state components and both define allowable state sequences in terms of a next-state transition relation. The state of the program module contains *more* components than for the state machine. This is due to the ability in the state machine to represent positionally, using multiple nodes, information such as the next sequence number or whether an acknowledgment is awaited. With the program module approach, all such information must be encoded within the state.

Correspondingly, the property-theoretic specification of possible transitions in the program module approach can sometimes simplify the machine specification. The method specifies *constraints* on possible transitions of the state machine, rather than complete elaboration. The program module statement (or lack thereof) indicating when it is allowable to call T_s illustrates this power. The expression of permitted asynchrony in dequeuing the next message in advance of transmission is another example.

The main improvement over the classical state transition specification is the ability to state liveness requirements. Liveness requirements based on single occurrence (A5 and A8), repeated occurrence (A6), and continual occurrence (A7) are all needed and expressed within the program module specification. It is not clear, however, that apart from the question of liveness, the program module approach leads to specifications that are fundamentally different than other state machine specifications.

As Lamport notes, state functions in the specification need not map directly to program variables within the implementation; any combination of implemented state and control structure may be mapped to state functions. Furthermore, atomic transitions in the specification need not be implemented by atomic implementation steps.

As in the case of any specification as an abstract program, a sufficiently comprehensive definition of program equivalence

will allow diverse implementation strategies. One would have considerable difficulty, however, in establishing that the sender process, as implemented in the previous section using two communicating processes, satisfies the program module specification. As an example of the difficulty, axiom A2 requires that as long as control is just after Dq, $packetready$ must remain true. Consider the case of the multiprocess state machine where concurrent processes perform the dequeuing and the A3a transition. The interaction between A2 and A3a then depends not only on the value of $packetready$ but also on the locus of control of the process calling dequeue—greatly complicating the proof. Similar difficulties would arise in attempting to establish that the single process abstract algorithm satisfies the multiprocess specification.

C. Bounded-State Temporal Logic Specification

In this section we illustrate the use of temporal logic specification with bounded-state components in the underlying model. In the underlying model, we retain only the S_o and S_i state components of the program module. The state for the overall node includes a sequence variable InQ, used to define the Dq and Enq operations; liveness requirements for the sender will make use of this variable. The auxiliary synchronization flags, $waiting$ and $packetready$, of the program module specification have been replaced by temporal properties relating between dequeuing and transmission. Fig. 6 illustrates the five temporal logic axioms comprising the specification.

Axioms A1 and A2 together correspond to safety requirements 1)–3). Axiom A1 states that a dequeued message a and the complement of the current sequence number must be placed next in the output variable S_o. Axiom A2 adds to this the requirement that, when a new packet value is placed in S_o, it must remain there until both another message has been dequeued and the corresponding uncorrupted acknowledgment has been received. Thus, successive messages will be transmitted in packets with alternating sequence numbers. Furthermore, the only requirement as to when a message may be dequeued is that exactly one message be dequeued per change to S_o. Requirement 3) follows from this: the strict alternation implies that no other packet values may be transmitted.

Axiom A4 directly expresses liveness requirement 4): if a new packet q is ever placed in S_o, it must be repeatedly transmitted (at least) until an uncorrupted acknowledgment is received. Axiom A3 expresses liveness requirement 5): if an awaited uncorrupted acknowledgment is present infinitely often, eventually a new message packet will be transmitted, provided further message service is requested. Axiom A5 ensures liveness requirement 6), guaranteeing that continued transmission occurs until all messages have been taken out of the queue.

Overall, the specification defines cause and effect relationships that must be true of any realization of the sender. The specification defines what effect on future transmission values is caused by dequeuing a message, how the sender must respond to continually receiving acknowledgments for a trans-

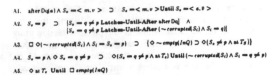

A1. $\text{after } D_s(a) \land S_a = < m, v > \supset S_e = < m, v > \text{Until } S_e = < a, v >$

A2. $S_e = p \supset \{S_e = q \neq p \text{ Latches-Until-After after } D_s\} \land \{S_e = q \neq p \text{ Latches-Until-After } (\sim corrupted(S_t) \land S_t = q\}$

A3. $\Box \Diamond(\sim corrupted(S_t) \land S_t = S_e = p) \supset \{\Diamond \sim empty(InQ) \supset \Diamond(S_e \neq p \land \text{ at } T_S)\}$

A4. $S_e = p \land \Diamond S_e = q \neq p \supset \Diamond(S_e = q \neq p \land \text{ at } T_e) \text{ Until } (\sim corrupted(S_t) \land S_t = q \neq p)$

A5. $\Diamond \text{ at } T, \text{ Until } \Box \; empty(InQ)$

Fig. 6. Bounded state temporal logic specification for the AB protocol.

mitted packet, and what must occur if transmission does not lead to an acknowledgment.

Apart from the liveness properties, the temporal logic specification expresses the same behavioral requirements as the previous state machine definition. The difference lies in how the behavior is specified. In the two previous state machine specifications, behavior is defined in terms of an abstract program, and of transitions between successive states of that program. This requires that the specifications include a complete set of state functions—complete in the sense that any property can be expressed in terms of the current program state. Thus, the specification has more the flavor of the operational description of the protocol given as our introduction to it. Each action used in the program has an effect on the defined state; one determines the overall effect by understanding the results on externally observable variables and function calls.

The bounded-state temporal logic model introduces sufficient state components to facilitate definition of how the state may change during execution—without introducing specific actions to cause the changes. This is achieved through the use of the more expressive binary temporal operators, capable of relating properties at distinct times. This brings the temporal specification closer to the spirit of the requirements given for the protocol. Flexibility in the temporal specification is achieved by stating only required cause-effect relationships, with all further details left unconstrained.

D. Unbounded-State Temporal Logic Specification

In the previous section we employed temporal logic to specify properties of an underlying model containing only bounded-state components. These state components were used to give a "behavioral" specification of the send process. We now modify the underlying model, eliminating any "internal" state components and introducing into the state unbounded history variables to record the sequence of prior values present at each of the visible interfaces. Fig. 7 illustrates this structure. The state variable X records the history of previously enqueued messages, α the history of previously transmitted packets, and δ the history of previously received packets. Thus, the state at each point in the execution sequence consists of the triple $\langle X, \alpha, \delta \rangle$. In this model we do not consider the operations that generate these sequences—we comment later on what is needed to define service operations.

The same temporal language described in the previous section is used here as well. Two additional general predicates are introduced to define unbounded growth of history variables. The predicates $u(A)$ and $uc(A, n)$, for history variable

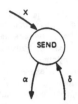

Fig. 7. Structure of unbounded-state AB sender.

A, element value m, and natural number n, are defined by

$$u(A) \equiv \forall n(\Diamond |A| > n)$$

$$uc(A, m) \equiv \forall n(\Diamond c(A, m) > n).$$

In the above, $|A|$ denotes the length of sequence A, and the function $c(A, m)$ denotes the number of times element m is present in sequence A. Predicate $u(A)$ asserts that the history variable A will grow without bound during system execution, while $uc(A, m)$ asserts that the value m will occur an unbounded number of times in A during system execution.

Two other functions on histories are needed to state the requirements for the sender process. For message number i occurring in input history X, we define the corresponding packet M_i by $M_i \equiv [i \bmod 2, X_i]$. Thus, the ith message will be associated with a packet with sequence number $i \bmod 2$. Finally, for output transmission line α, the function $\#(\alpha, n)$ is defined (we do not present the definition here) to return the number of changes of sequence number in α up to position n. The equivalent function on the input transmission history $\#(\delta, n)$ is a bit more complex. The history must be filtered to remove any erroneous packets before counting the number of sign changes. This is defined in terms of a filtered history value $\hat{\delta}$ and revised position value $\pi(n)$. Again, we omit formal definition here.

Fig. 8 illustrates the five axioms comprising the historical state specification of the sender. The specification follows the unbounded history approach used in Hailpern's thesis [4]. Axiom A1, together with the definition of M_i, expresses requirements 1) and 2). The axiom uses essentially a regular expression to proscribe the correspondence in every state between X and α. For some initial subsequence of messages in X, α must be composed of one or more packets for each successive message. The form of each packet is dictated by the definition of M_i, and the possible order of packet transmission is given by axiom A1. Axiom A2 expresses the stipulation of requirement 3) that the transmitted message must be acknowledged prior to initiating transmission of the next message. Stated here, the number of sequence number changes in α must be equal to or one greater than the number of sequence number changes in the (filtered) acknowledgment history δ.

Axioms A3 and A4 express liveness requirements 5) and 6). Axiom A3 contributes the requirement that, if the number of messages in X is equal to i, either the number of sign changes in α will eventually be equal to i, or the output history will grow unboundedly. Stated more simply, if there have been i message requests given, then either the ith message will even-

A1. $\exists n(|X| \geq n \quad \wedge \quad o - < M_i^+ > _{i-1}^+)$

A2. $\#(\delta, |\delta|) \leq \#(\alpha, |\alpha|) \leq \#(\delta, |\delta|) + 1$

A3. $|X| - i \quad \supset \quad u(\alpha) \quad \vee \quad \Diamond \#(\alpha, |\alpha|) - i$

A4. $u(\delta) \quad \supset \quad (\forall n |X| \geq n \supset \Diamond \#(\alpha, |\alpha|) - n)$

A5. $\#(\alpha, |\alpha|) - i \quad \supset \quad u(\alpha, M_i) \quad \vee \quad \Diamond \#(\delta, |\delta|) - i$

Fig. 8. Unbounded state temporal logic specification for the AB protocol.

tually be transmitted, or transmissions must continue without bound. Axiom A3 by itself allows the sender to systematically ignore uncorrupted acknowledgments and continuously retransmit the same packet. This is precluded by A4, which guarantees that if an unbounded number of acknowledgments is received, eventually all messages queued so far will be transmitted. Safety requirements dictate the possible values for continued retransmission.

Axiom A5 embodies liveness requirement 4): if the number of messages transmitted in α is i, either the corresponding packet M_i will occur an unbounded number of times in α or eventually the corresponding will occur in δ. More simply, if the ith message has been transmitted, either the corresponding packet will eventually occur in δ or the packet must be sent an unbounded number of times.

The axioms in this formulation have a distinctly different character from those of the previous two formulations. The state component of the underlying model is both enriched to include memory of all previous input and output parameter values and restricted to include only visible interface values. Rather than a cause-effect "behavioral" style, the axioms define properties of individual parameter histories, as in axiom A1, and relationships between histories, as done in axiom A2. With a state encoding of the entire history of past values, properties such as "successive messages must have alternating sequence numbers" can be stated quite naturally. Other properties may require complex filtering operations on the history values. The # was used to count the number of sign changes in the output history to determine the message currently being transmitted and the number of messages with uncorrupted acknowledgments. These operations are used in place of a more operational specification that encodes in the state the current message and its sequence number.

In general, the approach of Section V-B used current state to determine properties of future "current" states; here, the specification uses the entire past history to determine properties of future "past" history. In this specification method, several histories are interplayed: the history of states underpinning the model and the histories of individual variables present in each state. The history of states is reasoned about using temporal logic, while the history of individual variables is analyzed by explicit quantification over sequences. Auxiliary filtering operations are used to extract appropriate portions of the individual histories. An implementation correctness proof involves showing, in part, that the (necessarily) bounded-state component of an implementation is sufficient to guarantee that the properties expressed by unbounded histories can be realized.

The unbounded-state temporal logic specification, unlike the earlier specifications presented, does not described the flow of control associated with the Dq operation. Indeed, each module is specified in terms of input-output sequences, with no operation interface specification. By itself, this is not sufficient to express flow of control properties such as a Dq operation which, if called when the queue is empty, does not return until a message is available, or to express the semantics of "out of order operations," such as $Reset$. To handle the flow of control associated with the Dq operation, it would appear necessary to modify the input history X to be a sequence of prior "event values," each being at Dq or after $Dq(m)$. This history would have to be filtered to make available the current interpretation of X. Similar consequences arise from more complex interfaces involving several different operations.

E. Event Sequence Specification

At the far end of the spectrum is an event sequence approach with no state component in the underlying model other than an indication of whether a given parameterized event is occurring. We use temporal logic as the specification language to allow arbitrary properties of the underlying event model to be stated. An event sequence temporal logic specification expresses constraints on allowable sequences of events; any sequence that satisfies the constraints constitutes valid behavior.

Within our state-based temporal logic, the predicates at, in, and after are used to determine currently active actions. In a state-based model, it is possible to avoid any requirement that events be atomic or noninterruptable. However, where there is no notion of state, it may be difficult to reason about concurrent interaction without requiring that events be nonoverlapping in time. In our specification, at T_S and after T_S represent, in effect, distinct events.

We should stress that the approach illustrated here, using a state-based event model and a property-theoretic temporal language, has not been specifically reported in the literature. After presenting the sender process specification, we comment on variants of this approach that have appeared in the literature. It should be clear from the specification we present here that the temporal language chosen is not well suited for this form of specification. It appears, however, that much of the specification complexity is inherent and is caused by the lack of state component to establish context.

Fig. 9 illustrates the five axioms comprising the specification. While the axioms might appear completely unintelligible at first (and maybe second) glance, they can be structurally decomposed quite easily. Recall that the scheme P **Until** (Q **Until** R) indicates that P must hold until Q becomes true, which in turn, must hold until R becomes true. Similarly, for state variable x and free logical variable v, the scheme $x = v$ **Latches-Until** $x = 16$ indicates that variable x must retain its current value until it changes to 16. In the event sequence specification we use the derived predicate

$$\text{Transmits}\,(m, v) \equiv \forall m_1 v_1$$

$$\text{at } T_S(\langle m_1, v_1 \rangle) \supset \langle m_1, v_1 \rangle = \langle m, v \rangle$$

to denote the transmission of only $\langle m, v \rangle$. For parameterized

A1: Transmit⟨p, r⟩

Latches
Until ∃ n {Transmit⟨n, r⟩
Latches {after Dq₀(m)
Until ∃ m {∧ Transmit⟨n, r⟩ Until at Tᵣ{< m, r >}}}

A2: Transmit⟨n, r⟩

Latches {Transmit⟨m, r⟩
Until ∃ m {Latches-Until at Rᵣ{< m, r >, uncorrupted}}

A3: Transmit⟨n, r⟩

Latches {at Tᵣ{< m, r >} ⊃
Until ∃ m {{ ◇(at Rᵣ{< m, r >, uncorrupted}) ∨ □ ◇ at Tᵣ }}

A4: at Tᵣ{< n, r >} ∧ Transmit⟨n, v⟩ Until after Dq₀(m)
∧ ◇ at Rᵣ{< n, v >, uncorrupted} ∧ ◇ after Dq₀(m)
⊃ ◇ at Tᵣ{< m, r >}

A5: Transmit⟨p, r⟩

Latches
Until ∃ n {Transmit⟨n, v⟩
Latches {after Dq₀(m)
Until ∃ m {Latches {∧ Transmit⟨n, v⟩
Until {at Tᵣ{< m, v >} ∧
{(◇ Rᵣ{< m, v >} ⊃ ◇ at Dq₀}}}}}

Fig. 9. Event sequence temporal logic specification for the AB protocol.

events at $T_S(\langle m, v \rangle)$ and at $R_S(\langle m, v \rangle)$, the formula

Transmits (m, v) Latches–Until–After at $R_S(\langle m, v \rangle)$

states that if transmission of some packet $\langle m, v \rangle$ occurs, only that packet may be retransmitted until a receive event for $\langle m, v \rangle$ occurs.

Of the actual axioms, A1 and A2 represent safety properties and A3–A5 represent liveness requirements. Axiom A1 expresses requirements 1) and 2). The heart of the axiom is quite simple, and corresponds to axioms A1 and A2 of the bounded-state temporal logic specification: if packet $\langle n, v \rangle$ is "current" when a $Dq(m)$ occurs, the next change in packet transmitted must be to value $\langle m, \bar{v} \rangle$. The difficulty is that the state information giving the last packet value transmitted and the last message dequeued does not exist in this model. These prior values must be established using temporal operations over the state sequence. In doing so, one must use nested Until expressions to guarantee that the transmission of the packet $\langle n, v \rangle$ is the first transmission of that packet and, thus, prior to the dequeue action. Then, only the packet $\langle n, v \rangle$ can be transmitted until the next message m is dequeued and until $\langle m, \bar{v} \rangle$ is transmitted. Without the outer Until, a transmission of $\langle m, v \rangle$ following the dequeuing operation requires latching the transmitted value until a condition that does not occur.

Axiom A2, expressing requirement 3), has a similar structure. The outer level of Until operator is used to establish the *first* transmission of packet $\langle m, v \rangle$. From that point on, only that packet must be transmitted until an uncorrupted acknowledgment action occurs. Had we not established the point of first transmission, the axiom would have required that *any transmission* of a packet be followed by a corresponding acknowledgment, even if any acknowledgment had been previously received.

Axiom A3 rather directly expresses liveness requirement 4). Axioms A4 and A5 together embody liveness requirements

5) and 6). Axiom 4 contributes the requirement that transmission of packet $\langle n, v \rangle$, eventual uncorrupted acknowledgment, and eventual dequeuing of another message m must lead to transmission of packet $\langle m, \bar{v} \rangle$. Thus, if an acknowledgment for the outstanding packet is received and "noticed" by successfully dequeuing a further message, then the next message will eventually be transmitted.

Axiom A5 contributes the additional requirement that only the outstanding packet can be retransmitted until an acknowledgment is received and eventually noticed by attempting to dequeue another message. The outer two Latches–Until layers of axiom A5 are identical to axiom A1 and are needed to establish last packet value transmitted before dequeuing next message m. The inner structure expresses the requirement that, after next message m is dequeued, 1) only the prior packet may be retransmitted until the newly formed packet containing m has been transmitted and 2) if an uncorrupted acknowledgement is eventually received, it will be noticed by later calling dequeue to request the next message.

The statement of required behavior for the sender using this formulation of event sequences is significantly more complex than for the previous specifications. It can be argued that the use of an event-based temporal approach rather than a state-based approach, different operators for reasoning about temporal properties of sequences, or the use of a more generative language could have simplified this task. The use of Wolper's "grammar operators" [9], defining finite state recognizers for event sequences, could produce some simplification of the specification.

There does seem to be a fundamental problem with property-theoretic specification of allowable event sequences with no other notion of state. Without the context present in a (bounded or unbounded) state component, one is *always* forced to constrain the sequence from the earliest event bearing on the requirement. Requirements such as "successive messages from the queue must be transmitted in packets with alternating sequence numbers" necessitate correlation of five events in the sequence to overcome the lack of state information. Vogt's use [8] of an event-based temporal logic ameliorates the situation somewhat by allowing the specifier to make explicit use of a history variable representing *the* sequence of past events, in much the same manner as described in the previous section having established context in terms of properties of the past history, one uses a pure "stateless" approach to reason about the future.

Generative specification of allowable sequences does not have the problem of establishing sufficient context. In generative sequence expression languages, such as Schindler's RSPL [10] and the ISO Subgroup C Interaction Primitive Language [11], one large sequence expression explicitly generates the set of allowable sequences. This is in contrast to the property-theoretic approach in which a recognizer of allowable sequences is given as a set of independent properties that must be satisfied. In building one large ordering expression, the composition of ordering expressions implicitly builds context. But it is difficult to conceive how the very general requirements we impose on the sender process would be succinctly stated as one large sequence expression.

VI. RECONCILIATION

That none of the specifications given for the sender is completely satisfying seems clear. Moreover, even for this simple protocol, we find it difficult to achieve certainty that our specifications correctly reflect our abstract requirements. For a real protocol, formal mechanical verification that the protocol specification satisfies the service specification appears essential to precluding errors. We are currently extending our STP verification system [17] to include a decision procedure for temporal logic with embedded interpreted theories. With this we will be able to mechanically validate protocol specifications such as those above.

Of the specifications given, the state transition diagram seems to be the easiest to understand. This is disappointing for several reasons. First, it is unlikely that the transparency of specification can be maintained as the size and complexity of the protocol increases. Unless a designer copies exactly the states and transitions of the specification, he must glean requirements by understanding all possible behavior of a nondeterministic abstract model of the protocol, which places a heavy burden on him. Implementation flexibility is achieved only by elaborating the full range of desired solutions, using techniques such as nondeterministic transitions and asynchronous machines. Moreover, the user is given the burden of separating requirement from expedient in the specification; the set of conforming implementations for a given state transition specification is far from clear. Also, the state transition specification does not define liveness requirements for the protocol—key requirements for an implementation to support.

Our sample specifications do point out that more concrete state components and the use of state-transforming functions can facilitate statement of requirements, at the expense of complicating the detail of the specification and potentially biasing the choice of implementation. For more abstract specifications such as the temporal logic approaches to succeed, much higher level temporal abstractions are needed to succinctly capture temporal properties. Toward this end, we are currently developing a temporal interval logic. In addition, the specification method needs to be sufficiently flexible to allow the specifier to arbitrarily choose as to how much state information to include in the underlying model. The method itself should permit bounded and unbounded, internal and interface, state components. The tradeoff between implementation flexibility, ease of description, and historical versus behavioral specification can then be decided on a case-by-case basis. In this sense we argue for a midspectrum choice of specification approach.

REFERENCES

[1] ISO TC97/SC16/WG1 Subgroup A on Architecture. "Concepts for describing the OSI architecture." working draft, Ispra, Nov. 1981.
[2] D. Lehmann, A. Pnueli, and J. Stavi, "Impartiality, justice and fairness: The ethics of concurrent termination." in *Proc. ICALP 81*. New York: Springer Verlag, July 1981.
[3] Z. Manna and A. Pnueli, "Verification of concurrent programs. Part I: The temporal framework." Dep. Comput. Sci., Stanford Univ., Stanford, CA, Tech. Rep. STAN-CS-81-836, June 1981.
[4] B. Hailpern. "Verifying concurrent processes using temporal logic." Comput. Syst. Lab., Stanford Univ., Stanford, CA, Tech. Rep. 195, Aug. 1980.
[5] ISO TC97/SC16/WG1 Subgroup B on State Machines. "A FDT based on an extended state transition model." working draft. Boston, MA, Dec. 1981.
[6] O. Herzog. "Static analysis of concurrent processes for dynamic properties using Petri nets." in *Semantics of Concurrent Computation*. Evian, France: Springer Verlag, 1979.
[7] L. Lamport, "Specifying concurrent program modules." Comput. Sci. Lab., SRI Int., June 1981; also *TOPLAS*, to be published.
[8] F. Vogt. "Event-based temporal logic specification of distributed systems." Ph.D. dissertation, Hahn-Meitner Inst., Berlin, Germany, Feb. 1982.
[9] P. Wolper. "Specification and synthesis of communicating processes using an extended temporal logic." in *Proc. POPL 82*. ACM. Albuquerque, NM, Jan. 1982.
[10] S. Schindler, "Basic concepts of formal specification techniques and of RSPL." Tech. Univ. Berlin, Berlin, Germany, Tech. Rep., May 1980.
[11] ISO/TC97/SC16/WG1 Subgroup on Temporal Ordering Expressions. "Interaction primitives in formal specification of distributed systems." working paper. Washington, DC, Sept. 1981.
[12] P. E. Lauer, P. Torrigiani, and M. Shields. "COSY: A system specification language based on paths and processes." *Acta Inform.*, vol. 12, pp. 109–158, 1979.
[13] R. L. Schwartz and P. M. Melliar-Smith. "Temporal logic specification of distributed systems." in *Proc. IEEE Conf. Distributed Syst.*, Apr. 1981 (revised version available from the authors).
[14] L. Lamport, "Sometime is sometimes not never." in *Proc. POPL 1980*, ACM, Las Vegas, NV, Jan. 1980.
[15] B. Berthomieu, "Algebraic specification of communication protocols." Inform. Sci. Inst., Univ. Southern California, Los Angeles, Tech. Rep. RR-81-98, Dec. 1981.
[16] S. Gerhart *et al.*, "An overview of AFFIRM: A specification and verification system." in *Proc. IFIP Congress 80*, Oct. 1980.
[17] R. E. Shostak, R. L. Schwartz, and P. M. Melliar-Smith. "STP: A mechanized logic for specification and verification." in *Proc. 6th Conf. Automated Deduction* (Lecture Notes in Computer Science, vol. 138). New York: Springer Verlag, June 1982.

★

A Practical Approach to the Analysis

of Concurrent Systems

by J.R. ABRIAL

(August 1983)

Abstract

The main thesis of this paper is that the analysis of concurrent programs (i.e. their specifications, their proofs of correctness, deadlockfreeness, etc.), can be done by using methods very similar to those used for analysing sequential programs.

This approach, which is certainly not new (for instance see (1),(5),(12), and (13) among others), is illustrated by various examples.

The first group of examples shows the transformations of various sequential programs into equivalent pairs of concurrent programs.

The last example shows how a network of concurrent programs can be abstracted by a very special non-deterministic sequential program. Consequently, properties of the network can be proved by applying traditional methods on its abstraction.

Some of the programs constructed in the examples are written in (pidgin) ADA.

1. INTRODUCTION

The main purpose of this paper is to show how to use in practice the notion of trace ((1), (13)) to reason about concurrent programs. In this introduction we shall specify the kinds of programs in which we are interested. We shall then introduce the concept of trace and informally define the notion of cooperation among concurrent programs.

The concurrent programs we are interested in are those programs which communicate among themselves via some well defined mechanisms. Examples of such mechanisms are the Input/Output commands (? and !) of CSP (2), the entry call and "accept" statements of ADA (7), even the procedure call and "return" statements of, say, PASCAL or the less traditional "resume" statement used for communication between two coroutines (4), and finally the typical "send" and "receive" commands used to describe transmission protocols. We assume that the reader is familiar with such mechanisms.

There are, of course, other means by which concurrent programs might communicate: for instance a variable, the usage of which is shared among several programs, constitutes an obvious communication channel among them. However it is well known that the non-disciplined utilization of such variables leads to the construction of very fragile systems and it is also well known (2) that a shared variable can always be "encapsulated"into a concurrent program. Consequently, we shall not consider in this paper any communication performed through such shared variables. However, we shall bear in mind the pioneering work done by Owicki and Gries (5) which constitutes one of the first attempts ever made to formally analyze parallel programs.

Before beginning the technical developments, it is certainly worthwhile to clarify what is meant by an expression such as "to reason about concurrent programs". In fact, the meaning of such an expression, when applied to sequential programs, is quite clear, especially after the work of Floyd (6), Hoare (3), Dijkstra (8) and more recently that of Jones (11) among others. The message conveyed by all these people is essentially the following: a (sequential) program written in some well defined programming notation can be put into correspondance with some mathematical objects (for instance functions, relations or the associated predicates) and these objects, whatever their precise forms, all express in various ways the relationship between the input and the output of the program. As a consequence "to reason about sequential programs" consists of proving relevant properties which their associated mathematical objects should have (sometimes, such properties are called "specifications").

Concerning concurrent programs, the situation is, as expected, a little more delicate. One of the reasons for this lies in the fact that such programs do not have inputs and outputs defined as easily as is the case for sequential programs. For instance, what are the inputs of an Operating System ? its outputs? In fact, such inputs and outputs are made up of flows of data so intricately intertwined that it is hardly possible to imagine the existence of any mathematical object which could represent their relationship. Moreover, such flows of data are usually incomplete: for instance, considering an Operating System (a "program" which is not suppose to halt), there is no hope of ever reaching a point in time where its inputs and outputs could be contemplated as a whole.

This is the reason why the paradigm of Input/Output has to be abandoned in favor of the more promising concept of event. Roughly speaking a set of concurrent programs can be regarded as a huge "event producer". That some events correspond to the entry of some data and that some other events correspond to the exit of some other data, is in fact irrelevant. Rather, this is the concept of non-determinacy (10) which makes the distinction: an input is not determined by the actual state of the system, whereas an output certainly is. Consequently, and to summarize at this point, a set of concurrent programs is just a non-deterministic event producer. Moreover, because an event, when "produced" is already part of the past of the system, we might say that a system is a non-deterministic producer of its past.

As a consequence, "to reason about a system of concurrent programs" consists of reasoning about its past. For instance, we might specify a system by stating some of the properties of its possible pasts and, once constructed, we might prove that the system in question (i.e. the possible pasts in question) agrees with its specification. However, the very concept of past is not so easy to handle. In fact, as already noticed, the past of a system, especially that of a system that is supposed to run for ever, is never complete. In other words, the entire past of such a system must be regarded as an infinite object and our reasoning about it can only be an "approximate reasoning".

In order to make such a strange way of reasoning possible, we shall suppose that our systems, although capable of running forever, are not systems which have always been running: they should have been started at some point. This assumption helps us to transform the rather fuzzy notion of approximate reasoning into that of reasoning about approximations. Such (finite) approximations correspond to the various pasts-so-far that the system is able to produce in the course of its activity.

Finite approximations of the past might be represented in various ways. However, all such representations must have some common properties which correspond, more or less, to the Peano Axioms of Natural Numbers. For instance, there must exist a "zero" past, which is supposed to be the "past" of a not-yet-started system. Given an approximation of the past, a "better" approximation can be obtained (if the system is willing to proceed) by applying to the former certain "successor" functions. Finally, some sort of reasoning by induction should be applicable to prove properties of all these approximations of the past . Candidates having such properties are numerous, for instance the Natural Numbers, the tuples of such Numbers, the finite sequences, the tuples of such sequences, the finite trees, etc. Traditionally, the term "trace" is used to characterize past approximations which are represented by finite sequences.

Another outcome of this definition of a concurrent program by the set of approximations of its possible pasts, is that the cooperation of two (or more) such programs can be handled very easily. Such a cooperation is also defined by a set of past approximations, a set which must obviously be the intersection of the sets of past approximations corresponding to each individual cooperating program.

*

* *

The rest of this paper is organized as follows: we shall first give a brief review of some useful notations for handling finite sequences (Section 2); then we shall study various examples showing the transformations of various sequential programs into equivalent pairs of concurrent programs (Section 3); finally, we shall see how concurrent programs might be studied by representing the generation of their traces in the form of very special non-deterministic sequential programs.

2. NOTATIONS AND PRINCIPLES FOR SEQUENCES

In the following we shall extensively use the concept of finite sequence; in this section we shall briefly review a few notations and principles that may be applied to such sequences.

Given a set X , X^* denotes the set of all finite sequences of elements of X ; $\langle\rangle$ denotes the empty sequence, $\langle x\rangle$ the sequence containing the single element x , $\langle x,y\rangle$ one containing x and y in that order, and so on. If x is a member of X and s is a member of X^* then $s\,x$ is the result of postfixing x to s , likewise $x\,s$ is the result of prefixing x to s . Given a non-empty sequence belonging to X^* , that is, a sequence of the unique form $x\,s$ and also of the unique form $y\,t$ (for s and t in X^* and x and y in X), we shall frequently use the four functions frst , rest , last , and past defined as follows:

$$frst(x\ s) = x$$
$$rest(x\ s) = s$$
$$last(t\ y) = y$$
$$past(t\ y) = t$$

Subsets of X^* can be defined inductively by "equations" such as:

$$s = \begin{cases} f(s) \\ \\ t \end{cases}$$

where s and t denote elements of X^* and where f denotes a total monotone function from X^* to X^* (note that f may depend on some other free variables). Such an equation defines the smallest subset of X^* which contains the sequence t and also the sequence $f(s)$ provided it already contains the sequence s . This equation defines a set S and leads to two important principles.

Firstly, a <u>principle of (structural) induction</u>: in order to prove that all members of S have a certain property, it is sufficient to prove this property first for the sequence t (the basis) and then for sequences of the form f(s) , under the assumption that s already possesses the property (the induction step).

Secondly, a <u>principle of (primitive) recursion</u>: in order to define a function on all members of S , it is sufficient to give its value at t and then at "points" of the form f(s) in terms of its value at s . Note that this second principle can only be applied without further assumptions if f is a one-one function.

The set X^* may itself be defined inductively as follows

$$s = \begin{cases} s\ x & \text{for } x \text{ in } X \\ \\ <> \end{cases}$$

Consequently, the above principles are applicable to X^* . For instance the size of a sequence s , denoted |s| , can be recursively defined as follows

$$|<>| = 0$$
$$|s\ x| = |s| + 1$$

3. FROM SEQUENTIAL TO CONCURRENT PROGRAMS

In order to gradually introduce the concept and technique of traces, in this section, we shall study various examples showing how a single sequential program can be transformed into an equivalent pair of concurrent programs. The examples are very artificial and elementary: their purpose is to explain and to illustrate. We do not recommend that these transformations are to be done in practice!

3.1. DISTRIBUTING THE COMPUTATION OF FIBONACCI NUMBERS

The infinite sequence of numbers

$$0 \quad 1 \quad 1 \quad 2 \quad 3 \quad 5 \quad 8 \quad 13 \quad \ldots$$

in which each element is the sum of the preceding two, is called the Fibonacci sequence. Given a Natural Number n , the program

(3.1)
```
x,y : integer;
x := 0 ; y := 1 ;
for i in 1 to n do
    x := x+y ;   y := y+x
end
```

terminates and results in the final value of x (resp. y) being equal to that of the $2n^{th}$ (resp. $2n+1^{st}$) Fibonacci number. This result can be easily proved by induction. Note that a program fragment such as

```
for i in 1 to n do
    statement
end
```

is a mere shorthand for

```
begin
    i: integer;
    i := 0 ;
    while i < n do
        i := i+1 ;
        statement
    end
end
```

The apparent symmetry of program (3.1) with regard to x and y , suggests that it might be split into two parts, one responsible for the incrementation of x and the other for that of y .

(3.2)

```
x,y': integer;              x',y: integer;
x := 0 ;                    y := 1 ;
for i in 1 to n do          for i in 1 to n do
    x := x+y'                   y := y+x'
end                         end
```


However these two programs can hardly define any computation at all because the value of the variable x' (resp. y') in the right (resp. left) program is undefined.

In order for these programs to do something useful they must oooperate, that is, exchange some information from time to time. Consequently, we shall suppose that we have at our disposal two communication primitives s and r (for send and receive). These primitives need to be matched against each other in that each s(x) (send x) in one program has a corresponding r(x') (receive in x') in the other and vice versa. Moreover the parameter x in s(x) is supposed to be a "by value" parameter, whereas x' in r(x') is supposed to be a "by reference" parameter. Consequently, r(x') has the side effect of updating the local variable x' with the value of x in the matching s(x) (in CSP, s is ! and r is ?). Here are our two cooperating programs P and Q .

(3.3)

```
x,y': integer;              x',y: integer;
x := 0 ;                    y := 1 ;
for i in 1 to n do          for i in 1 to n do
    r(y');  ←───────────────── s(y);
    x := x+ŷ';  ──────────→   r(x');
    s(x)                      y := y+x'
end                         end
```

Although we can informally follow their cooperative computation, it is not so simple to prove that P and Q yield the desired result. Following the lead of (5), we shall first consider each program __individually__. For instance, if we trace the successive values received and sent by P (the left program), we may obtain the following results corresponding to three different experiments (where n=3)

(3.4)

r(y')	s(x)	r(y')	s(x)	r(y')	s(x)
7	7	3	10	2	12
2	2	5	7	1	8
1	1	2	3	5	8

As can be seen, P is able to produce various traces depending on the successive values of y' it receives from its __environment__. For the moment, we purposely __ignore__ that this environment is made up of the other program Q . Rather, we regard it as a mere sequential "file" of __sufficient size__.

An interesting question that may be raised at this point is one of characterizing the various traces our program P is able to produce for all possible "contents" of its environment (supposedly of sufficient "size"). Let A be the set of sequences inductively defined as follows:

(3.5)

$$a = \begin{cases} a \ y' \ y'+last(a) & \text{if } |a| \geqslant 1 \text{ and for } y' \text{ in } N \\ \langle y',y' \rangle & \text{for } y' \text{ in } N \\ \langle \ \rangle \end{cases}$$

The possible traces of program P correspond exactly to the members of size 2n of
A . In order to prove this result, it is sufficient to introduce in P a (dummy)
sequence variable a , whose role is to record the trace as it is generated. This
transformation of P yields the following program:

(3.6)

```
x,y': integer;
a: integer*;
x := 0 ;
a := <>;
for i in 1 to n do
    r(y') ;   a := a y' ;
    x := x+y' ;
    s(x)   ;   a := a x
end
```

Note that we have initialized the trace to the empty sequence. It is now easy to
prove that the final content of a is a member of size 2n of A and conversely
that all members of size 2n of A can be so generated by P . This proof, which
can be done by using conventional sequential program proof methods (3), uses the
following invariant for the main loop:

(3.7)
$$x = last(0\ a)$$
$$a \in A$$
$$|a| = 2i$$

We now turn our attention to program Q (the right program of (3.3)) and
similarly characterize its possible traces. We can prove, again by conventional
proof methods, that these traces are exactly the members of size 2n of the set
B , inductively defined as follows:

(3.8)
$$b = \begin{cases} b\ \ last(b)+last(past(b))\ \ x' & \text{if } |b| \geq 2 \text{ and for } x' \text{ in } N \\ \langle 1, x' \rangle & \text{for } x' \text{ in } N \\ \langle\,\rangle & \end{cases}$$

This time, the loop invariant is

(3.9)
$$y = last(0\ 1\ b)+last(past(0\ 1\ b))$$
$$b \in B$$
$$|b| = 2i$$

It must then be clear that the cooperation of P and Q requires a trace of size 2n which belongs to both A and B . Consequently, it is important to characterize the intersection of these sets. Their inductive definitions (3.5) and (3.8) suggest that we define a set C as follows:

(3.10)
$$c = \begin{cases} c\ y'\ x' & \text{if } |c| \geqslant 2 \\ \langle 1,1 \rangle \\ \langle \rangle \end{cases}$$

where

(3.11)
$$x' = y'+last(c)$$
$$y' = last(c)+last(past(c))$$

That members of C belong to both A and B is a direct consequence of their definitions. That members of A∩B are members of C can be proved by (structural) induction. In fact the statement to prove "for all members a of A " is

(3.12)
$$a \in B \Rightarrow a \in C$$

The two bases of the induction are simple; the induction step requires proving

(3.13)
$$(a\ y'\ y'+last(a)) \in C$$

under the following hypothesis

(3.14) $(a \quad y' \quad y'+last(a)) = (b \quad last(b)+last(past(b)) \quad x')$
                 $a = b \Rightarrow a \in C$

Condition (3.13) follows from the definition of C (in particular definitions
seen in (3.11)) and from elementary properties of sequences.

    Our initial goal was to prove that the final value of x (resp. y) was equal
to that of the $2n^{th}$ (resp. $2n+1^{st}$) Fibonacci number. To do so, it is obviously sufficient (after invariants (3.7) and (3.9)) to prove that C is the set of all initial
finite subsequences of even size of the Fibonacci infinite sequence. This last result
can be proved very easily by (structural) induction.

    From this example, we have learned a **method** for analysing concurrent programs.
This method can be summarized as follows:

    (i) Characterize the possible traces of each program considered
            individually. This results in the inductive definition of some sets.

    (ii) Express the cooperation of the programs by the intersection of
            these sets. Characterize this intersection.

    (iii) Prove the desired results on traces which belongs to the intersection.

    It is worth noting that proofs in (i) were done by using conventional proof
methods, ˙and that proofs in (ii) and (iii) were done by structural induction. The
only place where some creation was required was in part (i) for the inductive
definitions.

3.2. MUTUAL TRANSFORMATIONS OF TWO SETS

In the previous example, the two concurrent programs P and Q were mere
coroutines. They did not perform any computations in parallel. In this example, derived
from an exercise of E.W. Dijkstra (9) and also studied in (12) and (13), we shall
have more parallelism.

Given two finite, non-empty, and disjoint sets of integers S and T, the
program

(3.16)
```
X,Y: set of integer;
(X,Y) := (S,T);
while  min(Y) < max(X)  do
    (X,Y) := (X',Y')
end
```

where

(3.17)
$$X' = (X-\{max(X)\}) \cup \{min(Y)\}$$
$$Y' = (Y-\{min(Y)\}) \cup \{max(X)\}$$

terminates. It also results in two finite, non-empty, and disjoint sets of integers
X and Y , the union of which is equal to that of S and T . Moreover, all
members of X are smaller than those of Y . We shall now split this program, which
contains two "parallel" assignments, into two concurrent programs which do not.

(3.18)
```
X: set of integer;          Y: set of integer;
y: integer;                 x: integer;
X := S ;                    Y := T ;
while  y < max(X)  do        while  min(Y) < x  do
    X := (X-{max(X)}) ∪ {y}      Y := (Y-{min(Y)}) ∪ {x}
end                         end
```

As in the previous example, these two programs cannot perform any computation unless they cooperate. To do so, we shall suppose that we have at our disposal two matching primitives exchg1 and exchg2 which allow for a **full-duplex** communication between two partners. This leads to the following concurrent programs P and Q .

(3.19)

```
X: set of integer;            Y: set of integer;
y: integer;                   x: integer;
X := S ;                      Y := T ;
exchg1(max(X),y);  <------->  exchg2(x,min(Y));
while y < max(X)  do          while min(Y) < x  do
   X := (X-{max(X)})∪{y};        Y := (Y-{min(Y)})∪{x};
   exchg1(y,max(X))  <----->     exchg2(min(Y),x)
end                           end
```

Note that the first parameter in the primitive exchg1 is supposed to be a "by value" parameter, whereas the second one is "by reference". The situation is symmetric in exchg2 : the first one is "by reference" and the second one is "by value".

Such a full-duplex exchange mechanism can be implemented in ADA by means of a third concurrent program, a "task", having two "entries" exchg1 and exchg2 and whose "body" is:

(3.20)

```
loop
   accept  exchg2(out a',in b)  do
      accept  exchg1(in a,out b')  do
         a' := a ;  b' := b
      end
   end
end
```

Our task is now to prove that the two concurrent programs P and Q behave like the initial sequential program (3.16). To do so, we shall characterize the sets of possible traces that each program is able to produce whatever its environment, as in the previous example. Elements of these traces are the <u>pairs of</u> <u>numbers</u> which are supposed to be exchanged. Let A be the set of sequences inductively defined as follows

$$(3.21) \qquad a = \begin{cases} a \ \ (\max(f_S(a)),y) & \text{for all } y \text{ in } N \\ \\ <\,> \end{cases}$$

where f_S is a set function recursively defined (see Section 2) for all sequences of pairs of numbers

$$(3.22) \qquad \begin{aligned} &f_S(<\,>) = S \\ &f_S(s \ \ (x,y)) = (f_S(s)-\{\max(f_S(s))\}) \cup \{y\} \end{aligned}$$

It is not difficult to prove that the traces of program P belong to the set A. Hint: consider the following loop invariant

$$(3.23) \qquad \begin{aligned} &|a| \geqslant 1 \\ &X = f_S(\text{past}(a)) \\ &a \in A \\ &y < x \quad \text{for all } (x,y) \text{ in } \text{past}(a) \end{aligned}$$

More precisely the <u>while</u> statement in program P imposes that the possible traces of P are exactly the non-empty members a of A such that the following condition holds:

$$(3.24) \qquad \begin{aligned} &y < x \quad \text{for all } (x,y) \text{ in } \text{past}(a) \\ &x \leqslant y \quad \text{where } (x,y) = \text{last}(a) \end{aligned}$$

Likewise, we may inductively define the following set B

(3.25)
$$b = \begin{cases} b \ (x,\min(g_T(b))) & \text{for all } x \text{ in } N \\ \\ <> \end{cases}$$

where g_T is a set function recursively defined as follows

(3.26)
$$g_T(<>) = T$$
$$g_T(t \ (x,y)) = (g_T(t)-\{\min(g_T(t))\}) \cup \{x\}$$

The possible traces of program Q are exactly those members of set B which follow a condition similar to condition (3.24).

When programs P and Q cooperate, their common trace (if any) must belong to the intersection of A and B . It is not difficult to prove by induction that this intersection is equal to the set C inductively defined as follows

(3.27)
$$c = \begin{cases} c \ (\max(f_S(c)),\min(g_T(c))) \\ \\ <> \end{cases}$$

More precisely, and because of condition (3.24), this trace must be a member of C whose last element (x,y) is such that $x \leqslant y$. Moreover, it must be the <u>smallest</u> such element. Such a trace does exist (the proof is exactly the same as that of the termination of program (3.16)). Consequently the desired result follows easily.

3.3. DISTRIBUTING A SIMPLE COMPUTATION

At first glance, our third example might seem even more artificial than the previous ones. However we shall study it for two reasons. Firstly because it shows the cooperation of two concurrent programs which have different structures, and secondly because the traces of these programs will be made up of two sequences rather than a single one as before. Here is our initial sequential program

(3.28)
```
x: integer;
x := 0 ;
for i in 1 to n do
    x := x+i
end
```

Given a Natural Number n , the final value of x is obviously the sum 0+1+...+n .
We shall now suppose that the variable x is stored on an external device having two commands, read and write. Of course, we also need a local variable y (a buffer) to store the just read values. Here is our new program obtained from (3.28) after these transformations

(3.29)
```
y: integer;
write(0);
for i in 1 to n do
    read(y);
    write(y+i)
end
```

Note that the parameter in read is a "by reference" parameter whereas that in write is "by value". In order to analyse the behavior of program (3.29), we shall record the read and written values in two (dummy) sequence variables r and w as follows

(3.30)

```
          y: integer;
          r,w: integer*;
          r := <>;
          w := <>;
          write(0);        w := w 0 ;
          for i in 1 to n do
             read(y);        r := r y ;
             write(y+i);     w := w y+i
          end
```

Let A be the set of pairs of sequences inductively defined as follows

$$(3.31) \qquad (r,w) = \begin{cases} r\ y\ ,\ w & \text{if } |w|=|r|+1 \text{ and for } y \text{ in } N \\ r\ \ ,\ w\ last(r)+|w| & \text{if } |w|=|r| \text{ \& } |r| \geqslant 1 \\ <>\ ,\ <0> \end{cases}$$

Note that we have extended the notation used for the inductive definition of a set of sequences to that of a set of pairs of sequences. We can easily prove by conventional means that the set of pairs of traces generated by program (3.30) exactly corresponds to those members of A whose w component is of size n+1 . Hint: consider the following loop invariant:

(3.32)
$$|w|=|r|+1$$
$$i = |r|$$

The behavior of the "external device" that memorizes the value of variable x in program (3.28) may be specified by means of the set B , inductively defined as follows

$$(3.33) \qquad (r,w) = \begin{cases} r\ last(w)\ ,\ w & \text{if } |w| \geqslant 1 \\ r\ \ ,\ w\ x & \text{for } x \text{ in } N \\ <>\ \ ,\ < > \end{cases}$$

As can be seen, the element that may be read from the device is equal to the last element (if any) that has been written on it. This acts like a memory.

When program (3.30) cooperates with the memory, the common traces are obviously the pair of sequences (of size n and n+1) belonging to the set C defined as follows

$$(3.34) \qquad (r,w) = \begin{cases} r \ last(w) \ , \ w & \text{if } |w| = |r| + 1 \\ r & , \ w \ last(r) + |w| & \text{if } |w| = |r| \ \& \ |r| \geqslant 1 \\ \langle \ \rangle & , \ \langle \ 0 \rangle \end{cases}$$

It is then easy to prove by (structural) induction that these pairs of traces are such that

$$(3.35) \qquad r = w \quad \vee \quad r = past(w)$$
$$|w| \geqslant 1$$
$$last(w) = 0 + 1 + \ldots + (|w| - 1)$$

As a consequence, when program (3.30) terminates, we have $last(w) = 0 + 1 + \ldots + n$.

Note that an ADA "task" corresponding to the memory has the following "body" and two "entries" read and write .

(3.36)
```
x: integer;
accept write(in y)  do x:=y end;
loop
    select
        accept read(out y)  do y:=x  end
    or
        accept write(in y )  do x:=y  end
    end
end
```

4. FROM CONCURRENT TO SEQUENTIAL PROGRAMS

In the previous section we have studied various examples showing the transformation of various sequential programs into equivalent concurrent ones. In order to perform the proofs we have analysed the concurrent programs by studying their traces by means of inductively defined sets of sequences (in the last example the sets in question were even sets of <u>pairs</u> of sequences). The cooperation of two concurrent programs was then <u>abstracted</u> by the intersection of their sets of possible traces, resulting in a set which can also be inductively defined. For instance in the last example, we have obtained the following set definition

$$(3.34) \qquad (r,w) = \begin{cases} r \ last(w) \ , \ w & \text{if } |w| = |r| + 1 \\ r \qquad\quad , \ w \ last(r) + |w| & \text{if } |w| = |r| \ \& \ |r| \geqslant 1 \\ \langle \, \rangle \qquad\quad , \ \langle 0 \rangle \end{cases}$$

This representation of a trace by means of two sequences can obviously be generalized to more sequences. In this case the notation for defining corresponding inductive sets can become <u>very heavy</u>, especially because the sequence components that have not been modified must nevertheless be recopied. Another less heavy notation is that of guarded commands (12). For instance, the previous definition might be re-written as the following guarded command:

$$(4.1) \qquad r := \langle \, \rangle \ ; \ w := \langle 0 \rangle \ ;$$

$$\underline{do}$$

$$|w| = |r| + 1 \ \longrightarrow \ r := r \ last(w)$$

$$[]$$

$$|w| = |r| \ \& \ |r| \geqslant 1 \ \longrightarrow \ w := w \ last(r) + |w|$$

$$\underline{od}$$

In doing so, we have transformed the two concurrent programs defined in (3.30) and (3.36) into a single sequential program. There are some advantages in using guarded commands to denote the inductive definition of a set of tuples of sequences. Firstly the notation is very elegant and concise. Secondly all the conventional sequential program proof methods can be used.

We shall now study an example using this approach. In this example, we shall construct a small network of concurrent programs. This network is supposed to transmit a continuous flow of data, without reordering or loss, from one point, the Sender, to another one, the Receiver. To do so, we might first connect the points by a "channel" which acts as a one-place buffer. Later we shall have two (or more) redundant channels between the points.

The channel can obviously be specified by the following guarded command having two traces g and p (for get and put)

$$(4.2)$$

$$(g,p) := (\langle\rangle, \langle\rangle);$$
$$\underline{do}$$
$$|g| = |p| \longrightarrow g := g\,d \qquad \text{for all d}$$
$$\square$$
$$|g| = |p| + 1 \longrightarrow p := p\ last(g)$$
$$\underline{od}$$

An obvious ADA implementation of this one-place buffer is

$$(4.3)$$

```
d: data;
loop
    get(d) ; put(d)
end
```

In order to prove that this implementation is correct, we might consider the following loop invariant

$$g \neq \langle\rangle \Rightarrow d = last(g)$$
$$g = p$$

The Sender is specified by the following guarded command which has two traces r and g (for receive and get).

(4.4)
$$(r,g) := (\langle\rangle,\langle\rangle);$$
$$\underline{do}$$
$$(r,g) := (r\ d\ ,\ g\ d) \qquad\qquad \text{for all}\ \ d$$
$$\underline{od}$$

Likewise, the specification of the Receiver has two traces s and p (for send and put).

(4.5)
$$(s,p) := (\langle\rangle,\langle\rangle);$$
$$\underline{do}$$
$$(s,p) := (s\ d\ ,\ p\ d) \qquad\qquad \text{for all}\ \ d$$
$$\underline{od}$$

ADA implementations of these specifications are straightforward. For the Sender we have

(4.6)
```
loop
    accept get(out d: data) do rcv(d) end
end
```

where the parameter in rcv is supposed to be "by reference". For the Receiver we have

(4.7)
```
loop
    accept put(in d: data) do snd(d) end
end
```

where the parameter in snd is supposed to be "by´value".

The cooperative computation of the three programs (4.6), (4.3), and (4.7) is also a one-place buffer between r and s as shown by the following guarded command which correspond to the <u>common traces</u> of (4.4), (4.2), and (4.5). This can be proved by structural induction as in the previous section.

(4.8)

$$(g,p,r,s) := (<>,<>,<>,<>);$$

$$\textbf{do}$$

$$|g| = |p| \quad \longrightarrow \quad (r,g) := (r \ d \ , \ g \ d) \qquad \qquad \text{for all } d$$

$$\square$$

$$|g| = |p| + 1 \longrightarrow \quad (s,p) := (s \ \text{last}(g) \ , \ p \ \text{last}(g))$$

$$\textbf{od}$$

We shall now connect the Sender to the Receiver via two channels, instead of one. In adding an extra channel, our intention is to increase the reliability of the network. In case one channels fails, the system would work correctly with the other, as previously. When both channels work, however, redundant data received by the Receiver should be discarded. If we do not modify our previous specifications, we obtain the following guarded command for the common traces. Note that now we have two "gees", g_1 and g_2 , and two "pees", p_1 and p_2 , corresponding to each of our two channels.

(4.9)

$$(g_1,g_2,p_1,p_2,r,s) := (<>,<>,<>,<>,<>,<>);$$

$$\textbf{do}$$

$$|g_i| = |p_i| \quad \longrightarrow \quad (r,g_i) := (r \ d \ , \ g_i \ d) \qquad \qquad \text{for all } d$$

$$\square$$

$$|g_i| = |p_i| + 1 \longrightarrow \quad (s,p_i) := (s \ \text{last}(g_i) \ , \ p_i \ \text{last}(g_i))$$

$$\textbf{od}$$

where each guarded command has to be repeated <u>twice</u> (once for each value of i=1,2). The trouble with these traces is that they no longer correspond to a one-place buffer between r and s . In fact, one channel can easily "pass" the other, as shown by the following snapshots:

(4.10)   r g_1 g_2 p_1 p_2 s

$\langle \rangle$	$\langle \rangle$	$\langle \rangle$	$\langle \rangle$	$\langle \rangle$	$\langle \rangle$
$\langle a \rangle$	$\langle a \rangle$	$\langle \rangle$	$\langle \rangle$	$\langle \rangle$	$\langle \rangle$
$\langle a,b \rangle$	$\langle a \rangle$	$\langle b \rangle$	$\langle \rangle$	$\langle \rangle$	$\langle \rangle$
$\langle a,b \rangle$	$\langle a \rangle$	$\langle b \rangle$	$\langle \rangle$	$\langle b \rangle$	$\langle b \rangle$
$\langle a,b \rangle$	$\langle a \rangle$	$\langle b \rangle$	$\langle a \rangle$	$\langle b \rangle$	$\langle b,a \rangle$

In order to avoid such a disagreeable situation, each channel will be passed a serial
number together with the data sent to it by the Sender: This serial number corresponds
to the <u>rank</u> of the data in the Sender. This rank will be transmitted to the Receiver
by the channel. The Receiver may compare it with the previous rank received and thus
possibly refuse to re-emit the incoming data. This rank will also be <u>transmitted back</u>
by the channel to the Sender. The Sender may then compare it with the previous rank
sent and thus either retransmit an old data together with its old rank, or transmit
a new data together with its new rank.

Here is the specification of our new channel. The trace of the rank transmitted
back to the Sender is called j , that of the rank sent to the Sender is k , and
finally that transmitted to the Receiver is l.

(4.11) $(g,p,j,k,l) := (\langle \rangle, \langle \rangle, \langle \rangle, \langle 0 \rangle, \langle \rangle)$
          <u>do</u>
             $|g| = |p|$ $\longrightarrow$ $(j,g,k) := (j \; last(k) \; , \; g \; d \; , \; k \; x)$ for all d and x
          $\square$
             $|g| = |p|+1$ $\longrightarrow$ $(p,l) := (p \; last(g) \; , \; l \; last(k))$
          <u>od</u>

Note that we have initialized k to $\langle 0 \rangle$. This is because the "last rank"
transmitted (back) initially corresponds to 0 (which cannot be a rank). Here is
an ADA implementation of this new channel.

(4.12)
```
d: integer;
x: integer;
x := 0 ;
loop
    get(x,d,x) ; put(d,x)
end
```

The loop invariant is

(4.13)
$$g \neq \langle \rangle \;\Rightarrow\; d = last(g)$$
$$k \neq \langle \rangle \;\Rightarrow\; x = last(k)$$
$$g = p$$

The new Sender has the following specification

(4.14)
$$(g,r,j,k) := (\langle \rangle, \langle \rangle, \langle \rangle, \langle 0 \rangle);$$
```
do
    y = |r| ⟶ (g,r,j,k) := (g d , r d , j y , k|r|+1)   for all
                                                          y and d
 []
    y ≠ |r| ⟶ (g,j,k) := (g last(r) , j y , k |r|)
od
```

An ADA implementation of this specification is

(4.15)
```
i: integer;
d: data;
i := 0 ;
loop
    accept get(in y: integer, out e: data, out x: integer) do
        if y = i then i := i+1 ; rcv(d) end
        x := i ;  e := d
    end
end
```

As a loop invariant, we have

$$(4.16) \qquad i = |r|$$
$$r \neq <> \;\Rightarrow\; d = last(r)$$

Finally the specification of the new Receiver is

$$(4.17) \qquad (p,s,l) := (<>,<>,<>);$$

do

$\qquad x = |s|+1 \;\longrightarrow\; (p,s,l) := (p\ d\ ,\ s\ d\ ,\ l\ x)$ for all d and x

[]

$\qquad x \neq |s|+1 \;\longrightarrow\; (p,l) := (p\ d\ ,\ l\ x)$ for all d and x

od

and its ADA implementation is

$$(4.18)$$

```
i: integer;
i := 0 ;
loop
    accept put(in x: integer, in d: data) do
        if x = i+1 then snd(d) ; i := i+1 end
    end
end
```

The loop invariant obviously is

$$(4.19) \qquad i = |s|$$

By "putting together" specifications (4.11) (one for each channel) and specifications (4.14) and (4.17) of the Sender and Receiver, we obtain the following guarded command

(4.20) $(g_1,g_2,p_1,p_2,k_1,k_2,r,s) := (<>,<>,<>,<>,<0>,<0>,<>,<>);$

$\underline{do}$

$|g_i| = |p_i|$ & $last(k_i) = |r| \longrightarrow (g_i,k_i,r) := (g_i\ d\ ,\ k_i\ |r|+1\ ,\ r\ d)$ for all d

$\square$

$|g_i| = |p_i|$ & $last(k_i) \neq |r| \longrightarrow (g_i,k_i) := (g_i\ last(r)\ ,\ k_i\ |r|)$

$\square$

$|g_i| = |p_i|+1$ & $last(k_i) = |s|+1 \longrightarrow (p_i,s) := (p_i\ last(g_i)\ ,\ s\ last(g_i))$

$\square$

$|g_i| = |p_i|+1$ & $last(k_i) \neq |s|+1 \longrightarrow p_i := p_i\ last(g_i)$

$\underline{od}$

where all guarded commands have to be repeated twice (once for each value of $i = 1,2$). Note that we have eliminated traces j and l . Our final task is to prove that this guarded command corresponds to a one-place buffer between r and s . In other words, we have to prove that the following invariant holds

(4.21) $\qquad\qquad s = r \quad v \quad s = past(r)$

As usual the invariant to prove is a little stronger

(4.22) $\qquad\qquad s = r \quad v \quad s = past(r)$

$\qquad\qquad last(k_i) \leq |r|$

$\qquad\qquad last(g_i) = r(last(k_i))$

$\qquad\qquad (|g_i| = |p_i|$ & $last(k_i) = |r|) \Rightarrow s = r$

$\qquad\qquad (|g_i| = |p_i|+1$ & $last(k_i) = |s|+1) \Rightarrow s = past(r)$

We can also prove that the system does not deadlock, that is prove that traces r of any length can be transmitted.

5. CONCLUSION

We have shown, through various examples, that a concurrent program can be abstracted by an inductively defined set of tuples of sequences.

We have also shown that the cooperation of two (or more) such programs can, again, be abstracted by such a set. In fact this new set is just the intersection of the sets abstracting each cooperating program.

Finally, we have shown that inductively defined sets of tuples of sequences can be denoted by non-deterministic repetitive guarded commands working on sequence variables; the only possible operation on these variables being that of postfixing.

As a result, the analysis of concurrent programs can be reduced to that of non-deterministic sequential programs of this very special form.

References

(1) C.A.R. HOARE - A Calculus of Total Correctness for Communicating Sequential
     Processes - Science of Computer Programming - Volume 1 - 1981

(2) C.A.R. HOARE - Communicating Sequential Processes - CACM - Volume 21 - 1978

(3) C.A.R.HOARE - An Axiomatic Basis for Computer Programming - CACM - Volume 12 -
     1969

(4) M.E. CONWAY - Design of a Separable Transition-Diagram Compiler - CACM - Vo
     Volume 6 - 1963

(5) S. OWICKI & D. GRIES - Verifying Properties of Parallel Programs: an Axiomatic
     Approach - CACM - Volume 19 - 1976

(6) R.W. FLOYD - Assigning Meaning to Programs - Proc. Symposium Applied
     Mathematics - 1967

(7) UNITED STATES DEPARTMENT OF DEFENSE - Reference Manual for the ADA Programming
     Language - 1983

(8) E.W. DIJKSTRA - A Discipline of Programming - Prentice Hall - 1976

(9) E.W. DIJKSTRA - A Correctness Proof for Communicating Processes. A Small
     Exercise - in Selected Writings on Computing: a Personal Perspective -
     Springer Verlag - 1982

(10) E.W. DIJKSTRA - Guarded Commands, Non-determinacy and Formal Derivation of
     Programs - CACM - Volume 18 - 1975

(11) C.B. JONES - Software Development: a Rigorous Approach - Prentice Hall - 1980

(12) K.R. APT & N.FRANCEZ & W.P. DE ROEVER - A Proof System for Communicating
     Sequential Processes - ACM Transactions on Programming Languages - 1980

(13) J.MISRA & K.M. CHANDY - Proofs of Networks of Processes - IEEE Transactions
     on Software Egineering - Volume SE 7 - 1981

References

(1) C.A.R. HOARE - A Calculus of Total Correctness for Communicating Sequential Processes - Science of Computer Programming - Volume 1 - 1981

(2) C.A.R. HOARE - Communicating Sequential Processes - CACM - Volume 21 - 1978

(3) C.A.R.HOARE - An Axiomatic Basis for Computer Programming - CACM - Volume 12 - 1969

(4) M.E. CONWAY - Design of a Separable Transition-Diagram Compiler - CACM - Vo Volume 6 - 1963

(5) S. OWICKI & D. GRIES - Verifying Properties of Parallel Programs: an Axiomatic Approach - CACM - Volume 19 - 1976

(6) R.W. FLOYD - Assigning Meaning to Programs - Proc. Symposium Applied Mathematics - 1967

(7) UNITED STATES DEPARTMENT OF DEFENSE - Reference Manual for the ADA Programming Language - 1983

(8) E.W. DIJKSTRA - A Discipline of Programming - Prentice Hall - 1976

(9) E.W. DIJKSTRA - A Correctness Proof for Communicating Processes. A Small Exercise - in Selected Writings on Computing: a Personal Perspective - Springer Verlag - 1982

(10) E.W. DIJKSTRA - Guarded Commands, Non-determinacy and Formal Derivation of Programs - CACM - Volume 18 - 1975

(11) C.B. JONES - Software Development: a Rigorous Approach - Prentice Hall - 1980

(12) K.R. APT & N.FRANCEZ & W.P. DE ROEVER - A Proof System for Communicating Sequential Processes - ACM Transactions on Programming Languages - 1980

(13) J.MISRA & K.M. CHANDY - Proofs of Networks of Processes - IEEE Transactions on Software Egineering - Volume SE 7 - 1981

3. THE PROBLEM SET

The problems were given in advance to the workshop participants in order to provide a common focus for the different theories and methods. In choosing them an attempt was made to capture the essence of those applications of concurrent computation found in practical contexts.

Ten problems in all were presented and formal specifications of most of them were attempted between the participants. The reputed difficulty of the problems varied from easy to very hard. In fact the reputedly easy problems gave rise to considerable argument and discussion.

The participants were asked to provide specifications of the problems and to indicate how they might be solved. The descriptions of the problems were given in "standard English" with the explicit instructions not to attach specialised interpretations to words like "simultaneous", since the formalisations of such concepts and comparisons between them were among the objectives of the workshop. Whilst the organisers had attempted to make the descriptions of the problems precise, ambiguities and lack of completeness were to be expected and the participants were asked to make reasonable assumptions where necessary.

A distinction brought out before the workshop itself concerned the nature of specifications. A specification is generally considered to be a description of the behaviour of something without regard to how that behaviour is achieved. This presupposes an observer of that behaviour who thus has some interface with the system being specified. A completely closed system has no observable behaviour unless points of observation, that is interfaces through which information may pass from the system to an observer, are defined. The choice of such "observation ports" results in suppositions about the architecture of the system. This distinction was not identified by the organisers who set the problems, but was pointed out by one of the participants (L. Lamport); in practice the majority of the participants chose the same "points of observation" for the various problems.

In order to produce formal definitions of the systems described in the problem statements, a number of decisions must be made for each problem. These decisions are of two kinds: those which reflect the interpretation of phrases in the problem statement which are fundamentally associated with the concepts of time, communication and concurrency; and those consisting of choices about the viewpoints or "observation ports" that are chosen for the purpose of describing the system. This latter choice determines how much "mechanism" is put into the specification. Some of those decisions are dictated by the method and notation used for the formalisation of the problem. Other decisions are left open (with respect to the notation and method) and are made by the specifier trying to make the most reasonable assumptions possible about the intent behind the informal problem statement.

The problem of assessing the performance of an approach to specifying any particular problem requires one to separate the decisions dictated by the method or notation from those made freely by the specifier. (Of course, there are varying degrees of "dictating decisions" : some are really inescapable consequences of an underlying theory whilst others are "strong suggestions" that are the "obvious way" of using it.)

Rather than trying to provide a comparison of the solutions to each problem, which is a task fraught with the dangers of misunderstanding the solutions, we will attempt to illustrate the range of decisions that must be made for even a simple problem. The readers may then judge for themselves what decisions need to be made about each problem and to what extent these decisions are constrained or left open in each solution.

The Problem

For the purposes of illustration we choose problem 8.

Specify the object described as follows:

The object has two inputs and one output. The output and one of the inputs respectively send and receive data in packets at regular intervals. The remaining input is asynchronous, i.e. data appears at undetermined times.

The data packets which arrive at the synchronous input may be full or empty, and the object may only output data by forwarding packets from the synchronous input or filling an empty packet with data from the asynchronous input. All packets have the same size.

The problem is a simplified form of a node on a ring where the ring is clocked and only input to the ring is considered. Note that issues relating to overall performance of the ring (e.g. how empty packets are created, how fair usage is assured, if there are output nodes etc.) are not part of the problem.

A Closer Look at the Problem

The following are some simple working assumptions about what has been said and what is intended in the problem statement. Such assumptions will lie behind any attempt at formalising the problem.

Uniqueness: For each input and output, at any given time at most one event may occur (e.g. there will never be an instant at which two packets arrive at one synchronous input).

Regularity: Synchronous input and output occur at regularly spaced instants in time (i.e. time can be measured to some degree).

Coupling: The synchronous input and output are synchronised with respect to one another and as a consequence exactly the same number of outputs occur as synchronous inputs.

Transfer: Data (the content of packets) is transferred from the synchronous input to the synchronous output.

No-loss: No synchronous input data is lost.

No-gain: No synchronous input data is duplicated (i.e. a node does not, for example, fill an empty packet with the data of an arbitrary full packet unless that data was acquired from the asynchronous input).

These assumptions illustrate a number of trivial decisions which have to be made about the nature of the simplest part of a simple problem. One may disagree with the particular assumptions but the decisions they represent cannot be avoided.

Decisions About Synchronous Behaviour

To illustrate that further decisions about the synchronous behaviour of the system are necessary we raise two questions:-

Delay: What is the delay in the transfer of packets from the synchronous input to the output?

Time: To what extent can time be measured in the system i.e. what meaning can be given to the assumption of regularity?

The answer to delay is constrained by the synchrony requirement in that the delay can only be an integer multiple of the synchronous event interval but it may be negative, zero or positive and fixed or variable. Of course, negative delay means that the node is a predictor of its input and variable delay means that the node creates packets. Zero delay immediately raises the question of what is meant by instantaneous events. "Instantaneous" may typically refer only to the apparatus for measuring/observing events at a given level of specification, which naturally leads to the second question. How a specification deals with time (i.e. how it answers the question of Time above) depends on whether or not time is an intrinsic part of the specification language used or whether time must be modelled in the specification by some privileged set of events which are used as a clock. These events may be defined as a set which is ranged over or by giving a description of a clock and connecting this clock to other parts of the specification.

Decisions About Asynchronous Behaviour

The fundamental question is of course

Asynch: What do we mean by asynchrony?

In the current problem we have a set of synchronous events i.e. events which necessarily occur "at the same time". A collection of events may be taken as asynchronous if they do not necessarily have a fixed relationship between their times of occurrence. This leads to a number of possibilities in the context of the problem of how asynchrony is dealt with e.g:

(a)   Time is modelled as a dense linear ordering, the elements of which we may call "moments". The regular synchronous events form a (non dense) sub-ordering of moments. Asynchronous events may occur at any moment.

(b) Time is modelled as a non-dense linear ordering of moments and again the regular synchronous events form a sub-ordering. Asynchronous events may occur at any moment.

(c) As (b) but every moment is a moment of a regular synchronous event. Asynchronous events form a sub-ordering of moments. That is asynchronous events take place at the same times as synchronous events but there is no necessary relation between any particular synchronous and asynchronous events.

(d) It is not possible to talk about when an asynchronous event actually occurred between two adjacent synchronous events. It is only possible to talk about the effect at the moment of the next synchronous event.

A second question we can ask about the asynchronous events is how is their rate of occurrence bounded i.e.

Boundedness: How many asynchronous events can occur between two adjacent synchronous events?

Some possible answers include:

(a) Any number.
(b) Any finite number.
(c) At most some fixed finite number.
(d) (very special case) At most one.

The answer to the boundedness question leads to yet another question.

Policy: Are all asynchronous input messages eventually passed to the output (provided a sufficient number of empty packets can be obtained)?

In other words can the node buffer a sufficiently large number of asynchronous inputs or operate a "handshake" policy with its asynchronous inputs so it can prevent information loss occurring, or indeed can information loss be allowed?

Conclusion

Clearly the above assumptions, questions and answers are ad hoc. They are not derived from any general theory of what must be analysed in a communicating, concurrent or temporal system. It is probably fair to say that none of the approaches pursued to the specification of the different problems raised such a collection of questions systematically. That is, the "solutions" presented in section 4 are theories of communication, concurrency etc., not methods for the specification of communicating, concurrent systems. However, the theories do provide a possible sound basis for methods when and if such methods emerge.

The list of problems was as follows:

1. Two-way channel with disconnect

2. Simple network service

3. Synchronising firing squad (M. Minsky)

4. Railway

5. Array processor

6. Packet network with re-routing

7. Parallel combinator reduction machine

8. Mixing synchronous and asynchronous input

9. "Cash-point" service

10. m by n matrix switch

In the following subsections (3.1 to 3.10) the problems are described in detail as they were presented to the participants. An overview of the range of solutions is given, and a cross reference list of the participants' solutions to be found in section 4. These are in alphabetic order of author name so that the solutions to any given problem can be easily accessed through the cross reference list.

In several cases impromptu or first attempts at solutions were produced during the workshop which seemed sufficiently interesting to record. Where appropriate such solutions are included in the following subsections (i.e. section 3.i for problem number i). Readers of these proceedings should bear in mind that in these cases the solutions were typically devised "in real time" by a participant writing on an overhead projector in front of a small audience. We nonetheless feel that the first attempt solutions recorded here have in each case some specific point of interest which it would be a pity to lose.

Details of the particular problems and their solutions follow.

3.1 Two-way channel with disconnect

3.1.1 Motivation

This is a simple problem in communication often met in practice. Two parties can communicate with each other until one of them disconnects. It was intended as a "warming up" exercise.

3.1.2 Description

The problem is to specify the channel described as follows.

The "channel" between endpoints "a" and "b" can pass messages in both directions simultaneously, until it receives a "disconnect" message from one end, after which it neither delivers nor accepts messages at that end. It continues to deliver and accept messages at the other end until the "disconnect" message arrives, after which it can do nothing. The order of messages sent in a given direction is preserved.

3.1.3 Solutions

Written solutions have been prepared by the following participants:

    H.Barringer and R.Kuiper
    J.Y.Cotronis and P.E.Lauer
    A.Kaldewaij
    R.Koymans and W.P.de Roever
    L.Lamport
    G.Milne
    B.Moszkowski
    J.Sifakis

and are to be found in section 4 which is arranged in alphabetical order of author name.

The following two "first attempt" solutions were provided by A.W.Roscoe and V.Pratt respectively, at the workshop.

SPECIFYING PROBLEM ONE USING THE 'FAILURE' SETS MODEL FOR CSP
AND DERIVING CSP PROCESSES WHICH MEET THIS SPECIFICATION

A.W. Roscoe

Programming Research Group

University of Oxford

In this note we sketch how an abstract mathematical model can be used to specify the two-way channel. We see how theorems proved about the abstract specification suggest designs of processes which satisfy it. The model used can express safety and liveness properties and allows non-determinism. It does not deal with fairness however.

1. The Failure Sets Model

For a summary description of the failure sets model see the appendix to this paper.

The important points to note are:

(i) every process is represented by a set of pairs (s, δ), where s is a possible trace and δ is <u>either</u>

$\uparrow$ representing divergence (non-termination), <u>or</u>

X   representing a set of symbols to which the process can <u>refuse</u> to respond.

(ii) The model is good for expressing correctness conditions because it -
- . permits the banning of divergence
- . allows possible traces to be specified (safety)
- . allows the banning of refusal by the process (liveness).

If on operating some process A with current trace s we offer it a set X such that $(s, X) \notin A$, then we can guarantee that the process will eventually accept some element of X.

First, a notation for manipulating traces.

(i)   If $s, t \in \Sigma^*$, we say $s \leqslant t$ if $\exists u. su = t$.

(ii)   If $s \in \Sigma^*$, $X \subseteq \Sigma$, we say

$s \upharpoonright X = \langle \rangle$ if $s = \langle \rangle$

$\quad\quad = t \upharpoonright X$ if $s = t \langle a \rangle$ and $a \notin X$

$\quad = (t \upharpoonright X) \langle a \rangle$ if $s = t \langle a \rangle$ and $a \in X$.

(iii) If a is some name used for symbols, and $b \in \Sigma$, then

$$strip(a)(b) = c, \text{ if } b = ac$$
$$= b \text{ otherwise.}$$

(iv) If $s \in \Sigma*$, then

$$strip(a)(s) = <>, \text{ if } s = <>$$
$$= (strip(a)(t)) < strip(a)(b) >,$$
$$\text{if } s = tb, \text{ where } t \in \Sigma*, b \in \Sigma .$$

(v) $s \downarrow a = strip(a)(s \upharpoonright a.\Sigma)$

eg.: $< a.b, \ c.b, \ a.c > \downarrow a = < b,c >$

2.   Problem 1: Two-way Channel with Disconnect

What is a channel?

- Informally it passes messages either way.
- 'dis' is a message, so its order is preserved, and it is transmitted.
- To be a reliable channel it must accept all input it is offered while empty (in either direction?).
- When it contains a message this must eventually be delivered to a destination which does nothing but wait.
- On delivering or receiving a dis at either end it must die at that end.
  (To die without transmitting a 'dis' to the environment seems unreasonable.)

Specification of a Channel (Abstract)

- The set of ordinary messages is T (dis $\notin$ T).
- The alphabet $\Sigma_{CHAN(a,b)}$ of a channel, whose end ports are named a and b, is:
$$\{ a!t', \ a?t', \ b!t', \ b?t' \quad t' \in T \cup \{dis\} \}$$
- The predicate CHAN(a,b) is defined as follows:

   $CHAN(a,b)(C) = [(s,\delta) \in C \Rightarrow \delta \neq \uparrow]$

   $\& [(s,X) \in C \Rightarrow s \in (\Sigma_{CHAN(a,b)})^*]$

   $\& [s \downarrow a? \geqslant s \downarrow b! \ \& \ s \downarrow b? \geqslant s \downarrow a!]$

   ....order of messages preserved

   $\& [(s \downarrow a = u < d > v) \ \& \ d \in \{? dis, !dis\} \Rightarrow v = <>]$

   $\& [(s \downarrow b = u < d > v) \ \& \ d \in \{? dis, !dis\} \Rightarrow v = <>]$

   ....neither end can do anything after a di

   $\& \ \neg dis(a)(s) \ \& \ (s \downarrow a? = s \downarrow b!) \Longrightarrow X \cap (a?T \cup \{a?dis\}) = \emptyset$
   $\& \ \neg dis(b)(s) \ \& \ (s \downarrow b? = s \downarrow a!) \Longrightarrow X \cap (b?T \cup \{b?dis\}) = \emptyset$

   ....a non-disconnected end, all of whose communication has been received, must be able to transmit

$\& \neg dis(b)(s) \& (s\downarrow a? \geqslant (s\downarrow b!) < t'>) \Longrightarrow b!t' \notin X$
$\& \neg dis(a)(s) \& (s\downarrow b? \geqslant (s\downarrow a!) < t'>) \Longrightarrow a!t' \notin X$

....the channel can never refuse
to output a message it contains

where $dis(\alpha)(s) \equiv s \upharpoonright \{\alpha!dis, \alpha?dis\} \neq <>$.

A __buffer__ may be defined in the same way:

$\quad BUFF(B) \equiv \forall s(s,T) \notin B$

$\& (s,X) \in B \Longrightarrow s \in (?T'U!T')*$

$\qquad \& s\downarrow? \geqslant s\downarrow!$

$\qquad \&(s\downarrow? = s\downarrow! \Longrightarrow X \cap ?T' = \emptyset)$

$\qquad \&(s\downarrow? \geqslant (s\downarrow!)<t>) \dashv !t \notin X$

where $T' = TU\{dis\}$.

BUFF(a,b) is the same except that ! is replaced by b!

and ? is replaced by a?.

Assorted theorems can be proved concerning channels and buffers:

eg. $CHAN(a,b)(C) \& CHAN(b,d)(C*) \& d \neq a \Longrightarrow CHAN(a,d)(C \underset{b}{\divideontimes} C*)$

$\quad BUFF(A) \& BUFF(B) \Longrightarrow BUFF(A \gg B)$

$\quad BUFF(A) \& BUFF(A \gg B) \Longrightarrow BUFF(B)$

$\quad BUFF(A \gg B) \& BUFF(B) \Longrightarrow BUFF(A)$

$a \neq e, \& b \neq d \& CHAN(a,b)(C_1) \& BUFF(b,d)(B_1)$

$\qquad\qquad\qquad \& BUFF(d,b)(B_2) \& CHAN(d,c)(C_2)$

$\qquad\qquad \Longrightarrow CHAN(a,e)(C_1 \underset{b}{\divideontimes} (B_1 \| B_2) \underset{d}{\divideontimes} C_2)$

Such theorems are easy, if tedious, to prove.
Examples of buffers:

$B^1 = ?x:T' \to !x \to B^1$

$B^n = B^1 \gg \ldots \gg B^1 \quad (n \text{ times})$

$B^\infty = ?x:T' \to (B^\infty \gg !x \to B^1) \text{ (unbounded)}$

$B^* = ?x:T' \to (B^1 \gg !x \to B^*) \text{ (bounded but growing)}$

One obvious configuration for a channel is:

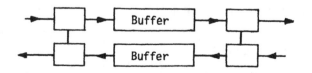

This can be realised:

$$INS(\alpha,\beta) = (\alpha?x{:}T \to (\beta!x{-}INS(\alpha,\beta) \;\square\; \alpha!dis{-}\underline{abort}\;))$$

$$\square\;(\alpha?dis{-}\beta!dis{-}\underline{abort}\;)$$

$$\square\;(\alpha!dis{-}\underline{abort}\;)$$

$$OUTS(\alpha,\beta) = (\beta?x{:}T \to (\alpha!x{-}OUTS(\alpha,\beta) \;\square\; \alpha?dis{-}\underline{abort}\;))$$

$$\square\;(\beta?dis{-}(\alpha!dis{-}\underline{abort} \;\square\; \alpha?dis{-}\underline{abort}\;))$$

$$\square\;(\alpha?dis{-}\underline{abort}\;)$$

If B_1 is any (b,a) buffer and B_2 is any (a,b) buffer, then

$$a \neq b \implies ((INS(a,b) \;\|\; OUTS(a,b)) \underset{b}{\overset{\times}{}} (B_1 \| B_2) \underset{a}{\overset{\times}{}} (INS(b,a) \| OUTS(b,a)))$$

satisfies $CHAN(a,b)$.

Appendix - A summary of the failure sets model for CSP

For a fuller description of this model the reader should consult any of [1, 2, 3, 4]. The model is similar to, and makes the same basic postulates about processes as, the well-known 'traces' model. It is, however, able to make some important distinctions between processes not made by simple traces.

The agents $\alpha.\gamma\, NIL + \alpha.\beta\, NIL$ and $\alpha.(\beta.NIL + \gamma.NIL)$ would be identified over traces, as would $(\mu p.\alpha.p)\backslash\alpha$ and NIL. There are good reasons for wishing to avoid these identifications: the idea is to record not only the possible traces (ie. sequences of atomic actions) of a process but also its refusals (the sets which it can reject in a 'stable' state after some trace), and divergences (the occasions when it can become involved in an infinite sequence of internal actions and never give any answer to its environment).

A process is thus a set of pairs (s,δ), the first component being a trace and the second either X, a refusal set ($X \subseteq \Sigma$, the alphabet), or $\uparrow$ indicating divergence.

A process Q will be any subset of $\Sigma^* \times (\mathbb{P}(\Sigma) \cup \{\uparrow\})$ such that

1. $dom(Q) = \{s \in \Sigma^* \mid \exists\delta.(s,\delta) \in Q\}$ is non-empty and prefix-closed
   $[<> \in dom(Q),\; st \in dom(Q) \implies s \in dom(Q)]$

2. $(s,X) \in Q\; \&\; Y \subseteq X \implies (s,Y) \in Q$

3. $(s,X) \in Q\; \&\; Y \cap (Q\; \underline{after}\; s)^0 = \phi \implies (s, X \cup Y) \in Q$

4. $(\forall \text{ finite } Y \subseteq X. \ (s,Y) \in Q) \Longrightarrow (s,X) \in Q$

5. $(s, \uparrow) \in Q \Longrightarrow (st, \delta) \in Q$

$Q \underline{\text{ after }} s = \{(t, \delta) \mid (st, \delta) \in Q\}$, $Q^0 = \{a \in \Sigma \mid \langle a \rangle \in \text{dom} Q\}$

Technical Notes

The space $\mathbb{M}$ of all processes is a complete semi-lattice under the reverse inclusion order $A \sqsubseteq B \Longleftrightarrow A \supseteq B$. This order is naturally interpreted as $A \supseteq B \equiv$ B is more non-deterministic than A. The bottom or minimal element of $\mathbb{M}$ is $\Sigma^* \times$ ($\mathbb{P}(\Sigma) \times \{\uparrow\}$) (called $\underline{\text{CHAOS}}$), one of whose many realisations is a process which can diverge immediately.

There is a natural map from boundedly non-deterministic synchronisation trees to $\mathbb{M}$, and a not-quite-so natural one from arbitrary synchronisation trees to $\mathbb{M}$. CSP can be given operational semantics which are in each case congruent to the abstract semantics given below.

The failure sets model gives a very expressive language for specification, since it regulates not only traces but also liveness (via divergence and refusals).

CSP can be given a semantics over $\mathbb{M}$:

$\underline{\text{abort}} = \{(\langle\rangle, X) \mid X \subseteq \Sigma\}$
          the process which does nothing at all

$\underline{\text{skip}} = \{(\langle\rangle, X), (\langle\checkmark\rangle, Y) \mid \checkmark \notin X\}$
          the process which immediately terminates successfully

$a \rightarrow A = \{(\langle\rangle, X) \mid a \notin X\} \cup \{(\langle a\rangle s, \delta) \mid (s, \delta) \in A\}$
          communicates 'a' and then behaves like A

$a.x{:}T \rightarrow A(x) = \{(\langle\rangle, X) \mid a.T \cap X = \emptyset\} \cup \{(\langle a.b\rangle s, \delta) \mid (b \in T \ \& \ (s, \delta) \in A(b)\}$
          inputs a value b named by 'a', then behaves like A(b).

$A \sqcap B = A \cup B$
          behaves like A or B at the $\underline{\text{process}}$' choice

$A \square B = \{(<>, X \cap Y) \mid (<>,X) \in A \;\&\; (<>,Y) \in B\} \cup \{(s,\delta) \mid s \neq <> \;\&\; (s,\delta) \in A \cup B\}$
$\qquad \cup \{(s,\delta) \mid (s,\uparrow) \in A \cup B\}$

behaves like A or B giving the <u>environment</u> the choice of <u>first</u> steps.

$A;B = \{(s,X) \mid s \text{ does not contain } \checkmark, \text{ and } (s, X \cup \{\checkmark\}) \in A\}$
$\qquad \cup \{(st,\delta) \mid s \text{ does not contain } \checkmark, \text{ and } (s,\uparrow) \in A\}$
$\qquad \cup \{(st,\delta) \mid s \text{ does not contain } \checkmark, (s<\checkmark>, \phi) \in A, (t,\delta) \in B\}$

behaves like A until it terminates successfully, then like B.

$A\backslash b = \{(s\backslash b, X) \mid (s, X \cup \{b\}) \in A\}$
$\qquad \cup \{((s\backslash b)t, \delta) \mid (s,\uparrow) \in A\}$
$\qquad \cup \{((s\backslash b)t, \delta) \mid \forall n \; (s<b>^{n}, \phi) \in A\}$

where $< >\backslash b = <>$

$\qquad s<a>\backslash b = (s\backslash b)<a> \quad \text{if } a \neq b$
$\qquad\qquad\qquad\quad = s\backslash b \qquad\qquad \text{if } a = b$

hides the event 'b' in A (note the divergence introduced by an infinite sequence of b's)

$A\backslash X = (\dots(A\backslash b_1)\dots)\backslash b_n, \quad \text{where } X = \{b_1 \dots b_n\}, \text{ is any finite set.}$

$(A_X \parallel_Y B) = \{(s, (U \cap X) \cup (V \cap Y) \cup Z) \mid s \in (X \cup Y)^{*}$
$\qquad\qquad \&\; (s \upharpoonright X, U) \in A \;\&\; (s \upharpoonright Y, V) \in B \;\&\; Z \cap (X \cup Y) = \phi\}$
$\qquad\qquad \cup \{(st,\delta) \mid s \in (X \cup Y)^{*} \;\&\; s \upharpoonright X \in \text{dom}A \;\&\; s \upharpoonright Y \in \text{dom}B$
$\qquad\qquad \&\; ((s \upharpoonright X, \uparrow) \in A \;\vee\; (s \upharpoonright Y, \uparrow) \in B)\}$

A, with alphabet X, operates in parallel with B which has alphabet Y.

$(A \parallel B)$ will be used as an abbreviation in the case where both A and B have as their alphabets the totality of symbols they can ever use.

$\backslash X$, $\parallel$ and easy alphabetical transformations can be used to derive operators.

$\gg$ which expects both arguments to have alphabet $?T \cup !T$, and connects the $!$ channel of its left-hand argument to the $?$ channel of its right-hand argument. Internal communication is hidden.

$\overset{x}{\underset{a}{}}$ which expects the intersection of the alphabets of its arguments to be $a?T \cup a!T$. The outputs $(a!)$ of each argument are connected to the input $(a?)$ of the other. Internal connection is hidden.

There are of course many theorems connecting these operators.

References

1. Hoare, C.A.R., Brookes, S.D., Roscoe, A.W. "A Theory of Communicating
    Sequential Processes". Oxford PRG monograph PRG-16 (1981)
    and JACM July 1984.

2. Brookes, S.D. Oxford D.Phil thesis, 1983 (SDB)

3. Roscoe, A.W. Oxford D.Phil thesis, 1982 (AWR)

4. Brookes, S.D., Roscoe, A.W. "An Improved Failure-Sets Model for Communicating
    Processes" To appear in Proceedings of NSF-SERC Seminar on concurrency,
    Springer-Verlag LNCS. Available as a Carnegie-Mellon Technical Report.

Note

The failures model has appeared in several forms. The original version
[1,2,3] was deficient in its treatment of divergence and was improved
in [2,3]. The version described in this note is the improved form from
[2]; this differs in presentation from the "standard" improved form of
[4] but is easily seen to be isomorphic to it.

TWO-WAY CHANNEL WITH DISCONNECT

V. Pratt

Stanford University

The "channel" is modelled as a process. A process is defined to be a set of pomsets (partially ordered multisets) of events on an event set $E = C \times D$, where C is the set of channels or ports of the process and D is the set of data to be sent over those channels.

In this example the channels of the process are as follows:

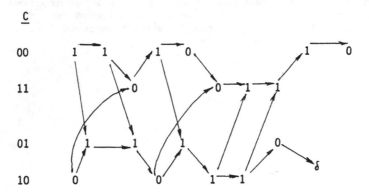

$$(0,0) \longrightarrow (0,1)$$
$$(1,1) \longleftarrow \;(a\;\;b)\; \longrightarrow (1,0)$$

Thus $C = 2 \times 2$, with the first bit giving direction and the second whether the message is entering or leaving. $\delta \in D$ is the disconnect message.

If $D = 2 \cup \{\delta\}\; (= \{0,1,\delta\}\;)$ then a typical pomset in the channel to be specified is:

<u>C</u>

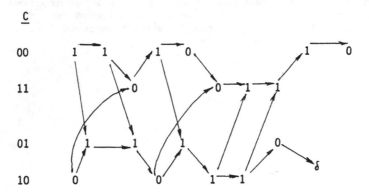

00
11
01
10

Any prefix of this pomset is also in the channel: any augmentation of the order is also permitted. This process contains only finite pomsets. δ may appear at the end of either or both of 00 and 11.

The reader should be able to infer from the diagram and attached remarks precisely which pomsets belong to this process. If so, then we have succeeded in specifying the process, in English.

The vagaries of natural language may be bypassed by using a formal language. We illustrate this by expressing the above using ordinary mathematical language. This particular choice of language further illustrates that the problem of modelling processes is more conceptual than linguistic in nature.

A pomset on E is, up to isomorphism, a structure $(L:U\to E, < \subseteq U^2)$, where L labels an "anonymous" carrier U with elements in E and $<$ partially orders U. In this example it is convenient to form these pomsets by restriction from structures enriched with a unary predicate "!", and to take $U = V \times 2$, where V is a set of "message carriers" and the extra bit distinguishes entry and exit. If $S = (L, <, !)$, we define $S \upharpoonright ! = (L \upharpoonright !, <\upharpoonright)$: that is, we select the domain of "!" and then discard "!" (since it is now vacuous).

Formal definition in full:

$\{ S \upharpoonright ! \quad | \exists V, U = V \times 2, \text{ dir}: V \to 2, \text{ data}: V \to D, E = C \times D$
$\qquad\qquad L: U \to E, < \subseteq U^2, ! \subseteq U, S = (L, <, !)$
$\qquad\qquad\qquad\qquad [|S| < \omega \wedge S \models \varphi] \}$

where the sentence φ is

$\qquad\qquad \forall v, v' \in V \quad \forall u, u' \in U \quad \forall i \in 2$
$[\quad (v,0) < (v,1)$
$\wedge \quad (v,0) < (v',0) \longrightarrow (v,1) < (v',1)$
$\wedge \quad \text{dir}(v) = \text{dir}(v') \longrightarrow (v,i) <=> (v',1)$
$\wedge \quad \text{dir}(v) = \text{dir}(v') \longrightarrow (v,i) <=> (v', 1-i)$
$\wedge \quad L(u)_1 = \delta \wedge u < u' \longrightarrow \sim !u'$
$\wedge \quad u < u' \longrightarrow (!u' \longrightarrow !u)$
$\wedge \quad L(v,i) = ((\text{dir}(v), i), \text{data}(v))$
$]$

where $C = 2 \times 2$ and $\delta \in D$.
(We write $u <=> v$ for $u < v \vee u = v \vee v < u$.)

Comment: Since the problem did not mention finiteness, we can justify the finiteness condition only by appealing to convention. Omitting it would permit dense pomsets, useful if the "messages" are the instantaneous values of a continuously sampled signal.

3.2 Simple Network Service

3.2.1 Motivation

This is a more demanding version of the first problem. Again it is a simplified version of a situation often met in practice. Most of the intrinsic problems remain, however.

3.2.2 Description

The problem is to specify the service described below. It is a simpli-fied version of the Network Service in the draft ISO standard for Open Systems Interconnect (OSI).

Introduction.

The service provides connections between ports called SAPs (Service Access Points), which can only support one connection at a time. The service could be extended to allow multiple connections, but this would require some way of identifying connection endpoints within a SAP, so we do not consider it here.

The messages recognised by the service have the form

<generic name> <specific name> (<parameters>).

The generic names are

```
1. CONNECT      ( abbreviated to CON ),
2. DISCONNECT   ( abbreviated to DIS ),
3. DATA         ( abbreviated to DAT ),
```

and the specific names are

```
1. request      ( abbreviated to req ),
2. indication   ( abbreviated to ind ),
3. response     ( abbreviated to res ),
4. confirm      ( abbreviated to con ).
```

CON can occur with all four specific names, DIS and DAT with req and ind only. Messages going into the service have specific names req or res, and those coming from the service ind or confirm.

Getting a Connection.

Each SAP has a unique address, and a user asks for a connection to a SAP with address 'b' by sending a CONreq(a,b) into SAP connection, will be delivered at 'b'. If the user of 'b' accepts with a CONres, a CON-con, indicating that the connection has been set up, will be delivered at 'a'. Data may then be sent in both directions by DATreq, delivered at the other end of the connection as a DATind. The order of transmit-ted data is preserved.

If 'b' is busy with a connection already, the network cannot get the connection for some reason, or the user at 'b' responds with a DISreq (

rejecting the connection), a DISind will be delivered at 'a', indicating that the connection cannot be set up.

Releasing a Connection.

Either party in a connection may release it at any time by sending a DISreq. The other end of the connection will then deliver a DISind, unless a DISreq is made there in the meantime, when nothing further is done.

Connections may also be released spontaneously by the network, resulting in the delivery of DISind at both ends of the connection, unless they have been disconnected already.

Any data, or other messages, sent to a SAP at one end of a connection which have not arrived when that SAP disconnects are lost. Although the relative order of data is preserved, DIS messages may overtake data.

The States of a SAP

Once a SAP has delivered a DISind, or accepted a DISreq, it is disconnected, and may only accept CONreq or deliver CONind, this is the initial state of all SAPs.

Once a SAP has delivered a CONind, or accepted a CONreq, it is busy. A SAP may not accept DATreq, or deliver DATind, unless a connection has been established.

3.2.3 Solutions

Written solutions have been prepared by the following participants:

> L.Lamport
> C.Morgan
> C.Morgan and C.A.R.Hoare
> A.Pnueli

and are to be found in section 4 which is arranged in alphabetical order of author name.

3.3 Synchronising Firing Squad

3.3.1 Motivation

This problem was chosen as an example of more complex synchronisation requirements. In engineering practice one encounters the problem of specifying either that a number of components come into synchronisation at a particular point in time or of specifying a mechanism by which synchronisation is achieved. (In the latter case one must be able to prove that synchronisation occurs.)

3.3.2 Description

The problem is to produce a formal description of the Firing Squad Problem (see below), and a solution if you have one.

We are given a line of FSMs (Finite State Machines), at one end is a 'general', at the other end any FSM and between identical copies of a 'soldier'. The problem is to design the machines so that all soldiers fire at the same time after the General has given the order (entered the state) 'Fire when ready' .

The machines operate in step, with the state of a machine at instant t+1 depending only on its state at time t and the state of its neighbours at time t.

The number of states in the machines must not depend on the length of the line, so that the same machines will work in a line of any length.

Hint

Propagate two waves down the line, one three times as fast as the other. Reflect the fast wave at the end so they meet in the centre, then do the same in each half and so on. A soldier fires when it is in a line of length one.

Reference

Marvin Minsky "Computation : Finite and Infinite Machines", Prentice-Hall, 1972, problem 2.7-5, p28 .

3.3.3 Solutions

Written solutions have been prepared by the following participants:

       E.Astesiano and G.Reggio
       R.Milner

and are to be found in section 4 which is arranged in alphabetical order of author name.

The following "first attempt" solution was provided by C.A.R.Hoare.

Workshop on Analysis of Concurrent Systems
Attempt at problem 3:
The Firing Squad

C.A.R. Hoare
9 September 1983

A soldier communicates with his left and right neighbours by input and
output on the left and right channels. He can also engage in the event
"fire". Neighbouring soldiers P and Q are combined by the operator >>.
In (P>>Q) the right channel of P is connected to the left channel of Q;
all communications along this connection are synchronised, and their
occurrence is concealed. The event "fire" requires simultaneous participation of both P and Q; so if P and Q decide to fire at "different
times", (P>>Q) will deadlock, and the prisoner will escape execution.

A firing line is made of a general, any number of soldiers, and a sergeant at the other end to the general:

$$LINE(n) = GENERAL >> (>>_{i<n} SOLDIER) >> SERGEANT$$

The line is started by a "go" signal on its (general's) left channel,
and it terminates with a volley of simultaneous shots from all the soldiers:

$$LINE(n) = (left.go \rightarrow fire \rightarrow STOP) \quad for\ all\ n$$

The problem is to construct the process GENERAL, SOLDIER, and SERGEANT
(independent of n) to meet this specification.

Unfortunately, CSP is such a powerful notation that this problem has a
very simple solution. To rule out such solutions, we must place additional constraints on the form of the SOLDIER process. It must be given
in the form:

$$SOLDIER = SOLDIER_0$$

where

$$SOLDIER_i = \underline{if}\ b(i)\ \underline{then}\ fire\ \underline{else}$$
$$left?j \rightarrow left!i \rightarrow$$
$$right!i \rightarrow right?k \rightarrow$$
$$SOLDIER_{f(i,j,k)}$$

where f is a function with finite range. Each soldier communicates its
current state with both its neighbours. They must simultaneously reach

the state i which satisfies b(i), in which they all fire.

Glossary

>> is a standard operator for forming chains of processes connected by their left and right channels. It is defined

$$P >> Q = (f(P) \parallel g(Q)) \setminus MESS$$

where

$$f(right.m) = g(left.m) = m \qquad for\ m \in MESS$$

$$f(x) = g(x) = x \qquad for\ all\ other\ events\ x$$

and MESS is the set of messages.

\ is the standard hiding operator, and || is the standard parallel combinator.

3.4 Railway

3.4.1 Motivation

The railway problem is a classic example of resource sharing and mutual exclusion problems encountered in computer systems.

3.4.2 Description

The problem is to produce a formal specification of a railway system as described below, and a design if you have one.

A railway system is made from lengths of single track joined at crossing points (a length of track may consist of one or more sections). A train may leave a crossing point on any unoccupied section of track connected to it. The system is to be run so that no section of track can have more than one train on it at any time. Any design should be independent of the number of trains in the system.

Suggested layout is three crossing points with two lines of track connecting each pair.

3.4.3 Solutions

Written solutions have been prepared by the following participants:

> P.Lauer
> B.Moszkowski
> A.W.Roscoe
> M.W.Shields

and are to be found in section 4 which is arranged in alphabetical order of author name.

3.5 Array Processor

3.5.1 Motivation

The synchronous and parallel operation of a large number of interconnected identical units occurs in VLSI design. This problem was intended to produce solutions which would reveal how the notations deal with synchrony and the replication and regular interconnection of a large number of components.

3.5.2 Description

The problem was to produce a formal specification of the machine described below.

The processor is a square array of ALUs (Arithmetic Logic Units), each connected to its horizontal and vertical neighbours, together with a 'controller'. Each ALU also has one connection for the controller to read its value, and one for instructions from the controller.

The computational instructions recognised by the ALUs are :

add, sub, mult, div, or, and, xor, not.

These instructions also need a part defining which inputs of the ALU they are applied to. The ALU has a register, where the result of a computation is put, and a 'move' instruction to make the value in the register appear on any output, or make it the 'value' of the ALU.

ALUs also recognise 'read' and 'write' instructions, these designate one ALU and have no effect on any other. The 'read' instruction gets the 'value' of a particular ALU and gives it to the controller, and the 'write' instruction deposits a value in a particular ALU.

ALUs on the boundary of the array always have the value zero on any input from a direction where there is no neighbouring ALU.

The controller is 'single instruction', i.e. it simultaneously gives the same instruction to all the ALUs. There is some mechanism for initialising all the ALUs to any values required.

3.5.3 Solutions

A written solution has been prepared by the following participant:

B.Moszkowski

and is to be found in section 4 which is arranged in alphabetical order of author name.

3.6 Packet Network with Re-routing

3.6.1 Motivation

This problem was chosen to investigate the issue of "time—out"s and how they are represented in different frameworks.

3.6.2 Description

The problem was to specify the system described below.

The network consist of a collection of 'nodes', each having a unique address. The objects transmitted are 'packets', which are grouped into 'messages'.

A node transmits a message by sending the packets it is made of with

send X to A via Z.

This means that packet X is to be delivered to node A, after going to node Z first. Node Z forwards the packet to another node with a similar instruction, with the same destination. The packet must eventually arrive at its destination. Packets are acknowledged on receipt, with the originating node retransmitting if an acknowledgement is not received within a specified time. Duplicate packets are discarded on receipt, and sets of packets making up a message are delivered in order to the user of a node.

3.6.3 Solutions

Written solutions have been prepared by the following participants:

>   H.Barringer and R.Kuiper
>   R.Koymans and W.P.de Roever
>   B.Moszkowski

and are to be found in section 4 which is arranged in alphabetical order of author name.

3.7 Parallel Combinator Reduction Machine

3.7.1 Motivation

This problem is the (potentially) asynchronous counterpart to the Array Processor.

3.7.2 Description

The problem is to specify a machine which can reduce 'combinations' (expressions consisting of function applications only) by performing all possible reductions in parallel. For an exposition of combinators see D.A.Turner: "A new implementation technique for applicative languages", Software - Practice and Experience, Vol. 9, 1979, pp 31-49.

The combinations to be reduced will consist of the following combinators and curried versions of +, *, -, / etc. called plus, times, minus, divide etc. Function application associates to the left.

Combinators.

```
S f g x  =  f x (g x)   *
K x y    =  x           *
I x      =  x           *
B f g x  =  f (g x)     *
C f g x  =  f x g       *
U f (x:y)=  f x y
P a b    =  (a:b)
Y f      =  f (Y f)     *
cond true x y  = x      *
cond false x y = y      *
```

Where ':' adds an element to the front of a list.

Reduction Rules.

The equations above marked *, taken left to right, and

```
U f (P x y)      -> f x y
plus m n -> m+n     if m,n reduced to numbers already,
et. sim. for times minus divide etc.
```

3.7.3 Solutions

Written solutions have been prepared by the following participants:

> J.R.Kennaway and M.R.Sleep
> P.Mosses

and are to be found in section 4 which is arranged in alphabetical order of author name.

An "impromptu" solution was provided by R.Milner as follows:

PARALLEL COMBINATOR REDUCTION MACHINE

R. Milner
University of Edinburgh

We use CCS in its original form - but with the addition of infinite sums, as justified by later work - to model combinator graph reduction as closely as possible, maintaining all possible sharing.

The principle of the model is that combinations are <u>agents</u>, not <u>values</u>. Though we take quite a few ideas from Kennaway and Sleep[1], we do not adopt their method of passing combinations (processes) as values in communication; we show instead how the more primitive idea of passing the <u>addresses</u> of combinations works well within CCS. Perhaps it is more appropriate too; one purpose of this modelling is to provide a bridge between the passing of higher-order objects as parameters (as in the lambda-calculus) and the more concrete intercommunication between physical machines.

Kevin Mitchell at Edinburgh University first produced a model of the kind presented here.

1. The Method, informally

The linkage of components of the composite agent which represents a combination (= term) is such that it looks just like the acyclic graph of the combination (graph, not tree, since the method must allow the sharing of sub-combinations). Throughout, arrows on outgoing arcs of agents in diagrams represent available combinations.

There are just two kinds of agent:

(1) AP, which is ready to receive a message from its rator;

(2) An incomplete combinator, ie. a combinator (S, K, I, ...) with pointers to a number of arguments - insufficient to yield a reduction.

Thus for S, there are incomplete combinators S_0 (= S, the bare combinator with no arguments), S_1 and S_2:

In general, then, an k-ary combinator C is modelled by k incomplete combinations C_0, C_1, ...C_{k-1}, where C_i points to i arguments. However, for I, though it is an unary combinator, we have both I_0 (= I) and I_1 as incomplete combinators; the latter will serve as an indirection node, as we shall see later. Each incomplete combinator is ready to send a message to any AP of which it is the rator, stating its identity and the addresses (indices) of its arguments. It will

do this repeatedly, since it does not know how often it will be used.
When AP receives a message from C_{k-1} - an <u>almost</u> complete combinator - it
reconfigures according to the reduction rule for C. The sequence of
communications corresponding to the reduction

$$SABC \longrightarrow AC(BC)$$

is as follows (extra arcs indicate possible sharing of combinations):

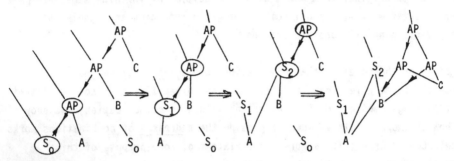

The arrows on arcs represent readiness to communicate; the circled agents
communicate at each stage.

2. Indices

Since an unbounded number of agents may be generated, and since their addresses
(indices) are passed in messages, a scheme for generating indices and keeping them
distinct seems unavoidable.

We keep things concrete here by choosing indices to be strings over a finite
alphabet $\{0, 1, 2, 3, ...\}$. We denote indices by m, n, q, r, s. It turns out
that only an AP node will ever need to generate indices. Accordingly, every node
will be uniquely indexed, and hold the indices of its sons; further, each AP node
will hold a distinct index for generation of further indices in case it
reconfigures (as in the last step of the example). All these distinct indices
will be also incomparable (none is an initial segment of any other) and this
property is preserved by all actions, including reconfigurations.

Another way of generating distinct indices is by reference to a global "name
server"; the present method is more distributed and seems perfectly implementable.

3. The Agents

An incomplete combination C_i with index r and argument indices m_1, m_2,
$m_3 ....m_i$ is written $C_i(r, m_1, m_2....m_i)$. It sends the message
$(\underline{C_i}, m_1, m_2, ... m_i)$ at label $\bar{\alpha}_r$.

$$C_i(r, m_1, \ldots m_i) = \bar{\alpha}_r(\underline{C}_i, m_1, \ldots m_i) \cdot C_i(r, m_1 \ldots m_i)$$

For S, K and I, this schema applies to S_0, S_1, S_2, K_0, K_1, I_0, I_1.
Note that the $\underline{C}_i$ part of the message is just a __symbol__, not an agent!
An AP node with index r, argument indices p, q, and index generator s is written
$AP_s(r, p, q)$. It receives a rator message $(\underline{C}_i, m_1, \ldots m_i)$;
if the arguments m_1, $m_2 \ldots m_i$, together with its rand q are enough for the
combinator C then it reconfigures; otherwise it merely becomes the incomplete
combinator $C_{i+1}(r, m_1 \ldots m_i, q)$.

We give the definition of AP just for S, K and I; note that it drops its index
generator s when it becomes an incomplete combinator; the only case where s is
used is in the reconfiguration for S, in which case it not only provides indices
for the new AP node but it also provides generators for them. In the definition
below, x and y are index variables, bound by the input label α_p;
they abbreviate infinite sums over the index set.

$$
\begin{aligned}
AP_s(r, p, q) =& \\
&\alpha_p(\underline{S}_0) \cdot S_1(r, q) + \alpha_p(\underline{S}_1, m) \cdot S_2(r, m, q) \\
+\ & \alpha_p(\underline{S}_2, m, n) \cdot (AP_{s0}(r, s3, s4) \mid AP_{s1}(s3, m, q) \mid AP_{s2}(s4, n, q)) \\
+\ & \alpha_p(\underline{K}_0) \cdot K_1(r,q) + \alpha_p(\underline{K}_1, m) \cdot I_1(r,m) \\
+\ & \alpha_p(\underline{I}_0) \cdot I_1(r,q) + \alpha_p(\underline{I}_1, m) \cdot AP_s(r,m,q)
\end{aligned}
$$

In the reconfiguration for S, the three new generators are s0, s1, s2; s3 and s4
are indices of new subsidiary AP nodes. Note that $(\underline{K}_1, m)$ and $\underline{I}_0$ messages
lead to the use of I_1 as an indirection node; on the other hand an
$(\underline{I}_1, m)$ message leads to a bypassing of the indirection node. Thus, I_1
indirection nodes are only bypassed when they occur as rators. (A more complex
scheme could bypass them whenever they occur as a son of any node, leaving only
the root node as an inevitable indirection node.)

4. Further Combinators

The above method of letting incomplete combinators pass upwards the addresses of
their arguments, needs a little adjustment to deal with reduction rules like

$$U\ f(P, x, y) \longrightarrow f\ xy$$
$$\text{cond true}\ x\ y \longrightarrow x$$

where the reduction depends not only upon the presence of enough arguments but
also upon the structure of one or more such arguments. The details are not
difficult, and we prefer to consider the problem of proving correctness of the
model, where the only combinators are S, K and I. The method adopted should also
generalise to handle the other combinators. (Later, we shall consider the presence
of __constant__ combinators $\underline{0}$, $\underline{1}$, ..., which will serve as possible results of
reductions.)

Configurations

Let $\alpha = \{\alpha_r \mid r \in N^*\}$, the set of possible indexed addresses. Then a
configuration C takes the form

$$C = (ROOT(m) \mid NODE_1 \mid \ldots \mid NODE_k)\backslash\alpha$$

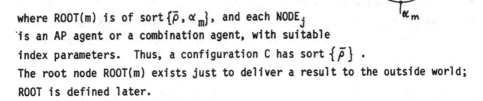

where ROOT(m) is of sort $\{\bar\rho, \alpha_m\}$, and each $NODE_j$
is an AP agent or a combination agent, with suitable
index parameters. Thus, a configuration C has sort $\{\bar\rho\}$.
The root node ROOT(m) exists just to deliver a result to the outside world;
ROOT is defined later.

To be admissible, C must satisfy a number of conditions. First, for every
argument index of a node there must exist a unique node with that index. Second,
all distinct index parameters (including index generators of AP nodes) must be
incomparable. (There may be a few further conditions). Then there is a unique
combination (term) M_C which is represented by C. Of course, every combination
is represented by infinitely many configurations; eg. the first three combinations
in the example shown earlier all represent SABC, and many more represent the same
term (due, for example, to the possibility of indirection nodes).

From now on, let us assume that all configurations considered are admissible;
one lemma to be proved is that every derivative of an admissible configuration is
also admissible, to justify this assumption.

5. Correctness

Our aim is to show that every configuration simulates the term which it
represents. Technically, this means first considering every combination M as an
abstract agent, such that $M \xrightarrow{\tau} M'$ iff M reduces to M' in one step; and second,
establishing that
$$\{<C, M_e> \mid C \text{ is an admissible configuration}\}$$
is a bisimulation.

The job is made easier by the Church-Rosser Theorem. For it will be easy to show
that whenever $C \xrightarrow{\tau} C'$, then $M_C(\xrightarrow{\tau})^*M_{C'}$ (one half of the bisimulation). On
the other hand it will not necessarily be the case that whenever $M_C \xrightarrow{\tau} M'$, then
$C (\xrightarrow{\tau})^*C'$, where C' is such that $M' = M_{C'}$. This is because C may contain only
one copy of a repeated subterm of M_C, and the reduction $M_C \xrightarrow{\tau} M'$ may reduce
only one occurrence of this subterm.
What will be the case is that $C \xrightarrow{\tau} C'$, where $M_C \xrightarrow{\tau} M'(\xrightarrow{\tau})^*M_C$. But for our
purpose it is enough to know that $M_{C'} \approx M'$, (ie. we show a bisimulation only "up
to observation equivalence") and this depends on the following lemma:

Lemma   If $M \xrightarrow{\tau} N$, then $M \approx N$.

Proof   We show that $\mathbb{R} = \{<M,N> \mid M(\xrightarrow{\tau})*N\}$ is a bisimulation.
Clearly, if $N \xrightarrow{\tau} N'$, then $M(\xrightarrow{\tau})*N'$ also.
On the other hand, if $M \xrightarrow{\tau} M'$, then

there exists, by the Church-Rosser Theorem, some N' such that $N(\xrightarrow{\tau})*N'$ and
$M'(\xrightarrow{\tau})*N'$, and since $<M', N'> \in \mathbb{R}$, we have shown $\mathbb{R}$ to be a bisimulation. ∞
To be realistic, we must of course deal with some visible ($\neq \tau$) action which
signifies that a reduction yields a result. There are many ways one might do
this; the simplest is perhaps to assume that there is a family

$$\underline{0}, \underline{1}, \underline{2}, \ldots.$$

of $\underline{\text{constant}}$ combinators, and that any combination M which starts with some
constant $\underline{k}$ is equipped (as an abstract agent) with an action

$$M \xrightarrow{\bar{\rho}(k)} M$$

ie. it can deliver "result" k.

Corresponding to constant $\underline{k}$ is its realisation (in configurations) by an
incomplete combination agent $k_0(r)$, with index address r, whose definition is
just as for any incomplete combinator agent, namely

$$k_0(r) = \bar{\alpha}_r(\underline{k}) \cdot k_0(r)$$

Now we see the proper definition for ROOT(m); it resides at the top of the
configuration waiting for a constant message $\underline{k}$ indicating that a constant has
reached the head of the corresponding combination.

$$\text{ROOT}(m) = \sum_k \alpha_m(\underline{k}) \cdot \bar{\rho}(\underline{k}).\text{ROOT}(m)$$

ROOT(m) merely transmits such messages (and only these) to the environment. With
these definitions, we now state the correctness theorem - in a slightly simplified
form (only because we have not fully taken into account the transitory state of
ROOT between receipt and delivery of result $\underline{k}$):

Theorem   The set of pairs $<C, M_C>$ for which C is an admissible
configuration is a bisimulation up to observation-equivalence.

Unfortunately, the full detail of the proof would take too much space - and would need detailed checking before we could be sure of the correctness of the model. But we have set the scene for it, and hope to have shown at least that such a model is possible in principle, and is not far from a physical realisation.

Reference [1] - J.E. Kennaway and M.R. Sleep, 'Applicative Objects as Processes'.

3.8 Mixing Synchronous and Asynchronous Input

3.8.1 Motivation

This problem was chosen to observe how different methods elucidated the distinction between synchrony and asynchrony.

3.8.2 Description

The problem was to specify the object described below.

The object has two inputs and one output. The output and one of the inputs respectively send and receive data in packets at regular intervals. The remaining input is asynchronous, i.e. data appears at undetermined times.

The data packets which arrive at the synchronous input may be full or empty, and the object may only output data by forwarding packets from the synchronous input or filling an empty packet with data from the asynchronous input. All packets have the same size.

3.8.3 Solutions

Written solutions have been prepared by the following participants:

> R.Koymans and W.P.de Roever
> G.Milne
> B.Moszkowski

and are to be found in section 4 which is arranged in alphabetical order of author name.

A "first attempt" solution was provided by C.A.R.Hoare as follows:

Workshop on Analysis of Concurrent Systems
Attempt at problem 8:
Mixing synchronous and asynchronous input

C.A.R. Hoare
9 September 1983

1. The Problem

A process normally copies messages from a regular input channel
(regin) to an output channel (out). It is also normally willing to
input a message on an occasional input channel (occin); and this message will be output on out in place of the next message from regin
which has the value "empty". After this, the process reverts to the
initial normal state.

2. The Specification

The events of interest are:

$$A = \{regin, occin, out\} \times \{MESS \cup empty\}$$

where MESS is the set of non-empty message values, and (c,x) denotes
communication of x on channel c.

Let tr be a trace of our process. The most fundamental property of the
system is that the real messages output are a merge of the two streams
of real messages input:

$$\exists t. \quad tr.out \lceil MESS \leqslant t$$
$$\land \ t.interleaves \ (tr.regin \lceil MESS,$$
$$tr.occin \lceil MESS)$$

We now need to place bounds on the number of messages output:

$$\#tr.out \leqslant^1 \#tr.regin$$

3. Glossary

tr.out = the sequence of communications on the out channel recorded in tr.

$t \restriction A$ = the sequence formed from t by omitting all symbols outside A.

$s \leq t$ = $\exists u.\ su = t$

#s = length of s.

$s \leq^n t$ = $t-n \leq s \leq t$

4. Implementation

START = (regin?x → out!x → START
  [] occin?y →
    (μX.regin?x →
      if x = empty then out!y → START
                   else out!x → X))

The implementation seems clearer than the specification in this case.

3.9 "Cash-point" Service

3.9.1 Motivation

This problem is one of ensuring reasonable control of a resource (money) using a mixture of global and local information (the data-base and the daily limit, and the information on the card). The problem can be made either very easy or very difficult by the choice of whether accounts are one-to-one with cards, and by the question of what constitutes an illegal card (e.g. is being overdrawn illegal). There are also considerable problems in updating the data-base when cash-points can operate while the data-base is temporally unavailable.

3.9.2 Description

The problem was to specify the service described below.

There are several 'tills' which can access a central resource containing the detailed records of accounts etc. A till is used by inserting a card and typing in a PIN (Personal Identification Number) which is encoded by the till and compared with a code stored on the card.

After successfully identifying yourself to the system you may try to

       1) Get the balance in your account.
       2) Make a withdrawal.
       3) Ask for a statement of account to be sent.

Information on accounts is held in a central database, and may be unavailable. So 1) may not always be possible. If the database is available, any amount up to the total in your account may be withdrawn, if it is not, there is a daily limit on withdrawals of £100 (so amount drawn in a day must be stored on the card).

"Illegal" cards are kept by the till.

The line to the database can be used to send data in only one direction at a time. Transactions at a till are recorded locally and sent downline to the centre, transactions occurring during transmission are treated as if the resource were unavailable and their results appended to the list of transactions held locally.

3.9.3

In fact this problem generated no interest in the workshop; no solutions were provided and no discussions on the problem took place.

3.10 m by n Matrix Switch

3.10.1 Motivation

The definition of the combination of concentrator, switch block and expander "switch" in which many routes through the switch are active simultaneously is a real problem in telephony. It also offers the problems of describing connections from many ports to many ports and of defining simultaneously active routes.

3.10.2 Description

The problem was to produce a formal description of the system below.

The system is made from two components, a 'concentrator', and a square 'matrix switch'. A nxn switch can make connections between two sets of n ports, A and B. Any port in A may be connected to any port in B, as long as ports are only connected in pairs i.e. a port may not be connected twice. A m into k concentrator has m 'inputs' and k 'outputs' , with m >= k. The concentrator connects an input to a free output when requested.

The system is built from a m into k concentrator connected to a k x k matrix switch, connected to a n into k concentrator.

Requests for connections arrive concurrently from all n+m users.

3.10.3 Solutions

A "first attempt" solution was provided by C.A.R.Hoare. Apart from this, no written solutions were provided for this problem.

Workshop on Analysis of Concurrent Systems
Attempt at Problem 10:
The Matrix Switch

C.A.R. Hoare
9 September 1983

1. Definition of an SMatrix

An *SMatrix* is defined by:

      in: the set of input ports

      out: the set of output ports

      lim: the maximum number of simultaneous connections,

             where

$$lim \leqslant \#in$$

$$\wedge\ lim \leqslant \#out$$

    conn: a one—one relation between in and out,

            where #conn $\leqslant$ lim

A *switch* is an SMatrix with #in = #out = lim.

A *concentrator* is an SMatrix with #in $\geqslant$ #out = lim.

Thus all switches are trivially concentrators.

2. Operations on SMatrices

The following operations are defined on SMatrices:

    if   M1 = (in1, out1, lim1, conn1)

    and   M2 = (in2, out2, lim2, conn2)

we define

1. $M1^{-1}$ = (out1, in1, lim1, conn1^{-1})

2. Provided out1 = in2,
   M1;M2 = (in1, out2, min(lim1, lim2), conn1;conn2)

3. Provided (in1 $\cap$ in2) = (out1 $\cap$ out2) = 0 ,

   M1+M2 = (in1 $\cup$ in2,
   out1 $\cup$ out2,
   lim1 + lim2,
   conn1 $\cup$ conn2)

4. If a$\in$in1 and b$\in$out1 and #conn1 < lim1
   with a$\notin$dom(conn1) and b$\notin$ran(conn1) ,
   then

   newcall$_{ab}$(M1) = (in1, out1, lim1, conn1 $\cup$ {(a,b)})

5. If (a,b)$\in$conn1, then

   breakcall$_{ab}$(M1) = (in1, out1, lim1, conn1 - {(a,b)})

3. A theorem, and conclusion

Theorem: Every SMatrix M can be decomposed into three components

C;D;E

where D is a switch and C, E^{-1} are concentrators.

The above has given a small mathematical theory for switching exchanges which may be useful in any further specifications. The problem as set by STL does not seem to require further specification: it certainly does not give the information which would be needed.

4. SOLUTIONS

ON THE SPECIFICATION OF THE FIRING SQUAD PROBLEM[*]

Egidio Astesiano - Gianna Reggio

Istituto di Matematica-Via L.B.Alberti 4 -16132
Genova (Italy)

Introduction.

Our approach uses SMoLCS methodology, a methodology of specification which provides a framework for describing transition systems as Structured Monitored Linear Concurrent Systems. Very roughly, a SMoLCS is a system in which some processes (entities) interact and every action of the system can be seen as obtained in three steps: first we look at the action capabilities of a single process in isolation (entity actions); then we consider the action capabilities of groups of processes, consisting of the synchronized occurrences of some entity actions ([prime] partial actions); finally an action of the overall system will be made of some contemporaneously happening compatible partial actions, whose choice may be influenced by an external observer-supervisor (monitoring). In that way the relationships and the dependencies of the behaviours of processes can be made explicit , to a certain extent, for discussing notions like parallelism, synchronization, distribution and for providing a formalization of the requirements of an informal specification.

In the first section we give the basic technical definitions and notations. The formal concepts of monitoring, structuring and linearization which characterize a SMoLCS are better defined,discussed and illustrated in [AR]. But note that SMoLCS is not a language and moreover that we do not fix, for the moment, a special metalanguage for describing SMoLCSes (though in future it could be convenient to have one for reference). Hence, as in [AR] we use the standard metalanguage used in partial data type specifications (see [BW]).

In the second section we give the formal specification of the problem; there it will be clear that the solutions are to be sought in a very simple subclass of SMoLCSes. Nevertheless our framework allows us to make precise many informal conditions: in particular, forgetting about other options related to less relevant points, we make explicit two different interpretations, A and B, of the clause requiring that an action of a soldier depends only on the state of the neighbours. Then, mainly in order to give examples of the technical concepts and to show the consistency of our specification, we present a solution for each option A and B. The different options give

[*] Work partially supported by a grant of CNR PFI-P1-CNET.

us an opportunity for illustrating the modularity of our methodology. Since the emphasis here is on specification,when discussing the correctness of the models we omit some technical details of the proof (though it has been carried out in full). We devote instead some lines to present possible "wrong solutions",in order to illustrate, by contrast,the meaning of some formal clauses.

The SMoLCS methodology has been developed in connection with the national project CNET (see   **[AMRZ]**   ), where it is currently applied to specify software architectures. For a   theory   which has some points of contacts with SMoLCS,but making more definite choices about the models to deal with,see also [DM].

We wish to thank our colleagues of the CNET project for many useful discussions on the subject (in particular U.Montanari,D.Mandrioli and F.Mazzanti).

1. Technical preliminaries on SMoLCS.

The style of our presentation will be an "abstract data type style",which we have found very convenient; the reference for the style and the concepts is the Broy and Wirsing's work [BW].

By a data type we mean a partial heterogeneous algebra;by a partially specified data type we mean a data type of which only some sorts and functions are specified. If T is a data type and srt,fnt,t denote respectively a sort,a function symbol and a term then SRT^T,fnt^T,t^T denote respectively the carrier of sort srt,the function corresponding to fnt in the interpretation and the element of the appropriate sort corresponding to t,if any, since we use partial algebras. We use a unique symbol D to denote definedness predicates (one for each sort and data type);i.e. for a data type T and any t :D(t) if t^T is defined. Equality of terms will be interpreted in a strong sense: t=t' in a data type T iff either t^T and t'^T are both defined and equal or both are undefined. When there is no ambiguity we drop the superscript to denote carriers,functions and interpretations of terms. Moreover, as standard notation, a generic element of SRT will be denoted by srt with subscripts and/or superscripts. It is not strictly essential to our treatment to have effectiveness (in the sense of recursion theory) conditions on the presentations of data types,though we can implicitly assume that every data type is effectively presented,since we are interested in constructive specifications.

1.1 Action systems. An action system (shortened AS) is a partially specified data type with sorts conf (for configurations),sa (for system actions) and bool (for boolean) and function symbols:

- s and t of type SA$\rightarrow$ CONF (for source and target of the action)
- init of type CONF$\rightarrow$ BOOL (for initial configurations of the system)
- / of type SA$\times$SA$\rightarrow$ SA (action composition) s.t.

$$D(sa_1/sa_2) \supset s(sa_1)=s(sa_2)=s(sa_1/sa_2)$$

/ is partial,associative and commutative.

If sa_1,sa_2 and sa_1/sa_2 are elements of SA,then the system in a certain stage $(s(sa_1))$ can execute action sa_1 or action sa_2 or both of them together.

Graphically we can represent an AS as in Fig. 1.

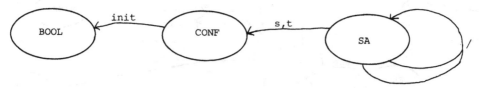

Fig. 1

Whenever init(conf) is true for any conf$\in$ CONF then the init operation is omitted.

If I is either $[0,...,k]$ or $\mathbb{N}$,then $\{sa_i\}_{i \in I}$ is a __partial execution__ iff $t(sa_i)=s(sa_{i+1})$ whenever $i,i+1 \in I$; a partial execution is an __execution__ iff moreover init$(s(sa_0))\wedge[I=\mathbb{N} \vee (t(sa_k)$ is normal$)]$;conf is said normal iff $\exists$ sa$\in$ SA s.t. s(sa)=conf.

Note that an AS is but a labelled transition system; our presentation is motivated by technical convenience,e.g. for defining the composition of actions.

In the following we shall need disjoint sums of ASes. Let N denote a set of names.

If A_n,for $n\in$ N,denotes an AS, then $\sum_{n\in N} A_n$ denotes an action system defined as follows. The sets of the configurations and of the system actions of $\sum_{n\in N} A_n$ are respectively the disjoint unions of $CONF_n$ and SA_n (the index n stands for the superscript A_n); i_n and j_n are the injections, while the functions s,t,init and / are obviously defined by:

if conf=i_n(c) where c$\in CONF_n$ then init(conf) = $init_n$(c);

if $sa_1=j_n(a_1)$ where $a_1 \in SA_n$ and $sa_2=j_m(a_2)$ where $a_2\in SA_m$,then

$$s(sa_1) = i_n(s_n(a_1)) \qquad t(sa_1) = i_n(t_n(a_1))$$

$$D(sa_1/sa_2) = [n=m\wedge D(a_1 /_n a_2)] \qquad sa_1/sa_2 = j_n(a_1 /_n a_2).$$

In the rest of the paper we will indicate i_n(c),for c$\in CONF_n$ and j_n(a),for a$\in SA_n$ respectively by c_n and by a_n.

1.2 SMoLCS with names. A Structured Monitored Linear Concurrent System with names, pictorially represented in Fig. 2,is an AS with configurations CONF and system actions SA,
describing the interactions of some processes, called entities with names in a set of
names N.

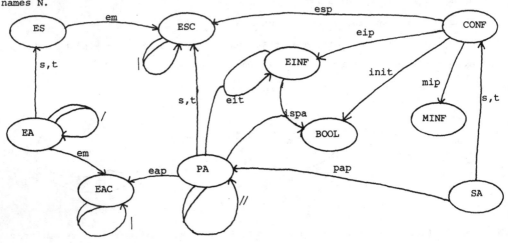

Fig. 2

An entity with name n is represented by an AS A_n; the overall behaviour of the entities is described by the AS $\sum_{n \in N} A_n$,with configurations ES (for entity stages)
and actions EA (for entity actions). We use s and t to denote source and target, both
for entity and system actions.

A configuration conf in CONF is characterized by three components:

- esp(conf),the entity stage part, which is an element of ESC (for entity stage col-
lection), the set of the finite sets of elements of ES;in ESC union is denoted by | and
the embedding of ES into ESC is denoted by em; we usually identify em(x) and x;

- eip(conf),the entity information part, which is an element of EINF, the set of the
entity informations; intuitively eip(conf) represents some global informations on the
relationships between processes (say e.g. dependencies,attributes,shared memories and
so on);

- mip(conf),the monitor information part,which is an element of MINF,the set of monitor informations; mip(conf) denotes informations which may be used to determine the
next action of the system at the monitor level,described below (say, e. g., priority).
We assume:

S1 $esp(conf) = es_n \mid es'_m \mid esc \supset n \neq m$

S2 $esp(conf) = esp(conf') \wedge eip(conf) = eip(conf') \wedge mip(conf) = mip(conf') \supset conf = conf'$

A system action is determined in a three steps procedure; entity actions (which we hav already introduced),partial actions and monitoring.

A partial action pa in PA represents the capability of simultaneous occurrence of some entity actions,eap(pa), the entity action part, which is an element of EAC (for entity action collection), the set of the finite sets of elements of EA (with union and embedding denoted as for ESC). A partial action pa is applicable in a configuration conf iff ispa(pa,eip(conf)) is true,and the happening of pa results in a change of eip(conf) to eit(pa,eip(conf)).

The relationship between pa and eap is given by

S3 $eap(pa) = ea_{n_1}^1 |...| ea_{n_k}^k \supset (\forall i,j \ \ 1 \geqslant i > j \geqslant k \ \ n_i \neq n_j) \wedge$

$s(pa)=s(ea_{n_1}^1)| ...| s(ea_{n_k}^k) \wedge t(pa)=t(ea_{n_1}^1)| ...| t(ea_{n_k}^k).$

To a system action sa is associated a partial action pap(sa),the partial action part, which determines the action as formalized in axiom S4.

S4 $isa(pap(sa),s(sa)) \wedge esp(t(sa)) = (esp(s(sa))-s(pap(sa))) | t(pap(sa)) \wedge$

$eip(t(sa)) = eit(pap(sa),eip(s(sa)))$

where $isa(pa,conf) = [s(pa) \subseteq esp(conf) \wedge ispa(pa, eip(conf))].$

For example, if $s(sa)=conf$, $t(sa)=conf'$, $esp(conf)=es_1|es_2|es_3|es_4$ and $eap(pap(sa))=ea_1|ea_2$ with $s(ea_1)=es_2$, $t(ea_1)=es_1'$, $s(ea_2)=es_4$ and $t(ea_2)=es_2'$, then we can graphically represent the change for esp(conf) to esp(conf') by

$$es_1 \ | \ es_2 \ | \ es_3 \ | \ es_4$$
$$\downarrow \qquad\qquad \downarrow$$
$$es_1 \ | \ es_1' \ | \ es_3 \ | \ es_2'$$

Moreover eip(conf')=eit(pa,eip(conf)) and possibly mip(conf') is different from mip(conf).

The monitoring step represents the observation and possibly the decisions of an observer-supervisor and can be explained as follows. The partial actions which can effectively happen,determining a system action, are the result of a choice, formally depending on the monitor information; moreover there is a partial binary operation on PA (//), meaning that some partial actions can be seen as happening together.

A partial action pa is prime iff $\not\exists p_1,p_2$ s.t. $pa=p_1 //p_2$. For a partial action being prime means that the entity actions of its entity action part are necessarily synchronized. The operation // satisfies the following axioms.

S5 // is commutative and associative

S6 $[D(pa_1 // pa_2) \wedge ea_n \in eap(pa_1) \wedge ea_n' \in eap(pa_2)] \supset D(ea_n/ea_n')$

S7 $[D(pa_1 // pa_2) \bigwedge eap(pa_1) = ea_{n_1}^1 |...| ea_{n_k}^k |ea_{n_{k+1}}^{k+1} |...| ea_{n_r}^r \bigwedge$

$$eap(pa_2) = ea_{n_1}^{1'} |...| ea_{n_k}^{k'} |ea_{n_{k+1}}^{k+1}, |...| ea_{n_s}^s, \bigwedge \{n_{k+1}, ..., n_r\} \cap \{n_{k+1}', ..., n_s'\} = \emptyset] \supset$$

$$eap(pa_1 // pa_2) = (ea_{n_1}^1 / ea_{n_1}^{1'}) |...| (ea_{n_k}^k / ea_{n_k}^{k'}) |ea_{n_{k+1}}^{k+1} |...| ea_{n_r}^r |ea_{n_{k+1}}^{k+1}, |...| ea_{n_s}^s,$$

When the composition of two partial actions is defined,if an entity performs an action in both the partial actions, say ea and ea' ,then its action in the composition is ea/ea

S8 $ispa(pa_1 // pa_2, einf) = ispa(pa_1, einf) \bigwedge ispa(pa_2, einf)$

Moreover we require that the choice depends only on the partial actions applicable to a configuration and on its mip part:

S9 $[(\bigvee pa'\ isa(pa', conf) = isa(pa', conf')) \bigwedge mip(conf) = mip(conf')] \supset$

$$ise(pa, conf) = ise(pa, conf')$$

where $ise(pa, conf) = [\exists sa\ s(sa) = conf \bigwedge pap(sa) = pa] \bigvee$

$$[\exists pa', pa''\ s.t.\ pa' = pa // pa'' \bigwedge ise(pa', conf)]$$

A SMoLCS with names is:

- monitor constant iff $\bigvee conf, conf' \in CONF\ mip(conf) = mip(conf')$,

- information constant iff $\bigvee conf, conf' \in CONF\ eip(conf) = eip(conf')$.

It is easily seen that if a system is monitor and information constant,then every configuration conf can be identified with its entity part esp(conf),so that we can simply write $conf = es_1 |es_2 |...| es_k$; analogously every partial action pa can be identified with its entity action part,eap(pa) ,since ispa(pa,eip(conf)) and eit(pa,eip(conf)) are constant for any pa and conf.

2. Formal specification of the problem.

We have to define a class FSQ of SMoLCSes with names such that $FSQ = \bigcup_{k \geqslant 2} FSQ_k$ where every FSQ_k is the class of the solutions for k machines.

Every F in FSQ_k has to satisfy the following conditions.

FS1 There exist two action systems G_F, M_F such that the entity part of F is

$$\sum_{n \in \{G, 1, ..., k\}} E_n \quad where\ E_G = G_F\ and\ E_i = M_F\ \forall i\ 1 \leqslant i \leqslant k.$$

(The k machines are identical,arranged in a line and there is a special machine,a General,at one of the two ends of the line).

FS2 F is information and monitor constant.

(The system is constituted only by the k machines and the General).

FS3 ES^{G_F} and ES^{M_F} are finite.

(A machine and the General have a finite number of states).

FS4 Two total predicates, isorder on EA^{GF} and isfire on EA^{MF} are defined s.t.

- $\exists\, ea \in EA^{GF}$ isorder(ea)

- $\exists\, ea \in EA^{MF}$ isfire(ea)

- for any execution of F $\{sa_i\}_{i \in I}$

$$[\,\exists\, ea_G \in eap(pap(sa_i))\ isorder(ea)\,] \supset$$
$$[\,\exists\, j \in I\ \ j > i \wedge (ea_1^1|\ldots|ea_k^k \subseteq eap(pap(sa_j)) \wedge (\forall r\ 1 \leqslant r \leqslant k\ isfire(ea^r)))\wedge$$
$$(\forall h \in I\ \ i < h < j\ \forall\, ea_n \in eap(pap(sa_h))\ (n \neq G\ \supset \neg isfire(ea)))\,].$$

(All the machines fire at the same moment after the General has given the order).

Note that this property of the F executions can also be expressed by means of a temporal logic formula on the executions.

Having defined the predicates on SA:

- order(sa) = $[\,\exists\, ea_G \in eap(pap(sa))\ isorder(ea)\,]$
- allfire(sa) = $[\,\exists\, ea_1^1|\ldots|ea_k^k\ ea_1^1|\ldots|ea_k^k \subseteq eap(pap(sa)) \wedge (\forall r\ 1 \leqslant r \leqslant k\ isfire(ea^r))\,)]$
- nofire(sa) = $[\,\forall\, ea_n \in eap(pap(sa))\ \ (n \neq G\ \supset \neg isfire(ea))\,]$

then FS4 can be expressed by

order $\supset$ [$\Diamond$ allfire] $\wedge$ [nofire until allfire] .

For a definition of the formal system of the linear temporal logic (with the operators $\Diamond$ and until) see [MP] .

FS5. The problem requires that the state of a machine at instant t+1 depends only on its state and the state of its neighbours at time t. This requirement can be interpreted in two ways: either word by word (that is formalized taking option B of the axiom) or, more permissively, requiring that a machine can interact only with its neighbours; in this second case no constraints are imposed on the kind of these interactions and hence the problem corresponds to the synchronization of identical processors using serial links. We formalize the second interpretation in the option A of the axiom.[☆] We need the following definitions:

- pa is maximal on conf iff isa(pa,conf) $\wedge$ [$\nexists$ pa' D(pa//pa') $\wedge$ isa(pa//pa',conf)=true]
- // is maximal iff D(pa//pa')= [$\forall$ ea$_n$,ea'$_n$ ea$_n$ $\in$ eap(pa) $\wedge$ ea'$_n$ $\in$ eap(pa') $\supset$ D(ea$_n$/ea'$_n$)]
- an entity action ea is a "condition action" iff

$s(ea)=t(ea) \wedge [\forall ea'\ s(ea')=s(ea) \supset D(ea/ea') \wedge ea/ea' =ea']$

An entity executing a condition action makes visible to other entities a property of its stage, which acts as a condition for the other entities; the condition action is compatible with any other action of the entity.

☆ It is worthwhile noting that if the interactions between the processes are like the CSP or CCS communications,then implicitly the second interpretation is assumed.

FS5-A i) // is maximal

ii) pa maximal on conf iff [$\exists$ sa$\in$ SA   s(sa)=conf $\wedge$ pap(sa)=pa]

iii) For any prime pa $\exists$ nb $\in$NB s.t. { n$\in$N| $\exists$ ea$_n$ $\in$eap(pa)} = nb, where

NB={{1},{G},{1,2},{G,1}}$\cup$ ($\bigcup_{1 < i < k}${{i-1,i,i+1},{i-1,i},{i,i+1},{i}})

(i) and ii) require that the monitoring does not interfere with the local decisions,

iii) that every machine can interact only with its neighbours).

FS5-B   FS5-A and moreover

iv) For any prime pa $\exists$ a unique ea$_n$ $\in$eap(pa)   s.t. ea$_n$ is not a condition action.

Note that FS5-A requires that the system is distributed in some sense (a machine be-haviour depends only on its neighbours). (It is possible to generalize that concept to a general SMoLCS with names N; giving a definition of N-strong distribution, for any $N \subseteq \mathcal{P}(N)$, meaning that there is no central control and that the interactions happen within the boundaries defined by the elements of N.)

FS1,...,FS5 characterize each FSQ$_k$, but there is a last constraint between the FSQ$_k$ for k $\geqslant$ 2: the form of the machines does not depend on k.

FS6 $\forall$ h,k $\geqslant$ 2 if F$\in$FSQ$_k$ then $\exists$F'$\in$FSQ$_h$ s.t. M$_F$ = M$_{F'}$ and G$_F$ =G$_{F'}$.

3. Solution.

3.1 Overview of the solution. We present two solutions of the problem, corresponding to the two options A and B in the specification of FS5 of the previous section.

Our solutions follow the hint given by the proposers: after the General has given the order two waves are propagated down the line starting from the left end; one goes three times as fast as the other and it is reflected at the end of the line so that they will meet in the middle of the line; then the procedure is reapplied to each half line (in the first half the waves move right to left, in the second one left to right) and so on until lines have length one. A machine in a line of length one is said in a ready state; a machine fires when it is ready together with its neighbours.

Now we give some examples to show how the procedure works out. We represent the propa-gation of the waves by using the flags $\overleftrightarrow{F}, \overrightarrow{F}, \overleftrightarrow{S}_i$, $\overrightarrow{S}_i$ (i=1,2,3): F for the fast wave, S for the slow wave; the arrows distinguish the waves moving either to right or left; the index is used for distinguishing the speeds of the waves.

In Fig.3 and Fig.4 we illustrate the synchronization procedure for k=3 (option A and B) and for k= 9 (option A), by means of matricial diagrams (as suggested in [M]), where the column n (n $\in$N) represents the sequence of the states of the machine named n, the row j the situation of the system at the j-th step. The machines at the ends of a synchronization line have the flag ） or ＜ ; the machines in a ready state , i.e. having the flags ） and ＜ , are graphically marked by ®; W (for waiting) and D (for done) represent the two General's states and FD (for firing done) the machine state after having fired.

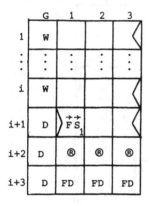

Left table (option A):

	G	1	2	3
1	W			
:	:	:	:	:
i	W			
i+1	D	）$\overrightarrow{F}\overrightarrow{S}_1$		
i+2	D	®	®	®
i+3	D	FD	FD	FD

Right table (option B):

	G	1	2	3
1	W			
:	:	:	:	:
i+1	W			
i+2	D			
i+3	D	）$\overrightarrow{F}\overrightarrow{S}_1$		
i+4	D	）$\overrightarrow{S}_2$	$\overline{F}$	
i+5	D	）$\overrightarrow{S}_3$		$\overleftarrow{F}$
i+6	D	）	®	
i+7	D	®	®	®
i+8	D	FD	FD	FD

Fig. 3

Synchronization procedure for 3 machines, option A and B.

3.2 Formal solution.

For any $k \geq 2$ we give two monitor and information constant SMoLCSes with names, S_k^A and S_k^B, which formally describe our solutions for k machines for option A and B.

S_k^A and S_k^B differ only for their prime partial actions. In the following we will use S_k as common name for S_k^A and S_k^B.

The entity part

The entity part of S_k is $\sum_{n \in \{G,1,\ldots,k\}} E_n$, where $E_G = G$ and $E_i = M$ for $i=1,\ldots,k$. G and M are the action systems specified below.

The General G

The set of the configurations is GS={W,D}; W and D are pictorially represented by ⬚W⬚ and ⬚D⬚ . The set of the actions is GACT={(W,W),(W,D)} (pictorially represented by ⬚W/W⬚ and ⬚W/D⬚); clearly s((W,W))=t((W,W))=s((W,D))=W and t((W,D))=D.

// is the totally undefined operator.

	G	1	2	3	4	5	6	7	8	9
1	W									
⋮	⋮	⋮	⋮	⋮	⋮	⋮	⋮	⋮	⋮	⋮
j	W									
j+1	D	$\vec{S}_1\,\vec{F}$								
j+2	D	$\vec{S}_2$	$\vec{F}$							
j+3	D	$\vec{S}_3$		$\vec{F}$						
j+4	D		$\vec{S}_1$		$\vec{F}$					
j+5	D		$\vec{S}_2$			$\vec{F}$				
j+6	D		$\vec{S}_3$				$\vec{F}$			
j+7	D			$\vec{S}_1$				$\vec{F}$		
j+8	D			$\vec{S}_2$					$\vec{F}$	
j+9	D			$\vec{S}_3$						$\overleftarrow{F}$
j+10	D				$\vec{S}_1$			$\overleftarrow{F}$		
j+11	D				$\vec{S}_2$		$\overleftarrow{F}$			
j+12	D				$\vec{S}_3$	$\overleftarrow{F}$				
j+13	D				$\overleftarrow{S}_1\,\overleftarrow{F}$	®	$\vec{S}_1\,\vec{F}$			
j+14	D			$\overleftarrow{F}$	$\overleftarrow{S}_2$	®	$\vec{S}_2$	$\vec{F}$		
j+15	D		$\overleftarrow{F}$		$\overleftarrow{S}_3$	®	$\vec{S}_3$		$\vec{F}$	
j+16	D	$\vec{F}$		$\overleftarrow{S}_1$		®		$\vec{S}_1$		$\overleftarrow{F}$
j+17	D		$\vec{F}$	$\overleftarrow{S}_2$		®		$\vec{S}_2$	$\overleftarrow{F}$	
j+18	D	$\overleftarrow{S}_1\,\overleftarrow{F}$	$\vec{S}_1\,\vec{F}$		®		$\overleftarrow{S}_1\,\overleftarrow{F}$	$\vec{S}_1\,\vec{F}$		
j+19	D	®	®	®	®	®	®	®	®	®
j+20	D	FD	FD	FD	FD	FD	FD	FD	FD	FD

Fig. 4

Synchronization procedure for 9 machines (option A)

A soldier machine M

The stages of M are characterized by the flags present in that stage on the machine, thus the set of the configurations of M is

$$MS= \mathcal{P}_F(\{\ \langle\ ,\ \rangle, \overrightarrow{F}, \overleftarrow{F}, \overrightarrow{S}_1, \overrightarrow{S}_2, \overrightarrow{S}_3, \overleftarrow{S}_1, \overleftarrow{S}_2, \overleftarrow{S}_3, FD\})$$

where $\mathcal{P}_F(X)$ is the set of the finite subsets of X.

Usually $\{fl_1, \ldots, fl_r\} \in MS$ is pictorially represented by $\boxed{fl_1 .. fl_r}$, $\emptyset$ by $\square$.

An element ms of MS represents a ready stage of the machine iff $\{\langle,\rangle\} \subseteq ms$, they are marked by ®. MACT, the set of the system actions, is a finite subset of $MS \times MS$ (s and t are the projection operations); hence we give it by listing its elements.

(ms,ms') is graphically represented by $\boxminus$ if $\square$ and $\square$ respectively represent ms and ms'.

Convention: here and in what follows $\square$ and $\square$ will be used to indicate generic elements of MS; $\boxed{\begin{smallmatrix}X\\Y\end{smallmatrix}}\left(\boxed{\begin{smallmatrix}X\\Y\end{smallmatrix}}\right)$ stands for $\boxed{\begin{smallmatrix}X\\Y\end{smallmatrix}}$ and $\boxed{\begin{smallmatrix}X\\Y\end{smallmatrix}}$ $\left(\boxed{\begin{smallmatrix}X\\Y\end{smallmatrix}}$ and $\boxed{\begin{smallmatrix}X\\Y\end{smallmatrix}}\right)$.

Elements of MACT

The machine passes $\overrightarrow{F}$ to its right neighbour

The machine passes $\overleftarrow{F}$ to its left neighbour

The machine takes $\overrightarrow{F}$ from its left neighbour

The machine takes $\overleftarrow{F}$ from its right neighbour

The machine takes $\overleftarrow{F}$ from its right neighbour

The machine takes $\overrightarrow{F}$ from its left neighbour

These actions permit the reflection of the fast wave.

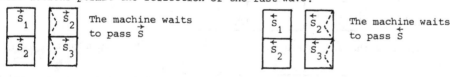

The machine waits to pass $\overrightarrow{S}$

The machine waits to pass $\overleftarrow{S}$

These actions permit to obtain the different speeds of the waves.

The machine passes $\overrightarrow{S}$ to its right neighbour

The machine passes $\overleftarrow{S}$ to its left neighbour

The machine takes $\overleftarrow{S}$ from its right neighbour

The machine takes $\overrightarrow{S}$ from its left neighbour

The machine passes $\overrightarrow{F}$ and waits to pass $\overrightarrow{S}$

The machine passes $\overleftarrow{F}$ and waits to pass $\overleftarrow{S}$

for every $\boxed{\diagdown}$ s.t. $\rangle \notin \boxed{\diagdown}$

The machine starts to synchronize the line to its right

for every $\boxed{\diagdown}$ s.t. $\langle \notin \boxed{\diagdown}$

The machine starts to synchronize the line to its left

for every $\boxed{\diagup}$ not marked by ®

The machine becomes ready

for every $\boxed{\diagdown}$ marked by ®

The machine fires

The action composition operation / on MACT is so defined:

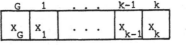

$$- \boxed{\diagdown} \Big/ \boxed{\diagup} = \boxed{\diagdown\!\!\!\diagup} \quad \text{for every} \quad \boxed{\diagdown} , \boxed{\diagup} \in \text{MACT},$$

- in all the other cases / is undefined.

Note that every action $\boxed{\diagdown\!\!\!\diagup}$ is a condition action (see discussion on FS5).

<u>Configurations</u>

Since S_k is monitor and information constant, every configuration can be identified by its entity stage part.

CONF = {$es_G|es_1|\ldots|es_k|$ $es_G=i_G$(gs) for some gs $\in$ GS,

for n=1,...,K $es_n=i_n$(ms) for some ms $\in$ MS}

If $\boxed{X_n}$ is a graphic representation of es_n then conf=$es_G|es_1|\ldots|es_k$ will be graphi-

cally represented by

G	1	. . .	k-1	k
X_G	X_1	. . .	X_{k-1}	X_k

.

The initial stages of the system are defined by init :CONF$\rightarrow$BOOL such that

init(conf)= [conf =

G	1	2	. . . . .	k-1	k
W			. . . .		$\rangle$

] .

<u>Partial actions</u>

Since S_k is monitor and information constant, we can assume PA $\subseteq$ EAC (for there is no need to define the eit and ispa operations).

There is a finite number of prime elements of PA, hence we give them by listing and after define the // operation.

An element of EAC $ea_{n1}|\ldots|ea_{nr}$ is graphically represented by

n1	...	..	nr
X_1	...	..	X_r
X'_1	...	..	X'_r

if for every $i=1,\ldots,r$ $ea_{ni}=j_{ni}(ea)$ for some $ea \in$ MACT $\cup$ GACT and ea is represented

by .

<u>The General waits</u>   A and B)

<u>The General gives the order</u>   A)   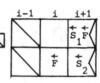   B)

Waves propagation start

A) (length of the line >3)

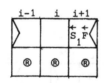   for every ◻ s.t. ⟨ ∉ ◻   for every ◻ s.t. ⟩ ∉ ◻
$(1 < i < k)$ $(1 < i < k)$

(length of the line $=3$)

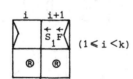 $(1 < i < k)$

(length of the line $=2$)

   $(1 \leq i < k)$

B) (length of the line ≥ 3)

   for every ◻ s.t. ⟨ ∉ ◻   for every ◻ s.t. ⟩ ∉ ◻
$(1 \leq i < k)$ $(1 \leq i < k)$

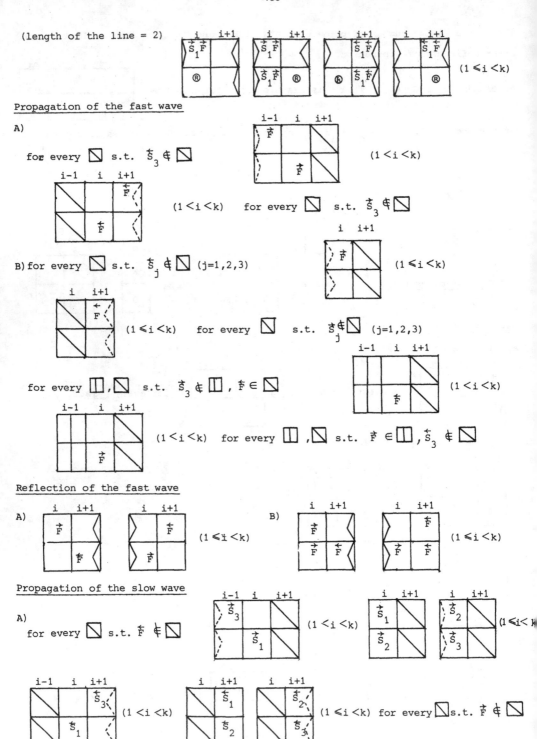

(length of the line = 2)

$(1 \leqslant i < k)$

Propagation of the fast wave

A)

for every ▢ s.t. $\vec{s}_3 \notin$ ▢ $(1 < i < k)$

$(1 < i < k)$ for every ▢ s.t. $\vec{s}_3 \notin$ ▢

B) for every ▢ s.t. $\vec{s}_j \notin$ ▢ $(j=1,2,3)$ $(1 \leqslant i < k)$

$(1 \leqslant i < k)$ for every ▢ s.t. $\vec{s}_j \notin$ ▢ $(j=1,2,3)$

for every ▢,▢ s.t. $\vec{s}_3 \notin$ ▢ , $\overset{\leftarrow}{F} \in$ ▢ $(1 < i < k)$

$(1 < i < k)$ for every ▢ ,▢ s.t. $\vec{F} \in$ ▢ , $\overset{\leftarrow}{s}_3 \notin$ ▢

Reflection of the fast wave

A) $(1 \leqslant i < k)$ B) $(1 \leqslant i < k)$

Propagation of the slow wave

A)
for every ▢ s.t. $\overset{\leftarrow}{F} \notin$ ▢ $(1 < i < k)$ $(1 \leqslant i < k)$

$(1 < i < k)$ $(1 \leqslant i < k)$ for every ▢ s.t. $\vec{F} \notin$ ▢

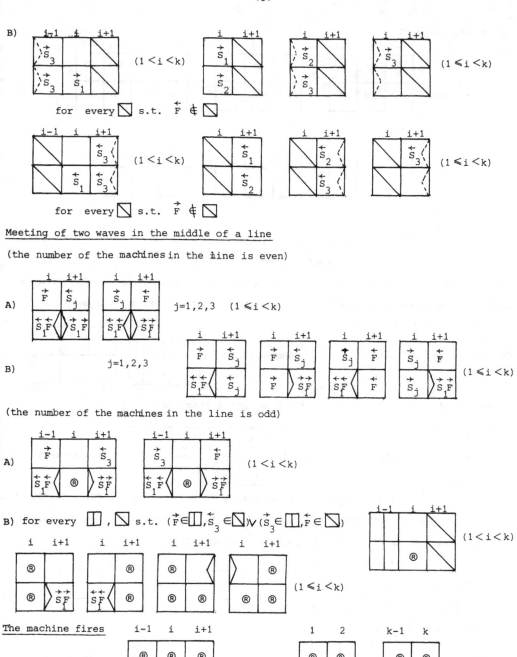

B) (1 < i < k)

for every ▧ s.t. $\overleftarrow{F} \notin$ ▧

(1 ≤ i < k)

for every ▧ s.t. $\overrightarrow{F} \notin$ ▧

Meeting of two waves in the middle of a line

(the number of the machines in the line is even)

A) j=1,2,3 (1 ≤ i < k)

B) j=1,2,3

(1 ≤ i < k)

(the number of the machines in the line is odd)

A) (1 < i < k)

B) for every ▯ , ▧ s.t. ($\overrightarrow{F} \in$ ▯, $\overleftarrow{S}_3 \in$ ▧) ∨ ($\overrightarrow{S}_3 \in$ ▯, $\overleftarrow{F} \in$ ▧)

(1 < i < k)

(1 ≤ i < k)

The machine fires   (1 < i < k)

Partial action composition

// is the maximal one; note that for a monitor and information constant SMoLCS, since every partial action pa coincides with eap(pa) there is a unique maximal //, by

SMoLCS axiom S7 .

For example:

(grids with symbols)

System actions

SA ={(conf,conf') | ∃ pa s.t. isa(pa,conf) ∧ pa is maximal on conf ∧

$$conf' = (conf - s(pa)) \mid t(pa)\}$$

For any conf,conf' there exists a unique pa s.t. conf'=(conf-s(pa)) | t(pa) (because pa=pa' iff s(pa)=s(pa') ∧ t(pa)=t(pa')). Then s̄,t and pap on SA are uniquely and obviously defined.

To clarify the definition note, for example, that

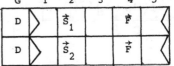

is not an element of SA, for the applicable partial action

(grid) is not executed; while (grid) belongs to SA.

3.3 Correctness of the solution.

It is very easy to see that axioms FS1,FS2,FS3,FS5-A (FS5-B) and FS6 are satisfied for S_k^A (S_k^B),k ≥ 2. To see that every S_k satisfies FS4 is sufficient the following Proposition and to note that:

- after the General has executed an order action the system stage becomes (grid),

- the General in the D state cannot more act,

(grid) is the unique system action with such source.

We indicate by S_k^+ the SMoLCS which has the same entity part, partial actions and monitoring as S_k and whose configuration set is

{es₁|...|es_r | for any j 1 ≤ j ≤ r ∃ n_j ∈ N, s ∈ MS ∪ GS s.t. es_j = i_{n_j}(s) and n_j ≠ n_i iff i ≠ j}.

Proposition.

For every S_k^+ $(k \geqslant 2)$ and h $(k \geqslant h \geqslant 2)$, for every configuration having one of the following forms:

$(0 \leqslant i \leqslant k-h)$,

there exists a partial execution $\{sa_j\}_{1 \leqslant j \leqslant m}$ s.t.

i) $t(sa_m) =$

ii) $s(sa_j)$, $1 \leqslant j < m$, does not contain

$(1 \leqslant j \leqslant h)$

iii) if $\{sa'_j\}_{1 \leqslant j \leqslant r}$ is a partial execution s.t. $s(sa'_1) = s(sa_1)$, then

$\{sa'_j\}_{1 \leqslant j \leqslant M} = \{sa_j\}_{1 \leqslant j \leqslant M}$ where $M = \min\{m,r\}$.

Proof. By arithmetic induction on h. (Omitted.)

3.4 A discussion on "wrong solutions". In this section we give two examples of systems which do not belong to FSQ (but satisfy FS4), for every machine can communicate with any other via shared memory or via handshaking.

Example1 T_k $(k \geqslant 2)$ is a monitor constant SMoLCS with names, defined as follows.

Entity part $\sum_{n \in \{G,1,\ldots,k\}} E_n$ where $E_G = G$ (defined in Section 3.2) and

$E_i = L$ for every i $1 \leqslant i \leqslant k$.

_ indicates the AS whose components are: CONF=$\{W,FD\}$, SA =$\{(W,FD)\}$ (W stands for waiting, FD for firing done) and $/$ is the totally undefined operator.

Configurations

CONF=$\{(W_G|W_1|\ldots|W_K,DNF), (D_G|W_1|\ldots|W_K,F), (D_G|FD_1|\ldots|FD_K,F)\}$

The first component of a configuration is the esp part while the second one is the eip part (DNF for do not fire, F for fire).

$(W_G|W_1|\ldots|W_K,F)$ is the only initial configuration.

Partial actions The set of the prime partial actions, which is a subset of EAC, is

$\{(W,W)_G, (W,D)_G\} \cup \{(W,FD)_i | 1 \leqslant i \leqslant k\}$ and the operations are defined by:

$ispa((W,W)_G,einf)=ispa((W,D)_G,einf)=true$; $eit((W,W)_G,einf)=einf$; $eit((W,D)_G,einf)=F$;

$ispa((W,FD)_i,einf)=[einf=F]$; $eit((W,FD)_i,einf)=einf$ for every i $1 \leqslant i \leqslant k$;

$/$ is maximal and

- $ispa(pa_1//pa_2,einf)=ispa(pa_1,einf) \wedge ispa(pa_2,einf)$

- $eit(pa_1//pa_2,einf)=einf'$ iff $eit(pa_1,einf)=einf'$ and $eit(pa_2,einf)=einf$;

these clauses completely define $//$, since for any $einf \in EINF$ there exists at most one pa s.t. ispa(pa,einf) and eit(pa,einf)$\neq$einf.

System actions

$$SA=\{((W_G|W_1|\ldots|W_k,DNF),(W_G|W_1|\ldots|W_k,DNF)),((W_G|W_1|\ldots|W_k,DNF),(D_G|W_1|\ldots|W_k,F)),$$
$$((D_G|W_1|\ldots|W_k,F),(D_G|FD_1|\ldots|FD_k,F))\}.$$

Their pap parts are respectively $(W,W)_G$, $(W,D)_G$ and $(W,FD)_1|\ldots|(W,FD)_k$.

T_k satisfies all the axioms of the problem specification except FS2; indeed this system is constituted by the General, the soldier machines and a shared memory (which can contemporaneously be read by several machines). This example shows the importance of FS2 about the absence of any global information.

Example 2

I_k (k$\geqslant$2) is a monitor and information constant SMoLCS with names, defined as follows.

Entity part

$$\sum_{n\in\{G,1,\ldots,k\}} E_n \text{ where } E_G=G \text{ (see Section 3.2) and for every } i \text{ } 1\leqslant i\leqslant k \text{ } E_i=X \text{ .}$$

X is the AS whose components are: CONF={W,OR,FD} (OR for order received),

SA={(W,OR),(OR,FD),(W,FD)} and / is the totally undefined operator.

Configurations

$$\{W_G|W_1|\ldots|W_k,D_G|OR_1|W_2|\ldots|W_k,D_G|FD_1|FD_2|\ldots|FD_k\}$$

The unique initial configuration is $W_G|W_1|\ldots|W_k$.

Partial actions

The set of the prime partial actions is $\{(W,W)_G,(W,D)_G|(W,OR)_1,(OR,FD)_1|(W,FD)_2\ldots\ldots|(W,FD)_k\}$ and // is the maximal one (which is unique, for I_k is monitor and information constant).

System actions

$$\{(W_G|W_1|\ldots|W_k,W_G|W_1|\ldots|W_k),(W_G|W_1|\ldots|W_k,D_G|OR_1|\ldots|W_k),$$
$$(D_G|OR_1|\ldots|W_K,D_G|FD_1|\ldots|FD_k)\}.$$

Their pap parts are respectively the three prime partial actions.

I_k satisfies all the axioms except FS5 iii), for any machine can communicate with the first and not only with its neighbours; thus it does not respect the request about distribution.

Concluding remarks.

Having shown our method on an example, we are now in a better position for discussing a bit further some of its general features.

Our specification consists in qualifying, via formal axioms, a class of systems, each one representing a solution of the problem. In order to express the formal properties, the solutions are sought in a special class of systems, the SMoLCSes, which are presented following a framework suitable for expressing requests on cooperation, concurrency and distribution.

Let us compare SMoLCS methodology against three basic issues.

The first is abstraction, (as opposed to overspecification);see,e.g.[B] and the first pages of [L]). How abstract is our specification? We think it is fair to say that our level of abstraction is intermediate between,say, temporal logic specifications and CCS specifications, i.e. between purely axiomatic specifications and purely constructive specifications which give models in a specific language (though rather abstract as CCS or CSP). But, while the difference with CCS or CSP specifications is clear, it is not so immediate to assess the difference in abstraction from using logic specifications (see for example the discussion on axiom FS4). The discriminating point is that SMoLCS methodology requires that a system is presented with features (summed up in the three steps: entity actions, partial actions and monitoring) which essentially make explicit its concurrent structure and can be used to specify distribution. In this (and only) sense a SMoLCS specification is more concrete. Also note that the use of abstract data types gives freedom from unnecessary details.

The second issue is comprehensibility (see [B]). Since we do not propose a fixed language, we do not need to translate: in other words we can adapt our specification to the level of the object to be specified. For example, when specifying ADA, we do not need to express high level constructs with lower level ones. That makes specification more understandable and especially it is easier to convince a user that the object formally specified does correspond to the object informally specified. Of course there is a price to pay: while the rules determining the transitions of the system are fixed when we translate in a specific language (see CCS), here they need to be specified for each system (in SMoLCS they are embedded in the three steps). In this respect the situation in SMoLCS is exactly the same as for Petri nets (see [AR] for a more precise relationship). Perhaps in future it could be convenient to single out some special subclasses of SMoLCSes expecially in order to have more concise descriptions and precise proof systems (analogously to what happens when we consider subclasses in Chomsky hierarchy). The disadvantage of defining directly the transitions is evident in our proposed solution for the firing squad. But note two facts. First, the presented solution is, in a sense, the most abstract in the class of systems following the two waves algorithm. Secondly, the solution could be expressed giving a system in another language and proving that it satisfies the formal requirements, i.e. it is a SMoLCS satisfying the specified axioms.

The third issue is distribution. It is well known that most current specification methods do not deal with it (see [L]). In SMoLCS there is an attempt at having structures for expressing requirements on distribution; consider, for example, our discussion about axiom FS5. A more formal discussion, though far from being complete, can be found in [AR].

As final remark, we would stress the fact that the firing squad problem is too simple, in some respect, for showing the use of some features of SMoLCS methodology, for example the use of entity and monitor informations. Moreover the modularity of our approach has not been fully exploited (except that for expressing the two options A and B of axiom FS5). In other cases it is more evident that the three steps allow us to express concisely specifications and solutions differing only in some points (e.g., some prime partial actions and various kind of monitoring). We refer to [AR] for illustrative examples on this point. In that paper SMoLCS is also put in perspective, discussing, more generally, the concepts of Structuring, Monitoring and Linearization.

Added during revision.The SMoLCS approach has now been given a new partly simpli
fied formalization by using the algebraic specification language ASL (see [AMRW]
for a formal presentation and [A] for a more explicative introduction).
In this new formalization a SMoLCS system is defined as an abstract data type obtained
by instantiating a parametrized abstract data type SMoLCS on the appropriate para
meters, related to entity transitions, synchronization, parallel composition and moni
toring. An application to the specification of a real communication architecture
is outlined in [AMRZ].

REFERENCES

[A]   E.Astesiano,"Combining an operational with an algebraic approach to the speci
        fication of concurrency", Quaderni CNET n.127, ETS Pisa, 1984, also to appear
        in the proceedings of the Workshop on Combining Methods,Nyborg (Denmark),
        May 1984
[AMRW] E.Astesiano, G.Mascari, G.Reggio, M.Wirsing,"On the parametrized algebraic
        specification of concurrent systems",Proceedings of CAAP '85-TAPSOFT Conferen
        ce, Berlin,LNCS n.185,Springer-Verlag, 1985.
[AMRZ] E.Astesiano, F.Mazzanti, G.Reggio, E.Zucca,"Formal specification of a concur
        rent architecture in a real project".Proceedings of ICS '85 ACM (Internatio
        nal Computing Symposium), North-Holland, 1985
[AR]   E.Astesiano,G.Reggio,"A unifying viewpoint for the construcive specification
        of cooperation,concurrency and distribution".Quaderni CNET n.115,ETS Pisa 1983.
[B]   D.Bjørner,"Requirements of a formal definition of ADA", ADA Europe Formal Defini
        tion Working Group, February 1983.
[BW]   M.Broy, M.Wirsing,"Partial abstract types", Acta Informatica 18, 47-64, 1982.
[DM]   P.Degano, U.Montanari, "A model for distribuited systems based on graph
        rewriting",Draft,Departement of Informatics,University of Pisa, November
        1983 (submitted for publication).
[L]   L.Lamport,"What good is temporal logic ?",Proceedings of the IFIP 9th World
        Computer Congress, North-Holland,September 1983.
[M]   M.Minsky."Computation: finite and infinite machines", Prentice-Hall,1972.
[MP]   Z.Manna,A.Pnueli,"How to cook a temporal proof system for your pet language",
        Proceedings of the ACM Symposium on Principles of Programming Languages,1983.

Towards the Hierarchical, Temporal Logic, Specification of Concurrent Systems

Presented at the
Workshop on the Analysis of Concurrent Systems
Cambridge, September 1983

Howard Barringer and Ruurd Kuiper
Department of Computer Science
University of Manchester
Oxford Road
Manchester, M13 9PL

Abstract

A hierarchical specification method is given which, through the use of a past time temporal logic, handles both safety and liveness requirements. The technique is applied to the specification of a "two way channel with disconnect", and in the partial development of a "packet switching communications network". An inference rule for the justification of parallel composition is indicated.

1: Introduction

In this paper we present a notion of specification which handles both safety and liveness requirements. A major goal of our approach is the support of hierarchic development, or modular decomposition. That is to say, given only the specifications of components (not their implementations) one can deduce whether some particular combination of the component implementations will satisfy some overall specification. This leads to the central notion of specifying a component in an environment (cf. [Jo83]).

At each level of development, the behaviour of a component in its environment is given by describing the changes that component can make to the interface with its environment and the changes its environment can make to that interface. This is essentially describing the externally observable behaviour of a component, however, one extra observational factor is added, namely, the ability to distinguish a change made by a component from one made by its environment. This is achieved by labelling the changes, i.e. labelling actions. This labelling, in fact, is crucial to the formulation of a rule for the parallel composition of processes.

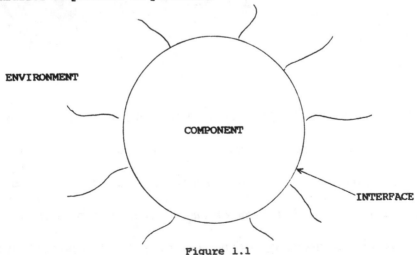

ENVIRONMENT

COMPONENT

INTERFACE

Figure 1.1

We assume throughout that the interface between a component and its environment is represented by shared variables. We describe a component by a temporal logic formula, *comp*, in an environment, described by *env*, over the set of interface variables, Σ, and we write specifications as triples of the form (Σ, env, comp). The use of temporal logic achieves our requirement for handling both safety and liveness.

The remainder of the paper is structured as follows. Section 2 presents the computational model and the semantics of a process. Section 3 covers the past time temporal logic we use and section 4 introduces the specification style. In section 5, we give a specification of the "two way channel" example (problem 1 of the STL problem set). In section 6, a partial development of a message based packet switching communications network (based around problem 6) is presented. Finally, in section 7, we indicate a rule for proving the parallel decomposition steps, as in section 6, correct.

2: The Computation Model

In the introduction, a description of behaviour by states of interface variables was indicated. The semantical model for system behaviour consists of a set of labelled state sequences which can be produced by that system. Given an execution sequence over an interface variable set, Σ,

$$\sigma_0 \cdots \sigma_n , \sigma_{n+1} \cdots$$

we first extend it to infinity at both ends by duplicating the initial state, σ_0, backwards and by duplicating the final state, if such exists, forwards. This extended sequence is indexed by the integers. Furthermore, we label actions by adding a label field, ℓ, into the state. Thus, the sequences, ρ, in our model are of the form:-

$$\ldots \ldots \langle\sigma_n, \ell_n\rangle \, , \, \langle\sigma_{n+1}, \ell_{n+1}\rangle \, \ldots \ldots$$

The label values are e, c or d. For any state indexed by n, the label values are interpreted as:-

a) e $\sigma_n \to \sigma_{n+1}$ is an environment action
b) c $\sigma_n \to \sigma_{n+1}$ is a component action
c) d $\sigma_n \to \sigma_{n+1}$ is a duplication of initial/final state

The semantics of a component, P, with interface, Σ, is now defined as the set of extended, labelled, computation sequences, generated by P in any environment, with all re-indexing, and is denoted by $M[P, \Sigma]$. The transitions labelled c are according to a given interpretation for the language in which P is expressed, e.g. a suitable operational semantics, however, no restrictions are placed on the transitions labelled e. This complies with the intuitive notion that the semantics of P is the set of execution sequences obtained from running P in any environment.

The interpretation of a specification (Σ, env, comp) will also be a set of such sequences, namely, those allowed by the specification. To be able to describe formally which set, we next introduce a logic to express env and comp.

3: Past Time Temporal Logic

To facilitate the description of sets of state sequences, a logic to express properties of sequences is required. For proving concurrent programs correct, linear future time temporal logic was introduced by Pnueli [Pn79], and further developed by Manna and Pnueli [MP82a,MP82b] and Owicki and Lamport [OL82]. In their approaches, "program locations" are used to infer the future behaviour of a program from only the present state. In the case of our specifications, we desire to use only the interface variables, and not introduce locations or other auxiliary, e.g. history, variables. As future behaviour might depend upon information about the past, now not encoded in the present state, we use a logic equipped with past time operators, [Pr67].

The extra symbols in this logic are:-

●	in the previous moment
◆	sometime in the (strict) past, i.e. not including now
▤	always in the (strict) past
◈	sometime (in the past, present or future)
⑪	always (in the past, present or future)

The interpretation of the temporal logic symbols in our model is as follows. Let ρ be any extended (labelled) state sequence. We define ρ^i to be the sequence $\rho[\sigma_{n-i}/\sigma_n]$ for all n, i.e. replacing every index n by index n-i. Intuitively, this means shifting the origin (i.e. the present time) i places forward in time. Firstly, we assume that the interpretation of a non-temporal formula, q, in a state is given, i.e. $\sigma \vDash q$, then we can interpret temporal formulae over sequences by induction over their structure, predicate logic symbols having the standard interpretation. Hence:-

$$\rho \vDash q \quad \triangleq \quad \sigma_0 \vDash q$$
$$\text{for non temporal formula q}$$
$$\rho \vDash \bigcirc w \quad \triangleq \quad \rho^1 \vDash w$$
$$\rho \vDash \Diamond w \quad \triangleq \quad \exists i \geqslant 0 . \rho^i \vDash w$$
$$\rho \vDash \Box w \quad \triangleq \quad \forall i \geqslant 0 . \rho^i \vDash w$$
$$\rho \vDash \bullet w \quad \triangleq \quad \rho^{-1} \vDash w$$
$$\rho \vDash \blacklozenge w \quad \triangleq \quad \exists i < 0 . \rho^i \vDash w$$
$$\rho \vDash \blacksquare w \quad \triangleq \quad \forall i < 0 . \rho^i \vDash w$$
$$\diamond w \quad \triangleq \quad \blacklozenge w \vee \Diamond w$$
$$\square w \quad \triangleq \quad \blacksquare w \wedge \Box w$$

Finally, we define a formula to be true for a set of sequences, S, if and only if it is true for each sequence in the set. I.e.

$$S \vDash w \quad \triangleq \quad \forall \rho \in S \ . \ \rho \vDash w$$

Example

Let ρ be a sequence of states denoting the value an integer variable z.   Take the origin (i.e. index 0) to be when z=1.

$$\rho \quad \triangleq \quad \ldots, \ -3, \ -1, \ 1, \ 3, \ 5, \ 7, \ 9, \ \ldots$$

The following formulae are true for **all** possible re-indexings of ρ, i.e' for any time we look at ρ.

```
    i)      is_odd(z)
   ii)      z=1  ⇥  ◊z=9
  iii)      z=1  ⇥  ⊟z=-1
   iv)      z=1  ⇥  □◊is_prime(z)
    v)      z=2  ⇥  □◊is_even(z)
```

The following formulae are false for **some** possible indexings of ρ:-

```
   vi)      ◊is_even(z)
  vii)      ◊z=9
```

4: Specifications

We now write our specifications as temporal formulae env and comp.   For methodological reasons, we suggest such formulae are presented in the following style. Env (and similarly comp) is formed from two parts.   The first part describes possible environment (component) actions.   It is given in a standard form , e ⇥ .... , (c ⇥ ....). By an abuse of notation, we use the predicates e, c (and d) to determine the "originator" of an action in the logic. Thus, the predicate e is true in the state $\langle\sigma, \ell\rangle$ if and only if ℓ is the label e, similarly for the predicate c (and d).   For example, a specification of a component with one interface variable, x, might assume the following about its environment, and have as part of its formula,

$$e \;\dashv\; \bigcirc x=5 \;\vee\; \bigcirc x=10$$

indicating the component expects that if the environment makes an action it will set x to 5 or to 10. The comp formula "action part" might be,

$$c \;\dashv\; x=\bigcirc x+1 \;\wedge\; \blacklozenge(e\text{-}\bigcirc x=5)$$

implying that the only correct action of the component is to subtract 1 from x if there has been an environment action setting x to 5.

The second part of the formula further restricts the possible sequences of actions made by the environment (component). There is no standard form and it is used to specify liveness assumptions about the environment (promises of the component). For example, the comp formula partially presented above may have the following "liveness part",

$$x=5 \;\dashv\; \Diamond\, c$$

indicating that if ever x = 5 then a component action will eventually occur.

The env (comp) formula is then taken as,

$$\text{"action part"} \;\wedge\; \text{"liveness part"}$$

i.e. every transition in a sequence satisfying env (comp) is in accordance with the env (comp) action part and the sequence satisfies the liveness part.

As our approach is to specify a component in an environment, the intuitive idea is to require the following from the component:

1) that it behaves in accordance with comp if the environment is behaving in

accordance with the assumptions, i.e. env;

2) that it may behave in any manner if the environment assumptions are not met, i.e. env does not hold;

3) that 1) and 2) above are the only allowed behaviours, i.e. misbehaviour of the component (comp not holding) if the environment is well behaved (env holding) is disallowed.

We thus take as the set of sequences allowed by a specification, Spec, (Σ, env, comp)

$$\{ \rho \mid \rho \vdash [\![ ]\!] \text{ env} \rightarrow [\![ ]\!] \text{ comp} \}$$

and is denoted by seq(Spec). Finally, we can now define the notion of a component, P, satisfying a specification, Spec,

$$P \text{ sat Spec} \quad \triangleq \quad M[P,\Sigma] \subseteq \text{seq(Spec)}$$

5: TWO WAY CHANNEL with DISCONNECT

The problem is to specify the channel described below.

The 'channel' between endpoints 'a' and 'b' can pass messages in both directions simultaneously, until it receives a 'disconnect' message from one end, after which it neither delivers nor accepts messages at that end. It continues to deliver and accept messages at the other end until the disconnect message arrives, after which it can do nothing. The order of mesages sent in a given direction is preserved.

Our technique is to specify a component in an environmment; here, the component is the channel. We consider each endpoint of the channel to be connected to the environment by two wires, an input and an output wire. The observable behaviour of the channel is then the appearance or disappearance of a message at the wires. We model this interface (i.e. the wires) by four variables, in_a, out_b, in_b and out_a, having as possible values messages, $m \in M$ or $\emptyset$. The disconnect message, $DISC$ is a member of M. We specify the behaviour of the channel in a "sensible" environment, i.e. an environment which does not put a message on an output wire or an already occupied input wire, nor removes a message from an input wire once there.

An interesting property of the channel is that the arrival of a disconnect message at endpoint a (b), after having travelled through the channel from b (a), is only passively noticed; messages are neither accepted nor delivered at that endpoint a (b) any more. In the specification given below, this property is expressed by the final clause of the liveness part in the component behaviour description. The formulation in terms of actions was suggested by A.Pnueli, originally we used just the state remaining static.

Figure 4.1

Notation

M is the set of messages including "disconnect", $DISC$

$w \in \{a, b\}$

$\neg w$ is a if w is b and vice versa

Spec CHANNEL $\triangleq$ $(\Sigma,\ env,\ comp)$

INTERFACE (Σ)

$in_a,\ in_b,\ out_a,\ out_b :\ M\ \cup\ \{\emptyset\}$

ENVIRONMENT BEHAVIOUR

$\quad env\ \triangleq\ env_a \wedge env_l$

Action Predicates

$\quad\quad send_w(m)\quad\triangleq\ in_w = \emptyset\ \wedge\ \bigcirc in_w = m$ { used to abbreviate send and
$\quad\quad receive_w(m) \triangleq\ out_w = m\ \wedge\ \bigcirc out_w = \emptyset$ { receive actions by environment

ACTIONS

$\quad env_a \triangleq$
$\quad\quad e\ \dashv\ \exists w.$
$\quad\quad\quad \boxed{}comp_a \dashv$ { -- see Remarks in text
$\quad\quad\quad (\exists m.\ send_w(m)\ \wedge\ \neg\diamondsuit send_w(m)\ \vee$ { Send any unique message
$\quad\quad\quad\quad\quad receive_w(m)\ )$ { Receive any message that appears

LIVENESS

$\quad env_l \triangleq true$ { no liveness assumptions

COMPONENT BEHAVIOUR

$\quad comp\ \triangleq\ comp_a \wedge comp_l$

Action Predicates

$\quad\quad acc_w(m)\quad\triangleq\ in_w = m\ \wedge\ \bigcirc in_w = \emptyset$ { used to abbreviate accept and
$\quad\quad del_w(m)\quad\triangleq\ out_w = \emptyset\ \wedge\ \bigcirc out_w = m$ { deliver actions of component

ACTIONS

$comp_a \triangleq$
  $c \;\Rightarrow\; \exists \omega.$
  $(\; \neg \lozenge acc_\omega(DISC)$ { This end is not disconnected and
    $\wedge$ { there is a message such that
    $\exists m. ((\; m \neq DISC \quad \wedge$ { either it is not *DISC*, and
          $del_\omega(m) \qquad \wedge$ {   it is delivered, and
          $\lozenge acc_{\neg\omega}(m) \quad \wedge$ {   it has been accepted, and
          $\neg \lozenge del_\omega(m) \quad \wedge$ {   it is not yet delivered, and
          $\forall m_1. (\lozenge del_\omega(m_1) \;\Rightarrow\; \lozenge(acc_{\neg\omega}(m) \wedge \lozenge acc_{\neg\omega}(m_1))))$
                                                                        {   it is delivered in order
    $\vee$ { or
          $acc_\omega(m) \;)$ {   it is accepted

LIVENESS

$comp_l \triangleq \forall \omega.$
  $\forall m. (\; in_\omega = m \quad \wedge$ { If the environment sends m and
    $\neg \lozenge acc_\omega(DISC) \quad \wedge$ { this end is not disconnected
    $\square \neg acc_{\neg\omega}(DISC) \;)$ { and the other end never
    $\Rightarrow$ { accepts a disconnect, then
      $\lozenge acc_\omega(m)$ { eventually m will be accepted

  $\wedge$ {   and

  $((out_\omega = \emptyset \quad \wedge$ { if the environment can receive
   $\neg \forall m. (\lozenge acc_{\neg\omega}(m) \;\Rightarrow\; \lozenge del_\omega(m)) \quad \wedge$ { and the channel is not empty
   $\square \neg acc_\omega(DISC) \quad \wedge$ { and this end never accepts *DISC*
   $\neg \lozenge acc_{\neg\omega}(DISC))$ { and the other end is not
   $\Rightarrow$ { disconnected, then
      $\exists m. \lozenge del_\omega(m))$ { some message will be delivered

  $\wedge$ {   and

  $\forall m. (\; acc_\omega(DISC)$ { if *DISC* is accepted here
    $\Rightarrow$ { then
      $\lozenge \square (\neg acc_{\neg\omega}(m) \wedge \neg del_{\neg\omega}(m)))$ { the other end will become dead

REMARK

Intuitively, the clause ▊$comp_a$ in env_a states that an action by the
environment only has to live up to the requirements in env_a if all previous
actions by the component have been in accordance with $comp_a$. Leaving this
clause out would allow strange sequences, where illegal component actions are
justified by future misbehaviour of the environment. For example, assuming

$\langle in_a, out_a, in_b, out_b \rangle$ as the state configuration, the following labelled sequence

$$\ldots \langle\langle\emptyset,\emptyset,\emptyset,\emptyset\rangle,d\rangle \ , \ \langle\langle\emptyset,\emptyset,\emptyset,\emptyset\rangle,c\rangle \ , \ \langle\langle m,\emptyset,\emptyset,\emptyset\rangle,e\rangle \ , \ \langle\langle m,m,\emptyset,\emptyset\rangle,d\rangle \ , \ \ldots$$

would be allowed, as the illegal e action (i.e. the environment placing m onto the output channel out_a) makes ($[\![env=[\![comp)$ trivially true. However, before this illegal e action, the component made an illegal move by outputting m onto the input. Such strange sequences of behaviour are ruled out by adding the clause $\blacksquare comp_a$.

6: Partial Development of a Packet Switching Network

In this section we present an incomplete development of a packet switching network. The network example used is based on problem 6 of the STL problem set. Namely:-

> The network consists of a collection of 'nodes', each having a
> unique address. The objects transmitted are 'packets', which
> are grouped into 'messages'.

> A node transmits a message by sending the packets it is made
> of with

> > send X to A via Z.

> This means that packet X is to be delivered to node A, after
> going to node Z first. Node Z forwards the packet to another
> node with a similar instruction, with the same destination.
> The packet must eventually arrive at its destination. Packets
> are acknowledged on receipt, with the originating node
> retransmitting if an acknowledgement is not received within a

specified time. Duplicate packets are discarded on receipt, and sets of packets making up a message are delivered in order to the user of a node.

Rather than attempt to give a specification of this system in total, with all the complexities of rerouting and possible retransmission at the packet level, we have adopted a hierarchical approach. Initially, we specify the system at an "abstract" level, i.e. as a reliable message network. Then, through succesive stages of development, we specify components such that when these components (i.e. implementations satisfying the specifications) are combined (in fact, in parallel) they will implement the original, top level, system specification.

6.1: Network Development Approach

Fig. 6.1 below characterises the structure of a node in the system we wish to develop; each node is identically structured. Each layer in the diagram represents a layer of the software implementing the node.

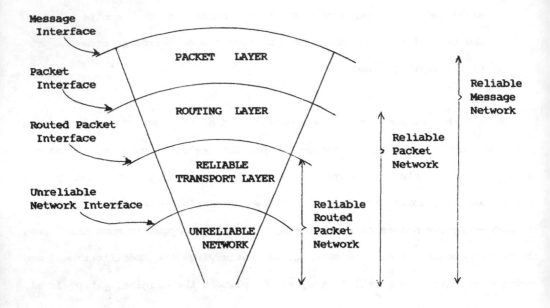

Figure 6.1: Node Structure

The top level specification of the system is given by specifying a component,
the reliable message network, in an environment. The network is specified as
having *n* ports. The first stage of development realises the reliable message
network as n *packet processing nodes* running in parallel with a *reliable
packet network* in the same environment as before. These "new components" are
again given as specifications and must be further developed towards an
implementation. We only present further development of the reliable packet
network.   The second stage of development realises this packet network as n
routing nodes running in parallel with a *reliable routed packet network* in the
environment of the reliable packet network.   We do not present further
developments of the system, however, Fig. 6.1 indicates the obvious
continuation.

6.2: Level 0 — Reliable Message Network Specification

The observable behaviour of the message network is the appearance/disappearance of messages at the n ports of the network. Each port has both an input and output channel. We thus model the interface, between the network and its environment, by 2n variables, in_i^1, out_i^1, for $i \in \{1..n\}$, each having as possible values messages, $m \in M$ or $\emptyset$. This top level view is displayed in Fig. 6.2.

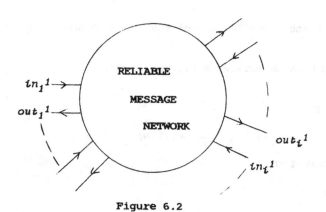

Figure 6.2

We do not formally define the structure of a message, i.e. define M, but do assume that the message has a destination address, selected by $dest(..)$, and, of course, some contents. Since the network can be viewed as a multiport unbounded buffer and as in [SCFG82] it is proved that the externally observable behaviour of an unbounded buffer allowing identical messages is not expressible in linear temporal logic, we assume that all messages in the lifetime of the network are distinct.

Fig. 6.3 shows the "actions" performed on a port interface by both the environment and the component (i.e. the reliable message network).

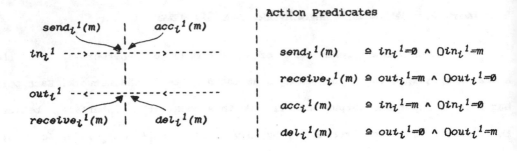

$$send_i{}^1(m) \quad \triangleq \quad in_i{}^1 = \emptyset \wedge \bigcirc in_i{}^1 = m$$

$$receive_i{}^1(m) \triangleq out_i{}^1 = m \wedge \bigcirc out_i{}^1 = \emptyset$$

$$acc_i{}^1(m) \quad \triangleq \quad in_i{}^1 = m \wedge \bigcirc in_i{}^1 = \emptyset$$

$$del_i{}^1(m) \quad \triangleq \quad out_i{}^1 = \emptyset \wedge \bigcirc out_i{}^1 = m$$

Figure 6.3

We now present the specification of the reliable message network.

Spec RELIABLE MESSAGE NETWORK $\triangleq$ (Σ, *env*, *comp*)

INTERFACE (Σ)

$in_i{}^1$, $out_i{}^1$: $M \cup \{\emptyset\}$ for $i \in \{1..n\}$

ENVIRONMENT BEHAVIOUR

$env \quad \triangleq \quad env_a \wedge env_l$

ACTIONS

$env_a \triangleq$
    $e^1 \rightarrow \blacksquare comp_a \rightarrow$
                $\exists i, m.\ send_i{}^1(m) \wedge \forall j.\neg \blacklozenge send_j{}^1(m)$ { send any unique message
                          $\vee$ { or
                    $receive_i{}^1(m)$ { receive any message, anywhere

LIVENESS

  $env_l \triangleq true$ { no liveness assumptions

COMPONENT BEHAVIOUR

$comp \quad \triangleq \quad comp_a \wedge comp_l$

ACTIONS

$comp_a \triangleq$
$\quad c^1 \Rightarrow \exists l,m. \quad acc_l{}^1(m)$ { accept any message
$\qquad\qquad\qquad \lor$ { or
$\qquad\qquad\qquad (del_l{}^1(m) \land$ { deliver a message
$\qquad\qquad\qquad\;\; dest(m)=l \land$ { with the correct destination
$\qquad\qquad\qquad\;\; \exists j.\Diamond acc_j{}^1(m) \land$ { which was accepted
$\qquad\qquad\qquad\;\; \neg\Diamond del_l{}^1(m))$ { and has not been delivered

LIVENESS

$comp_l \triangleq$
$\quad \forall l,m. \;(in_l{}^1{=}m \Rightarrow \Diamond acc_l{}^1(m) \;) \quad \land$ { all messages will be accepted
$\qquad\;\; \land$ { and provided
$\qquad (\Box\Diamond out_l{}^1{=}\emptyset \land$ { there are sufficient requests
$\qquad\;\; \exists j.\Diamond acc_j{}^1(m) \land$ { and a message with correct
$\qquad\;\; dest(m)=l \land$ { destination is present (which
$\qquad\;\; \neg\Diamond del_l{}^1(m)$ { has not been delivered)
$\qquad\qquad \Rightarrow$ { then
$\qquad\qquad\quad \Diamond del_l{}^1(m) \;)$ { it will be delivered

6.3: Level 1 — First Stage of Development

We now develop the reliable message network as n packet sequencer nodes together with a reliable packet network as indicated in Fig. 6.4 below. This level of specification (level 1) thus consists of n+1 specifications. In order to be a correct development step, one must show that the parallel composition of processes, each satisfying an appropriate level 1 specification, does indeed satisfy the top level specification, i.e. the reliable message network specification. We indicate an inference rule for just that purpose in section 7.

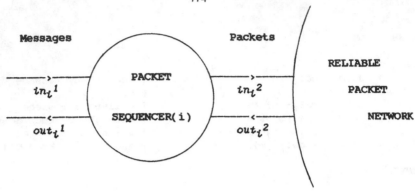

Figure 6.4.

Informally, the packet sequencer takes a complete message, m, in from the outside environment and disassembles it into packets, p. These packets are then sent by the sequencer into the *reliable packet network*. The packet sequencer also receives packets delivered by the packet network and reassembles them into messages. Only complete messages are delivered by the packet sequencer to the outside environment. As the n packet sequencers differ only in node index, a generic specification for the packet sequencers is presented in section 6.3.1.

The reliable packet network is completely analogous to the reliable message network. To obtain its specification one can substitute packet, i.e. p and P, for message, i.e. m and M, in the specification given in section 6.2, and hence we omit the specification here.

As before, we do not formally define P but do assume obvious selectors, e.g. $dest(..)$ which would appear in the reliable packet network specification. We also assume that $p \epsilon m$ is true if and only if p is a constituent packet of the message m.

6.3.1: Specification of the Packet Sequencer

Fig. 6.5 shows the actions performed on the sequencer interfaces with the outside environment and with the reliable packet network. Note that the complete environment of the packet sequencer is formed by that outside environment together with the reliable packet network.

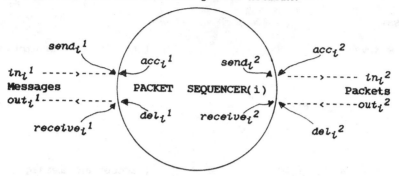

where the new action predicates are defined as:-

$$send_i{}^2(p) \quad \triangleq \quad in_i{}^2 = \emptyset \land \bigcirc in_i{}^2 = p$$

$$receive_i{}^2(p) \quad \triangleq \quad out_i{}^2 = p \land \bigcirc out_i{}^2 = \emptyset$$

$$acc_i{}^2(p) \quad \triangleq \quad in_i{}^2 = p \land \bigcirc in_i{}^2 = \emptyset$$

$$del_i{}^2(p) \quad \triangleq \quad out_i{}^2 = \emptyset \land \bigcirc out_i{}^2 = p$$

Figure 6.5

The packet sequencer specification of level 1 is now presented.

Spec PACKET SEQUENCER (i) $\triangleq$ (Σ, env, $comp$)

INTERFACE (Σ)

$in_i{}^1$, $out_i{}^1$: $M \cup \{\emptyset\}$ -- messages
$in_i{}^2$, $out_i{}^2$: $P \cup \{\emptyset\}$ -- packets

ENVIRONMENT BEHAVIOUR

env $\triangleq$ $env_a \land env_l$

ACTIONS

env_a $\triangleq$
$e_i{}^2$ $\Rightarrow$ $\blacksquare compa$ $\Rightarrow$
    $((\exists m. \ send_i{}^1(m) \land \neg\diamond send_i{}^1(m)$ { send any unique message
          $\lor$ { or
        $receive_i{}^1(m))$ { receive any message
        $\lor$ { or

$$(\exists p.\ del_i{}^2(p)$$
$$\lor$$
$$acc_i{}^2(p)))$$

{ deliver any packet
{ or
{ accept any packet, see Remark

LIVENESS

$$env_i \ \triangleq \ true$$

{ no liveness assumptions

COMPONENT BEHAVIOUR

$$comp \ \triangleq \ comp_a \land comp_i$$

ACTIONS

$$comp_a \ \triangleq$$
$$c_i{}^2 \ \rightarrow \ (\exists m.\ acc_i{}^1(m)$$
$$\lor$$
$$del_i{}^1(m) \land$$
$$(\forall p.\ p \in m \rightarrow \Diamond receive_i{}^2(p)) \land$$
$$\neg \Diamond del_i{}^1(m))$$
$$\lor$$
$$(\exists p.\ receive_i{}^2(p)$$
$$\lor$$
$$send_i{}^2(p) \land$$
$$(\exists m.\ p \in m \land \Diamond acc_i{}^1(m)) \land$$
$$\neg \Diamond send_i{}^2(p))$$

{ accept any message
{ or
{ deliver a message which
{ has all packets received
{ and has not been delivered
{or
{ receive any packet
{ or
{ send a packet which is
{ part of an accepted message
{ but has not been sent

LIVENESS

$$comp_i \ \triangleq$$
$$(\forall m.\ in_i{}^1 = m \rightarrow \Diamond acc_i{}^1(m)$$
$$\land$$
$$(\Box \Diamond out_i{}^1 = \emptyset \land$$
$$(\forall p.\ p \in m \rightarrow \Diamond receive_i{}^2(p)) \land$$
$$\neg \Diamond del_i{}^1(m)$$
$$\rightarrow$$
$$\Diamond del_i{}^1(m)))$$
$$\land$$
$$(\forall p.\ out_i{}^2 = p \rightarrow \Diamond receive_i{}^2(p)$$
$$\land$$
$$(\Box \Diamond in_i{}^2 = \emptyset \land$$
$$(\exists m.\ p \in m \land \Diamond acc_i{}^1(m)) \land$$
$$\neg \Diamond send_i{}^2(p)$$
$$\rightarrow$$
$$\Diamond send_i{}^2(p)))$$

{ all messages will be accepted
{ and provided
{ there are sufficient requests
{ and all packets are present of
{ a message which has not been
{ delivered then
{ it will be delivered
{and
{ all packets will be received
{ and provided
{ there are sufficient requests
{ and a packet of an accepted
{ message has not been sent
{ then
{ it will be sent

Remark

Here, we do not need to require the packet to be unique as the reliable packet network will only produce unique packets.

6.4: Level 2 — Second Stage of Development

We now develop the reliable packet network as n router nodes and a reliable packet routing network as is indicated by Fig. 6.6. Again, we obtain n+1 specifications for this level, and, of course, similar steps as hinted in section 6.3 should be taken to show correctness of the development.

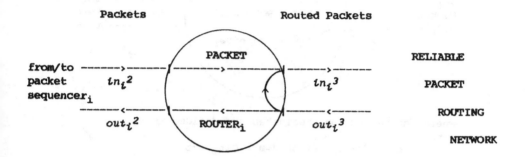

Figure 6.6.

Essentially, the packet router has two tasks.

1)   It must supply an intermediate destination for an incoming packet, p, from the packet sequencer and then transmit the routed packet, rp, into the *reliable packet routing network*.

2)   It must take an incoming routed packet, rp, from the reliable packet routing network and either deroute it to obtain p and pass p on to the packet sequencer if the final destination of rp is this node, or reroute rp with a new intermediate destination and send the rerouted packet back into the routing network.

The generic specification of the packet routers is given in section 6.4.1.

The reliable packet routing network is again specified analogously to the reliable message network, using routed packets instead of messages and intermediate destinations instead of destinations. We omit the specification.

6.4.1: Specification of the Packet Router

Fig. 6.7 shows the actions performed on the router interfaces with the packet sequencer and the reliable packet routing network.

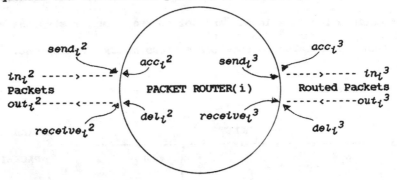

where the new action predicates are defined as:-

$$send_i^3(rp) \quad \triangleq \quad in_i^3 = \emptyset \wedge \bigcirc in_i^3 = rp$$

$$receive_i^3(rp) \quad \triangleq \quad out_i^3 = rp \wedge \bigcirc out_i^3 = \emptyset$$

$$acc_i^3(rp) \quad \triangleq \quad in_i^3 = rp \wedge \bigcirc in_i^3 = \emptyset$$

$$del_i^3(rp) \quad \triangleq \quad out_i^3 = \emptyset \wedge \bigcirc out_i^3 = rp$$

Figure 6.7

As in section 6.3, we do not formally define the type of routed packets RP but do assume two functions for routing and derouting. The general routing function, $route:PXI\text{->}RP$, supplies the next intermediate destination for the packet, p, which is dependent upon the ultimate destination of p and on the current node address, i. To ensure liveness for the packet network, this routing function must be well founded in the sense that there are no infinite chains of rerouting. The function, $deroute:RP\text{->}P$, retrieves a packet from its intermediate routed version.

We now present the specification of the packet router.

Spec PACKET ROUTER (i) $\triangleq$ (Σ, env, $comp$)

INTERFACE (Σ)

in_i^2, out_i^2 : $P \cup \{\emptyset\}$ -- packets
in_i^3, out_i^3 : $RP \cup \{\emptyset\}$ -- packets with intermediate routing

ENVIRONMENT BEHAVIOUR

env $\triangleq$ $env_a \wedge env_l$

ACTIONS

$env_a \triangleq$
$\quad e_i^3 \rightarrow \blacksquare comp_a \rightarrow$
$\qquad ((\exists p.\ send_i^2(p) \wedge \neg\!\blacklozenge send_i^2(p)$ { send any unique packet
$\qquad \quad \vee$ { or
$\qquad\qquad receive_i^2(p))$ { receive any packet
$\qquad \vee$ {or
$\qquad (\exists rp.\ del_i^3(rp)$ { deliver any routed packet
$\qquad\quad \vee$ { or
$\qquad\qquad acc_i^3(rp)))$ { accept any routed packet

LIVENESS

$env_l \triangleq true$ { no liveness assumptions

COMPONENT BEHAVIOUR

$comp$ $\triangleq$ $comp_a \wedge comp_l$

ACTIONS

$comp_a \triangleq$
$\quad c_i^3 \rightarrow (\exists p.\ acc_i^2(p)$ { accept any packet
$\qquad \vee$ { or deliver a packet which
$\qquad del_i^2(p) \wedge$ { has the correct ultimate
$\qquad dest(p)=i \wedge$ { destination and was received
$\qquad (\exists rp.\blacklozenge receive_i^3(rp) \wedge p=deroute(rp)) \wedge$ { from the network
$\qquad \neg\!\blacklozenge del_i^2(p))$ { and has not been delivered
$\qquad \vee$ {or
$\qquad (\exists rp.receive_i^3(rp)$ { receive any routed packet
$\qquad\quad \vee$ { or
$\qquad send_i^3(rp) \wedge$ { send a routed packet which
$\qquad ((\exists p.\blacklozenge acc_i^2(p) \wedge rp=rout(p,i))$ { was either accepted as a
$\qquad\quad \vee$ { packet or has come from
$\qquad (\exists rp'.\blacklozenge receive_i^3(rp') \wedge$ { the network with this node
$\qquad\qquad dest(deroute(rp'))\neq i \wedge$ { as just intermediate (not
$\qquad\qquad rp=route(deroute(rp'),i))) \wedge$ { ultimate) destination
$\qquad \neg\!\blacklozenge send_i^3(rp))$ { and has not been sent yet

LIVENESS

$comp_i \triangleq$
$(\forall p.\ (in_i{}^2=p \rightarrow \Diamond acc_i{}^2(p))$ { all packets accepted
  $\wedge$ { and provided there are
  $(\Box\Diamond out_i{}^2=\emptyset \wedge$ { sufficient requests and
   $(\exists rp.\ \Diamond receive_i{}^3(rp) \wedge$ { there is a packet
          $p=deroute(rp) \wedge$ { which has come from the
          $dest(p)=i \wedge$ { the network but not yet
          $\neg\Diamond del_i{}^2(p))$ { delivered
      $\rightarrow$ { then
          $\Diamond del_i{}^2(p)))$ { it will be delivered
$\wedge$ {and
$(\forall rp.(out_i{}^3=rp \rightarrow \Diamond receive_i{}^3(rp))$ { all routed packets will be
  $\wedge$ { received from the network
  $(\Box\Diamond in_i{}^3=\emptyset \wedge$ { and provided there are
   $((\exists p.\ \Diamond acc_i{}^2(p) \wedge$ { sufficient requests and
          $rp=route(p,i) \wedge$ { either there is a packet
          $\neg\Diamond send_i{}^3(rp))$ { waiting to be sent out
      $\vee$ { or
      $(\exists rp'.\Diamond receive_i{}^3(rp') \wedge$ { there is a packet waiting
          $rp=route(deroute(rp),i) \wedge$ { to be rerouted through
          $\neg\Diamond send_i{}^3(rp)))$ { to another node
      $\rightarrow$ { then
          $\Diamond send_i{}^3(rp)))$ { it will be sent

6.5: Further Stages of Development

The next stage in the development of this network example is to realise the reliable routing packet network from an *unreliable routing packet network* together with n *reliability* nodes. The task of the reliability node is to achieve reliable transmission through the unreliable network. The problem specification (see section 6.1) suggested the use of a simple retransmission protocol, i.e. if an acknowledgement for a packet is not received within a certain time period then that packet is retransmitted, and so on. The success of such a protocol clearly depends on the property, of the unreliable network, that if a packet is sent infinitely often then eventually it will reach the destination uncorrupted.

We do not give further specifications of these components, but mention briefly how time-outs might be expressed in the specification. We assume that the processes update a global time variable, t. Retransmission until reception of an acknowledgement after a *fixed* time, k, can then be expressed by the liveness requirement

$$\forall rp, t1.\ send(rp) \wedge t=t1 \ \Rightarrow\ (\square\square\neg send(rp) \wedge \Diamond(ack(rp) \wedge t-t1<k))$$
$$\vee$$
$$(\neg ack(rp)\ until\ (send(rp) \wedge t-t1 \geqslant k))$$

where $ack(rp)$ denotes the reception of an acknowledgement for the routed packet rp.

7: An Inference Rule for Parallel Process Composition

The development steps made in the previous section were parallel decomposition. Below we informally present a rule for showing that such parallel decomposition steps are correct, i.e. if n processes p_i satisfy the specifications $spec_i$ then the rule shows what conditions on the specifications $spec_i$ in relation to a specification $spec$ must be fulfilled in order for the parallel composition of the p_i processes to satisfy that specification $spec$.

$$
\begin{array}{c}
Pi\ \ sat\ \ (\Sigma_i,\ env_i,\ comp_i)\ \ ,\ \ i=1,..,n \\
G1..G4\ \ |\!-\ \ \wedge_{i=1,n}\ (env_i \Rightarrow comp_i)\ \Rightarrow\ (env \Rightarrow comp) \\
\hline
P_1||...||P_n\ \ \ sat\ \ \ (\Sigma,\ env,\ comp)
\end{array}
$$

Intuitively, this requires that the execution sequences which are "common" in the sets described by the specifications, $spec_i$, must be contained in the set described by $spec$. Essentially, common sequences are those which have identical states and a labelling which matches in accordance with the axioms G1..G4 given below.

$$G1 \qquad \text{⬚} (\Lambda_{i=1,n} \; e_i \quad <=> \quad e \;)$$
$$G2 \qquad \text{⬚} (V_{i=1,n} (c_i \wedge \Lambda_{j \neq i} \; e_j) \quad <=> \quad c \;)$$
$$G3 \qquad \text{⬚} (\Lambda_{i=1,n} \; d_i \quad <=> \quad d \;)$$
$$G4 \qquad \text{⬚} (\Lambda_{i=1,n} (e_i \oplus c_i \oplus d_i) \wedge (e \oplus c \oplus d) \;)$$

where e_i $(c_i, \; d_i)$ is the environment (component, duplicate) action predicate used in the specification of the ith process of the parallel composition, and e $(c, \; d)$ refer to the composition as a whole.

Further information about this rule and the semantics of parallel composition in our model can be found in the extended abstract [BK83].

Acknowledgements

We are sincerely grateful to Amir Pnueli for the keen interest he has shown in our work. An early version of our parallel decomposition rule was briefly introduced at the actual workshop in Cambridge, September 1983. At that time, Amir Pnueli pointed out some flaws with the rule and helped us formulate the current version.

We are also grateful to Willem P. de Roever for interesting discussions and for providing much cleaner "black" past time temporal symbols.

This work has been supported under S.E.R.C grant GR/C/05670. Both authors acknowledge their support.

References

[BK83] H.Barringer and R.Kuiper
        A Temporal Logic Specification Method Supporting Hierarchical
        Development
        Extended Abstract
        Dept. of Computer Science, University of Manchester.
        Nov. 1983

[Jo83]   C.B.Jones
           Specification and Design of (Parallel) Programs
           Proc. IFIP 83, Paris, North Holland, 1983.

[MP82a]   Z.Manna and A.Pnueli
           Verification of Concurrent Programs: The Temporal Framework
           in "The Correctness Problem in Computer Science"
           ed. R.S.Boyer and J.S.Moore
           International Lecture Series in Computer Science, pp215-273,
           Academic Press, London, 1982.

[MP82b]   Z.Manna and A.Pnueli
           Verification of Concurrent Programs: A Temporal Proof System
           Computer Science Report, Stanford University, 1983.

[OL82]   S.S. Owicki and L. Lamport
           Proving Liveness Properties of Concurrent Programs
           ACM TOPLAS, Vol. 4, No. 3, pp455-495, July 1982.

[Pn79]   A.Pnueli
           The Temporal Semantics of Concurrent Computation
           in Proc. of the Symp. on Semantics of Concurrent Computation,
           Evian, France, July 1979
           Springer-Verlag LNCS, Vol. 70, pp1-20.

[Pr67]   A.Prior
           Past, Present and Future
           Oxford University Press, 1967.

[SCFG82]   A.P.Sistla, E.M.Clarke, N.Francez and Y.Gurevich
           Can Buffers be Specified in Linear Temporal Logic?
           Proc. 1st ACM SIGACT/SIGOPS Conf. on PODC, Ottawa, Aug. 1982.

TWO WAY CHANNEL WITH DISCONNECT

J.Y.Cotronis P.E.Lauer

Computing Laboratory
University of Newcastle upon Tyne

1 INTRODUCTION

In this paper we use the COSY formalism to give the behavioural specification of a two way channel capable of being disconnected, which was suggested for discussion at the Workshop on the Analysis of Concurrent Systems, Cambridge 12-16 September, 1983.

As it was pointed out in the companion paper [L83] in this volume, COSY is a formalism intended to simplify the study of synchronic aspects of concurrent and distributed systems where possible by abstracting away from all aspects of systems except those which have to do with synchronisation.

In COSY we may specify behaviours of concurrent and distributed systems in a purely language theoretical way. COSY is intended to facilitate the derivation of dynamic properties of systems, such as absence of deadlock, starvation, from static or structural properties of the specification, where possible. A COSY specification may be vindicated using interpretations of behaviours of the model.

The syntax and semantics of basic COSY is formally outlined in the companion paper [L83]. We will only informally explain COSY in the context of the development of the problem. The macro notation will not be formally defined in either of the papers here but illustrations of the macro expansions should allow the reader to understand what is meant.

In this paper we shall develop two specifications of a two-way channel. One with no disconnection and a second capable of being disconnected. Due to space constraints we shall not use the formal tools of COSY for analysis and vindication. We shall only show snapshots of behaviours of the specification of the two way channel capable of being disconnected which were obtained using our Computer Based Analysis Environment, called BCS. For a formal treatment of COSY specifications see the accompanying paper [L83] in this volume. The bibliography of this paper may also be found in [L83].

2   THE TWO WAY CHANNEL WITH NO DISCONNECT

problem

Specify the channel described below.

Description

The ´channel´ between endpoints ´a´ and ´b´ can pass messages in both directions simultaneously. The order of messages sent in a given direction is preserved.

In the specification of the two-way channel with no disconnect we need two queues through which messages from node a to node b and, respectively, from node b to node a are sent. We assume that the queues are finite but of arbitrary size. We shall use a ring buffer discipline. The ring buffer consists of frames each having the following behavioural description:

1. the frame is initially empty, and

2. deposits and removes strictly alternate with a deposit occuring first.

In COSY such a behaviour may be specified by the path:

    F1 path m_deposit;m_remove end

where m_deposit reads "a message is deposited", and likewise for m remove. The path F1 specifies a cyclic sequential system and the ";" denotes sequentialisation of execution of operations. Thus, the path F1 specifies that a deposit should occur first followed by a remove, and because of the cyclic property of COSY paths this sequence of execution of operations m_deposit and m_remove may be repeated.

A single frame may be tested for being empty by modifying F1 to path F2:

    F2 path empty,(m_deposit;m_remove) end

The "," in the above path denotes arbitrary choice. As "," binds stronger than ";" we use "( )" to override this precedence. Thus F2 specifies that initially, we may either test the frame for being empty or we may deposit a message into the frame. After a deposit, only a remove is possible, taking the frame into its initial state.

For a queue of size n we need n of these frames, each having its own operations for testing for empty, depositing and removing messages. Let us specify three frames by the paths F3:

    F3 path empty(1),(m_deposit(1);m_remove(1)) end
       path empty(2),(m_deposit(2);m_remove(2)) end
       path empty(3),(m_deposit(3);m_remove(3)) end

where we have distinguished the operations for empty, m_deposit, m_remove in each of the paths of F3 by indexing. The three paths in F3 have no operations in common and therefore specify three independent frames each following the behaviour of F2 concurrently with the other two.

To test if all three of the frames are full we introduce one new operation, allfull, as follows:

```
F4 path empty(1),(m_deposit(1);allfull*;m_remove(1)) end
   path empty(2),(m_deposit(2);allfull*;m_remove(2)) end
   path empty(3),(m_deposit(3);allfull*;m_remove(3)) end
```

Operation allfull occurs in all three paths. In the COSY semantics this means that for this operation to execute all three of the paths must permit its execution, that is, we assume a "handshake" synchronisation of all paths involving an operation name shared by all. The star, "*", denotes the Kleene-star, permitting the execution of an operation zero or more times. Thus, operation allfull may only be executed after a deposit has been done in all three frames. While all three frames are full, operation allfull may be executed zero or more times.

Let us examine a vector of histories of F4. The i'th sub-history, indexed by Pi, corresponds to the i'th sub-system (i.e. path) of F3, for i=1,2,3.

```
P1 empty(1).          .m_deposit(1).allfull.          .m_remove(1)
P2          .empty(2).m_deposit(2).allfull.          .m_remove(2)
P3          .empty(3).m_deposit(3).allfull.m_remove(3).m_deposit(3)
```

Initially the first frame is found empty, by executing operation empty(1). As empty(1) only appears in the first path, it only appears in the first sub-history. Then, the operations empty(2) and empty(3) are executed concurrently. This is possible as each operation appears only in one path, permitting its execution. As we have pointed out, all three operations empty(i) for i=1,2,3 could have been executed concurrently. This could be inferred from the first two steps of the above history vector. Where there is an operation in one step, the empty string is in the other, for all sub-histories. Therefore, the operations executed in the first two steps could have been executed in one.

The history continues by executing the operations m_deposit(i) for i=1,2,3 concurrently. Operation allfull then is executed which appears in all three of the sub-histories as it appears in all three paths. The three paths therefore, synchronize at this point. Then a message is removed from the third frame, and the final step the messages in the first and second frame are removed, and a message is deposited into the third frame, concurrently.

We may specify the paths F4 more concisely by using the macro notation, as follows:

```
F4m C1 array empty m_deposit m_remove(1:3) endarray
       R1 #i:1,3,1[path empty(i),(m_deposit(i);allfull*;m_remove(i)) end]
```

In the above specification, the construct array...endarray is called a collectivisor and it is used to declare subscripted operations which may be used or generated by a macro program. The collectivisor Cl declares the operations :

    empty(1), empty(2), empty(3),
    m deposit(1), m_deposit(2), m_deposit(3),
    m remove(1), m_remove(2), m_remove(3)

The construct R1 is a <u>replicator</u> which is used to represent and generate regularities of basic COSY programs, such as the paths in F4, which differ only in the subscripts of the operations they use. Replicators define an index associated with a specification, and a regularity of structure in which subscripts of operations may depend on the replicator index.

The index in R1 is "i" and its specification "1,3,1", which means that the index takes values from 1 to 3 in steps of 1. The regularity of R1 is inside "[...]", namely

    <u>path</u> empty(i),(m_deposit(i);allfull*;m_remove(i)) <u>end</u>

Upon expansion of the replicator the values the index takes are substituted in distinct copies of the regularity. Thus after expansion, R1 generates the three paths in F4.

Let us modify F4 or F4m to specify the ring buffer discipline. According to this discipline, a ring buffer should have the following behaviour:

1. the order of removing must be the same as the order of depositing into the frames.

We may specify the above behaviour in COSY by constraining the execution of deposits and removes in F4, in such a way that the deposits (respectively the removes) are sequentialised in ascending order of indices, as in F5:

    F5 <u>path</u> m_deposit(1);m_deposit(2);m_deposit(3) <u>end</u>
       <u>path</u> m_remove(1);m_remove(2);m_remove(3) <u>end</u>

We may represent each of the paths in F5 more concisely using some more features of the macro notation:

    F5m <u>path</u> ;[m_deposit] <u>end</u>
        <u>path</u> ;[m_remove] <u>end</u>

The construct ;[...] is called a <u>distributor</u> and it generates regularities of structure inside "[...]" similarly to the replicators, but upon expansion it takes values which subscript the operations implicitly from the collectivisors. Assuming that m deposit and m remove have been declared by the collectivisor Cl in F4m, then the expansions of the two paths in F5m are respectively the paths in F5.

The complete three frame ring buffer which may be tested for being full, and each of whose frames may be tested for empty, is specified in macro COSY by:

```
RB3
C1 array empty m_deposit m_remove(1:3) endarray
R1 #i:1,3,1[path empty(i),(m_deposit(i);allfull*;m_remove(i)) end]
   path ;[m_deposit] end
   path ;[m_remove] end
```

As both ports a and b may send messages to each other simultaneously, we need two such queues. Let us specify the queue by which a sends messages to b by prefixing all operations in RB3 by "ab-", and similarly, the queue by which b sends to a by pefixing all operations in RB3 by "ba-". Thus the two queues become:

```
{a to b queue}
array ab-empty ab-m_deposit ab-m_remove(1:3) endarray
#i:1,3,1[path ab-empty(i),(ab-m_deposit(i);allfull*;ab-m_remove(i)) end]
path ;[ab-m_deposit] end
path ;[ab-m_remove] end

{b to a queue}
array ba-empty ba-m_deposit ba-m_remove(1:3) endarray
#i:1,3,1[path ba-empty(i),(ba-m_deposit(i);allfull*;ba-m_remove(i)) end]
path ;[ba-m_deposit] end
path ;[ba-m_remove] end
```

To complete the specification of the two way channel with no disconnect we need to specify the actions of the two nodes. Let us describe the actions of a:

1. node a may be either requested to accept a message, or remove a message from buffer ba.

2. If requested to accept a message, it should accept it and deposit it into ab only if there is space in ab.

3. If node a removes a message from ba, it should deliver it.

Here we refined the original specification in that node a does not accept any messages if the queue ab is full. The reason is that for finite queues, if both queues are full and both nodes accept a message each waits for their respective queues to be non-full, and the whole channel gets into a deadlock. The path which specifies the behaviour of node a is

```
{actions of a}
path
   ( a-m_req_accept
   ; (,[ab-empty];a-m_accept;,[ab-m_deposit])
     ,ab-allfull)
   ;(,[ba-m_remove];a-m_deliver)
end
```

The distributor

    ,[ab-empty]

expands to

    ab-empty(1),ab-empty(2),ab-empty(3)

and it may be read as:

    "test if there is an empty frame in queue ab".

The behaviour of node b is symmetric to that of node a. Thus the actions of node b may be obtained from the actions of node a by substituting all prefices "ab-", "ba-", "a-" by "ba-", "ab-", "b-", respectively. Thus the complete COSY specification for the two way channel with no disconnect is the following:

```
program {2WC-ND}
{ab queue}
array ab-empty ab-m_deposit ab-m_remove(1:3) endarray
#i:1,3,1[path ab-empty(i),(ab-m_deposit(i);allfull*;ab-m_remove(i)) end]
path ;[ab-m_deposit] end
path ;[ab-m_remove]  end
{ba queue}
array ba-empty ba-m deposit ba-m remove(1:3) endarray
#i:1,3,1[path ba-empty(i),(ba-m_deposit(i);allfull*;ba-m_remove(i)) end]
path ;[ba-m_deposit] end
path ;[ba-m_remove]  end
{a node}
path
    ( a-m_req_accept
    ; ( ,[ab-empty];a-m_accept;,[ab-m_deposit])
      ,ab-allfull)
   ;(,[ba-m_remove];a-m_deliver)
end
{b node}
path
    ( b-m_req_accept
    ; ( ,[ba-empty];b-m_accept;,[ba-m_deposit])
      ,ba-allfull)
   ;(,[ab-m_remove];b-m_deliver)
end
endprogram
```

3   THE TWO WAY CHANNEL CAPABLE OF BEING DISCONNECTED

Here we modify and extend the 2WC-ND program to specify the two way channel capable of disconnection.

<u>problem</u>

Specify the channel described below.

<u>Description</u>

The ´channel´ between endpoints ´a´ and ´b´ can pass messages in both directions simultaneously, until it receives a ´disconnect´ message from one end, after which it neither delivers nor accepts messages at that end. At the other end messages are not accepted but only delivered until the ´disconnect´ message arives, after which the node can do nothing. The order of messages sent in a given direction is preserved.

First of all the queues have to be modified

1. to distinguish between depositing of ordinary messages and disconnect messages, and

2. to be able to be reset to empty.

In order to distinguish between ordinary messages and disconnect messages in the queue, every frame should be modified to distinguish them as well. By distinguish we mean that if an ordinary message (respectively disconnect) is deposited into a frame, then an ordinary message (respectively disconnect) will be removed from that frame. The modified first frame of the ab queue thus becomes:

```
path ab-empty(1)
    ,(ab-m_deposit(1);ab-allfull*;ab-m_remove(1))
    ,(ab-d_deposit(1);ab-allfull*;ab-d_remove(1)) end
```

This path specifies that either an m_deposit may occur or a d_deposit. But the path guarantees that after an m_deposit (respectively d_deposit), an m_remove (respectively d_remove) will occur. Similar modifications must be performed on the rest of the frames of ab and to the frames of ba.

The operations d_deposit(i) and d_remove(i) in each queue must be constrained to preserve the order of messages. Thus

```
path ;[ab-m_deposit] end
```

should become

```
path ;[ab-m_deposit,ab-d_deposit] end
```

and similarly, the path

```
path ;[ab-m_remove] end
```

should become

    <u>path</u> ;[ab-m_remove,ab-d_remove] <u>end</u>

When a node accepts a disconnect message it should empty its incoming queue. Thus each frame should be able to be reset to empty as an alternative way of removing, and the queue has also to be testable for empty to verify that the resetting has been done, for all frames. Thus the first frame of ab must be further modified to

```
path ab-empty(1),ab-allempty
     ,(ab-m_deposit(1);ab-allfull*;ab-m_remove(1),ab-reset(1))
     ,(ab-d_deposit(1);ab-allfull*;ab-d_remove(1),ab-reset(1)) end
```

The complete queues in the macro notation thus become:

```
{ab queue}
array ab-empty ab-m_deposit ab-m_remove ab-reset(1:3) endarray
#i:1,3,1
 [path
    ab-empty(i),ab-allempty
  ,(ab-m_deposit(i);ab-allfull*;ab-m_remove(i),ab-reset(i))
  ,(ab-d_deposit(i);ab-allfull*;ab-d_remove(i),ab-reset(i))
  end]
path ;[ab-m deposit,ab-d deposit] end
path ;[ab-m remove,ab-d remove] end
{ba queue}
array ba-empty ba-m_deposit ba-m_remove ba-reset(1:3) endarray
#i:1,3,1
 [path
    ba-empty(i),ba-allempty
  ,(ba-m_deposit(i);ba-allfull*;ba-m_remove(i),ba-reset(i))
  ,(ba-d_deposit(i);ba-allfull*;ba-d_remove(i),ba-reset(i))
  end]
path ;[ba-m_deposit,ba-d deposit] end
path ;[ba-m_remove,ba-d_remove] end
```

As some of the actions of each node depend on the state of the other node, which may be connected or disconnected, we need to specify the conditions for change, and a way of determining the state of each node. The two nodes must

1. be connected together, and

2. after accepting or delivering a disconnect message become disconnected.

The paths specifying the conditions for connection and disconnection, and also the state of nodes a and b are:

```
{state of node a}
path connect_both;a-connected*;a-d_accept,a-d_deliver;a-disconnected* end
{state of b}
path connect_both;b-connected*;b-d_accept,b-d_deliver;b-disconnected* end
```

respectively. As operation connect_both occurs in both the above paths, for it to be executed, both paths should permit it, after which both nodes are in their connect state. After accepting a disconnect message or delivering a disconnect message a node becomes disconnected and remains disconnected. Only after the other node gets disconnected, may both be connected again.

Let us now describe in detail the actions of node a.

connect together with b, then

repeat zero or more times:

either acknowledge request for accepting an ordinary message, then

if b is connected then

if ab is not full, accept and deposit into ab

if ab is full, do not accept

if b is disconnected then ignore message

or   remove ordinary message from ba and deliver it

until

either accepting a disconnect message and disconnects, followed by

if b is connected then deposit disconnectmessage into ab

if b is disconnected then do nothing, then

empty queue ba, taking care of any pending messages

or   removing a disconnect message, deliver it and disconnect

We believe that the above description of the actions of node a are precise, apart from the phrase "taking care of any pending messages" which needs some explanation. We call pending messages those which are to be deposited in queue ab after node b has been found connected, but before they are actually deposited node b accepts a disconnect message and disconnects itself. As node b must reset queue ab and ab must be left empty, care must be taken to reset any pending messages as well. The actions of a may be specified by the path below which follows directly from the above description of the actions of node a:

```
{actions of a}
path
   connect_both
  ; ( ( a-m_req_accept
       ; ( b-connected
         ; ( ab-empty(1),ab-empty(2),ab-empty(3)
           ;a-m_accept
           ;ab-m_deposit(1),ab-m_deposit(2),ab-m_deposit(3))
           ,ab-allfull)
        ,(b-disconnected;a-ignored) )
      ,(ba-m_remove(1),ba-m_remove(2),ba-m_remove(3);a-m_deliver))*
  ; ( a-d_accept
     ; ( b-connected
       ; ( ab-d_deposit(1),ab-d_deposit(2),ab-d_deposit(3)) )
      ,(b-disconnected)
      ;(ba-reset(1),ba-reset(2),ba-reset(3))*;ba-notpending
      ;(ba-reset(1),ba-reset(2),ba-reset(3))*;ba-allempty)
    ,( ba-d_remove(1),ba-d_remove(2),ba-d_remove(3)
      ;a-d deliver;a-disconnect)
  end
```

or more concisely by using the macro notation by:

```
{actions of a}
path
   connect_both
  ; ( ( a-m_req_accept
      ; (b-connected;(,[ab-empty];a-m_accept;,[ab-m_deposit]),ab-allfull)
       ,(b-disconnected;a-ignored) )
     ,(,[ba-m_remove];a-m_deliver))*
  ; ( a-d_accept
      ; ( b-connected;,[ab-d_deposit]),(b-disconnected)
      ;(,[ba-reset])*;ba-notpending;(,[ba-reset])*;ba-allempty)
     ,( ,[ba-d_remove];a-d_deliver;a-disconnect)
end
```

The above path resets pending messages. The reseting of ba is done in two stages. During the first stage we guarantee that there is space in ab for any pending messages to be deposited. After testing that there are no pending messages the reseting is completed. We may specify the actions of node b symmetrically, by replacing all prefices "a-", "b-", "ab-", "ba-" of operations in the above path by "b-", "a-", "ba-", "ab-", respectively. Finally, we must specify the conditions under which a message is pending to be deposited to a queue. The conditions and the state of pending messages to queue ab are:

1. initially no message is pending,

2. after b is found connected, indicating the intension of node a to deposit a message into ab, a deposit is pending

3. after a deposit or when ab is found full (in the case where node b is connected and there is no room for depositing), no deposit is pending.

The path specifying the above behaviour is

```
     {for emptying ba completely}
     path ba-notpending*;a-connected
        ; ba-d_deposit(1),ba-d_deposit(2),ba-d_deposit(3)
         ,ba-m_deposit(1),ba-m_deposit(2),ba-m_deposit(3),ba-allfull
     end
```

Similarly we may specify the conditions and the state of pending messages to queue ba. The complete program is thus:

```
program{2WC-D}
{ab queue}
array ab-empty ab-m_deposit ab-m_remove ab-reset(1:3) endarray
#i:1,3,1
  [path
     ab-empty(i),ab-allempty
    ,(ab-m_deposit(i);ab-allfull*;ab-m_remove(i),ab-reset(i))
    ,(ab-d_deposit(i);ab-allfull*;ab-d_remove(i),ab-reset(i))
  end]
path ;[ab-m_deposit,ab-d_deposit] end
path ;[ab-m_remove,ab-d_remove]  end
{ba queue}
array ba-empty ba-m_deposit ba-m_remove ba-reset(1:3) endarray
#i:1,3,1
  [path
     ba-empty(i),ba-allempty
    ,(ba-m_deposit(i);ba-allfull*;ba-m_remove(i),ba-reset(i))
    ,(ba-d_deposit(i);ba-allfull*;ba-d_remove(i),ba-reset(i))
  end]
path ;[ba-m_deposit,ba-d_deposit] end
path ;[ba-m_remove,ba-d_remove]  end
{state of node a}
path connect_both;a-connected*;a-d_accept,a-d_deliver;a-disconnected* end
{state of b}
path connect_both;b-connected*;b-d_accept,b-d_deliver;b-disconnected* end
{actions of a}
path
    connect_both
  ; ( ( a-m_req_accept
       ; (b-connected;(,[ab-empty];a-m_accept;,[ab-m_deposit]),ab-allfull)
       ,(b-disconnected;a-ignored) )
      ,(,[ba-m_remove];a-m_deliver))*
  ; ( a-d_accept
     ; ( b-connected;,[ab-d_deposit]),(b-disconnected)
     ;(,[ba-reset])*;ba-notpending;(,[ba-reset])*;ba-allempty)
     ,( ,[ba-d_remove];a-d_deliver;a-disconnect)
end
{actions of b}
path
    connect_both
  ; ( ( b-m_req_accept
       ; (a-connected;(,[ba-empty];b-m_accept;,[ba-m_deposit]),ba-allfull)
       ,(a-disconnected;b-ignored) )
      ,(,[ab-m_remove];b-m_deliver))*
  ; ( b-d_accept
     ; ( a-connected;,[ba-d_deposit]),(a-disconnected)
     ;(,[ab-reset])*;ab-notpending;(,[ab-reset])*;ab-allempty)
     ,( ,[ab-d_remove];b-d_deliver;b-disconnect)
end
{for emptying ab completely}
path ab-notpending*;b-connected
     ; ab-d_deposit(1),ab-d_deposit(2),ab-d_deposit(3)
      ,ab-m_deposit(1),ab-m_deposit(2),ab-m_deposit(3),ab-allfull
end
{for emptying ba completely}
path ba-notpending*;a-connected
     ; ba-d_deposit(1),ba-d_deposit(2),ba-d_deposit(3)
      ,ba-m_deposit(1),ba-m_deposit(2),ba-m_deposit(3),ba-allfull
end
endprogram
```

Due to space constraints we will not formally analyse or vindicate the above progam. For a more formal treatment of a COSY specification see the companion paper in this volume [L83]. Here we will only show some snapshots of histories of the above specification.

The first history H1, shows both nodes being connected together, then requesting acceptance of a message, test each other for being connected and that their respective queues are not full, accept their messages and deposit them in the first frame of their queues.

```
P1      .            .                .                .
P2      .            .        .ab-empty(1).        .ab-m_deposit(1)
P3      .            .                .                .
P4      .            .                .                .
P5      .            .                .        .ab-m_deposit(1)
P6      .            .                .                .
P7      .            .        .ba-empty(1).        .ba-m_deposit(1)
P8      .            .                .                .
P9      .            .                .                .
P10     .            .                .        .ba-m_deposit(1)
P11 connect_both.        .a-connected.        .                .
P12 connect_both.        .b-connected.        .                .
P13 connect_both.a-m_req_accept.b-connected.ab-empty(1).a-m_accept.ab-m_deposit(1)
P14 connect_both.b-m_req_accept.a-connected.ba-empty(1).b-m_accept.ba-m_deposit(1)
P15     .            .b-connected.        .        .ba-m_deposit(1)
P16     .            .a-connected.        .        .ab-m_deposit(1)
                                                    .ba-m_deposit(1)
```

<u>History   H1</u>

The second history H2, is a continuation of H1. Here both nodes accept disconnect messages and disconnect themselves, then find each other disconnected, check that no messages are pending and reset their appropriate queues.

```
P1      .            .        .ab-reset(1).ab-allempty
P2      .            .                .        .ab-allempty
P3      .            .                .        .ab-allempty
P4      .            .                .                .
P5      .            .                .                .
P6      .            .        .ba-reset(1).ba-allempty
P7      .            .                .        .ba-allempty
P8      .            .                .        .ba-allempty
P9      .            .                .                .
P10     .            .                .                .
P11 a-d_accept.a-disconnected.        .                .
P12 b-d_accept.b-disconnected.        .                .
P13 a-d_accept.b-disconnected.ba-notpending.ba-reset(1).ba-allempty
P14 b-d_accept.a-disconnected.ab-notpending.ab-reset(1).ab-allempty
P15     .        .ab-notpending.        .
P16     .        .ba-notpending.        .
```

<u>History   H2</u>

The history H3 below shows that when a queue is full and a node is requested to accept a message, the message is not accepted, although the other node is connected.

```
P1                          .              .         .ab-allfull
P2                          .              .         .ab-allfull
P3   ab-m_deposit(3).       .              .         .ab-allfull
P4   ab-m_deposit(3).       .              .         .
P5                          .              .         .
P6                          .              .         .ba-allfull
P7                          .              .         .ba-allfull
P8   ba-m_deposit(3).       .              .         .ba-allfull
P9   ba-m_deposit(3).       .              .         .
P10                         .              .         .
P11                         .         .a-connected.
P12                         .         .b-connected.
P13  ab-m_deposit(3).a-m_req_accept.b-connected.ab-allfull
P14  ba-m_deposit(3).b-m_req_accept.a-connected.ba-allfull
P15  ab-m_deposit(3).       .b-connected.ab-allfull
P16  ba-m_deposit(3).       .a-connected.ba-allfull
```

History   H3

The history H4 is a continuation of H3. In the first part of the history, in H4a, node a accepts a disconnect message and finds node b connected but cannot deposit into ab since ab is full. Node b is requested to accept a message, finds a is disconnected and ignores the message. Node b removes the first message from ab.

```
P1   ab-allfull.        .              .              .         .ab-m_remove(1).
P2   ab-allfull.        .              .              .         .
P3   ab-allfull.        .              .              .         .
P4        .             .              .              .         .ab-m_remove(1).
P5        .             .              .              .         .
P6        .             .              .              .         .
P7        .             .              .              .         .
P8        .             .              .              .         .
P9        .             .              .              .         .
P10       .             .              .              .         .
P11          .a-d_accept.       .    .a-disconnected.            .
P12       .        .b-connected  .              .         .
P13  ab-allfull.a-d_accept.b-connected   .              .         .
P14       .        .b-m_req_accept.a-disconnected.b-ignored.ab-m_remove(1).
P15  ab-allfull.       .b-connected   .              .         .
P16       .             .              .              .         .
```

History   H4a

In the second part of H4, H4b, node a deposits the disconnect message to ab. The rest of the history shows node b removing messages from ab until it removes the disconnect message delivers it and disconnects itself, whilst node a is reseting ba.

The only operation which may be executed at the end of the history below is the operation connect_both.

```
P1   ab-d_deposit(1).          .           .           .           .
P2                 .ab-m_remove(2).         .           .           .
P3                 .           .           .ab-m_remove(3).         .
P4   ab-d_deposit(1).          .           .           .           .
P5                 .ab-m_remove(2).         .ab-m_remove(3).         .
P6                 .           .ba-reset(1).           .           .
P7                 .           .           .ba-reset(2)  .           .
P8                 .           .           .           .ba-reset(3).
P9                 .           .           .           .           .
P10                .           .           .           .           .
P11                .           .           .           .           .
P12                .           .           .           .           .
P13  ab-d_deposit(1).ba-notpending .ba-reset(1).ba-reset(2)   .ba-reset(3).
P14  b-m_deliver    .ab-m_remove(2).b-m_deliver.ab-m_remove(3).b-m_deliver.
P15  ab-d_deposit(1).          .           .           .           .
P16                .ba-notpending .          .           .           .


P1   ab-d_remove(1).           .
P2                 .           .
P3                 .           .
P4                 .           .
P5   ab-d_remove(1).           .
P6   ba-allempty   .           .
P7   ba-allempty   .           .
P8   ba-allempty   .           .
P9                 .           .
P10                .           .
P11                .           .
P12                .           .b-disconnect
P13  ba-allempty   .           .
P14  ab-d_remove(1).b-d_deliver.b-disconnect
P15                .           .
P16                .           .
```

History   H4b

The final history H5 demonstrates that upon resetting of the queues, any pending messages should be reset as well. The history below shows the following behaviour: Both nodes are connected, then node a is requested to accept a message; node a finds b connected but before even testing queue ab for being full or not full, node b accepts a disconnect message. The message of node a is now pending. Node b finds node a connected and deposits the disconnect message into ba. Node b cannot reset ab before the pending message has been deposited into ab. The only possible progress is for node a to test ab for being not full, accept the message and deposit it into ab. Then node b resets ab while node a removes the disconnect message delivers it and disconnects itself.

```
P1        .              .              .              .              .
P2        .              .              .              .              .
P3        .              .              .              .              .
P4        .              .              .              .              .
P5        .              .              .              .              .
P6        .              .              .              .              .ba-d_deposit(1).
P7        .              .              .              .              .
P8        .              .              .              .              .
P9        .              .              .              .              .ba-d_deposit(1).
P10       .              .              .              .              .
P11 connect_both.        .              .              .a-connected.
P12 connect_both.               .b-connected.b-d_accept.        .
P13 connect_both.a-m_req_accept.b-connected.            .        .
P14 connect_both.        .              .b-d_accept.a-connected.ba-d_deposit(1).
P15       .        .b-connected.        .              .        .
P16       .              .        .              .a-connected.ba-d_deposit(1).


P1  ab-empty(1).        .ab-m_deposit(1).            .ab-reset(1).ab-allempty
P2        .              .              .            .         .ab-allempty
P3        .              .              .            .         .ab-allempty
P4        .        .ab-m_deposit(1).    .            .         .
P5        .              .              .            .         .
P6        .              .        .ba-d_remove(1)    .         .
P7        .              .              .            .         .
P8        .              .              .            .         .
P9        .              .              .            .         .
P10       .              .        .ba-d_remove(1)    .         .
P11       .              .              .            .     .a-disconnect
P12       .              .              .            .         .
P13 ab-empty(1).a-m_accept.ab-m deposit(1).ba-d_remove(1).a-d_deliver.a-disconnect
P14       .              .        .ab-notpending .ab-reset(1).ab-allempty
P15       .        .ab-m_deposit(1).ab-notpending     .         .
P16       .              .              .            .         .
```

<u>History   H5</u>

4   ACKNOWLEDGEMENTS

This work was partially supported by the Science and Engineering Research Council of Great Britain.

AN EXAMPLE OF SPECIFICATION AND VERIFICATION IN CESAR

J. Cl. Fernandez, J. Ph. Schwartz and J. Sifakis

Laboratoire Genie Informatique, Institut IMAG BP 68

38402 SAINT MARTIN D'HERES CEDEX, FRANCE

1. INTRODUCTION

The aim of this paper is to illustrate by an example the use of the system CESAR for the specification and verification of systems of communicating processes.

Cesar is a verification tool which allows to compare a program with its specifications given by a set of formulas of temporal logic. The verification principle - in the version presented - consists in translating the program into a state graph which is functionally equivalent to it. The conformity of the program to its specifications is verified by evaluation of the formulas on the state graph thus obtained. The description of programs is done in a CSP-like language. A program is a set of tasks communicating by exchanging messages. For the verification method to be effective, we require that all program variables are of type integer and bounded. Specifications are a set of formulas of a branching time logic and express properties which must be satisfied by the program. Using branching time logic instead of linear time logic is one of the pecularities of the method presented. In CESAR, the program under study is translated into an equivalent non-deterministic "flat" program of the form, DO c1-->a1 |..|cn-->an OD, where the c_i's are conditions and a_i's are (vectorial) assignments. A state graph is generated by exhaustive simulation of the "flat" program. Formulas are verified by evaluation on this state graph. The verification method is based on the fact that temporal operators are fixed points of monotonic predicate transformers obtained from the state graph. CESAR is a project which has started in 1981 [Qu1], [Qu2], [QS1]. In this paper, we present the second version of the tool [Sc] and illustrate its use for the specification and verification of a program, solution to problem 1. This paper is organized in four parts. In part 2, the main features of the description language are given. In part 3, we present the specification language. In part 4 are exposed the analysis principle applied in CESAR and the theorical results on which it is based.

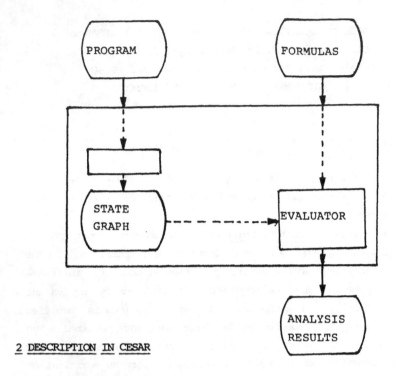

2 DESCRIPTION IN CESAR

2-1 The description language

The language of CESAR is an algorithmic language allowing to describe systems as a set of tasks communicating by exchanging messages. A
system is described in a hierachical manner by parallel composition of
elementary tasks.
The syntax of the language is given by the following grammar. We use
the notations :

<xxx> : non terminal symbol

 xxx : key-word

[xxx]* : optional occurence of xxx

[xxx]$^+$: optional occurence of xxx an arbitrary number of times

[xxx] : occurence of xxx a positive number of times

As usual, the character "|" is used to delimit alternatives. The termi-
nal symbols "[", "]" and "|" of the grammar are written respectively _[,
_], _|.

<program> ::= <task>

<task> ::= <elementary task> | <composed task>

```
<elementary task> ::= TASK <identifier> ;
                         [<input>]
                         [<output>]
                         [<declaration>]
                         [<initialization>]
                         DO
                            <guarded command>
                            [_| <guarded command>]*
                         OD


<input> ::= INPUT <identifier> [, <identifier>] *;

<ouput> ::= OUTPUT <identifier> [, <identifier>]* ;

<declaration> ::= DECLARE [<dcl>]+

<dcl> ::= <identifier> : <number> .. <number> ;

<initialization> ::= INIT <assignment> [, <assignment>]* ;

<guarded command> ::= [<label>]*
                      <condition> : [<exchange> [, <assignment>]*]

<label> ::= {[<character>]+}

<exchange> ::= !<identifier> [:= <expression>]                    |
               [<identifier>,]+ ! <identifier> := <expression> |
               [[<identifier>,]*<identifier> := ]? <identifier>|
               <assignment>

<assignment>  ::=  <identifier> := <expression>

<composed task> ::= COTASK <identifier> ;
                      [<input>]
                      [<output>]
                      [<task> ;]+
                      [<diffused variables>]
                      [<anonymous variables>]
                      BODY
```

```
                    <instance of task>
                    [// <instance of task>]
```

<diffused variables> ::= BROAD <identifier> [, <identifier>] * ;

<anonymous variables> ::= PORT <identifier> [, <identifier>] * ;

```
<instance of task> ::= <identifier>
                       [(<identifier> [, <identifier>]*)]
```

The following non terminals are defined according to the syntax of
PASCAL :
  <identifier> : the symbol "_" is admitted
  <number> : signed integer
  <condition> : boolean expression
  <expression> : integer expression

    An elementary task is declared by the key-word TASK followed by its
name   and the (optional) definition of the exchanged parameters.
Received parameters are declared by means of INPUT and emitted parameters by means of OUTPUT. All the exchanged formal parameters must have
distinct names and are of type integer. The order of declaration of the
parameters is relevant.

    Internal variables of elementary tasks are of type interval. Their
declaration, introduced by the key-word DECLARE, gives the bounds of the
interval of definition. Declaration may be followed by initializations
introduced by the key-word INIT. Non initialized variables are supposed
to take an arbitrary value of their interval of definition.

    The body of an elementary task is a unique statement DO ... OD con-
taining a set of guarded commands. Each guarded command is formed by a
condition followed by the symbol ":" and a set of vectorial assignments
optionally preceded by an exchange.

    An emission (resp. reception) is an assignment whose left member
(resp. right member) is a name of a formal exchanged parameter preceded
by an exclamation mark (resp. a question mark).   This parameter must
belong to the output (resp. input) parameter list. A received or emitted value may be simultaneously assigned to one or more internal variables. When the value emitted is non relevant (pure synchronization) it
can be omitted and the assignment symbol ":=" as well.

    Guarded commands may be preceded by a set of labels, which are used
in the formulas of the specification.

All the expressions used in the body of an elementary task must respect the syntax of Pascal.

A composed task is declared by the key-word COTASK followed by its name and optional definitions of exchanged formal parameters. As for elementary tasks, these parameters must have distinct names and are of type integer.

The declaration of a composed task is followed by :
- The declaration of tasks (elementary or composed) from which it is constructed.
- The declaration of names of exchanged variables used to etablish connections between the exchanged parameters of the component tasks.
- The body of the task.

An exchanged variable is the name of a communication channel used by one or more component tasks. Exchanged variables are declared by means of the key-words BROAD and PORT corresponding respectively to two different communication modes : one-to-many (diffusion) and one-to-one. In the first case communication takes place by rendez-vous between an emitter and all the possible receivers while in the second case communication takes place by rendez-vous between an emitter and only one possible receiver.

The body of a composed task is introduced by the key-word BODY and it contains a set of instances of its component tasks separated by the symbol"//". An instance of a task is given by its name followed by a list of names of echanged variables or parameters of the composed task. The correspondance between names of exchanged variables (or parameters of composed tasks) and formal parameters is done by position.

2-2 Algorithmic description of problem 1

We describe this system by a set of three tasks ENDA, ENDB and LINE. The values of the messages exchanged are not relevant. To preserve the order of the messages, we represent the task LINE with two bounded circular buffers (one for each direction of transmission). We obtain the following description :

```
COTASK CHANNEL ;

TASK ENDA ;
  INPUT mb ;
  OUTPUT ma, da ;
```

```
   DO
      {sendal}   true : !ma     | (* emission of a message *)
      {senddisa} true : !da     | (* emission of a disconnection order *)
      {recla}    true : ?mb       (* reception of a message *)
   OD ;


TASK ENDB ;
   INPUT mma ;
   OUTPUT mmb, db ;


   DO
      {sendbl}   true : !mmb    | (* emission of a message *)
      {senddisb} true : !db     | (* emission of a disconnection order *)
      {reclb}    true : ?mma      (* reception of a message *)
   OD ;


TASK LINE ;
   INPUT ia, ib, dia, dib ;
   OUTPUT oa, ob ;
   DECLARE
      inxab:1..2 ;
      outxab:1..2 ;
      countab:0..2 ;
      (* input and output pointers, number of elements of the buffer of
       messages from "a" to "b" *)
      inxba:1..2 ;
      outxba:1..2 ;
      countba:0..2 ;
      (* input and output pointers, number of elements of the buffer of
       messages from "b" to "a" *)
      disca:0..1 ;
      discb:0..1 ;
      (* disca = 1 means ENDA is disconnected *)
   INIT countab:=0, countba:=0,
        disca:=0, discb:=0,
        inxab:=1, inxba:=1,
        outxab:=1, outxba:=1 ;


   DO
      {recal} (disca=0) and (countab<2) : ?ia,inxab:= (inxab mod 2) + 1,
```

```
                                    countab:=countab+1     |
(* reception of a message from "a" *)
disca=0 : ?dia,disca:=1                                    |
(* message of disconnection *)
{recbl} (discb=0) and (countba<2) : ?ib,inxba := (inxba mod 2) +1,
                                    countba:=countba + 1   |
(* reception of a message from "b" *)
discb=0 : ?dib,discb:=1                                    |
(* message of disconnection *)
{sendla} (disca=0) and (countba>0) : !oa,outxba:=(outxba mod 2) + 1,
                                    countba:=countba - 1 |
(* emission of a message to "a" *)
{sendlb} (discb=0) and (countab>0) : !ob,outxab:=(outxab mod 2) + 1,
                                    countab:=countab - 1
(* emission of a message to "b" *)
OD ;
```

PORT ma1, mb1, mla, mlb, disa, disb ;

BODY
  ENDA(mla,ma1,disa) //
  ENDB(mlb,mb1,disb) //
  LINE(ma1,mb1,disa,disb,mla,mlb).

3 SPECIFICATION IN CESAR

3-1 The specification language

In this section, we present a simplified version of the specification language of CESAR. The complete language is in fact more
powerful ; in particular, this language contains "until" operators and
allows to express properties under some assumption of fairness [QS2].
The syntax of the specification language L is given by :

```
<formula> ::= <term> <> <term>       |
              <term> => <term>       |
              <term> [AND <term>]* |
              <term> [OR <term>] * |
              <term>
```

```
<term> ::= [<operator>]* <predicate>


<operator>  ::= NOT | ALL | POT | SOME | INEV


<predicate> ::= <predicate on program variables> |
                <position predicate>              |
                (<formula>)


<position predicate> ::= INIT                  |
                         ENABLE                |
                         ENABLE<list of actions> |
                         ENABLE<list of tasks>   |
                         AFTER <list of actions> |


<list of actions> ::= (<program label> [,<program label>]*)


<list of tasks> ::= (<name of program task> [,<name of program task>]*)
```

That is , the specification language for a given program is a set of formulas constructed from predicates on program variables and position predicates by using logical connectives and four unary temporal operators : ALL, POT SOME and INEV. The meaning of position predicates is defined as follows :

- INIT represents the set of all the possible initial states of a program,

- ENABLE(l) represents the set of the states from which the action named by label l can be executed ; ENALBLE (l,l',l"...) is an abbreviation for ENABLE(L) OR ENABLE(l') OR ENABLE(l") OR ...

- ENABLE(T) represents the set of the states from which at least one action of the task named T can be executed ; ENABLE(T,T',T"...) is an abbreviation for ENABLE(T) OR ENABLE(T') OR ENABLE(T") OR .... Finally, ENABLE represents the set of the states from which at least a task of the program is not blocked.

- AFTER (l) represents the set of the states reached just after the execution of the action named by l ; AFTER (l,l',l"...) is an abbreviation for AFTER (l) OR AFTER (l') OR AFTER (l") OR ....

Each formula f of the specification language is an assertion about the behaviour of a program and represents a set of states |f| which satisfy the property expressed. The function | | is defined as follows.

Consider a program as a state graph $S = (Q,->)$ where Q is its set of states and $->$ a binary relation on Q (i.e. its transition relation). An <u>execution sequence</u> from a state $q0 \in Q$ is a sequence $s = q0\ q1..\quad qi\ qi+1..$ such that $qi->qi+1$ and if it is finite then its least element is a sink state. Denote by $EX(q)$ the set of the execution sequences starting from state q and by $s(k)$ the k-th element of the sequence s (if it is defined). We take,

$q\in|true|$ always,

$q\in|f$ AND $f'|$ iff $q\in|f|$ and $q\in|f'|$,

$q\in|f$ OR $f'|$ iff $q\in|f|$ or $q\in|f'|$,

$q\in|$NOT $f|$ iff $q\notin|f|$,

$q\in|POT(f)|$ iff $\exists s\in EX(q)\exists k\in N.s(k)\in|f|$,

$q\in|INEV(f)|$ iff $\forall s\in EX(q)\exists k\in N.s(k)\in|f|$.

The operators ALL and SOME are defined as the duals of POT and INEV respectively i.e. ALL(f)=NOT POT (NOT(f)) and SOME(f)=NOT INEV(NOT(f)). Obviously, POT(f) represents the set of the states q of S such that there exists an execution sequence starting from q and containing a state which satisfies f. Thus, POT expresses the modality "it is possible that". In the same way, INEV expresses the modality "it is inevitable that".

The interpretation of the dual operators ALL and SOME is,

$q\in|ALL(f)|$ iff $\forall s\in EX(q)\forall k\in N.s(k)\in|f|$

$q\in|SOME(f)|$ iff $\exists s\in EX(q)\forall k\in N.s(k)\in|f|$

Thus, ALL(f) represents the set of the states from which "f is always true".

3-2 Specifications of problem 1

We give hereafter a set of formulas expressing the part of the specifications of problem 1 which can be given in the language presented. We use the predicates,

fina=(disca=1) ; (*disconnection of ENDA *)

finb=(discb=1) ; (*disconnection of ENDB *)

notemptyab=(countab>0) ; (* the buffer a->b is not empty *)

notfullab=(countab<2) ; (* the buffer a->b is not full *)

notemptyba=(countba>0) ; (* the buffer b->a is not empty *)

notfullba=(countba<2) ; (* the buffer b->a is not full *)

Properties relative to disconnection

a) Disconnection of ENDA and ENDB is possible :

  INIT => POT fina (* disconnection of ENDA *)

  INIT => POT finb (* disconnection of ENDB *)

  INIT => POT (fina AND finb) (* disconnection of ENDA and ENDB *)

Notice that the properties obtained by substituting INEV to POT in the given formulas are not valid. However, the specification language of CESAR has an operator FINEV expressing inevitability under some assumption of fairness for which these properties are valid [QS2].

b) if ENDA or ENDB is diconnected it cannot communicate with LINE.

  INIT => ALL(fina => ALL fina)

  INIT => ALL(fina => ALL NOT ENABLE (sendal))

  INIT => ALL(fina => ALL NOT ENABLE (recla))

  INIT => ALL(finb => ALL finb)

  INIT => ALL(finb => ALL NOT ENABLE (sendbl))

  INIT => ALL(finb => ALL NOT ENABLE (reclb))

c) Sending a disconnection message leads to effective disconnection.

  INIT => ALL (AFTER (senddisa) => fina)

  INIT => ALL (AFTER (senddisb) => finb)

Properties of response to action

a) Sending a message from an endpoint leads to its transmission through the line to the other endpoint if it is not disconnected.

  INIT => ALL (AFTER (recal) => notemtpyab)

  INIT => ALL (AFTER (recal) AND NOT finb) => ENABLE(sendlb))

  INIT => ALL (AFTER (recbl) => notemtpyba)

  INIT => ALL (AFTER (recbl) AND NOT fina) => ENABLE(sendla))

b) Sending a message from an endpoint makes possible its reception from the other.

  INIT => ALL (AFTER (recal) => POT (finb OR AFTER (sendlb))

  INIT => ALL (AFTER (recbl) => POT (fina OR AFTER (sendla))

For these formulas, the remark concerning the substitution of POT by FINEV to obtain strong properties holds.

4 PROVING SPECIFICATIONS IN CESAR

The verification method applied in CESAR consists in evaluating the formulas which express specifications, on a state graph obtained from the algorithmic description by exhaustive simulation. In this section, we present basic theoretical results used by the formula evaluator.

Let $S = (Q, \rightarrow)$ be the state graph obtained from a program under study. We define the predicate transformer PRE : for P a unary predicate on Q, $\text{PRE}(P)(q) = \exists q'.(q \rightarrow q' \text{ and } P(q'))$.

Proposition [SI] [QS]

Let f be a formula of the specification language L and $S = (Q, \rightarrow)$ a state graph.

$|\text{POT }(f)| = \lim Xk$ where $Xk+1 = Xk \cup \text{PRE}(Xk)$ with $X0 = |f|$

$|\text{INEV }(f)| = \lim Xk$ where $Xk+1 = Xk \cup (\text{PREXk} \cup \text{NOT PRE}(\text{NOT}(Xk)))$ with $X0 = |f|$

According to the results of this proposition, it is possible to compute iteratively the interpretation of the temporal operators. In order to prove a formula f, the evaluator first computes the set of states representing the predicates on program variables or position predicates which occur in f. Then, it computes the interpretation of its temporal operators. The formula f represents a valid property iff it evaluates to Q.

CESAR is an interactive system programmed in PASCAL under MULTICS on HB-68. All the commands of MULTICS can be used in CESAR. A typical session of analysis of a program in CESAR is composed of the following steps.

- Definition under the editor "ted" of MULTICS,of two files containing respectively the program under study and the predicates on program variables used in specifications.
- Activation of the system. The user disposes of commands for generating the "flat" non-deterministic program or the state graph.
- Evaluation of the formulas.
- The user also disposes of a command which allows to compare non-interpreted formulas of the specification language (detection of redundancies or inconsistencies in specifications). This command activates a decision procedure for the specification language.

For problem 1 the state graph has 479 states and its generation has taken 40 seconds of CPU time. All the properties given in specifications have been proved valid ; the verification of each property has taken at most 1 second of CPU time.

5 DISCUSSION

We have presented a tool for the verification of concurrent programs. This tool, in its present version, is a prototype realized in order to validate our ideas and results concerning the specification and analysis of systems. The description language of CESAR is certainly too poor but it can be enriched to make description easier by introducing more elaborated types, sequenciality and composed statements.

The main limitation of CESAR is obviously the restriction to programs having a finite number of states. This restriction is not imposed by the proof method itself but it has been adopted for reasons of efficiency. Removing it, makes necessary the use of methods of theorem proving and the analysis process becomes non-automatic. However, CESAR seems to be an adequate tool for the analysis of protocols. As a matter of fact, the main aspects of the behaviour of this type of applications can be described by using finite state machines.

REFERENCES

[Qu1] : J.P. QUEILLE "The CESAR system : an aided and certification system for distribued applications". Proc. of the 2nd inter. conf. on distribued computing systems Computer Society Press pp149-161 1981.

[Qu2] : J.P. QUEILLE "Le système CESAR : Description, spécification et analyse des applications réparties"Thèse docteur-ingénieur, Grenoble, 1982.

[QS1] : J.P.QUEILLE and J.SIFAKIS :"Specification and verification of concurrent systems in CESAR" Inter. Symp. on Programming L.N.C.S 137 pp337-350, 1982.

[Sc] : J.Ph. SCHWARTZ :"QUASAR, une réalisation du système CESAR : Description,spécification et analyse des applications réparties. Thèse docteur-ingénieur, Grenoble, 1983

[Si] : J. SIFAKIS :"A unified approach for studying the propeties of transition systems" TCS 19, pp227-258, 1982.

Trace Theory and the Specification of Concurrent Systems

Anne Kaldewaij

(Department of Mathematics and Computing Science,
Eindhoven University of Technology, The Netherlands)

Abstract

In this paper we show how trace theory can be used to describe the behaviour of "concurrent systems". We present a short introduction to trace theory. We also discuss a program notation that specifies the trace set of a component. As an example we derive a solution for one of the problems of the STC Workshop [5].

1. Introduction

The behaviour of a component (e.g. a channel) will be presented in the form of a program text. The program text will express all possible communication patterns between the component and its environment. Such a sequence of communication actions between a component and its environment is called a trace. A program text defines a trace structure consisting of an alphabet (a set of symbols) and a trace set (a set of traces). Each symbol may be interpreted as a type of communication. The trace set reflects all possible communication patterns.

In the sequel we give a short introduction to trace theory and mention some results. At the end we give an example of its use. For a detailed treatment of trace theory and its applications we refer to [3]. An introduction to trace theory can also be found in [1]. Readers familiar with trace theory may skip sections 2 and 3.

2. Trace theory

An alphabet is a finite set of symbols. If B is an alphabet then B^* denotes, as usual, the set of all finite-length sequences of elements of B, including the empty sequence which is denoted by ε. A *trace structure* is a pair $<\underline{t}T,\underline{a}T>$ in which $\underline{a}T$ is an alphabet and $\underline{t}T \subseteq (\underline{a}T)^*$. $\underline{a}T$ is called the alphabet of T, and $\underline{t}T$ is called the trace set of T.

The *projection* of a trace t on an alphabet B, denoted by $t{\upharpoonright}B$, is defined by

$$\varepsilon{\upharpoonright}B = \varepsilon$$
$$(tb){\upharpoonright}B = (t{\upharpoonright}B)b \qquad \text{for trace } t \text{ and symbol } b \text{ with } b \in B$$
$$(tb){\upharpoonright}B = t{\upharpoonright}B \qquad \text{for trace } t \text{ and symbol } b \text{ with } b \notin B$$

(Concatenation is denoted by juxtaposition).

The projection of a trace structure T on an alphabet B, denoted by $T{\upharpoonright}B$ is the trace structure $< \{t{\upharpoonright}B \mid t \in \underline{t}T\} , \underline{a}T \cap B >$.

We define two composition functions. The first one is called *weaving* and is a kind of "synchronized interleaving". The weave of two trace structures T and U, denoted by $T \underline{w} U$, is defined by

$$T \underline{w} U = <\{t \in (\underline{a}T \cup \underline{a}U)^* \mid t{\upharpoonright}\underline{a}T \in \underline{t}T \wedge t{\upharpoonright}\underline{a}U \in \underline{t}U\} , \underline{a}T \cup \underline{a}U>$$

For disjoint alphabets weaving amounts to the shuffle operation. We mention that weaving is symmetric, idempotent and associative.

As we will see in the next section, components may be specified using previously defined subcomponents. Relations between the subcomponents will be expressed by equalities between symbols of the alphabets of the subcomponents. We do not want the specifications to exhibit the internal structure of a component. To hide such internal relations we introduce a second composition function, called *blending*, which is weaving followed by the elimination of common symbols. The blend of two trace structures T and U, denoted by $T \underline{b} U$, is defined by

$$T \underline{b} U = (T \underline{w} U){\upharpoonright}(\underline{a}T \div \underline{a}U)$$

where $\div$ denotes symmetric difference, i.e. $A \div B = (A \cup B) \setminus (A \cap B)$.

We mention that blending is symmetric. Under the restriction that each symbol occurs in at most two alphabets of the constituting trace structures, blending is associative.

A trace structure of a component describes all sequences of communication actions the component may be involved in. The order of the symbols in a trace is the order of the communication actions in time.

An initial segment of a trace is called a *prefix* of that trace. Whenever a component "accepts" a trace it will have accepted the prefixes of it as well. For a trace structure T we call the trace structure that contains all traces of T and prefixes thereof the prefix closure of T and denote it by PREF(T) :

$$\text{PREF(T)} \quad = \quad <\{t \in (\underline{a}T)^* \mid (\underline{E}s: s \in (\underline{a}T)^* : ts \in \underline{t}T)\} \ , \ \underline{a}T>$$

Trace structure T is called prefix-closed if T = PREF(T) . We mention that the weave of prefix-closed trace structures is prefix-closed.

Example 1

Let T = <{ε, xy, xyxy, xyxyxy, ... } , {x,y}> then
PREF(T) = <{ε, x, xy, xyx, xyxy, ... } , {x,y}>

PREF(T) is the prefixed-closed set of all traces t of {x,y}* for which

$$0 \leq t\underline{N}x - t\underline{N}y \leq 1$$

where t$\underline{N}$x denotes the number of occurrences of x in t .
PREF(T) describes the behaviour of a binary semaphore, initialized at 0. We may also interpret PREF(T) as the description of a one-place buffer which is initially empty. Then x corresponds to the event "value enters the buffer" and y to the event "value leaves the buffer".

Let U = <{ε, yz, yzyz, yzyzyz, ... } , {y,z}> then PREF(U) describes a one-place buffer. The blend of PREF(T) and PREF(U) yields the trace structure

$$<\{t \in \{x,z\}^* \mid (\underline{A}t' : t' \text{ prefix of } t : 0 \leq t'\underline{N}x - t'\underline{N}z \leq 2)\}, \{x,z\}>$$

as the reader may verify.
This blend corresponds to a two-place buffer.

(End of example 1)

3. The specification of a component

In this section we introduce a program notation to which a trace structure corresponds. The simplest form is

<u>com</u> C(A) : S <u>moc</u>

where C is the name of the component specified, A is an alphabet, and S is a *command* .

With command S a trace structure TR(S) is associated. A command has one of the following forms.

(i)   A symbol is a command. Command b has trace structure $<\{b\}, \{b\}>$.

            If S and T are commands then

(ii) $S|T$ is a command with

$$TR(S|T) = <\underline{t}TR(S) \cup \underline{t}TR(T), \underline{a}TR(S) \cup \underline{a}TR(T)>$$

(iii) $S;T$ is a command with

$$TR(S;T) = <\{st \mid s \in \underline{t}TR(S) \wedge t \in \underline{t}TR(T)\}, \underline{a}TR(S) \cup \underline{a}TR(T)>$$

(iv) S,T is a command with

$$TR(S,T) = TR(S) \underline{w} TR(T)$$

(v) $S*$ is a command with

$$TR(S*) = <(\underline{t}TR(S))*, \underline{a}TR(S)>$$

            where $(\underline{t}TR(S))*$ is the set of all finite concatenations of zero or more traces of $\underline{t}TR(S)$.

The trace structure TR(C) of component C given by

            $\underline{com}$ C(A) : S $\underline{moc}$

is defined by

            TR(C) = PREF(TR(S))

As a syntactic restriction we impose $A = \underline{a}TR(C)$. We introduce the rule that the comma has the highest priority, followed by the semicolon, and then the vertical bar.

Example 2

A one-place buffer can be defined as

            $\underline{com}$ $buf_1(x,y)$: $(x;y)*$ $\underline{moc}$

(End of example 2)

A second way of specifying a component is by a program text of the following form:

<u>com</u> C(A):

    <u>sub</u> s_0: C_0, $\ldots$ s_{n-1}: C_{n-1}

    $a_0 = b_0$, $\ldots$, $a_{m-1} = b_{m-1}$

<u>moc</u>

Component C has n subcomponents, named s_i, $0 \le i < n$. The n names are distinct. We call s_i a subcomponent of type C_i . C_i is a component with a given trace struc- ture $TR(C_i)$. Replacing each symbol b of $\underline{a}TR(C_i)$ by $s_i.b$, in the alphabet and in the traces of $TR(C_i)$, yields a trace structure denoted by $s_i.TR(C_i)$ with alpha- bet denoted by $s_i.\underline{a}TR(C_i)$ and trace set denoted by $s_i.\underline{t}TR(C_i)$. By doing so we en- sure that the alphabets $s_i.\underline{a}TR(C_i)$ have no elements in common.

The symbols a_i and b_i , $0 \le i < m$, are chosen from the set B defined by $B = A \cup s_0.\underline{a}TR(C_0) \cup \ldots \cup s_{n-1}.\underline{a}TR(C_{n-1})$. Each symbol of this set B should occur exactly once in the equalities. Moreover, for all i, $0 \le i < m$, we demand that a_i and b_i belong to two different (of the n+1) alphabets.
Two symbols occurring in one equality are considered to be the same symbol. Due to the given restrictions each symbol of

$$s_0.\underline{a}TR(C_i) \cup \ldots \cup s_{n-1}.\underline{a}TR(C_{n-1})$$

is either equal to a symbol in A or common to exactly two alphabets of the trace structures of the subcomponents. That implies that the blending of the $s_i.TR(C_i)$, $0 \le i < n$, is associative and its result has alphabet A.
We define TR(C) by

$$TR(C) = s_0.TR(C_0) \underline{b} \ldots \underline{b} s_{n-1}.TR(C_{n-1})$$

<u>Example 3</u>

A one-place buffer has been defined as

    <u>com</u> $buf_1(x,y)$: $(x;y)^*$ <u>moc</u>

We define a two-place buffer as follows:

    <u>com</u> $buf_2(x,z)$:

        <u>sub</u> s0,s1: buf_1

        x = s0.x, s0.y = s1.x, s1.y = z

    <u>moc</u>

We have s0.TR(buf_1) = <{ε, s0.x, s0.x s0.y, s0.x s0.y s0.x, $\ldots$} , {s0.x,s0.y}>
    and s1.TR(buf_1) = <{ε, s1.x, s1.x s1.y, s1.x s1.y s1.x, $\ldots$} , {s1.x,s1.y}>

Replacing s0.x by x , s0.y by s1.x , and s1.y by z yields

$<\{\epsilon, x, x\,s1.x, x\,s1.x\,x, ...\}, \{x,s1.x\}> \underline{b} <\{\epsilon, s1.x, s1.x\,z, ...\}, \{s1.x,z\}>$

which results, as we have seen in a previous example, in

$<\{t \epsilon \{x,z\}^* \mid (\underline{A}t' : t' \text{ prefix of } t : 0 \leq t'\underline{N}x - t'\underline{N}z \leq 2)\}, \{x,z\}>$

a trace set corresponding to a two-place buffer.

(End of example 3)

The third and most general form of a component is a combination of the previous two. It is a text of the form

> $\underline{com}$ C(A):
>
> > $\underline{sub}$ $s_0: C_0, \cdots s_{n-1}: C_{n-1}$
> > $a_0 = b_0, \cdots , a_{m-1} = b_{m-1}$
> > S
>
> > $\underline{moc}$

where S is a command. With again B defined by

$$B = A \cup s_0.\underline{a}TR(C_0) \cup ... \cup s_{n-1}.\underline{a}TR(C_{n-1})$$

we impose the following restrictions (which differ slightly from [3]):

- $a_i \epsilon B$ and $b_i \epsilon B$ for all $0 \leq i < m$
- a_i and b_i belong to two different alphabets for all $0 \leq i < m$
- each symbol of B occurs exactly once in the m equalities
- $\underline{a}TR(S) \subseteq A$

The trace structure TR(C) of component C is defined by

$$TR(C) = (s_0.TR(C_0) \underline{b} ... \underline{b} s_{n-1}.TR(C_{n-1})) \underline{w} PREF(TR(S))$$

Due to the restrictions we have $\underline{a}TR(C) = A$. An example will be given in the next section.

4. The example

As an example of the use of trace theory we shall derive a solution for problem 1 of
the STC Workshop [5].:

" The 'channel' between endpoints a and b can pass messages in both
directions simultaneously, until it receives a 'disconnect' message
from one end, after which it neither delivers nor accepts messages at
that end. It continues to deliver and accept messages at the other end
until the 'disconnect' message arrives, after which it can do nothing.
The order of messages sent in a given direction is preserved. "

We distinguish the following events.

    ina : "input into the channel arrives at endpoint a "
   outa : "output from the channel arrives at endpoint a "
  disca : "a disconnect message into the channel arrives at endpoint a "

and similarly for endpoint b : inb, outb, and discb .

Input arriving at endpoint a will be followed by output arriving at endpoint b .
It is also possible that a disconnect message arrives at endpoint a. These together
are expressed by the command

$$(ina ; outb \mid disca)*$$

After the arrival of a disconnect message at endpoint a there will be no more ina
or outa events. This is expressed by

$$(ina \mid outa)* ; disca$$

For reasons of symmetry we also have $(inb ; outa \mid discb)*$
                                    and $(inb \mid outb)* ; discb$

The traces of the desired component should satisfy these four requirements. According
to the definition of weaving we obtain the following component using the comma :

        com   channel$_1$(ina,outa,disca,inb,outb,discb):

            (ina ; outb | disca)*
           ,((ina | outa)*;disca)
           ,(inb ; outa | discb)*
           ,((inb | outb)*;discb)

        moc

We did not take into account that a disconnect message at endpoint a eventually arrives at endpoint b . To that end we introduce two other events.

rdisca : "disconnect message from endpoint a is received at endpoint b "

rdiscb : "disconnect message from endpoint b is received at endpoint a " .

According to the specifications there will be no ina or outa event after an rdiscb event (and the same for inb, outb, and rdisca respectively). Thus, we obtain the next version :

<u>com</u> channel$_1$(ina,outa,disca,rdiscb,inb,outb,discb,rdisca) :

   (ina ; outb | disca ; rdisca)*

   ,((ina | outa)* ; (disca | rdiscb))

   ,(inb ; outa | discb ; rdiscb)*

   ,((inb | outb)* ; (discb | rdisca))

<u>moc</u>

The reader may verify that the following traces belong to channel$_1$:

   ε

   ina outb inb disca

   ina outb disca inb rdisca

and the following traces do not belong to channel$_1$:

   ina inb outa disca outb rdisca inb

   ina outb disca outa

The command (ina ; outb | disca ; rdisca)* resembles a one-place buffer. We will replace it by a k-place buffer which is order preserving. To that end we first define a two-valued 1-place buffer which is a generalization of example 2.

<u>com</u> buf$_1$(xin,yin,xout,yout) :

   (xin ; xout | yin ; yout)*

<u>moc</u>

As a generalization of example 3 we define for $k \geq 2$ a two-valued k-place buffer as follows :

```
com   bufₖ(xin,yin,xout,yout) :

   sub  s0: buf₁,  s1: bufₖ₋₁

   xin = s0.xin,  yin = s0.yin,

   s0.xout = s1.xin,  s0.yout = s1.yin,

   s1.xout = xout,  s1.yout = yout

moc
```

We use the two-valued buffer to construct a k-buffered channel. The two values are
"normal input" and "disconnect messages". We replace the first and the third line
of the command of channel$_1$ by two buffers.

```
com   channelₖ(ina,outa,disca,rdiscb,inb,outb,discb,rdisca) :

   sub  s0,s1: bufₖ

   ina = s0.xin,  disca = s0.yin,  outb = s0.xout,  rdisca = s0.yout,
   inb = s1.xin,  discb = s1.yin,  outa = s1.xout,  rdiscb = s1.yout

   ((ina | outa)*;(disca | rdiscb))
   ,((inb | outb)*;(discb | rdisca))

moc
```

In the component above we did not distinguish between different input messages. We
shall now, however, assume that the "normal" input messages form a bitstream. Instead
of the event ina we consider two events :

  ina0 : " a zero arrives as input at endpoint a "
  ina1 : " a one arrives as input at endpoint a "

Similarly we have outa0, outa1, inb0, inb1, outb0, and outb1 .
A three-valued 1-place buffer is given by

```
com   buf₁(xin0,xin1,yin,xout0,xout1,yout) :

   (xin0 ; xout0 | xin1 ; xout1 | yin ; yout)*

moc
```

The specification of a three-valued k-place buffer, buf$_k$, is left to the reader. Our
final solution is now given by:

<u>com</u> channel$_k$ (ina0,ina1,outa0,outa1,disca,rdiscb,

inb0,inb1,outb0,outb1,discb,rdisca) :

<u>sub</u> s0,s1: buf$_k$

ina0 = s0.xin0, ina1 = s0.xin1, outb0 = s0.xout0, outb1 = s0.xout1,

inb0 = s1.xin0, inb1 = s1.xin1, outa0 = s1.xout0, outa1 = s1.xout1,

disca = s0.yin, rdisca = s0.yout,

discb = s1.yin, rdiscb = s1.yout

((ina0 | ina1 | outa0 | outa1)*;(disca | rdiscb))

,((inb0 | inb1 | outb0 | outb1)*;(discb | rdisca))

<u>moc</u>

5. Final remarks

The theory, given in section 3, may be extended by allowing recursively defined components. With that extension an unbounded buffer can be obtained. For the interested reader we refer to [4].

An important property of our specification method is that it leads very smoothly from the original problem definition to a specification (program text) that is close to a possible implementation. As a matter of fact, Jan L.A. van de Snepscheut demonstrates in [2],[3] how our program notation can be implemented as a VLSI circuit.

6. Acknowledgements

Acknowledgements are due to Martin Rem, Jan L.A. van de Snepscheut and the other members of the Eindhoven VLSI Club.

Syntax and informal semantics of DyNe, a parallel language

J.R. Kennaway and M.R. Sleep
Computing Studies Sector
University of East Anglia
Norwich, U.K.

Introduction

DyNe (Dynamic Networks) is a language for parallel processes. It is founded on two basic ideas. Firstly, in spirit it resembles actor languages. A process consists of an actor executing a script, or more generally, several scripts at once. This latter possibility makes actor names behave more like ports, in that a message sent to a named actor may be received by any one of the scripts it is executing which is able to accept it. Secondly, it embodies the idea that a function call in conventional functional languages should correspond in a parallel language to the sending of an argument to a process representing the function, which replies with the result. Each communication in DyNe is therefore an exchange of messages. In keeping with this intuition, the built-in arithmetic operators of DyNe look to processes using them like ordinary scripts. They differ only in that their behaviour is predefined.

After giving an informal description of DyNe we will show how it can be applied to describe a parallel implementation of combinator reduction.

Context-free syntax

The variant of BNF used here presents alternative productions on successive lines. $\acute{|}\acute{}$ is a symbol of DyNe, not a meta-symbol of BNF. Curly brackets enclose optional parts.

Scripts

S ::=	S . S	(sequential composition)
	S + S	(alternative composition)
	({I:}S | ... | {I:}S)	(parallel composition)
	A	(basic action)
	O	(built-in script)
	I	(free occurrence of identifier)

Actions

A ::=	S -> S´ ? T	(active offer)
	GET T DO S REPLY S	(passive offer)
	LET T = S ENDLET	(definition)

7. References

[1] Rem, Martin ; Snepscheut, Jan L.A. van de ; Udding, Jan Tijmen. Trace theory and
     the definition of hierarchical components. In: Proceedings of the third
     Caltech Conference on VLSI. Computer Science Press 1983, pp 225-239.

[2] Snepscheut, Jan L.A. van de. Deriving circuits from programs. In: Proceedings
     of the third Caltech Conference on VLSI. Computer Science Press, 1983,
     pp 241-256.

[3] Snepscheut, Jan. L.A. van de . Trace theory and VLSI design. Ph.D. thesis.
     Eindhoven University of Technology, 1983.

[4] Udding, Jan Tijmen. On recursively defined sets of traces. Technical Note.
     Eindhoven University of Technology, Department of Mathematics and Computing
     Science, 1982.

[5] Problem set for the workshop on the analysis of concurrent systems.
     In these proceedings.

Built-in scripts

```
O ::= B           (built-in constants)
      PLUS
      MINUS
      EQ
      LT
      GT
      LESSEQ
      GRTREQ
          ...etc.
```

Basic constants

```
B ::= (any of some standard repertoire. Here we assume integers, booleans
      (TRUE and FALSE), and tokens (denoted by initially capitalised words)
```

Identifiers: a countable set, ranged over by I, whose members are denoted by
lower-case words

Templates

```
T ::= B           (basic constant)
      I           (free identifier)
      I:t         (bound identifier)
      t           (type)
      (T|...|T)   (tupling)
```

Types

```
t ::= INT
      BOOL
      TOKEN
      NAME
      DEAD
      PASSIVE
      ACTIVE
      (t|...|t)   (tupling)
      t + t       (union)
      t - t       (difference)
```

Binding occurrences and scoping

Occurrences of the identifier I of the following forms are binding occurrences:

    I:t   (in a template)

    I:S   (in a parallel script)

Given a phrase Z, the scope of a binding occurrence of an identifier in Z consists of the whole of Z, with the following exclusions:

(1) Let an action of the form ({I:}S|...|{I:}S) occur in Z. The scope of a binding occurrence of an identifier within any component script excludes the other components and the rest of Z.

(2) Let GET T DO S REPLY S´ occur in Z. The scope of a binding occurrence of I in S´ excludes T, S, and the rest of Z. The scope of a binding occurrence of I in S excludes T.

(3) Let S->S´?T occur in Z. The scope of a binding occurrence of I in S (resp. S´) excludes S´ and the rest of Z (resp. S and the rest of Z). The scope of a binding occurrence of I in T excludes S and S´.

(4) Let LET T=S ENDLET occur in Z. The scope of a binding occurrence of an identifier in S excludes T and the rest of Z.

(5) In S.S´, the scope of a binding occurrence of I in S´ excludes S.

(6) In S+S´, the scope of a binding occurrence of I in either component excludes the other. When S+S´ occurs in a larger phrase Z, only those identifiers which are bound in both S and S´, and to the same type, are visible to the rest of Z.

(7) In (T1|..|Tk), the scope of a binding occurrence of I in any component excludes the others.

(8) If an identifier has two (or more) binding occurrences in a script, one of which lies within the scope of the other, then the scope of the inner occurrence is excluded from the scope of the outer. This is the usual Algol-like rule for nested scopes.

To appreciate the significance of these rules it is helpful to state explicitly some features of DyNe scoping which they define by omission. In S.S´, a free occurrence of I in S´ is bound by a binding occurrence of I in S, even if S is enclosed in parentheses. In the declaration LET T=S ENDLET, a free occurrence of I in S is bound by a binding occurrence of I in T. That is, recursive definitions are allowed. The scope of the identifiers bound by a parallel script include each of the component scripts and the script following it. The scope of an identifier bound by the DO part of an action includes both the REPLY part of that action and the following part of the script in which the action occurs.

Where there are multiple definitions of an identifier, for the most part the later definition supercedes the earlier. Thus in S.S´, if I is bound by both S and S´, then the second binding will supercede the first. Neither component of an alternative script is thought of as being "later" than the other. This is to exclude the possibility of a script such as (S+S´).S", where S binds I but S´ does not, and I occurs free in S". When the script runs, only one of S or S´ will be selected for execution. If S´ were selected, then I would be undefined in S". The scope rules above remove this difficulty, by restricting the scope of such an identifier to S.

Syntactic constraints

1. A free occurrence of an identifier in a template may only be bound to a dead script.

2. In LET T=S ENDLET, T and S must have the same shape.

3. A recursive LET definition must be "well-guarded", a term we borrow from [1], with much the same meaning. We shall not give a formal definition, but informally it means that in a definition such as LET I=S ENDLET, any free occurrences of I in S must be after some communication action. Thus definitions such as the following are ruled out: x=x, x = PAR y=S ENDPAR.x, x = LET y=S ENDLET.x.

The first two of these conditions can in general only be checked at run time.

Initial actions, passive actions, and active actions

The initial actions of a script are defined by the function IA:

$$IA(\ S.S'\ ) \ = \ IA(\ S'\ ) \qquad \text{(if IA(S) is empty)}$$
$$\qquad\qquad = \ IA(\ S\ ) \qquad \text{(otherwise)}$$
$$IA(\ S + S'\ ) \ = \ IA(\ S\ )\ u\ IA(\ S'\ )$$
$$IA(\ (\ \{I1:\}S1\ |\ \dots\ |\ \{Ik:\}Sk\ )\ ) \ = \ IA(\ Sil\ )\ u.\ \dots\ u\ IA(\ Sil\ )$$
where Sil,...,Sil are the anonymous components
of the parallel composition
$$IA(\ A\ ) \ = \ \{\ A\ \}$$
$$IA(\ B\ ) \ = \ \{\}$$
$$IA(\ PLUS\ ) \ = \ \{\ GET\ (x|y)\ REPLY\ z\ |\ x,y,z\ \text{integers},\ z{=}x{+}y\ \}$$
and similarly for the other built-in scripts

The GET action is called passive; the others are active. A script having an initial active action is called active; one having only passive actions (and at least one such) is passive. The remainder are called dead scripts.

Types and values

The sets of values of various types may be represented as follows:

INT = { integers }
BOOL = { TRUE, FALSE }
TOKEN = { tokens }
NAME = { run-time actor names }
DEAD = { all scripts having no initial actions }
ACTIVE = { all scripts having an initial active action }
PASSIVE = { all scripts which are neither DEAD nor ACTIVE }
(t1|...|tk) = t1 * ... * tk

The + and - operations on types are set union and difference.

Shapes of scripts

A shape is a template with no bound variables. Every script and template has a shape, given by the following rules.

The shape of a template is the result of replacing every component I:t by t.

If S is active or passive, the shape of S is, respectively, ACTIVE or PASSIVE.

The shape of (S|...|S) is the tuple consisting of the shapes of its anonymous components.

The shape of a script which is a basic expression is the script itself.

Execution of scripts (an informal operational semantics)

A script is constructed from actions and built-in scripts. A script without free identifiers (a closed script) may be executed as follows.

(1) Dead scripts have terminated. They cannot be executed any further. They are the final result of executing a script. The dead scripts are the basic values and tuples of dead scripts.

(2) Each of the built-in operators (PLUS, MINUS, EQ, etc.) repeatedly accepts a tuple of values (of the shape appropriate to the operator) to which it replies with the result of applying the operator to the values. It can be represented semantically as an infinite sum with one component for every possible tuple of arguments.

(3) The three basic actions are executed as follows.

(a) To execute S->S'?T, first send (S,T') to S', where T' is the shape of T. If S' is not an actor name, then this implies that an actor is created to execute S'. Await a reply from S', which will have T' as its shape. Bind the bound identifiers of T to the corresponding components of the reply.

(b) To execute GET T DO S REPLY S', await a message (S",T') such that the shape of S" matches T. Bind the bound identifiers of T to the corresponding components of S". Execute S. Execute S' until its shape matches T', and send the result as the reply. (It is an error for execution of S' to terminate with a dead script of any other shape.) Note that S' may contain identifiers that received bindings from the execution of S.

(c) To execute LET T=S ENDLET, bind the bound identifiers of T to the corresponding components of S (which is required to be the same shape).

(4) Scripts are combined by '.', '+', and parallel composition.

(a) To execute S.S', execute S until it terminates, then execute S'.

(b) To execute S+S', do any of the following which is possible (making an arbitrary choice if more than one is).

(i) If S is active, execute it.

(ii) If S' is active, execute it.

(iii) If S or S' has an initial passive action for which there is a matching input available, then execute any such action. Then execute the remainder of the script - S or S' - in which that action occurred.

The first two of these cases rarely arise in practice, the usual use of + being to perform a pattern-matching choice among passive communications.

(5) To execute a script of the form ({I:}S|...|{I:}S), let I1,..,Ik be the distinct identifiers which appear. Create k actors, generating names n1,..,nk. Bind I1,..,Ik to these names. For each Ii, give the corresponding actor all those scripts S for which Ii:S is a component of the parallel composition; it will execute these concurrently. The anonymous components are given to the actor executing the original script. The result of executing them is the parallel composition of all the results.

Sugar

Parentheses may be used ad lib to indicate grouping. To minimise their use, the following are ranked in precedence from the tightest-binding to the loosest: REPLY, ->, ., +. Furthermore, -> is deemed to be left-associative. It is unnecessary to specify left or right associativity for `.` and `+`, as the semantics makes these associative operators. Note in particular that GET T DO S1 REPLY S2.S3 groups as (GET T DO S1 REPLY S2).S3, not GET T DO S1 REPLY (S2.S3).

It is sometimes convenient to write the arrow symbol the other way round:

$$S <- S` ? I \quad == \quad S` -> S ? I$$

One often wishes to send a message to an actor and use the reply as the subsequent script.

$$S => S` : T \quad == \quad S -> S` ? T . S"$$

where S" the the script resulting from replacing every component I:t of T by I. We also write

$$S => S` \quad == \quad S => S` : I:ANY$$
$$S <= S` : T \quad == \quad S` => S : T$$
$$S <= S` \quad == \quad S` => S$$

When the DO part of a passive communication is the token NIL it may be omitted:

$$GET\ T\ REPLY\ S \quad == \quad GET\ T\ DO\ NIL\ REPLY\ S$$

Unidirectional synchronised communication (as is used in, e.g. CSP and CCS) can be expressed by using some standard token for the reply half of a communication. We use OK, and allow REPLY OK to be omitted:

$$GET\ T\ DO\ S \quad == \quad GET\ T\ DO\ S\ REPLY\ OK$$
$$GET\ T \quad == \quad GET\ T\ DO\ NIL\ REPLY\ OK$$

DyNe's parallel composition combines two functions: tupling and process creation. When we wish to emphasise the former interpretation we may use commas instead of `|` to separate the components. When we are more concerned with the latter we may use PAR and ENDPAR as brackets, and require (without loss of generality) that each component have a distinct name. This also applies to templates.

The type DEAD + ACTIVE + PASSIVE may be denoted by ANY, and INT + BOOL + TOKEN by BASE.

We introduce the following abbreviations.

(1) Lists of definitions.

$$T1=S1, \ldots ,Tk=Sk \quad == \quad (T1,..,Tk) = (S1,..,Sk).$$

(2) Fixed points.

$$FIX\ I\ .\ S \quad == \quad LET\ I:ANY = S\ ENDLET\ .\ I$$

(3) Coercion.

$$S :: T \quad == \quad S \rightarrow (\ GET\ I:ANY\ REPLY\ I\ )\ ?\ T$$

(4) Conditional.

$$IF\ S\ THEN\ S'\ ELSE\ S"\ FI \quad == \quad S::I:BOOL\ .\ I =>$$
$$(\ GET\ TRUE\ REPLY\ S'$$
$$+\ GET\ FALSE\ REPLY\ S"\ )$$

In keeping with the idea that a function is represented as a script which cyclically accepts a message (an argument for the function) and replies with a result, we introduce sugar to allow such scripts to be written in the form of conventional pattern-matching definitions:

$$I(T1) = S1, \ldots, I(Tk) = Sk \quad ==$$
$$I = FIX\ I.\ (\ GET\ T1\ REPLY\ S1 + \ldots + GET\ Tk\ REPLY\ Sk\ )\ .\ I$$

If the shapes of the templates overlap, the result is a nondeterministic function – any branch of the alternative script which matches the incoming argument may be chosen.

Lastly, we give names to two commonly useful scripts.

$$IND\ (n:NAME) = FIX\ x.\ (\ GET\ y\ DO\ y \rightarrow n\ ?\ z:ANY\ REPLY\ z\ )\ .\ x$$

$$WAIT\ (s:ANY) = GET\ x:ANY\ DO\ PAR\ I:s\ ENDPAR\ REPLY\ x=>I\ .\ IND(I)$$

IND<=n is an "indirection script". It behaves indistinguishably from the script of the actor named n, relaying active offers from other processes and the replies to them. WAIT<=s waits until some other script makes it an active offer. It then creates an actor executing s, sends it the message x, and relays the reply. It then becomes an indirection process pointing at the actor it created. From the point of view of any other actor, WAIT<=s behaves just like s, except that execution of s is delayed until it is made an active offer.

Example: Parallel combinator reduction

We can construct a parallel model of combinator reduction by translating a combinator graph into a network of processes, with one process for each node. The edges of the graph are represented by the possibilities of communications between processes.

A node representing a constant is represented by a script which replies to the offer of a token VAL with the constant it holds.

$$const\ (n:INT+BOOL) = GET\ VAL\ REPLY\ n\ .\ (const <= n)$$

A built-in operator such as plus is represented by a script which sends a VAL token to the processes representing its arguments, and on receiving the replies becomes a const script representing the sum as above.

```
plus (x:NAME, y:NAME)  =  ( VAL -> x ? i:INT | VAL -> y ? j:INT ) .
                          ( (i,j) -> PLUS ? k:INT ) .
                          ( const <= k )
```

A list node cons(x,y) is represented by a script which repeatedly accepts offers of three forms: ISNIL, to which it replies with the boolean value FALSE; HEAD to which it replies with its first argument; and TAIL, to which it replies with its second.

```
cons (x:NAME, y:NAME)  =  ( GET ISNIL REPLY FALSE +
                            GET HEAD REPLY x +
                            GET TAIL REPLY y ) .
                          ( cons <= (x,y) )
```

The empty list is represented by:

```
nil  =  GET ISNIL REPLY TRUE . nil
```

and the test for an empty list is:

```
isnil x:NAME  =  ISNIL -> x ? y:BOOL . (const <= y)
```

The head operator, which selects the first argument of a cons, is represented by a script which sends a HEAD token to the actor representing its argument and becomes an indirection script pointing to the actor named by the reply.

```
head (x:NAME)  =  HEAD -> x ? (y:NAME) . (IND <= y)
```

Tail is modelled similarly.

The apply node is represented by a script which, given two actor names, sends the second name to the first actor and becomes the script received as the reply.

```
apply (l:NAME, r:NAME)  =  l <= r
```

A combinator node need not be supplied with all the arguments it needs for its reduction rule.   For each combinator of arity n we therefore define a series of n+1 scripts to represent nodes containing that combinator but having different numbers of arguments from 0 to n. Each of the first n of these scripts will take much the same form. It will accept an offer of an actor name (from an apply node such as above, and representing the next argument to be supplied to the combinator) and reply with the next most complete form of itself. The last script in the series will implement the reduction rule for the combinator. We illustrate this with the scripts for S, K, and I. B and C are very similar to S.

```
S0  =  GET x:NAME REPLY (S1<=x) . S0
S1 x:NAME  =  GET y:NAME REPLY (S2 <= (x,y)) . (S1 <= x)
S2 (x:NAME, y:NAME)  =  GET z:NAME REPLY (S3 <= (x,y,z)) . (S2 <= x,y))
S3 (x:NAME, y:NAME, z:NAME)  =  PAR v:apply<=(x,z) | w:apply<=(y,z) ENDPAR .
                               (apply <= (v,w))
K0  =  GET x:NAME REPLY (K1<=x) . K0
K1 x:NAME  =  GET y:NAME REPLY x . (K1<=x)
I0  =  GET x:NAME REPLY x . I0
```

Note that we have made a slight optimisation with K and I, in that it is not necessary to define K2 or Il, which we nevertheless give for completeness.

K2 (x:NAME, y:NAME) = IND <= x

Il = IND

These definitions model parallel-everywhere reduction. Other reduction orders can be modelled by other translations. For example, evaluations can be delayed by introducing some WAITs in the active scripts above to turn them into passive scripts.

[1] R. Milner. "A Calculus of Communicating Systems   Lecture Notes In Computer Science, vol.92. Springer-Verlag, 1980.

EXAMPLES OF A REAL-TIME TEMPORAL LOGIC SPECIFICATION

Ron Koymans and Willem P. de Roever*
University of Nijmegen
Nijmegen, the Netherlands

1. Introduction

In this contribution we give specifications for the STL/SERC problems nrs. 1, 6
and 8, mentioned below. Our specification method is based on a real-time temporal
logic very like the one in [KV de R]. We describe our logic in Section 2.
The specification of each problem is split into the following parts:

- 0. the informal specification as given to the authors
- 1. our interpretation of the informal specification including the meaning
  of the primitive notions to be specified
- 2. our notations specific for this problem
- 3. the atomic formulas of this specification (the atomic formulas are the
  formulas without operators)
- 4. the axioms specifying the primitive notions from point 1 interleaved
  with comments and remarks (comments rephrase the axioms in words and
  remarks indicate interesting points and consequences of the axioms).

2. The logic and its model

Our model is different from the usual temporal logic model, because real-time must
be considered. The model still is ultimately state-based but a state now has a
real-time component. This real-time component will be an element of the real-time
domain $\mathbb{R}$:

> $\mathbb{R}$ is a structure $(|\mathbb{R}|,<,+)$ with a linear ordering $<$ and addition $+$ and the
> following constraint: $\mathbb{R}$ is a superstructure (an extension) of $(\omega,<,+)$ where ω
> is the set of natural numbers (including 0) with its usual ordering and
> addition.

<u>Notation:</u> Let $\leqslant$ be the usual analog of $<$. By $|\mathbb{R}|_{\geqslant 0}$ we denote $\{t\epsilon|\mathbb{R}| |\ 0\leqslant t\}$.

For our logic we assume a many-sorted language with the standard operators
$\perp$ (falsity), $\rightarrow$ (implication) and $\forall$ (universal quantifier, for all sorts) and the
temporal operators $\bigcirc$ (next), $\blacklozenge$ (before) and $\mathcal{U}_{=t}$ (strong until in real-time t).
We demand that $|\mathbb{R}|_{\geqslant 0}$ is one of the sorts of the language. We assume
$=$ (equality) to be part of the language.

*W.P. de Roever is now at the Department of Mathematics and Computing
Science, Eindhoven University of Technology

The formulas of the language are formed by means of these operators and a set A of atomic formulas which denote state predicates. In our model a state s is a pair $<t,B>$ where $t\epsilon|R|$ and $B \subseteq A$ is the set of atomic formulas valid in that state.

Note that the real-time domain R occurs in both the logic and its model; in fact, we have a new logic and its accompanying model for every specification of R to a concrete structure.

In our model there is a unique initial state I. This initial state has real-time component 0.

An execution is considered as an infinite sequence $<s_i>_{i=0}^{\infty}$, where s_i is a state for all $i\epsilon\omega$, $s_0=I$ and $\pi_1(s_i) < \pi_1(s_{i+1})$ for all $i\epsilon\omega$, where π_j is the projection function on the j-th coordinate, i.e. time increases.

Let $\sigma=<s_i>_{i=0}^{\infty}$ be an execution.
For $i\epsilon\omega$ define σ_i to be s_i.
Implication, universal and existential quantification in the metalanguage are denoted respectively by $\Rightarrow$, $\forall$ and $\exists$. We now inductively define the relation $(\sigma,j)\models \varphi$ for all pairs (σ,j) (where σ is an execution and $j\epsilon\omega$) and any real-time temporal logic formula φ as follows:

$(\sigma,j)\models P :\overset{\text{def.}}{=} P\epsilon \pi_2(\sigma_j)$ for all $P\epsilon A$

$(\sigma,j)\not\models \bot$

$(\sigma,j)\models P\to Q: \overset{\text{def.}}{=} (\sigma,j)\models P \dashv (\sigma,j)\models Q$

$(\sigma,j)\models \forall v\epsilon D\ P(v):\overset{\text{def.}}{=} \forall v\epsilon D\ ((\sigma,j)\models P(\underline{v}))$ for all sorts D

$(\sigma,j)\models oP :\overset{\text{def.}}{=} (\sigma,j+1)\models P$

$(\sigma,j)\models \blacklozenge P :\overset{\text{def.}}{=} \exists n\epsilon\omega\ [0{\leqslant}n{\leqslant}j \wedge (\sigma,j-n)\models P]$

$(\sigma,j)\models PU_{=t}Q :\overset{\text{def.}}{=} \exists n\epsilon\omega[(\sigma,j+n)\models Q \wedge \pi_1(\sigma_{j+n}) = \pi_1(\sigma_j)+t \wedge$
$\forall i\epsilon\omega[0{\leqslant}i<n \Rightarrow (\sigma,j+i)\models P]]$

In this logic the operator $U_{=t}$ is considered as a ternary operator with formulas as its first two arguments and an element from $|R|_{\geqslant 0}$ as its third argument.

We define furthermore the following derived operators for formulas P and Q:

$\neg P \overset{\text{def.}}{=} P \to \bot$ (negation)

$P\wedge Q \overset{\text{def.}}{=} \neg(P \to \neg Q)$ (conjunction)

$P\vee Q \overset{\text{def.}}{=} \neg P \to Q$ (disjunction)

$\exists x\epsilon D\ P(x) \overset{\text{def.}}{=} \neg\forall x\epsilon D\ \neg P(x)$ for all sorts D (existential quantification)

$\top \overset{\text{def.}}{=} \neg\bot$ (truth)

$\Diamond_{=t}P \overset{\text{def.}}{=} \top U_{=t}P$ (eventually in real-time t)

$$\Diamond P \overset{\text{def.}}{=} \exists t_\epsilon \ |R|_{>0} \ \Diamond_{=t} P \qquad \text{(eventually)}$$

$$\Diamond_{<t} P \overset{\text{def.}}{=} \exists t' \ \epsilon \ |R|_{>0} \ (t'<t \wedge \Diamond_{=t'} P) \quad \text{(eventually before real-time t)}$$

$$\Diamond_{\leqslant t} P \overset{\text{def.}}{=} \Diamond_{=t} P \vee \Diamond_{<t} P \qquad \text{(eventually within real-time t)}$$

$$\square P \overset{\text{def.}}{=} \neg \Diamond \neg P \qquad \text{(henceforth)}$$

$$P \, U \, Q \overset{\text{def.}}{=} \exists t_\epsilon \ |R|_{>0} \ (P \, U_{=t} \, Q) \qquad \text{(strong until)}$$

$$P \, \hat{U} \, Q \overset{\text{def.}}{=} \neg Q \wedge P \, U \, Q \qquad \text{(not immediate strong until)}$$

The defined operators O, $\Diamond$, $\square$ and U above correspond indeed to the well-known
linear time temporal logic operators of the same name.

3. Common properties of the specifications

In all three specifications we consider a system and users requesting services
from the system. The users can request services from the system by certain
actions which will always be primitive notions (e.g. the sending of a message).
The system responds upon these requests by actions which provide the requested
service (e.g. the delivery of a message). These system actions will also be
primitive notions.

We call the objects given by the users to the system data elements. Logically
speaking, these data elements remain in the system until they are removed (e.g. by
their delivery at their destination). For technical reasons these data elements
all have an identification which makes them unique. Technically we can insure
this uniqueness by time-stamping the data elements: if a user requests a service
by some action then the data elements involved with this action are time stamped
with the time at which the action was initiated. Anyway, all actions are modelled
in our specifications by the satisfaction of the corresponding atomic formulas
(see Section 2) in the state in which the action is initiated. Prima facie, this
unique identification assumption seems overly restrictive. Logically speaking,
there are two positions, however. Either the system accepts possibly identical
data elements and wraps them up differently by placing them in an auxiliary
buffer, thereby providing a unique identification to the combination of data
element plus wrapping; a prerequisite for this kind of position is the
introduction of auxiliary states, or auxiliary state functions in Lamport's
parlance.

In the other position one does not want to introduce auxiliary state-components,
and hence, necessarily can only distinguish between data elements by their
histories in the models in question. In case a data element is handed to the
system by a user there is no distinction in their histories associated with data
elements anymore, and hence we need unique identification of data elements.

We adopt this latter position. An important consequence of our position is the following. Typical of our kind of specification is that we axiomatize the primitive notions and nothing more. (The primitive notions are a subset of the atomic formulas, see Section 2, relevant to the problem under consideration). Hence our formal specifications contain only objects explicitly specified by the informal specifications, e.g. when it is given that an object preserves the order of its data elements we do not model the object by an auxiliary state-component such as a queue because we find this too implementation biased.

In all three specifications we assume <u>perfect communication</u> in the sense that the following two conditions are satisfied:

1. The system under consideration does not create data elements by itself. In other words: the system can only manipulate data elements received by actions of users.
2. The system does not copy data elements. In other words once a data element is removed from the system (e.g. by delivering it to a user), this data element never reappears in the system. This is made possible by the unique identification of data elements.

In all specifications there is also a condition about the delivery of data elements once they are accepted by the system from a user:

3. The system must guarantee the delivery of accepted data elements under certain (problem dependent) circumstances.

Note that the three conditions above are relevant in practice because it is known that in the real world it is impossible to guarantee completely (any one of) these three conditions. Therefore we formulate these requirements explicitly as axioms so as to have the option of dropping some of them (and thereby specifying something else).

In all three specifications the given axioms in part 4 are always invariants, i.e. they are valid for every state in an execution, so in fact they should all be preceded by the operator □. Furthermore, we use free variables in these axioms; this should be understood as an implicit universal quantification over the domains of data elements which are specified for these variables in the notations specific to the problem under consideration (part 3 of each specification).

4.   Problem 1

4.0   The informal specification

Problem

Specify the channel described below.

Description

The 'channel' between endpoints 'a' and 'b' can pass messages in both
directions simultaneously, until it receives a 'disconnect' message from
one end, after which it neither delivers nor accepts messages at that
end. It continues to deliver and accept messages at the other end until
the 'disconnect' message arrives, after which it can do nothing. The
order of messages sent in a given direction is preserved.

4.1   Our interpretation

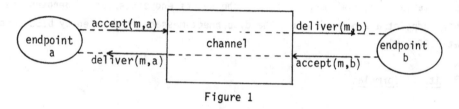

Figure 1

Let e be an element of {a,b}, the set of endpoints.
The primitive notions here are:
- accept (m,e): the channel accepts the message m from the endpoint e
- deliver (m,e): the channel delivers the message m at the endpoint e.

(As can also be seen in figure 1 the nomenclature of the primitive notions is
taken with the channel as viewpoint).

In our interpretation the channel cannot accept (and the same for deliver) two
different messages at the same time at one endpoint.

Let $\bar{e}$ denote the other endpoint $\bar{a} = b$ and $\bar{b} = a$. The idea of perfect
communication (see section 3) leads here to the assumption of a perfect channel:

1.   The channel does not create messages by itself (in other words: the channel
     can only deliver accepted messages)
2.   The channel does not copy messages (in other words: the channel delivers a
     message at most once)
3.   All accepted messages from endpoint e will eventually be delivered at $\bar{e}$
     unless $\bar{e}$ is already disconnected.

Concerning 3 above: in the informal specification nothing is said about losing messages (note the phrase 'can pass messages') but we think it to be natural to assume that all messages will be delivered. However, in Section 4.4 we indicate how to change the specification to incorporate a possible loss of messages.

A further assumption is that the disconnect-message is considered as a normal message which can be accepted by the channel at an endpoint e and then be delivered by the channel at $\bar{e}$. In particular, the disconnect-message obeys the preservation of ordering with respect to other messages. Again we give in Section 4.4 an indication how the specification should be adjusted to incorporate a special treatment of the disconnect-message.

4.2 Notations

Let M denote the domain of messages.
Variables m and m' range over M.

The variable e is an element of {a,b}, the set of endpoints, and $\bar{e}$ denotes the other endpoint: $\bar{a}$ = b and $\bar{b}$ = a. The disconnect-message is denoted by DISC (note that DISC ϵ M).

4.3 Atomic formulas

The only atomic formulas here are the primitive notions:
accept (m,e) and deliver (m,e) for all mϵ M and e ϵ {a,b}.

4.4 The axiomatization

Ax 1.1 $[accept(m,e) \wedge accept(m',e)] \rightarrow m' = m$
Ax 1.2 $[deliver(m,e) \wedge deliver(m',e)] \rightarrow m'=m$

Comment: The channel cannot accept two different messages at the same time at one endpoint. The same holds for the delivery of messages.

Ax 1.3 $deliver(m,e) \longrightarrow \Box\Box\neg deliver(m,e)$

Comment: Once a message is delivered, it can never be delivered again (in other words: the channel does not copy messages).

Ax 1.4 $accept(m,e) \rightarrow \Diamond(deliver(m,\bar{e}) \vee \blacklozenge accept(DISC,\bar{e}))$

Comment: An accepted message at e will eventually be delivered at ē unless ē has issued a disconnect.

Remarks:

1. Because $\Diamond(P \lor Q) \leftrightarrow (\Diamond P \lor \Diamond Q)$ and $\Diamond \blacklozenge P \leftrightarrow \blacklozenge \Diamond P \leftrightarrow (\blacklozenge P \lor \Diamond P)$ hold (for all formulas P and Q), it follows that the disconnect-message accepted at ē can have taken place any time (i.e. past, present or future): $\Diamond \blacklozenge$ accept (DISC, ē).

2. The axiom implies that there can be no loss of messages as long as both endpoints are connected.

3. We allow the theoretical possibility of an infinite transmission speed, i.e. accept $(m,e) \land$ deliver $(m,\bar{e})$ is not excluded; a finite transmission speed can be forced by adding the conjunctive $\neg$ deliver$(m,\bar{e})$ after the implication:

$$\text{Ax } 1.4^{FIN} \quad \text{accept}(m,e) \to [\neg \text{ deliver}(m,\bar{e}) \land$$
$$\Diamond(\text{deliver}(m,\bar{e}) \lor \blacklozenge \text{ accept}(DISC,\bar{e}))].$$

Ax 1.5   deliver$(m,e) \longrightarrow \blacklozenge$ accept$(m,\bar{e})$

Comment: The channel can only deliver accepted messages; in other words: the channel does not create messages by itself.

Remark: Axioms 1.3, 1.4 and 1.5 formalize the assumption of a perfect channel (see Section 4.1).

Ax 1.6   [accept(DISC,e) v deliver(DISC,e)]$\to O\square$ ($\neg$ accept$(m,e) \land$
$$\neg \text{deliver}(m,e))$$

Comment: The effect of a disconnect-message for e (either accepted from e or coming from ē) is that nothing can be accepted or delivered any more at e.

Remarks: 1. Note that Ax 1.4 guarantees that the acceptance of a disconnect-message at e leads to the delivery of that message at ē unless ē already disconnected itself.

2. From axioms 1.4 and 1.6 it follows that we allow deliver $(m,e) \land$ accept(DISC, e) to hold, i.e. the channel can deliver a message at e while _at_the_same_time_ it accepts a disconnect-message at e (note the phrase 'can pass messages in both directions simultaneously' in the informal specification).

Ax 1.7 $[\text{accept}(m,e) \wedge \bigcirc\Diamond\text{accept}(m',e)] \rightarrow \square(\text{deliver}(m,\bar{e}) \rightarrow$
$\neg \blacklozenge \text{deliver}(m',\bar{e}))$

Comment: The order of messages sent in a given direction is preserved.

Remarks: 1.   Note that this axiom does not depend on whether m will be delivered
or not (in other words: this axiom is independent of the loss of
messages, see axiom 1.4).

2.   The premise of the axiom implies m' ≠ m because of the unique
identification of messages by means of timestamps (see Section 3).

3.   If the disconnect-message is not considered as a normal message we
should change Ax 1.7 into

Ax 1.7' $[\text{accept}(m,e) \wedge \bigcirc\Diamond \text{accept}(m',e) \wedge m' \neq \text{DISC}] \rightarrow$
$\square(\text{deliver}(m,\bar{e}) \rightarrow \neg \blacklozenge\text{deliver}(m',\bar{e}))$
and furthermore Ax 1.4 should be changed into
Ax 1.4' $\text{accept}(m,e) \rightarrow$
$\Diamond (\text{deliver}(m,\bar{e}) \vee \blacklozenge \text{deliver}(\text{DISC},\bar{e}) \vee \blacklozenge\text{accept}(\text{DISC},\bar{e}))$.

Note that we do not need Ax 1.4' instead of Ax 1.4 anyway because
deliver(DISC,$\bar{e}$) → ♦accept(DISC,e) holds according to Ax 1.5 and for all
three possibilities of precedence of the acceptance of a message m relative to acceptance of DISC, the addition of a disjunctive
♦deliver(DISC,$\bar{e}$) in Ax 1.4 is useless:

(i) $[\text{accept}(m,e) \wedge \bigcirc\Diamond \text{accept}(\text{DISC},e)] \rightarrow$
$\square(\text{deliver} (m,\bar{e}) \rightarrow \neg\blacklozenge \text{deliver} (\text{DISC},\bar{e}))$ by Ax 1.7

(ii) $[\text{accept}(m,e) \wedge \text{accept}(\text{DISC},e)] \rightarrow m=\text{DISC}$ by Ax 1.1

(iii) $\neg[\text{accept} (\text{DISC},e) \wedge \bigcirc\Diamond \text{accept}(m,e)]$ by Ax 1.6

4.   In the case that loss of messages is allowed, we have to replace Ax
1.4 by a version reflecting fairness:
Ax 1.4^{FAIR} $[\square\Diamond\exists m \text{ accept}(m,e)] \rightarrow \Diamond(\exists m \text{ deliver}(m,\bar{e}) \vee$
$\blacklozenge\text{accept}(\text{DISC},\bar{e}))$.
The existential quantification in this axiom ranges over M.
This is indeed the only axiom that needs to be changed; as
indicated in remark 1, Ax 1.7 is independent of Ax 1.4. Instead of
expressing that every message accepted at e will eventually be
delivered at $\bar{e}$ unless $\bar{e}$ is already disconnected (see Ax 1.4), axiom
1.4^{FAIR} expresses the following: if infinitely often a message is
accepted at e then eventually at least one message will be
delivered at $\bar{e}$ unless $\bar{e}$ is already disconnected. In the case that
$\bar{e}$ is never disconnected, it follows that even infinitely many

messages accepted at e will eventually be delivered at $\bar{e}$.

Note that from the premise $\square\lozenge\exists$ m accept (m,e) and axiom 1.6 it follows that $\square\neg\blacklozenge$ accept(DISC,e) and hence $\square\neg\blacklozenge$ deliver(DISC,$\bar{e}$) by axiom 1.5.

This means that analogous to remark 3 the clause $\blacklozenge$ deliver(DISC,$\bar{e}$) need not be added to the disjunction of Ax 1.4^{Fair}. However, the clause $\blacklozenge$ accept(DISC,$\bar{e}$) in the disjunction of Ax 1.4^{Fair} is still essential: consider the situation in which the disconnect-message is accepted at $\bar{e}$ but this disconnect-message gets lost and so is never delivered at e (this is quite possible as we consider in this remark the disconnect-message as a normal message and we are just handling the loss of messages); meanwhile infinitely many messages are accepted at e.

In this situation no messages should be delivered at $\bar{e}$ after the disconnect-message has been accepted at $\bar{e}$. Note that the premise $\square\lozenge\exists$m accept(m,e) and axiom 1.6 also imply $\square\neg\blacklozenge$ deliver(DISC,e) so an accepted disconnect-message at $\bar{e}$ must indeed get lost.

5. If the disconnect-message is not considered as a normal message and loss of messages is allowed (remarks 3 and 4 combined), then we can combine the changes to the axioms: it is sufficient to take Ax 1.7' and Ax 1.4^{FAIR} instead of Ax 1.7, respectively Ax 1.4. If we furthermore assume that the disconnect-message cannot get lost, then the clause $\blacklozenge$ accept(DISC,$\bar{e}$) in the disjunction of Ax 1.4^{FAIR} is no longer essential and this axiom can be replaced by the simpler

Ax $1.4^{FAIR'}$ [$\square\lozenge\exists$m accept(m,e)] $\longrightarrow\lozenge\exists$ m deliver(m,$\bar{e}$).

6. For this problem we only used a small part of the logic of section 2, viz.

$\square$, $\lozenge$, $\bigcirc$ and $\blacklozenge$

as the only temporal operators.

5.   Problem 6

5.0 The Informal Specification

Problem

Specify the system described below.

Description

The network consists of a collection of 'nodes', each having a unique address. The objects transmitted are 'packets', which are grouped into 'messages'.

A node transmits a message by sending the packets it is made of with

send X to A via Z.

This means that packet X is to be delivered to node A, after going to node Z first. Node Z forwards the packet to another node with a similar instruction, with the same destination. The packet must eventually arrive at its destination. Packets are acknowledged on receipt, with the originating node retransmitting if an acknowledgement is not received within a specified time. Duplicate packets are discarded on receipt, and sets of packets making up a message are delivered in order to the user of a node.

5.1 Our Interpretation

A message is considered as a sequence of packets $<p_1, \ldots, p_k>$ where $k \geq 1$.
The primitive notions here are:

- sendmessage $(<p_1, \ldots, p_k>)$:   send the message consisting of the packets $p_1, \ldots, p_k$ (in that order) to their joint destination by means of sending each individual packet from their joint source.

- delivermessage $(<p_1, \ldots, p_k>)$:   deliver the message consisting of the packets $p_1, \ldots, p_k$ (in that order) to the user of their joint destination.

- $send_n(p, t)$:   node n sends packet p to its destination via node t.

As we have to express that a message can only be delivered if all of its packets have arrived at their joint destination, we also introduce the counter-part of send:

-   $\text{receive}_n(p)$:   node n receives the packet p (this receive must be the result of an earlier $\text{send}_s(p,n)$ for some node s).

Note that we suppose that the destination of a packet can be derived from the packet itself (so one parameter can be omitted in send) and that the same is true for the source of a packet (this is needed anyway as destination of the acknowledgement of the packet). We assume for all packets that their destination is different from their source. Just as for problem 1 we assume perfect communication:

1.   the network does not create messages by itself
2.   the network does not deliver messages and packets more than once
3.   all messages eventually arrive at their destination.

Concerning 3 above: this seems to be implied by the informal specification (note the phrase 'the packet must eventually arrive at its destination'). We furthermore assume that an acknowledgement is transmitted by the network as a normal packet from the destination of the acknowledged packet to its source. Again we assume that an acknowledgement does not need to be acknowledged! As nothing is said in the informal specification about acknowledging duplicate packets (getting duplicate acknowledgements), our formal specification does not express this either. The same holds for the return of packets in their originating node: as nothing is said in the informal specification about this, our formal specification does not forbid this.
One point in the informal specification is unclear to us: <u>why are packets acknowledged on receipt if all packets must eventually arrive at their destination?</u>

5.2   Notations

Let $\mathbb{P}$ denote the domain of packets, $\mathbb{N}$ the domain of nodes and ω the domain of natural numbers. Variable p (also with superscripts and subscripts) ranges over $\mathbb{P}$. By $\langle p_1, \ldots, p_k \rangle$ we denote the sequence of packets (the message) consisting of $p_1, \ldots, p_k$ in that order. Variables i, j, k and ℓ (also with subscripts) range over ω. Variables n, n', t and t' range over $\mathbb{N}$. By p^i we denote the ith duplicate of the packet p (for i=0 we have the original packet). Note that all duplicates of a packet are different packets because data elements are uniquely identifiable (see Section 3). By source(p) we denote the originating node of packet p, by dest(p) the destination node of packet p and by ack(p) the acknowledgement-packet corresponding to p. The following relations hold between source(p), dest(p) and ack(p): source(ack(p)) = dest(p) and dest(ack (p)) = source(p).

By acktime we denote the time after which an originating node retransmits if it did not receive an acknowledgement within that time.

5.3 Atomic Formulas

The atomic formulas are sendmessage $(<p_1,...,p_k>)$, delivermessage $(<p_1,...,p_k>)$, $send_n(p,t)$, $receive_n(p)$ and isack(p) for all p, $p_i \varepsilon P$, $1 \leq i \leq k$ and n, t ε N. The predicate isack(p) is true if and only if p is an acknowledgement-packet (hence isack(ack(p)) holds for all pε P).

5.4 The Axiomatization

AX 6.1 $[k \geqslant 1 \wedge$ delivermessage $(<p_1,...,p_k>)] \rightarrow$

$$\bigcirc \square \neg \text{ delivermessage } (<p_1,...,p_k>)$$

Comment: Once a message $<p_1,...,p_k>$ is delivered it can never be delivered again.

Ax 6.2 $[k \geqslant 1 \wedge$ sendmessage$(<p_1,...,p_k>)] \rightarrow$

$[\forall i [1 \leqslant i \leqslant k \rightarrow (\text{source}(p_i) = \text{source}(p_1) \wedge \text{dest}(p_i) =$

$\text{dest}(p_1) \wedge \text{source}(p_1) \neq \text{dest}(p_1) \wedge \Diamond \exists t \ send_{\text{source}(p_1)} (p_i^o, t))]$

$\wedge \Diamond$ delivermessage$(<p_1,...,p_k>)]$.

Comment : Packets making up a message have the same originating node and the same destination node and these two nodes are different; the packets are distributed in the sense that each packet is sent individually from the joint originating node via some node (need not be the same for all packets) to the joint destination node; eventually the packet will be delivered as a message in the same order as specified in sendmessage.

Ax 6.3 $[k > 1 \wedge \text{delivermessage}(<p_1, \ldots, p_k>)] \rightarrow$

$$[\blacklozenge \text{sendmessage}(<p_1, \ldots, p_k>) \wedge \forall i [1 \leq i \leq k \rightarrow \blacklozenge \exists j \\ \text{receive}_{\text{dest}(p_1)}(p_i^j)]]$$

Comment: A message can only be delivered if it was sent before (with the packets in the same order) and all its packets (or duplicates thereof) have arrived at their joint destination.

Remark: Axioms 6.1, 6.2 and 6.3 formalize the assumption of perfect communication of messages.

Ax 6.4 $[\text{send}_n(p^i, t) \wedge \text{send}_{n'}(p^i, t')] \rightarrow [n' = n \wedge t' = t]$

Ax 6.5 $[\text{receive}_n(p^i) \wedge \text{receive}_{n'}(p^i)] \rightarrow n' = n$

Comment: The network cannot at the same time send the same packet from or via different nodes or receive a packet in different nodes.

Ax 6.6 $\text{send}_n(p^i, t) \rightarrow [[\neg \exists n' \, \text{receive}_{n'}(p^i) \wedge \bigcirc \neg \, \text{send}_n(p^i, t)] \\ \mathring{U} \text{receive}_t(p^i)]$

Comment: If a packet is sent via a node t it will eventually, but not immediately, be received in t and cannot be received or sent again anywhere in the meantime.

Ax 6.7 $[\text{receive}_n(p^i) \wedge \text{dest}(p) \neq n] \rightarrow$

$$[[\neg \exists n' \exists t' \, \text{send}_{n'}(p^i, t') \wedge \bigcirc \neg \, \text{receive}_n(p^i) \, \mathring{u} \\ \exists t \, \text{send}_n(p^i, t)]$$

Comment: If a packet is received in a node that is not the destination node of the packet, then it will eventually, but not immediately, be sent on to another node and cannot be sent or received again anywhere in the meantime.

Ax 6.8 $\text{Send}_n(p^i, t) \rightarrow \lozenge \text{receive}_{\text{dest}(p)}(p^i)$

Comment: A packet will eventually arrive at its destination.

Remark: From Ax 6.6 it follows that again the eventually cannot be immediate.

Ax 6.9 $\text{receive}_{\text{dest}(p)}(p^i) \longrightarrow \bigcirc \square \neg \text{receive}_{\text{dest}(p)}(p^i)$

Comment: A packet can only arrive once at its destination (in other words: a packet is removed from the network at the first receipt at its destination).

Remark: Note that axiom 6.9 and the remark of axiom 6.8 imply $\text{send}_n(p^i,t) \rightarrow \neg \blacklozenge \text{receive}_{\text{dest}(p)}(p^i)$ which means that there cannot be packets in transit that already have been received at their destination.

Ax 6.10 $[\text{receive}_{\text{dest}(p)}(p^i) \wedge \neg \exists\, j \neq i\ \blacklozenge\ \text{receive}_{\text{dest}(p)}(p^j) \wedge \neg$
$\text{isack}(p)] \longrightarrow \diamondsuit \exists\, t\ \text{send}_{\text{dest}(p)}(\text{ack}(p)^0,t)$

Comment: The <u>first</u> acknowledgement (indicated by the zero) is sent whenever a (possibly duplicate) packet is <u>for the first time</u> received at its destination unless the packet itself is an acknowledgement.

Remark: Recall that $\text{dest}(p) = \text{source}(\text{ack}(p))$.

Ax 6.11 $\text{receive}_n(p^i) \longrightarrow \blacklozenge \exists\, t\ \text{send}_t(p^i,n)$

Comment: This axiom is more or less the counterpart of Ax 6.6: a node n can only receive a packet if this packet was previously sent to n.

Ax 6.12 $[\bigcirc \text{send}_n(p^i,t) \wedge ((\blacklozenge\ \exists\, t'\ \text{send}_n(p^i,t')) \vee \text{source}(p) \neq n)]$
$\longrightarrow \blacklozenge\ \text{receive}_n(p^i)$

Comment: If a packet is sent, but not <u>for the first time</u> from its <u>originating</u> node, then it must have been previously received.

Remarks: 1. The next-operator $\bigcirc$ is needed to contrast with the before operator $\blacklozenge$ of $\blacklozenge \exists\, t'\ \text{send}_n(p^i,t')$ expressing that the packet was not for the first time sent from this node.

       2. We allow that a packet returns to its originating node because there is no reason to forbid this.

       3. In this axiom $n \neq \text{dest}(p)$ holds because of the axiom itself and the formula in the remark of axiom 6.9.

4. The axioms 6.4 through 6.9, 6.11 and 6.12 imply that for each duplicate of a packet there is a <u>unique</u> chain of nodes (starting from the originating node of the packet) through which the packet is sent and received until it eventually arrives at its destination (axiom 6.8) and is thereafter never seen again (axiom 6.9). In other words: each duplicate packet can be uniquely localised; that is, at any time it can be at only one place in the network. For example, axioms 6.6, 6.7, 6.11 and 6.12 imply that a chain of nodes through which a packet is sent and received can be traced back eventually to the first time it was sent in the originating node. As a corollary of these remarks we have the following strengthenings of axioms 6.6 and 6.7:

$$\text{send}_n(p^i,t) \longrightarrow [[\neg\exists n' \; \text{receive}_{n'}(p^i) \wedge O\neg\exists n' \; \exists t' \; \text{send}_{n'}(p^i,t')] \; \mathring{U} \; \text{receive}_t(p^i)]$$

and

$$[\text{receive}_n(p^i) \wedge \text{dest}(p) \neq n] \longrightarrow$$

$$[[\neg\exists n' \; \exists t' \; \text{send}_{n'}(p^i,t') \wedge O\neg\exists n' \; \text{receive}_{n'}(p^i)]$$
$$\mathring{U}\exists t \; \text{send}_n(p^i,t)]$$

Ax 6.13 $[\text{send}_n(p^i,t) \wedge \neg \; \text{isack}(p)] \longrightarrow \exists\alpha \; \exists\beta \; \blacklozenge\text{sendmessage}(\alpha*_{<p>}*\beta)$

Remark: The existential quantification ranges over the domain of sequences of packets and * is the concatenation-operator of sequences of packets.

Comment: All packets which are not an acknowledgement eventually originated from a sendmessage.

Ax 6.14 $[O \; \text{send}_n(p^i,t) \wedge \neg\blacklozenge\exists t' \; \text{send}_n(p^i,t') \wedge \text{source}(p) = n \wedge \neg \; \text{isack}(p) \wedge$
$O\neg\lozenge_{\leq\text{acktime}}\exists j \; \text{receive}_n(\text{ack}(p)^j)]$

$\rightarrow O(\lozenge_{=\text{acktime}}\exists t' \; \text{send}_n(p^{i+1},t') \wedge\neg\lozenge_{<\text{acktime}}\exists j>i \; \blacklozenge\exists t'$

$$\text{send}_n(p^j,t'))$$

Comment: If a packet that is not an acknowledgement is sent from its originating node for the first time and there arrives no acknowledgement within acktime time units then the next duplicate of the packet is sent and before that moment no next duplicate can be or has been sent.

Remark: The next-operator $\bigcirc$ is needed everywhere in this axiom to shift the timepoint one state in the execution to be able to compare this with the $\neg\blacklozenge$ in the premise (we want to express that $send_n(p^i,t)$ occurs for the first time, cf. remark 1 of axiom 6.12).

Ax 6.15 $[\bigcirc send_n(p^i,t) \wedge \neg\blacklozenge \exists t' \, send_n(p^i,t') \wedge source(p) = n \wedge$
$\neg isack(p) \wedge \bigcirc\diamondsuit_{\leqslant acktime} \exists j \, receive_n(ack(p)^j)]$

$\rightarrow \square\neg\blacklozenge\exists \, j > i \; \exists t' \, send_n(p^j,t')$

Comment: The premise is the same as in axiom 6.14 except that now an acknowledgement arrives indeed within acktime time units; in that case no next duplicate can ever be sent or have been sent.

Ax 6.16 $send_{dest(p)}(ack(p)^i,t) \longrightarrow$

$\exists \ell_0 \ldots \exists \ell_i \, \forall j \leqslant i [\blacklozenge receive_{dest(p)}(p^{\ell_j}) \wedge$
$\neg\exists \ell \neq \ell_0, \ldots \ell_j \, \blacklozenge receive_{dest(p)}(p^\ell)]$

Comment: The i-th duplicate (note that we start counting from zero) of an acknowledgement can only be sent if previously <u>exactly</u> $i + 1$ duplicates of the acknowledged packet have arrived at the destination of the acknowledged packet.

Remarks: 1. The sequence of natural numbers $\ell_0, \ldots, \ell_i$ can be coded into one natural number so that the axiom can be rewritten in a more regular form.

   2. Axioms 6.4 through 6.16 formalise the communication via packets and can be divided into two parts: axioms 6.4 through 6.10 (and part of axiom 6.14) formalise the chain of effects caused by sending a packet for the first time from its source, while axioms 6.11 through 6.16 formalize which chains of effects are allowed in the network by prohibiting the network to create by itself the various sorts of possible packets (note the special role of axiom 6.13 which relates the sending of packets which are not an acknowledgement to the sending of a message).

6. Problem 8

6.0 The Informal Specification

Problem 8 Mixing Synchronous and Asynchronous Input

Problem

Specify the object described below.

Description

The object has two inputs and one output. The output and one of the inputs respectively send and receive data in packets at regular intervals. The remaining input is asynchronous, i.e. data appears at undetermined times.

The data packets which arrive at the synchronous input may be full or empty, and the object may only output data by forwarding packets from the synchronous input or filling an empty packet with data from the asynchronous input. All packets have the same size.

6.1 Our Interpretation

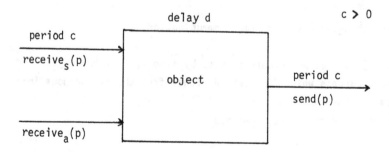

Figure 2

The primitive notions here are:

- receive$_s$(p):   the object receives the packet p from the synchronous input
- receive$_a$(p):   the object receives the packet p from the asynchronous input
- send(p):   the object outputs packet p

(As also can be seen in figure 2 the nomenclature of the primitive notions is taken with the object as viewpoint).

As can be seen in figure 2 we assume that the arrival of packets from the synchronous input and the output of packets occurs at regular intervals with the same period c (this seems to us a natural interpretation of the informal specification). Furthermore we assume that there is a finite delay of d time units between the arrival of a packet p from the synchronous input and the sending of a packet (not necessarily packet p). With these assumptions we interpret the possibilities of outputting a packet as follows:

1. each non-empty packet from the synchronous input will be output with delay d
2. an empty packet from the synchronous input may be output with delay d or alternatively a previously received packet from the asynchronous input may be output with delay d instead.

Of course, we again assume perfect communication:

1. the object does not create packets by itself, c.q. the object can only output packets which it received either from the synchronous input or from the asynchronous input
2. the object does not copy packets.

6.2 Notations

Let P denote the domain of packets.
All variables range over P.

6.3 Atomic Formulas

The atomic formulas are receive$_s$(p), receive$_a$(p), send(p) and isempty(p) for all p ε P. The predicate isempty(p) is true if and only if p is an empty packet.

6.4 The Axiomatization

Ax 8.1   send(p) $\longrightarrow$

$$[\mathsf{L}(\neg\exists p' \neq p \; send \; (p')) \wedge \bigcirc\neg \; send \; (p)] \; \mathsf{U}_{=c}(\exists p' \; send \; (p'))]$$

Comment: Packets are sent at a regular interval of c time units.

Remark: This axiom implies [send (p) $\wedge$ send (p')] $\longrightarrow$ p' = p.

Ax 8.2   [receive$_s$(p) $\wedge$ receive$_s$(p')] $\longrightarrow$ p' = p

Comment: The object cannot receive two different packets at the same time
          from the synchronous input.

Ax 8.3   [receive$_s$(p) $\wedge \neg$ isempty(p)] $\longrightarrow \Diamond_{=d}$ send (p)

Comment: Each non-empty packet from the synchronous input will be output with
          a delay of d time units.

Ax 8.4   [receive$_s$(p) $\wedge$ isempty(p)] $\longrightarrow$
          [$\Diamond_{=d}$ send(p) v $\exists$p' L($\Diamond_{=d}$ send (p')) $\wedge \blacklozenge$ receive$_a$(p')]]

Comment: If an empty packet arrives from the synchronous input there are two
          choices:
          either the object sends (with delay d) this empty packet on or it
          fills the empty packet with a packet already received from the
          asynchronous input and sends (with delay d) this filled packet.

Remark: Axioms 8.3 and 8.4 guarantee that whenever a packet is received from
          the synchronous input there will be output a packet with delay d.

Ax 8.5   receive$_s$(p) $\longrightarrow \Diamond_{=c} \exists$p' receive$_s$(p')

Comment: If a packet is received from the synchronous input, then after c
          time units again a packet will be received from the synchronous
          input.

Remark: Note that axioms 8.1 through 8.4 imply that nothing can be received
          from the synchronous input in between the period of c time units:

As already indicated in the remark of axiom 8.4 we have $\text{receive}_s(p) \longrightarrow \Diamond_{=d} \exists p'$ send (p'), so if two different packets are received from the synchronous input in a period of c time units (note that according to axiom 8.2 they cannot be received at the same time), it follows that there will also be output two packets at different times in a period of c time units which is in contradiction with axiom 8.1.

Ax 8.6 $[\text{O receive}_s(p) \wedge \neg \exists p' \blacklozenge \text{receive}_s(p')] \longrightarrow$

$[(\neg \exists p' \blacklozenge \text{send}(p')) \wedge \text{O} \neg \Diamond_{<d} \exists p' \text{ send}(p')]$

Comment: There cannot be output any packets before d time units have elapsed after the receipt of the <u>first</u> packet from the synchronous input.

Remarks: 1.   Axioms 8.1 through 8.6 guarantee that the communication is perfect because receiving from the synchronous input and the corresponding sending occur at regular intervals with period c.

           2.   Nothing is expressed in these axioms about the handling of packets received from the asynchronous input: it is only mentioned in axiom 8.4 that a packet from the asynchronous input may be output instead of an empty packet from the synchronous input; but whether the packets from the asynchronous input are buffered or not etc. is deliberately left unspecified as there is nothing said about this in the informal specification.

7.   Comparison with other Methods

Some methods in these proceedings do not tackle the specification of liveness properties, although these are explicitly stated as to be specified. Other methods do not tackle the problem of time, and duration of time, although again this is an essential part of some of the given specification problems. We regard both liveness and/or time duration to be essential to the problems whose specification is given in this contribution.

Concerning liveness the only related work concerns that of more standard temporal logics such as those of Lamport, Barringer and Kuiper, and possibly Pnueli.

To the casual reader it may seem that there exists a wide gap between the style of specification as e.g. suggested by L. Lamport [L] and our method. For us there is no such gap. Lamport introduces auxiliary state-components to simplify his temporal formulas at the expense of expanding this state. We pursue the other extreme: just by way of exercise, we would like to demonstrate how these specifications end up if one does not introduce auxiliary state-components, at the expense of complicating one's temporal formulas (cf. e.g. [S and M-S]). An excellent example of this occurs in the specifications of problem 1: in [L] a queue is introduced as auxiliary state-component while in this contribution the order preservation property is expressed in the logic itself. Also Lamport does not wish to use the next-state operator O because what is regarded as an atomic operation at an abstract level need not be implemented as an atomic operation at a more concrete level. Our only comment on this observation is that we agree with this obviously correct point of view, but do not wish to consider this as a reason to expel O from our formalism. The observation merely indicates that in distinguishing between levels of abstraction one also has to distinguish between the meaning of one's O operator, in other words: the meaning of the O operator depends on the level of one's abstraction, and should be related to the meaning of the O operator on lower levels of abstraction. Whether this necessarily leads to Lamport's formalism remains to be seen. Finally, our use of user actions and system actions and Lamport's interface state functions and internal state functions are obviously two sides of the same coin.

8. References

[KV de R] Koymans, R., Vytopil, J. and de Roever, W.P. "Real-time Programming and Asynchronous Message Passing", Proceedings of the Second Annual ACM Symposium on Principles of Distributed Computing, Montreal, Canada, August 1983.

[L] Lamport, L. "STL/SERC Problems", August 25, 1983, paper distributed at the Cambridge Workshop.

[S and M-S] Schwartz, R.L. and Melliar-Smith, P.M. "Temporal Logic Specification of Distributed Systems", report SRI International Computer Science Laboratory, 20 January 1981.

Problems from the
Workshop on the Analysis of Concurrent Systems

Leslie Lamport
SRI International

In my approach, as in all temporal logic specification methods, the specification is a set of temporal logic formulas that the system is required to satisfy. This assumes that there is an operational model of the system in which an execution consists of a sequence of atomic actions starting from some initial state, where each action produces a new (possibly the same) state. The system is correct if the temporal logic formulas that comprise the specification are true for every possible execution.

I use a temporal logic in which there is no "nexttime" operator. If a formula is true on an execution, then it is true of the execution obtained by adding "stuttering" actions that don't change the state. This means that a specification does not specify the grain of atomicity of the implementation. For example, the following specification can be satisfied just as well by an implementation in which an atomic actions is the execution of a single microcode instruction on a computer as in one in which adding or deleting a message to/from a queue is an atomic action. (Of course, verifying that the implementation meets the specification will be harder for in former case than in the latter.) This is discussed in my IFIP paper *What Good Is Temporal Logic?*

In my method, one specifies *state functions* (mappings from the system state to some set of values), the initial states of the state functions, and how these state functions change with time. To show that a particular implementation meets the specification, one must show the existence of the appropriate state functions which change as specified.

There are two kinds of state functions: *interface* state functions and *internal* state functions. In showing that the specification is satisfied, the implementer is free to define the internal state functions as he wishes. However, the implementer and the user must agree in advance about how the interface state functions are to be defined. The interface state functions are implementation dependent. For example, if the user is to call the system as a machine-language subroutine, then the address of that subroutine must be specified as part of the interface state functions. (Saying that there exists an address which, when branched to, does the appropriate things won't help the user if he can't find out what the address is.)

The problem set says absolutely nothing about the interface in any of the problems. For example, does one present a message to the channel in Problem 1 by calling a Pascal subroutine or by setting voltage levels on some wires? This may seem like too low-level a concern, but imagine asking someone to build a channel with which two processes in Concurrent Pascal can communicate and receiving a box with a bunch of wires sticking out. In most specifications, there is no indication of whether one is specifying a Pascal program or a piece of hardware. If the specification doesn't even tell us this, how can it hope to help us avoid subtle misunderstandings in the interface? I suspect that in practice, a misunderstanding in these "low-level" concerns is likely to be a lot more disastrous than the failure to correctly implement some subtle aspect of the protocol.

My method permits one to specify the interface in exactly the same manner as he specifies the internal part, enabling one to state whether the implementation is supposed to be a Pascal subroutine or a box with a bunch of wires. More precisely, it can be used to specify the interface in terms of a commonly understood underlying semantics, such as assertions about Pascal programs or about voltage levels. However, since the problem set doesn't mention the interface, I will ignore it in my specifications.

As I said above, to specify a system, one must specify the state functions, their initial values, and how they change. Formal specification of the state functions is essentially the problem of formally specifying data types, and is not my concern. I will just use informal notations to do this. Specification of the initial values is simply a matter of writing assertions that they must satisfy. My concern is the specification of how the state functions change. This is done in terms of *transition axioms*, where a transition is simply an atomic action in which some state function changes. All possible transitions are described in terms of axioms. Safety properties are specified by restricting when the transitions can take place and what they may do, and liveness properties are specified by stating under what conditions a transition must eventually take place.

This is all done by giving names to every possible transition (the names are parameterized by, for example, process identifiers), stating what transitions may change each state function (any other transitions must not change the state function), and giving an axiom for each transition. The transition axioms are given in the following three parts, where the transition takes the system from an "old" to a "new" state.

- An *enabling condition*, stating a condition that must hold in the old state when the transition occurs.
- An *action*, which is an assertion describing relations that must hold between the values of state functions in the old state (denoted by the subscript *old*) and the values of state functions in the new state (denoted by the subscript *new*) of the transition.
- A *liveness* axiom. A liveness axiom is usually of the form "*condition⤳ action*" which means that at any time when *condition* holds, the *action* must take place at some time in the future. (In general, *condition* can be an arbitrary temporal logic assertion.)

This splitting of the transition axioms into three parts is really syntactic sugar. The enabling condition could be made part of the action by simply subscripting every state function in it by *old*. The action axiom can be translated into an ordinary temporal logic assertion, but the resulting assertion would be quite hard to understand.

Transitions can be divided into *interface* and *internal* transitions. The interface transitions are the ones that change interface state functions, so they are externally visible to the user; the internal transitions change only internal state functions, so they are not directly visible. Since I am omitting the interface state functions, it is not clear from looking at the transitions which are interface transitions and which are internal. I will therefore indicate which are which.

The two specifications that follow were done quickly—I spent about about three hours reading the problems and figuring out how to write the specifications, and another five hours typesetting them—and they haven't been checked, so they undoubtedly contain errors. My intent is to illustrate the method, not to convince you of its infallability.

At the end of this document are the pure specifications, devoid of all comments. (They take three pages.)

[*In the following specifications, material formatted like this is explanatory, and is not part of the formal specification.*]

1. Problem 1

Note: I assume a theory of queues (finite sequences of elements), with the operators *head, tail* and *last* having the obvious meanings, with * denoting concatenation.

1.1. Clarification

The following assumptions have been made about things that were not clearly determined by the informal specification.

1. Delivery of a message is effected solely by the channel, with no need for any action by the user.

2. There is unbounded buffering of messages.

3. A disconnect message "arrives" only after preceding messages have been delivered.

In 1.7, I indicate how the specification would change if different assumptions were made.

1.2. Transitions

All of the following are interface transitions (transitions that are "visible" to the user).

We assume a set M of messages. For any element $e \in \{a, b\}$ we let $\neg e$ denote the other element.

$acc_e(m)$: $e \in \{a, b\}$, $m \in M$. [*Endpoint e accepts message m. Note that there is a set of "accept" transitions—one for each e, m pair.*]

$del_e(m)$: $e \in \{a, b\}$, $m \in M$. [*Endpoint e delivers message m.*]

1.3. State Functions

We use the notation that a formula like $f(x, \cdot)$ is an abbreviation for "$f(x, y)$ for any y", and likewise for similar uses of ".".

state: A mapping from $\{a, b\}$ to $\{connected, disconnected\}$. Changed by $acc.(disconnect)$. [*state(e) indicates the state of endpoint e.*]

$e \to \neg e$: $(e \in \{a, b\})$ A queue of messages. Changed by $acc_e(\cdot)$, $del_e(\cdot)$ and $acc_{\neg e}(disconnect)$. [*Indicates the messages in transit from e to $\neg e$.*]

1.4. Initial Conditions

$\forall e \in \{a, b\} : state(e) = connected$

$\forall e \in \{a, b\} : e \to \neg e = \emptyset$

1.5. Invariants

The following assertions are always true—i.e., are true for all states in any execution. This can easily be proved by showing that they are true of the initial state and that they are left true by every transition. Thus, they are not part of the specification. They are included here to help you understand the specification.

$\forall e \in \{a, b\} : state(e) = disconnected \supset \neg e \to e = \emptyset$

$disconnected \in e \to \neg e \supset$
$\quad (state(e) = disconnected \wedge disconnected = last(e \to \neg e))$

[*If there is a disconnected message in a queue, then it is the last message in the queue and the sender is disconnected.*]

1.6. Transition Axioms

$acc_e(m)$, $m \neq disconnect$

$\quad$ *Enabling Condition:* $state(e) = connected$

$\quad$ [*This transition can occur only when e is in the connected state.*]

$\quad$ *Action:* $state(\neg e)_{old} = connected \supset e \to \neg e_{new} = e \to \neg e_{old} * m$
$\quad\quad \wedge \ state(\neg e)_{old} = disconnected \supset e \to \neg e_{new} = e \to \neg e_{old}$

$\quad$ [*This transition puts m onto the message queue, unless $\neg e$ has already disconnected, in which case it does nothing.*]

$\quad$ *Liveness:* — [*No liveness axiom, because the user need never try to send a message.*]

$acc_e(disconnected)$

Enabling Condition: $state(e) = connected$

Action: $state(e)_{new} = disconnected \wedge \neg e \rightarrow e_{new} = \emptyset$

Liveness: —

$del_e(m)$

Enabling Condition: $head(\neg e \rightarrow e) = m$

[*A message can be delivered only if it's at the head of the queue.*]

Action: $\neg e \rightarrow e_{new} = tail(\neg e \rightarrow e_{old})$

[*The transition simply removes the message from the queue. In a complete specification, there would also be changes to interface state functions indicating how the message is actually delivered.*]

Liveness: $head(\neg e \rightarrow e) = m \rightsquigarrow del_e(m)$

[*The message at the head of the queue must eventually be delivered.*]

$del_e(disconnected)$

Enabling Condition: $\neg e \rightarrow e = \{disconnected\}$

Action: $\neg e \rightarrow e_{new} = \emptyset \wedge state(e)_{new} = disconnected$

Liveness: $\neg e \rightarrow e = \{disconnected\} \rightsquigarrow del_e(disconnected)$

1.7. Alternative Assumptions

Changing the assumptions stated in 1.1 would require the following changes.

1. If message delivery requires some action on the part of the user, then an additional enabling condition is needed for the $del_e(m)$ transitions.

2. Bounded buffering requires the extra enabling condition on the $acc_e(m)$ transitions that there is room in the buffer.

3. Allowing a *disconnected* to be processed before all messages have been delivered is handled most easily by changing the enabling condition of $del_e(disconnected)$ to be

$$disconnected \in \neg e \rightarrow e$$

This appears to require that an implementation keep all messages in the queue before the $del_e(disconnected)$ transition, forbidding an implementation in which messages get thrown away before the closing *disconnected* message is delivered. However, there is a mechanism in the formalism for allowing an implementation to "throw away" unnecessary information about the internal state functions.

2. Problem 2

2.1. Clarification

The following assumptions have been made about things that were not clearly determined by the informal specification.

1. Delivery of a message is effected solely by the channel, with no need for any action by the user.

2. There is unbounded buffering of messages.

3. The informal specification seems to imply that after delivering to s a CONind from t, the system cannot break the impending connection before s has replied with a CONres or a DISreq. This will be difficult to implement, and probably not what one wants to do. For example, it requires that the requester be hung up until s responds. However, this requirement is reflected in my formal spec.

In 2.7, I indicate how the specification would change if different assumptions were made.

It should also be noted that the informal specification is satisfied by an implementation that never makes any connections, but always responds to a CONreq(a, b) with a DISreq. My specification also allows this.

2.2. Transitions

We let M denote the set of all messages, D the set of all data items, S the set of all SAPs, and C the set $\{(s, t) : s, t \in S \text{ and } s \neq t\}$.

The following are all the transitions.

$acc_s(m)$: $s \in S,\ m \in M$. (Interface)
[*Endpoint s accepts message m.*]

$del_s(m)$: $s \in S,\ m \in M$. (Interface)
[*Endpoint s delivers message m.*]

$refuse(s, t)$: $(s, t) \in C$. (Internal)
[*The action in which a CONreq(s, t) request is refused by the system. This refusal is eventually indicated by a del_s(DISind) action "at SAP s".*]

release(s, t): (s, t) $\in C$. (Internal)

> [*The action in which the system spontaneously breaks the connection between s and t. Both ends of the connection are eventually notified of the break by* DISind *messages.*]

2.3. State Functions

state: A mapping that takes an element from $s \in S$ to one of the following possible states, where ($t \in S - \{s\}$):

> *free*   [*The SAP is free.*]
>
> *connected*(t) [*The SAP is connected to t.*]
>
> *requesting*(t) [*The SAP has issued a connection request to t for a connection.*]
>
> *requested*(t) [*The SAP has delivered a request for a connection from t.*]

> *state*(s) is changed by acc_s(CONreq($s, \cdot$)), acc_s(CONres), acc_s(DISreq), del_s(CONind(t, s)), del_s(CONcon), del_s(DISind).

$s \rightarrow t$: ((s, t) $\in C$) A queue of messages. Changed by $acc_s(\cdot)$, $del_t(\cdot)$, acc_t(DISreq), *release*($s, \cdot$), *release*($\cdot, s$), *refuse*($s, \cdot$).

> [*Indicates the messages in transit from s to t.*]

2.4. Initial Conditions

$\forall s \in S : state(s) = free$

$\forall(s, t) \in C : s \rightarrow t = \emptyset$

2.5. Invariants

The following assertions are always true—i.e., are true for all states in any execution. This can be proved by showing that they are true of the initial state and that they are left true by every transition. Thus, they are not part of the specification. They are included here to help you understand the specification.

I use the notation that α^* denotes any finite number (including 0) of repetitions of the sequence α, and $\alpha^{0,1}$ denotes a sequence consisting of zero or one instance of α.

$\forall (s,t) \in C : state(s) = free \supset t \rightarrow s = \text{CONreq}(t,s)^{0,1}$

[*If s is free, then the only message that could be in the queue of messages from t is a* CONreq(t,s) *message.*]

$\forall (s,t) \in C : state(s) = connected(t) \supset t \rightarrow s = \text{DATreq}(\cdot)^* * [\text{DISreq} * [\text{CONreq}(t,s)]^{0,1}]^{0,1}$

[*If s is connected to t, then the queue of messages from t consists of a sequence of data messages, possibly followed by a* DISreq *which may then be followed by a* CONreq.]

$\forall (s,t) \in C : state(s) = requested(t) \supset t \rightarrow s = \emptyset$

$\forall (s,t) \in C : state(s) = requesting(t) \supset t \rightarrow s = \emptyset \text{ or } \text{DISreqCONreq}(t,s)^{0,1}$
$\qquad$ or $\text{CONcon} * \text{DATreq}(\cdot)^* * [\text{DISreq} * [\text{CONreq}(t,s)]^{0,1}]^{0,1}$

[*The second possibility results from the connection being refused–either by an explicit refusal or by the internal refuse(s,t) transition. In the third case, t sent a* CONcon, *initiating its end of the connection, then followed it by a sequence of messages it can ordinarily send to s when the connection has been established.*]

2.6. Transition Axioms

In the following transition axioms, an unquantified variable is assumed to be existentially quantified over all parts of the specification. For example, the t appearing in the axioms for the $acc_s(\text{CONres})$ transition denotes some SAP t, which is the same t in both the enabling condition and the action. (This is just some syntactic sugar.)

$acc_s(\text{CONreq}(s,t))$

$\quad$ *Enabling Condition:* $state(s) = free$

$\quad$ *Action:* $state(s)_{new} = requesting(t) \wedge s \rightarrow t_{new} = s \rightarrow t_{old} * \text{CONreq}(s,t)$

$\quad$ *Liveness:* —

$acc_s(\text{CONres})$

$\quad$ *Enabling Condition:* $state(s) = requested(t)$

$\quad$ *Action:* $state(s)_{new} = connected(t) \wedge s \rightarrow t_{new} = s \rightarrow t_{old} * \text{CONres}$

Liveness: —

$acc_s(\text{DISreq})$

Enabling Condition: $state(s) = connected(t)\,\text{or}\,requested(t)$

Action: $state(s)_{new} = free\,\wedge$
    $s \to t_{new} = \textbf{if}\,\text{DISreq} \in s \to t_{old}\,\textbf{then}\,s \to t_{old}\,\textbf{else}\,s \to t_{old} * \text{CONres}\,\wedge$
    $t \to s_{new} = \textbf{if}\,\text{CONreq}(t, s) \in t \to s_{old}\,\textbf{then}\,\text{CONreq}(t, s)\,\textbf{else}\,\emptyset$

[*Note that the DISreq is put into $s \to t$ only if a DISreq hasn't already been put there by a release(s, t) transition; and all messages in $t \to s$ are deleted except for a CONreq which can be there if t had also issued a DISreq and then issued a subsequent CONreq.*]

Liveness: —

$acc_s(\text{DATreq}(m))$

Enabling Condition: $state(s) = connected(t)$

Action: $s \to t_{new} = s \to t_{old} * \text{DATreq}(m)$

Liveness: —

$del_s(\text{CONind}(t, s))$

Enabling Condition: $state(s) = free\,\wedge\,head(t \to s) = \text{CONreq}(t, s)$

Action: $state(s)_{new} = requested(t)\,\wedge\,t \to s_{new} = tail(t \to s_{old})$

Liveness: $\Box\,enabling\,condition \rightsquigarrow del_s(\text{CONind}(t, s))$

[*Literally, this says that if the enabling condition holds forever, then the transition must take place. This way of reading the formula tends to be confusing, since the transition makes the enabling condition false, so the enabling condition can't hold forever. It is therefore better to read this condition as: "If the enabling condition is true, then it must eventually become false or else the transition must eventually occur." This together with the action axiom implies that the enabling condition cannot hold forever.*]

$del_s(\text{CONcon})$

Enabling Condition: $head(t \to s) = \text{CONres}$

[It follows from the invariants that state(s) must be requesting(t).]

Action: $state(s)_{new} = connected(t) \wedge t \rightarrow s_{new} = tail(t \rightarrow s_{old})$

Liveness: $\Box$ *enabling condition* $\rightsquigarrow del_s(\text{CONcon})$

$del_s(\text{DISind})$

Enabling Condition: $(t \rightarrow s) = \alpha * \text{DISreq} * \beta$

[The enabling condition is that there is a DISreq in the queue, since this message can "jump over" data messages.]

Action: $state(s)_{new} = free \wedge t \rightarrow s_{new} = \beta$

[This is the same β as in the enabling condition. The invariants imply that β must be either $\emptyset$ or consist of a single CONreq message.]

Liveness: $\Box$ *enabling condition* $\rightsquigarrow del_s(\text{DISind})$

$del_s(\text{DATind}(m))$

Enabling Condition: $head(t \rightarrow s) = \text{DATreq}(m)$

Action: $t \rightarrow s_{new} = tail(t \rightarrow s_{old})$

Liveness: $\Box$ *enabling condition* $\rightsquigarrow del_s(\text{DATind}(m))$

$release(s, t)$

Enabling Condition: $state(s) = connected(t) \wedge$
$\quad state(t) = connected(s) \text{ or } requesting(t)$

[See item 3 of 2.1.]

Action: $s \rightarrow t_{new} = s \rightarrow t_{old} * \text{DISreq} \wedge t \rightarrow s_{new} = t \rightarrow s_{old} * \text{DISreq}$

Liveness: —

$refuse(s, t)$

Enabling Condition: $last(s \rightarrow t) = \text{CONreq}(s, t)$

[The invariants imply that a CONreq must be the last element in the queue.]

Action: $s \rightarrow t_{new} = s \rightarrow t_{old} - \text{last element} \wedge t \rightarrow s_{new} = t \rightarrow s_{old} * \text{DISreq}$

Liveness: —

[*As I observed above, the liveness property of the del$_t$(CONind(s,t)) transition implies that the enabling condition cannot hold forever. Since these are the only transitions that can make the enabling condition false, it follows that if the enabling condition ever becomes true then one of these two transitions must occur.*]

2.7. Alternative Assumptions

Changing the assumptions stated in 2.1 would require the following changes.

1. If message delivery requires some action on the part of the user, then an additional enabling condition is needed for the $del_s(m)$ transitions.

2. Bounded buffering requires the extra enabling condition on the $acc_s(m)$ transitions that there is room in the buffer.

3. The current specification allows a connection to be broken spontaneously (the *release*(s,t) transition) only after at least one of the parties believes that it is connected–i.e., only after the CONres has been sent. To allow the connection to be broken between the time the CONind has been delivered and the time the CONres or DISreq is accepted adds a bit more complexity to the specification, since there are a few more cases to consider, but is not difficult.

PROBLEM 1

State Functions

$state$:   mapping $\{a, b\} \rightarrow \{connected, disconnected\}$.
Changed by $acc.(disconnect)$.

$e \rightarrow \neg e$: $(e \in \{a, b\})$ A queue of messages.
Changed by $acc_e(\cdot)$, $deL_{\neg e}(\cdot)$ and $acc_{\neg e}(disconnect)$.

Initial Conditions

$\forall e \in \{a, b\} : state(e) = connected$

$\forall e \in \{a, b\} : e \rightarrow \neg e = \emptyset$

Transition Axioms

$acc_e(m)$, $m \neq disconnect$

    Enabling Condition: $state(e) = connected$

    Action: $state(\neg e)_{old} = connected \supset e \rightarrow \neg e_{new} = e \rightarrow \neg e_{old} * m$
             $\wedge\ state(\neg e)_{old} = disconnected \supset e \rightarrow \neg e_{new} = e \rightarrow \neg e_{old}$

$acc_e(disconnected)$

    Enabling Condition: $state(e) = connected$

    Action: $state(e)_{new} = disconnected \wedge \neg e \rightarrow e_{new} = \emptyset$

$del_e(m)$

    Enabling Condition: $head(\neg e \rightarrow e) = m$

    Action: $\neg e \rightarrow e_{new} = tail(\neg e \rightarrow e_{old})$

    Liveness: $head(\neg e \rightarrow e) = m \rightsquigarrow del_e(m)$

$del_e(disconnected)$

    Enabling Condition: $\neg e \rightarrow e = \{disconnected\}$

    Action: $\neg e \rightarrow e_{new} = \emptyset \wedge state(e)_{new} = disconnected$

    Liveness: $\neg e \rightarrow e = \{disconnected\} \rightsquigarrow del_e(disconnected)$

Problem 2

State Functions

$state$: mapping $S \rightarrow \{free, connected(t), requesting(t), requested(t) : t \in S\}$
$state(s)$ changed by $acc_s(\text{CONreq}(s, \cdot))$, $acc_s(\text{CONres})$, $acc_s(\text{DISreq})$, $del_s(\text{CONind}(t, s))$, $del_s(\text{CONcon})$, $del_s(\text{DISind})$.

$s \rightarrow t$: $((s,t) \in C)$ Queue of messages. Changed by $acc_s(\cdot)$, $del_t(\cdot)$, $acc_t(\text{DISreq})$, $release(s, \cdot)$, $release(\cdot, s)$, $refuse(s, \cdot)$.

Initial Conditions

$\forall s \in S : state(s) = free$

$\forall (s,t) \in C : s \rightarrow t = \emptyset$

Transition Axioms

$acc_s(\text{CONreq}(s, t))$

Enabling Condition: $state(s) = free$

Action: $state(s)_{new} = requesting(t) \wedge s \rightarrow t_{new} = s \rightarrow t_{old} * \text{CONreq}(s, t)$

$acc_s(\text{CONres})$

Enabling Condition: $state(s) = requested(t)$

Action: $state(s)_{new} = connected(t) \wedge s \rightarrow t_{new} = s \rightarrow t_{old} * \text{CONres}$

$acc_s(\text{DISreq})$

Enabling Condition: $state(s) = connected(t)$ or $requested(t)$

Action: $state(s)_{new} = free \wedge$
$s \rightarrow t_{new} = $ **if** $\text{DISreq} \in s \rightarrow t_{old}$ **then** $s \rightarrow t_{old}$ **else** $s \rightarrow t_{old} * \text{CONres} \wedge$
$t \rightarrow s_{new} = $ **if** $\text{CONreq}(t, s) \in t \rightarrow s_{old}$ **then** $\text{CONreq}(t, s)$ **else** $\emptyset$

$acc_s(\text{DATreq}(m))$

Enabling Condition: $state(s) = connected(t)$

Action: $s \rightarrow t_{new} = s \rightarrow t_{old} * \text{DATreq}(m)$

$del_s(\text{CONind}(t, s))$

  Enabling Condition: $state(s) = free \wedge head(t \to s) = \text{CONreq}(t, s)$

  Action: $state(s)_{new} = requested(t) \wedge t \to s_{new} = tail(t \to s_{old})$

  Liveness: $\square$ *enabling condition* $\rightsquigarrow del_s(\text{CONind}(t, s))$

$del_s(\text{CONcon})$

  Enabling Condition: $head(t \to s) = \text{CONres}$

  Action: $state(s)_{new} = connected(t) \wedge t \to s_{new} = tail(t \to s_{old})$

  Liveness: $\square$ *enabling condition* $\rightsquigarrow del_s(\text{CONcon})$

$del_s(\text{DISind})$

  Enabling Condition: $(t \to s) = \alpha * \text{DISreq} * \beta$

  Action: $state(s)_{new} = free \wedge t \to s_{new} = \beta$

  Liveness: $\square$ *enabling condition* $\rightsquigarrow del_s(\text{DISind})$

$del_s(\text{DATind}(m))$

  Enabling Condition: $head(t \to s) = \text{DATreq}(m)$

  Action: $t \to s_{new} = tail(t \to s_{old})$

  Liveness: $\square$ *enabling condition* $\rightsquigarrow del_s(\text{DATind}(m))$

$release(s, t)$

  Enabling Condition: $state(s) = connected(t) \wedge$
    $state(t) = connected(s) \text{ or } requesting(t)$

  Action: $s \to t_{new} = s \to t_{old} * \text{DISreq} \wedge t \to s_{new} = t \to s_{old} * \text{DISreq}$

$refuse(s, t)$

  Enabling Condition: $last(s \to t) = \text{CONreq}(s, t)$

  Action: $s \to t_{new} = s \to t_{old} - \text{last element} \wedge t \to s_{new} = t \to s_{old} * \text{DISreq}$

Extension to Problem 1

When specifications are considered in isolation, comparing them becomes a matter of aesthetics. The real test of a specification method is how useful the specifications are. There are two ways in which a specification is used:

- To reason about another system that uses the specified system.
- To determine the correctness of an implementation of the specified system.

To judge how well specification methods perform these functions, I propose the following addition to Problem 1. (I chose this problem because it is the simplest of the three problems for which I could figure out what was to be specified.)

The extension of the problem is to prove the correctness of an implementation of the channel. The implementation is a concurrent program—or, more precisely, a collection of concurrent processes—that utilize lower-level message-passing operations. Process a sends a message msg to process b by executing the subroutine call send(b, msg). Process b can receive a message sent by process a by executing the subroutine call receive(a, m), where m must be a program variable. Upon return from this subroutine call, the variable m will have as its value some message that was sent by process a with a send(b, msg).

The send and receive subroutine calls have the following properties:

1. A call of receive returns a message that was sent by a corresponding call of send. (Hence, it cannot return if there is no such message.)

2. Each message sent can be received at most once—i.e., messages are not duplicated by the protocol.

3. Control will eventually return from a call to receive if there is a waiting message—i.e., one that was sent but not yet received.

4. If a message msg has been sent, then it will eventually be received if the receiving process issues enough calls of receive. In other words, no message will remain unreceived forever while an infinite stream of messages are received.

5. A call of *send* always returns.

(The first two properties are saftey properties, the rest are liveness properties.) Note that messages are *not* necessarily delivered in the order they are sent. The first part of the problem is to specify these message-passing operations.

In the implementation, messages are sent with sequence numbers. I assume a data type *numbered message*. A numbered message consists of an ordered pair with components *num*, which is a nonnegative integer and *msg*, which is a message of the type assumed for Problem 1.

To simplify the program, I assume a data type *numbered-message queue*, which is a set of numbered messages, together with the following operations, where Q is a numbered-message queue.

insert(msg, Q): Adds the numbered message msg to Q.

low(Q): A function that returns the smallest *num* component of all the messages in Q, or zero if Q is empty.

get(m, Q): Sets the variable m equal to the *msg* component of a lowest-numbered message in Q, and deletes that message from Q.

In the implementation, the endpoint a accepts a message msg when the subroutine call $accept_a(msg)$ is executed. I assume that the subroutine $accept_a$ cannot be called while it is being executed—i.e., that calls to $accept_a$ are sequential. Endpoint a delivers a message msg by executing the subroutine call $deliver_a(msg)$. I assume that the latter subroutine is given.

The implementation of endpoint a consists of the subroutine $accept_a$ plus a concurrently executed *delivery* process. The programs for the subroutine and process are given below. The implementation of endpoint b is the same, except for the interchange of "a" and "b". Atomic actions are enclosed by angle brackets.

global variables
  connected : **boolean** *initially* **true**

subroutine accept$_a$(msg)

variables
  msgno : **integer** *initially* 0

begin
  while not connected **do** ⟨ skip ⟩ **od**;
  ⟨ msgno := msgno + 1 ⟩;
  send(b, (msgno, msg));
  ⟨ **if** msg = "disconnect" **then** connected := **false** **fi** ⟩;
  ⟨ return ⟩
end

process *delivery$_a$*

variables
  nextnum : **integer**   *initially* 1
  m :   **numbered message**
  v :   **message**
  Q :   **numbered-message queue** *initially* ∅

begin
  while ⟨ connected = **true** ⟩
    do while ⟨ *low*(Q) ≠ nextnum ⟩
        do *receive*(v, Q);
            ⟨ *insert*(v, Q) ⟩
        od;
      ⟨ **if** connected **then** deliver$_a$(v) **fi** ⟩;
      ⟨ **if** v = "disconnect" **then** connected := **false** **fi** ⟩;
      ⟨ nextnum := nextnum + 1 ⟩
    od

A SIMPLE RAILWAY SYSTEM

P.E.Lauer

Computing Laboratory
University of Newcastle upon Tyne

1   INTRODUCTION

In this paper we will use the COSY formalism to give a behavioural specification
of a simple railway system, consisting of a layout of sections on which an arbitrary
number of trains may run asynchronously. Such a system has been implemented in terms
of a model train set at the University of Newcastle upon Tyne, Computing Laboratory,
and a number of memos dealing with problems arising in the system have been written
in the past years (cf. [MR78],[S79],[R78],[JL82],[D82]). In the present paper we
will only deal with the railway system and the simple problem stated in the problem
set for the Cambridge workshop.

2   THE COSY FORMALISM

The following remarks are important for an understanding of the role of the COSY
formalism for specifying and analyzing concurrent and distributed systems.

1. Specification : Our method of "specification" is proposed as an additional and
    complementary method to the method of logical specification by, for example,
    Hoare Logic or Temporal Logic. We specify behaviours of concurrent and
    distributed systems in a purely language theoretical way, that is, no programming
    language constructs are used, such as channels and communication primitives in
    CSP, or shared data and semaphores in ALGOL68.

2. Analysis : General Properties of Systems : Freedom from Deadlock : Adequacy. Our
    formalism is intended to facilitate the derivation of dynamic global properties
    of systems, such as, absence of deadlock and starvation, from static or
    structural properties of the specification, where possible and as far as
    possible. Such properties may be expressed and demonstrated in terms of
    uninterpreted specifications.

3. Vindication : Does my specification say what I want to say ? To vindicate a COSY
    specification one will need to use interpretations of behaviours of the model in
    terms of the domain to be modelled.

4. Computer   Based Analysis Environment The formalism turns out to be surprisingly

comfortable for non-mathematicians to use. The formalism has recently been implemented in a computer based development system called BCS [L83]. This environment has been used by a number of students and colleagues to specify and analyze various concurrent system strategies.

The COSY formalism consists of a notation and its corresponding formal semantics. A basic COSY (concurrent system) specification may be thought of as a "vector" of cyclic regular expressions (grammars). To each regular expression there corresponds a regular language which it generates (its sequential behaviour or, as we shall say, its set of firing sequences, FS). To the vector of regular expressions there corresponds a vector of regular languages (concurrent and synchronised behaviours or, its set of vector firing sequences, VFS) which are related as follows :

If the alphabets (as we shall say, sets of operations, Ops) of two or more component regular expressions share a letter, this is interpreted to mean that the regular expressions involved must synchronise (hand shake) every time that letter is appended to any string belonging to their respective languages. This ensures that in any synchronised concurrent behaviour (vector of languages) all component languages will agree on the number and order of letters which their alphabets share.

If, however, two letters occur in no alphabet of any single component regular expression, that is, if they are not sequentialised, then they may be concurrently appended to any strings belonging to the languages of the regular expressions which involve that letter.

A macro COSY specification consists of a vector of regular expression schemata which represent corresponding expanded basic COSY specifications in a short and perspicuous manner. This feature is required by the notation to specify concurrent systems of arbitrary size, since regular expressions can only be used to specify systems of some definite and fixed size.

The figure below indicates what has been said schematically, and additionally shows that there exits an equivalent standard semantics for COSY in terms of labelled condition event (Petri) nets (cf.[B79], [B82], [LBS77], [LC75], [LSB79a]).

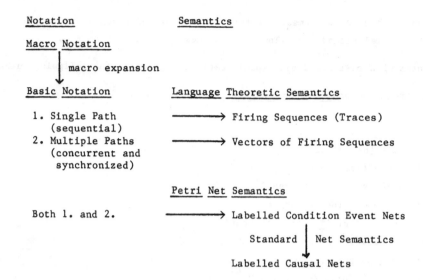

Notation	Semantics

Macro Notation

  ↓ macro expansion

Basic Notation   Language Theoretic Semantics

1. Single Path   ——→ Firing Sequences (Traces)
   (sequential)
2. Multiple Paths   ——→ Vectors of Firing Sequences
   (concurrent and
   synchronized)

                    Petri Net Semantics

Both 1. and 2.   ——→ Labelled Condition Event Nets

                    Standard ⏐ Net Semantics
                            ↓
                Labelled Causal Nets

To make the above discussion more precise we will introduce some formal definitions and illustrate them by means of simple examples.

2.1 THE SYNTAX OF THE BASIC COSY PATH NOTATION

A basic COSY path specification is a string derived from the production rules given below. The following meta-language conventions have been used in the syntax rules: The symbols "=", "[", "]", "/", "*", "+", "@" are used as meta-symbols. The symbol "=" denotes replacement of its left hand side by the string on its right hand side. The braces "[ ]" are used to group items together, "/" indicates alternate productions, "[item]*" indicates production of "item" zero or more times, "[item]+" production of "item" one or more times. The notation

   [item1 @ item2]+

is used as a shorthand for

   item1 [item2 item1]*

In the syntax rules for basic COSY specifications "item2" may be one of the terminal symbols ";" and ",". Non-underlined lower case words, except single lower case letters and digits, are non-terminal symbols, and all other symbols like ";", ",", "(", ")", "*", underlined lower case words and single lower case letters and digits and a number of special characters and other graphic characters are terminal symbols. We shall additionally use the following convention: in right parts of production rules the concatenation of terminals and non-terminals has precedence over alternation. Thus A B/C means either A B or C. When necessary we use "[ ]" to override the normal precedence. Thus A [B/C] means either A B or A C.

The syntax of a basic COSY path specification is given by the following rules:

BN1. basicprogram = program body endprogram

BN2. body = [path]+

BN3. path = path sequence end

BN5. sequence = [orelement @;]+

BN6. orelement = [starelement @,]+

BN7. starelement = element/element*

BN8. element = operation/(sequence)

BN9. operation = [digit]* letter [letter/digit]*

BN10. digit = 0/.../9

BN11. letter = alphabetic/other

BN12. alphabetic = a/b/.../z/A/B/.../Z

BN13. special = (/)/;/,/*/{/}

BN14. other = any graphic character except specials

Comments can be inserted anywhere where blanks can be inserted above the level of operations. They are enclosed in opening parentheses "{" and closing parentheses "}".

A simple example of a basic COSY path program is :

program{ Example1 }

    {P1}path a;b;a end
    {P2}path a,c;d end

endprogram

2.2 VECTOR FIRING SEQUENCE SEMANTICS FOR BASIC COSY PATHS

In the regular expressions produced by the non-terminal "sequence" the symbols ";" and "," denote sequentialization and arbitrary choice respectively; the symbol "*" is the Kleene star, which denotes zero or more repetitions.

All the regular expressions in paths are considered to be cyclic in the sense that constituent operations may be executed repeatedly subject to the constraints of sequentialization and arbitrary choice. For this reason the outermost star and parentheses are always omitted, their presence being implicit. The semantics of single basic path P are given in terms of its set of firing sequences denoted by FS(P). The infinite set FS(P) is constructed from a set consisting of the cycles of P by the function "Cyc". The function "Cyc" applies to syntactic components of basic paths, that is to substrings produced by non-terminals. Syntactic components of paths are denoted by syntactic variables. A path P is represented by path SEQ end where SEQ denotes a sequence, which is represented by OREL1;...;ORELn where ORELi for i=1,...,n denote orelements. An orelement is represented by STAREL1,...,STARELn where STARELi for i=1,...,n denote starelements. A starelement is represented by ELEM* or ELEM where ELEM denotes an element which is represented by (SEQ) when it is produced by the second option of the syntax rule for element BN8, or by OP when produced by the first option.

2.2.1 The cycles of single paths

"Operation" denotes the set of all operations which may be generated from the non-terminal "operation" by productions BN9-BN12 and BN14.

"Terminal" denotes the set of terminal symbols consisting of program,endprogram,path,end, digits,alphabetics,specials and others.

"Expression" denotes the set of all strings of terminal symbols which can be obtained by applying appropriate productions to any of the non-terminals "path","sequence","orelement","starelement","element", and "operation".

Given E∈Expression,Ops(E) denotes the set of operations occurring in expression E,that is:

Ops:Expression ---> P(Operation)

where "P(Operation)" denotes the power set (set of all subsets) of the set Operations.It is defined by:

Ops(E)=cases E:

1. path SEQ end   → Ops(SEQ)
2. OREL1;...;ORELn   → Ops(OREL1) U...U Ops(ORELn)
3. STAREL1,...,STARELn   → Ops(STAREL1) U...U Ops(STARELn)
4. ELEM*   → Ops(ELEM)
5. (SEQ)   → Ops(SEQ)
6. OP   → {OP}

If we consider the two paths of Example 1 we obtain :

Ops(P1) = {a,b}
Ops(P2) = {a,c,d}

Given a single path P, "Exp(P)" denotes the set of expressions,terminal strings,which may be generated from Ops(P), that is Exp(P) c Expression.

Given a single path P and E∈Exp(P), "Cyc(P)" denotes the set of cycles of P. It can be characterized by:

Cyc:Exp(P) ---> $\underline{P}$(Ops(P)*-{e})

where "e" denotes the empty string, and Cyc is defined as follows:

Cyc(E)=<u>cases</u> E:

1. <u>path</u> SEQ <u>end</u>   → Cyc(SEQ)
2. OREL1;...;ORELn   → Cyc(OREL1) ..... Cyc(ORELn)
3. STAREL1,...,STARELn   → Cyc(STAREL1) U...U Cyc(STARELn)
4. ELEM*   → Cyc(ELEM)*
5. (SEQ)   → Cyc(SEQ)
6. OP   → {OP}

In the above definition of "Cyc" the symbol "U" denotes the set-union operator and the symbol "." the concatenation of sets of strings operator. The operation

   X.Y

where X,Y are sets of strings is defined as:

   X.Y={x.y|x ∈ X,y ∈ Y}

where "." denotes string concatenation and " ∈ " element of a set.

In the definition of "Cyc" a starred set X* indicates the set obtained by concatenation of zero or more times of elements of the set X. Formally X* is defined by

   X*=X0 U X1 U X2 U ...

where X is a set of strings and Xi is defined recursively by

   Xi = X(i-1) . X
   X0 = {e}

For the two paths of Example 1 we obtain :

   Cyc(P1) = {a.b.a}
   Cyc(P2) = {a.d,c.d}

2.2.2 The firing sequences of single paths

From the set Cyc(P) we construct the set of firing sequences of P denoted by FS(P) as follows:

FS(P)=Pref(Cyc(P)*)

where Pref(X) is defined as

Pref(X)={x|x.y $\in$ X, for some y}

where X is a set of strings.

The set FS(P) is the set of sequences of operation executions permitted by the path P.

For the two paths of our example we obtain :

FS(P1)=Pref({a.b.a}*)={a.b.a}*.Pref({a.b.a})={a.b.a}*.{e,a,a.b}
FS(P2)=Pref({a.d,c.d}*)={a.d,c.d}*Pref({a.d,c.d})={a.d,c.d}*.{e,a,c}

2.2.3 Vectors of strings

As already mentioned, to model the non-sequential behaviour of a basic path specification R consisting of paths P1,...,Pn partial orders of occurrences of operations will be constructed which are represented by vectors of strings. An n-vector $\underline{x}$

$\underline{x}$=(x1,...,xn)

is a possible behaviour of R if each xi for $1 \leq i \leq n$ is a possible firing sequence of Pi for i=1,...,n and furthermore, if the xi's agree on the number and the order of occurrences of operations they share.

To formally define the set of possible behaviours or histories of R, vectors of strings are introduced together with a composition operation on them. Let S1,...,Sn be a family of sets of strings and let

$$\mathop{X}_{i=1}^{n} Si*=S1* X...X Sn*=\{ (s1,...,sn)|\text{for all } i, si \in Si*\}$$

where "X" denotes the cross product operator. If the vectors $\underline{x}$ and $\underline{y}$ belong to the above set then their composition $\underline{x}.\underline{y}$ is defined as

$\underline{x}.\underline{y}$=(x1,...,xn).(y1,...,yn)=(x1.y1,...,xn.yn)

where "." denotes the vector concatenation operation.

2.2.4   The vector operations

To each specification R consisting exclusively of paths

R=P1...Pn

we associate its <u>set of operations</u> Ops(R) defined by

Ops(R)=Ops(P1)U...U Ops(Pn)

and its <u>set of vector operations</u> Vops(R) defined as follows: For each operation "a" in R we construct an n-vector $\underline{a}$. The i'th component of this vector for $1 \leq i \leq n$ denoted by $[\underline{a}]i$ is given by

$[\underline{a}]i=|$ a if a$\in$Ops(Pi)
$\quad\quad|$ e otherwise

The set of vector operations of R, Vops(R) is then defined as

Vops(R)={$\underline{a}$|a $\in$ Ops(R)}

Let us define Vops(R)* to be the submonoid of

$\overset{n}{\underset{i=1}{X}}$ Ops(Pi)*

by Vops(R) and $\underline{e}$=(e,...,e) under the vector composition operation.

For Example 1 = P1P2 we obtain :

Ops(Example 1) = Ops(P1) U Ops(P2) = {a,b} U {a,c,d} = {a,b,c,d}

and

Vops(Example 1) = {$\underline{h}$| h$\in$Ops(Example 1) &
$\quad\quad\quad\quad\quad\quad$($\forall$ 2$\geq$i$\geq$1:(h$\in$Ops(Pi) --> $[\underline{h}]i$ = h) &
$\quad\quad\quad\quad\quad\quad$(h$\notin$Ops(Pi) --> $[\underline{h}]i$ = e))}

$\quad\quad\quad\quad\quad\quad\quad$= {(a,a),(b,e),(e,c),(e,d)}

2.2.5   The vector firing sequences or congreable behaviours

The set of all possible behaviours or histories of R, the <u>vector firing sequence</u> of R, denoted by VFS(R) is defined by:

VFS(R)=($\overset{n}{\underset{i=1}{X}}$ FS(Pi)) $\cap$ Vops(R)*

The set

$$\overset{n}{\underset{i=1}{X}} FS(Pi)$$

in the definition of VFS(R) guarantees that each string component of a history $\underline{x} \in$ VFS(R) is a firing sequence of the corresponding path, i.e. it represents the individual and independent views of each sequential subsystem, and the set Vops(R)* guarantees that all these firing sequences agree on the number and order of activations of the operations they share, i.e. it represents the common view all synchonised subsystems must have of the system. VFS(R) of course represents these two types of view combined.

By the construction of VFS(R) each of its elements $\underline{x}$ represents everything that has happened in some possible period of activity of R. We may write $\underline{x}$ as a composition of vector operations $\underline{a1},...,\underline{am}$ of Vops(R) as in (V1)

(V1) $\underline{x} = \underline{a1}.....\underline{am}$

Consequently, for every $\underline{x} = (x1,...,xn) \in$ Vops(R)*, the symbol $[\underline{x}]i$ denotes the string xi, i.e. , $[\underline{x}]i = xi$, for $i = 1,...,n$.

For Example 1 we obtain :

VFS(Example 1) = (FS(P1)XFS(P2)) $\cap$ Vops(Example 1)*
            = (({a.b.a}*.{e,a,a.b})X({a.d,c.d}*.{e,a,c})) $\cap$
                 {(a,a),(b,e),(e,c),(e,d)}*
            = {(e,e),(e,c),(e,c.d),(a,a),(a.b,a),(a,a.d),(a.b,a.d),
                 (a.b,a.d.c),(a.b.a,a.d.a),(a.b.a.b,a.d.a), ... }

2.2.6   Independent operations and concurrency

If for some operations "ak" and "ar" for $1 \leq k, r \leq m$ and $k \neq r$, $[\underline{ak}]i \neq e$ implies $[\underline{ar}]i = e$ for $i = 1,...,n$ then the composition $\underline{ak}.\underline{ar}$ is the same as $\underline{ar}.\underline{ak}$. Such operations are said to be **independent** and we write **ind(ak,ar)**. If furthermore $r = k+1$ that is $\underline{ak}$ and $\underline{ar}$ are neighbouring vectors in (V1), as in (V2)

(V2) $\underline{x} = \underline{a1}....\underline{ak}.\underline{ar}....\underline{am}$

then $\underline{x}$ may also be written as (V3)

(V3) $\underline{x} = \underline{a1}.....\underline{ar}.\underline{ak}.....\underline{am}$

The **commutativity** of vector operations in a vector firing sequence is interpreted to mean that the operations corresponding to these vector operations may execute concurrently. We say that two operations "a" and "b" are <u>concurrent</u> at a history <u>x</u> and we write

   a <u>co</u> b <u>at</u> <u>x</u>

if <u>ind</u>(a,b) and <u>x.a</u> , <u>x.b</u> $\in$ VFS(R). This definition implies that only independent operations may execute concurrently. However, independent operations may not always execute concurrently or may never execute concurrently at all.

   For Example 1 we obtain, for example :

<u>b</u> <u>co</u> <u>d</u> <u>at</u> <u>a</u> since <u>ind</u>(b,d) & <u>a.b</u>$\in$VFS(Example 1) & <u>a.d</u>$\in$VFS(Example 1)

2.2.7 Dynamic properties of COSY systems

   As we have mentioned, a basic COSY specification describes a system by specifying partial orders on the execution of its operations and therefore, the only properties of interest are behavioural in nature.

   The formal model of behaviour, the vector firing sequences of path-specifications permit us to speak formally of dynamic properties of a system specified by a path-specification R. All properties of R may be expressed in terms of its corresponding vector firing sequences VFS(R). Such properties fall into two classes, the <u>general</u> and the <u>specific</u> properties.

   The <u>general</u> <u>properties</u> are those which apply to any specification, properties such as absence of deadlock or starvation, which may be defined in terms of uninterpreted operations. We say that a path-specification R is <u>deadlock-free</u> if and only if

   $\forall$<u>x</u> $\in$ VFS(R) $\exists$a $\in$ Ops(R):<u>x.a</u> $\in$ VFS(R)

that is if and only if every history <u>x</u> may be continued. We say that a specification R is <u>adequate</u> if and only if

   $\forall$<u>x</u> $\in$ VFS(R) $\forall$a $\in$ Ops(R) $\exists$<u>y</u> $\in$ Vops(R)*: <u>x.y.a</u> $\in$ VFS(R)

that is, if and only if every history of R may be continued enabling eventually every operation in R. Adequacy is a property akin to absence of partial system deadlock(see also [B79 and B82]).

   The <u>specific</u> <u>properties</u> involve the interpretation of a COSY specification as a description of an actual system. The operations of a COSY specification are interpreted as actions of a system and the behaviour of the specification as the behaviour of the system.

   As far as specific properties of specifications are concerned, various specifications have been shown to satisfy some design requirements. The most involved of these is the parallel resource releasing mechanism [SL80a, SL80b and LS81b].

We will consider a system with a maximum number t of trains capable of running asynchronously on a simple layout. We will :

1. give an intuitive description of the system,

2. construct a COSY specification for it, and

3. characterize and analyze the behaviours of the specification and show how simple properties of the system are modelled.

2.3   TRANSLATION OF COSY TO LABELLED PETRI NETS

We will briefly explain the translation from basic COSY programs to labelled marked place/transition nets [Br80].

The current net semantics of basic COSY programs is obtained by translating each component sequential path into a labelled state machine represented as a net, i.e. representing transitions by boxes. For example, the paths :

{Pl}<u>path</u> a;b;a <u>end</u> {P2}<u>path</u> a,c;d <u>end</u>

would individually give rise to :

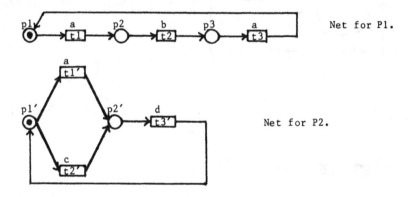

Net for Pl.

Net for P2.

Once the nets corresponding to the individual paths have been obtained, for example, two nets called Nl and N2, one applies a composition rule denoted by "⊕" to the two nets, written Nl⊕N2, constructed from Nl and N2 by the identification of transitions with the same label.

We may now give the construction of Nl⊕N2 from nets Nl and N2, and illustrate it with the two example paths above :

1. The set of places of N1⊕N2 is the set theoretic union of the sets of places of N1 and N2, with inherited markings.

2. Suppose t is a transition in either N1 or N2 such that no transition in the other net is labelled with the label of t, then N1⊕N2 contains a transition t, with the same label as t, whose input and output places are the same as those of t (recall 1).

3. Suppose t1 and t2 are transitions of N1 and N2, respectively, with the same label, then N1⊕N2 contains a transition (t1,t2) with the same label as t1 and t2 and whose set of input (respectively output) places is the union of the sets of input (respectively output) places of t1 and t2.

"⊕" may be shown to be <u>commutative</u> and <u>associative</u>. If P=P1...Pm and Ni is the marked labeled state machine associated with Pi, then the net associated with P is defined to be N1⊕...⊕Nm.

The result of applying these rules to our example paths P1 and P2 is then :

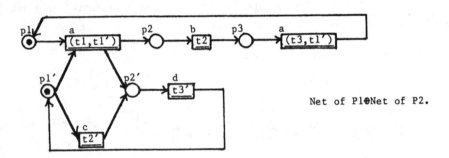

Net of P1⊕Net of P2.

3   THE RAILWAY

3.1   A DESCRIPTION OF THE RAILWAY

Problem

Produce a formal specification of a railway system as described below, and a design if you have one.

Description

A railway system is made from lengths of single track joined at

crossing points (a length of track may consist of one or more
sections). A train may leave a crossing point on any unoccupied
section of track connected to it. The system is to be run
so that no section of track can have more than one train on it
at any time. Any design should be independent of the number of
trains in the system.

Suggested layout is three crossing points with two lines of
track connecting each pair.

3.2   COSY SPECIFICATION OF THE RAILWAY

We develop a COSY specification for the railway system described above and in the
process we will need to sharpen the above description. The following conditions   may
be formulated :

1. At most one train may occupy any one section at any one time;

2. A train may leave a section which it occupies only if there exists some
   unoccupied section connected to it, and its departure from the section it leaves
   is coincident with its entrance into the section it moves to;

3. Any design should be independent of the number of trains in the system, which we
   interpret to mean that the solution will be parametrized relative to some
   arbitrary maximum number t of trains that may be in the system.

4. What has not been stated but seems to be an important property of the railway
   example is that when the system is run it does not lead to deadlock.

3.2.1   Towards a COSY specification of the railway system

We will use a slightly larger example of layout than the one suggested.   The
layout may be represented by an undirected graph, the nodes of which represent the
sections of track where trains reside, and the arcs of which indicate the possible
moves of trains from section to section :

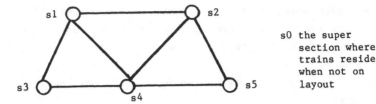

s0 the super
   section where
   trains reside
   when not on
   layout

Figure 1 : An example layout.

We treat the layout as consisting of a number n of <u>sections</u> together
with an additional section s0 which trains occupy when they have been taken off the
track. Then condition 1 above translates to the condition :

1'. No section, except s0, should contain more than one train at any one time.

We will represent the moves from section i to section j by writing the operation
name ss(i,j).   We assume the existence of a relation Adj on pairs (i,j) and write :
(i,j)∈Adj if it is true that si is adjacent to sj.   Note that (0,i),(i,0)∈Adj is
always true if i≠0.

Since at most one train may be in a section at a time, moves into and out of a
section must strictly alternate; we can express this in COSY by a path resembling a
single frame buffer (cf.[CL83], this volume) :

{si} <u>path</u> arrival(i);departure(i) <u>end</u>

for section si, i≠0.

If we denote the graph of a given layout by G=(S,Adj), where S is the set of nodes
(sections) and Adj the relation of adjacency, expressed in terms of the indices of
the sections, then for our example we obtain :

S = {s0,s1,s2,s3,s4,s5}

and

Adj = {(0,1),(0,2),(0,3),(0,4),(0,5),(1,0),(1,2),(1,3),(1,4),
       (2,0),(2,1),(2,4),(2,5),(3,0),(3,1),(3,4),
       (4,0),(4,1),(4,2),(4,3),(4,5),(5,0),(5,2),(5,4)}.

The operation arrival(i) may be read as "any of the possible moves into section si"
and hence we can consider the operation as consisting of an exclusive choice of any
of the possible moves into si written as an or-element :

arrival(i) = ss(0,i),ss(i1,i),...,ss(im,i)

where 0,i1,...,im are the indices of the sections adjacent to si.

Using the macro notation (cf.[CL83]) we can write this as :

```
    array #i,j:(i,j)∈Adj [ss(i,j) ss(j,i)]endarray
    operation arrival(i) = ,[ss( ,i)] endoperation
```

and similarly for departures :

```
    operation departure(i) = ,[ss(i, )] endoperation
```

Using these definitions we obtain the following path for the i-th section for an arbitrary layout :

```
    {P(si)}path ,[ss( ,i)] ; ,[ss(i, )] end
```

The COSY specification of a whole layout involving n sections may be obtained by concatenating the paths for appropriate n≥i≥1 using a macro replicator :

```
{Program(Adj,n):No trains}
program

        array #i,j:(i,j)∈Adj [ ss(i,j) ss(j,i) ]

        {P(S)} #i:1,n,1[{P(si)} path ,[ss( ,i)] ; ,[ss(i, )] end]

endprogram
```

The expansion of the macro program results, for our example layout, to :

```
    program {P(S)}
        {P(s1)}path ss(0,1),ss(2,1),ss(3,1),ss(4,1) ;
                    ss(1,0),ss(1,2),ss(1,3),ss(1,4) end
        {P(s2)}path ss(0,2),ss(1,2),ss(4,2),ss(5,2) ;
                    ss(2,0),ss(2,1),ss(2,4),ss(2,5) end
        {P(s3)}path ss(0,3),ss(1,3),ss(4,3) ;
                    ss(3,0),ss(3,1),ss(3,4) end
        {P(s4)}path ss(0,4),ss(1,4),ss(2,4),ss(3,4),ss(5,4) ;
                    ss(4,0),ss(4,1),ss(4,2),ss(4,3),ss(4,5) end
        {P(s5)}path ss(0,5),ss(2,5),ss(4,5) ;
                    ss(5,0),ss(5,2),ss(5,4) end

    endprogram
```

So far we have not represented trains in any way. One fact that follows from the stated requirements for the railway system is that the arrival of a train at a section must be followed by a departure of the same train from that section. We will express a move of a train k from section i to section j by the operation name tss(k,i,j) and we construct a new version of P(S) called P(t,S) :

program {Example with Trains}

   array #k:1,t,1[#i,j:(i,j)∈Adj [tss(k,i,j) tss(k,j,i)]]

{P(t,S): With trains}
  #i:1,n,1[{P(t,si)} path ,1[(,[tss(, ,i)];,[tss(,i,)])] end]

endprogram

The expansion of this macro path for our example is :

      program {P(3,S)}
      {P(3,sI)}
      path (tss(1,0,1),tss(1,2,1),tss(1,3,1),tss(1,4,1);
          tss(1,1,4),tss(1,1,3),tss(1,1,2),tss(1,1,0)),
        (tss(2,0,1),tss(2,2,1),tss(2,3,1),tss(2,4,1);
          tss(2,1,4),tss(2,1,3),tss(2,1,2),tss(2,1,0)),
        (tss(3,0,1),tss(3,2,1),tss(3,3,1),tss(3,4,1);
          tss(3,1,4),tss(3,1,3),tss(3,1,2),tss(3,1,0))
     end
     {P(3,s2)}
      path (tss(1,0,2),tss(1,1,2),tss(1,4,2),tss(1,5,2);
          tss(1,2,5),tss(1,2,4),tss(1,2,1),tss(1,2,0)),
        (tss(2,0,2),tss(2,1,2),tss(2,4,2),tss(2,5,2);
          tss(2,2,5),tss(2,2,4),tss(2,2,1),tss(2,2,0)),
        (tss(3,0,2),tss(3,1,2),tss(3,4,2),tss(3,5,2);
          tss(3,2,5),tss(3,2,4),tss(3,2,1),tss(3,2,0))
     end
     {P(3,s3)}
      path (tss(1,0,3),tss(1,1,3),tss(1,4,3);
          tss(1,3,4),tss(1,3,1),tss(1,3,0)),
        (tss(2,0,3),tss(2,1,3),tss(2,4,3);
          tss(2,3,4),tss(2,3,1),tss(2,3,0)),
        (tss(3,0,3),tss(3,1,3),tss(3,4,3);
          tss(3,3,4),tss(3,3,1),tss(3,3,0))
     end
     {P(3,s4)}
      path (tss(1,0,4),tss(1,1,4),tss(1,2,4),tss(1,3,4),tss(1,5,4);
          tss(1,4,0),tss(1,4,1),tss(1,4,2),tss(1,4,3),tss(1,4,5)),
        (tss(2,0,4),tss(2,1,4),tss(2,2,4),tss(2,3,4),tss(2,5,4);
          tss(2,4,0),tss(2,4,1),tss(2,4,2),tss(2,4,3),tss(2,4,5)),
        (tss(3,0,4),tss(3,1,4),tss(3,2,4),tss(3,3,4),tss(3,5,4);
          tss(3,4,0),tss(3,4,1),tss(3,4,2),tss(3,4,3),tss(3,4,5))
     end
     {P(3,s5)}
      path (tss(1,0,5),tss(1,2,5),tss(1,4,5);
          tss(1,5,0),tss(1,5,2),tss(1,5,4)),
        (tss(2,0,5),tss(2,2,5),tss(2,4,5);
          tss(2,5,0),tss(2,5,2),tss(2,5,4)),
        (tss(3,0,5),tss(3,2,5),tss(3,4,5);
          tss(3,5,0),tss(3,5,2),tss(3,5,4))
     end
     endprogram

From the above expansion it may be seen that the "1" associated with the outermost distributor in the macro path

    ,1[(,[tss(, ,i)]; ,[tss(,i,)])]

specifies that the comma distributes over the first dimensions of

    tss(, ,i) and tss(,i,)

If the dimension were not explicitly specified, then according to the default rule, the innermost comma would distribute over the leftmost available dimension and therefore the outermost comma would distribute over the second and respectively third dimensions of

    tss(, ,i) and tss(,i,)

One restriction which was not mentioned in the original description of the railway is that : the same train can not be placed on the layout before it has been previously removed . This restriction can be enforced by adding new paths of the form :

{All possible journeys of train k with uniqueness condition}
{P(k,G)}
path ,[tss(k,0,)] ; (,#i:i>0[,#j:j>0[tss(k,i,j)]])* ; ,[tss(k, ,0)] end

The full program for n sections, t trains and a layout described by an adjacency relation Adj has the form :

program {t Train, n Sections, Adj Layout : P(t,S,G) }

    array #k:1,t,1[#i,j:(i,j)∈Adj [tss(k,i,j) tss(k,j,i)]] endarray
    {P(t,S)}
    #i:1,n,1[{P(t,si)} path ,1[(,[tss(, ,i)];,[tss(,i,)])] end]
    {P(t,G)}
    #k:1,t,1[{P(k,G)} path ,[tss(k,0,)]
                        ; (,#i:i>0[,#j:j>0[tss(k,i,j)]])*
                        ; ,[tss(k, ,0)]
                end]

endprogram

The expansion of P(t,G) with 4 trains is :

```
{4 Train, 5 Sections, Adj Layout : P(4,G) }
{P(1,G)}
path tss(1,0,1),tss(1,0,2),tss(1,0,3),tss(1,0,4),tss(1,0,5);
     (tss(1,1,2),tss(1,1,3),tss(1,1,4),
      tss(1,2,1),tss(1,2,4),tss(1,2,5),
      tss(1,3,1),tss(1,3,4),
      tss(1,4,1),tss(1,4,2),tss(1,4,3),tss(1,4,5),
      tss(1,5,2),tss(1,5,4))*;
      tss(1,1,0),tss(1,2,0),tss(1,3,0),tss(1,4,0),tss(1,5,0) end
{P(2,G)}
path tss(2,0,1),tss(2,0,2),tss(2,0,3),tss(2,0,4),tss(2,0,5);
     (tss(2,1,2),tss(2,1,3),tss(2,1,4),
      tss(2,2,1),tss(2,2,4),tss(2,2,5),
      tss(2,3,1),tss(2,3,4),
      tss(2,4,1),tss(2,4,2),tss(2,4,3),tss(2,4,5),
      tss(2,5,2),tss(2,5,4))*;
      tss(2,1,0),tss(2,2,0),tss(2,3,0),tss(2,4,0),tss(2,5,0) end
{P(3,G)}
path tss(3,0,1),tss(3,0,2),tss(3,0,3),tss(3,0,4),tss(3,0,5);
     (tss(3,1,2),tss(3,1,3),tss(3,1,4),
      tss(3,2,1),tss(3,2,4),tss(3,2,5),
      tss(3,3,1),tss(3,3,4),
      tss(3,4,1),tss(3,4,2),tss(3,4,3),tss(3,4,5),
      tss(3,5,2),tss(3,5,4))*;
      tss(3,1,0),tss(3,2,0),tss(3,3,0),tss(3,4,0),tss(3,5,0) end
{P(4,G)}
path tss(4,0,1),tss(4,0,2),tss(4,0,3),tss(4,0,4),tss(4,0,5);
     (tss(4,1,2),tss(4,1,3),tss(4,1,4),
      tss(4,2,1),tss(4,2,4),tss(4,2,5),
      tss(4,3,1),tss(4,3,4),
      tss(4,4,1),tss(4,4,2),tss(4,4,3),tss(4,4,5),
      tss(4,5,2),tss(4,5,4))*;
      tss(4,1,0),tss(4,2,0),tss(4,3,0),tss(4,4,0),tss(4,5,0) end
```

3.3 ANALYSIS OF THE CORRESPONDING RAILWAY BEHAVIOURS

For the COSY specification of the railway given above, we :

1. Characterize histories in terms of interpretive functions representing the location of trains and the local states of sections,

2. show that any such history is uniquely determined by train itineraries and sequences of train arrivals at sections, and

3. show adequacy, or absence of partial system deadlock.

We will denote a t train railway program whose layout is defined by the graph $G=(S,Adj)$ by $P(t,S,G)$. That is,

$$P(t,S,G) = P(t,s1)P(t,s2)...P(t,sn)P(1,G)P(2,G)...P(t,G)$$

Then the behaviours defined by $P(t,S,G)$ are the vector firing sequences of $P(t,S,G)$, denoted by $VFS(P(t,S,G))$.

Briefly, the elements of VFS(P(t,S,G)) are vectors :

  (x1,...,xn,y1,...,yt)

if there are n=|S| sections in the layout, and where :

  xi is an element of FS(P(t,si)), i.e., a sequence of arrivals and departures of
  trains at section si, and

  yk is an element of FS(P(k,G)), i.e., a sequence of moves of train k.

To see what VFS(P(t,si)) is like, we can define <u>interpretive</u> <u>functions</u> on its
elements :

When <u>x</u> ϵ VFS(P(t,S,G)) , we can define functions :

  At(<u>x</u>,k) - where train k <u>is</u> after history <u>x</u> , and

  Empty(<u>x</u>,si) - is there a train at si ?

With these functions we can demonstrate that the model is <u>correct</u>. First some
preliminary definitions :

Suppose xϵOps(P(t,S,G))* :

  let last(x) be the last operation occurring in x :

$$last(x) = \begin{cases} - e \text{ (the empty sequence) if } x=e \\ - \text{ the unique } aϵOps(P(t,S,G)) \text{ such that} \\ \qquad \nexists x'ϵOps(P(t,S,G))^*: x'a=x \text{ otherwise.} \end{cases}$$

<u>Fact</u> 1 :

Let <u>x</u>ϵVFS(P(t,S,G)) and t$\geq$k$\geq$1 :

  Then last([<u>x</u>]n+k) = tss(k,j,i) <==> last([<u>x</u>]i) = tss(k,j,i) .

Supposing <u>x</u>ϵVFS(P(t,S,G)). Let k be a train. Then [<u>x</u>]n+k is the
set of moves of k in <u>x</u>. If last([<u>x</u>]n+k)$\neq$e, then it is the
<u>last</u> <u>move</u> made by k. Otherwise, k is still off the layout.
We define :

$$At(\underline{x},k) = \begin{cases} - s0 \text{ if } [\underline{x}]n+kϵCyc(P(k,G))^* \\ - si \text{ if } last([\underline{x}]n+k)=tss(k,j,i) \text{ some k.} \end{cases}$$

If si is a section, then si is empty if si=s0 (by convention) or
At($\underline{x}$,k)$\neq$si for any k.

Empty($\underline{x}$,si) <==> (i=0 or ($\forall$k:At($\underline{x}$,k)$\neq$si)).

From Fact 1, we obtain Fact 2 :

Fact 2 :

Let $\underline{x}\theta$Vops(P(t,S,G))* and a=tss(k,j,i) , then :

At($\underline{x}$,k)=sm and Empty($\underline{x}$,si) and $\underline{x}\theta$VFS(P(t,S,G)) <==>

At($\underline{xa}$,k)=si and Empty($\underline{x}$,sm) and $\underline{xa}\theta$VFS(P(t,S,G)).

Fact 2 tells us that VFS(P(t,S,G)) is the set of all possible
(asynchronous) histories of the railway running under
constraint 2 (section 4.2). It also allows one to deduce :

Fact 3 :

Let $\underline{x}\theta$VFS(P(t,S,G)), then if t$\geq$k$\geq$1,

$$[\underline{x}]n+k = \begin{cases} - e & \text{or} \\ - tss(k,0,i1)tss(k,i1,i2)tss(k,i2,i3)... \end{cases}$$

that is, trains do not 'jump'.

Next, let us use the notion of arrival sequence
to state another fact which states that arrival sequences
completely characterise histories.

Let xθFS(P(t,si)). Then x will be of the form :

tss(k1,i1,i)tss(k1,i,j1)tss(k2,i2,i)...tss(kr,i´,j´).

Define the arrival sequence of x :

as(x) = k1.k2....kr

where we use '.' to indicate concatenation for readability.

Fact 4 :

Let x,y$\in$VFS(P(t,S,G)), then

(a) $\forall n \geq i \geq 1$: as([x]i) = as([y]i) and

(b) $\forall t \geq k \geq 1$: [x]n+k = [y]n+k

$$==> \quad x = y .$$

Finally, let us state the fact that there is no partial system deadlock possible and sketch a proof of this fact :

Fact 5 :

P(t,S,G) is __adequate__ for any t, S and G.

Proof : (sketch)

Take all trains from the layout, move the chosen one along the chosen arc - having put it on the layout on the required section.

4   ACKNOWLEDGEMENTS

This work was partially supported by the Science and Engineering Council of Great Britain. The solution to the railway problem was obtained in collaboration with Mike Shields who was responsible for the statement and proof of the various facts about the model given above (cf.[S79]).

5   BIBLIOGRAPHY

[B79]   E Best : Adequacy of Path Programs. In : Net Theory and Applications: Proc. of the Advanced Course on General Net Theory of Processes and Systems, Hamburg, 1979 (Ed. W Brauer). __Lecture__ __Notes__ __in__ __Computer__ __Science__ __84__, Springer Verlag, 1980.

[B82]   E Best : Adequacy Properties of Path Programs, Theoretical Computer Science 18 (1982), pp 149-171, North-Holland Publishing Co.

[Br80]   W Brauer (ed.) : Proceedings of the Advanced Course on General Net Theory of Processes and Systems, Hamburg, 1979. Lecture Notes in Computer Science 84, Springer Verlag, 1980

[CL83]   J Y Cotronis, P E Lauer : Two way channel with disconnect, this Volume.

[D82]   R E Devillers : The train set strikes again !, Report ASM/105, Computing Laboratory, University of Newcastle upon Tyne, 17 December 1982.

[JL82]   R Janicki, P E Lauer : Towards a solution of the Merlin-Randall problem of train journeys, Report ASM/95, Computing Laboratory, University of Newcastle upon Tyne, 5 October 1982.

[L82]   P E Lauer : Computer System Dossiers, Proc. Int. Seminar on Synchronisation, Control and Communication in Distributed Computing Systems, London, Sept. 20 through 24, 1982. To appear in a Book by Academic Press.

[L83]   P E Lauer : Users' introduction to BCS : A computer based environment for specifying analysing and verifying concurrent systems, Report ASM/107, Computing Laboratory, University of Newcastle upon Tyne, June 1983.

[LBS77] P E Lauer, E Best, M W Shields : On the problem of achieving adequacy of concurrent programs. In the book : IFIP TC-2 Working Conference on the Formal Description of Programming Concepts, St Andrews, Canada, 1977. North-Holland Pub. Co.

[LC75]   P E Lauer, R H Campbell : Formal Semantics for a class of high level primitives for coordinating concurrent processes. Acta Informatica 5, pp 247-332, 1975.

[LS81b] P E Lauer, M W Shields : Interpreted COSY programs : Programming and Verification, Proceedings 2nd International Conference on Distributed Computing Systems, Paris, 8-10 April 1981, IEEE Computer Society Press, (Ed. E Gelenbe), 1981, pp.137-148.

[LSB79a] P E Lauer, M W Shields, E Best : The design and certification of asynchronous systems of processes. Advanced Course on Abstract Software Specification, Lyngby, Denmark, January 1979. Lecture Notes in Computer Science 86, Springer Verlag, 1979.

DESCRIPTION AND ANALYSIS USING CIRCAL

by

George J. Milne
Department of Computer Science
University of Edinburgh
James Clerk Maxwell Building
The King's Buildings
Mayfield Road
Edinburgh EH9 3JZ

The following introduction to the CIRCAL model is taken from
"A Model for Hardware Description and Verification" [3] where CIRCAL
is proposed as a circuit description and analysis model. It can
equally well be used to model software systems or systems of hard
and soft components, as illustrated by its use in modelling problems
1 and 8. A full description of the model together with circuit
examples is given in "CIRCAL : A Calculus for Circuit Description" [1].

CIRCAL

CIRCAL provides a framework in which to represent both the behaviour
of a circuit as it evolves through time and the connectivity properties
of the circuit being modelled.   The behaviour of a circuit component
such as a transistor, gate or a much larger device is the sequence of
events which the component wishes to perform in conjunction with other
components in its environment using a number of predetermined communication
ports.   We may model the occurrence of these events relative to each other,
or with respect to an absolute timescale.   The latter is examined closely
here since we aim to demonstrate how time may be represented and used for
device analysis within the model.

The linkage conventions of the system being modelled may be shown by
picturing devices as boxes with arcs connecting their labelled ports.

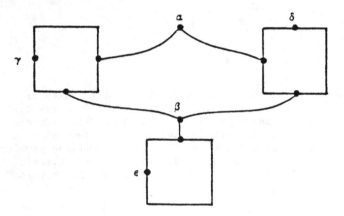

We use the convention that two or more ports with the same label are joined
and the labels are moved to the midpoint.   The three devices pictured above
are all linked via their β ports while only two are linked using the α por
These ports can then be used to attach further devices to construct a larger
system.

Technically the set of port names for a device is known as its sort,
as in a sorted algebra.   The devices pictured above have their behaviour

specified by CIRCAL expressions with each expression having the associated
sort.   The expression denoting the whole system, which is obtained from
the component expressions, has as its sort the union of the component
sorts.   The sort labels indicate where a device may interact with others
but its corresponding behaviour expression will indicate how and when the
ports are actually used.   Sorts are frequently not explicitly defined but
the context should indicate what would be an appropriate sort.

CIRCAL expressions are constructed from a number of primitive and
derived operators as listed below.

For D_L being the domain of behaviour expressions with sort L   (a set
of labels remember) we have the following operators and their type:-

guarding	$\lambda :$	$D_L \rightarrow D_L$	where $\lambda \subseteq L$
choice	$+ :$	$D_L \times D_L \rightarrow D_L$	
nondeterminism	$\oplus :$	$D_L \times D_L \rightarrow D_L$	
termination	$\Delta :$	D_L	
composition	$\bullet :$	$D_L \times D_M \rightarrow D_{LUM}$	
abstraction	$-\alpha:$	$D_L \rightarrow D_{L-\{\alpha\}}$	where $\alpha \in L$

Meaning is given to these operators (and so to any CIRCAL expression)
using an operational semantics called acceptance semantics which is described
in [4].   This semantics is used to prove the soundness of a set of CIRCAL
axioms which allow equivalence proofs to be performed without constant recourse
to the underlying semantics.

The CIRCAL operators may be described informally.

guarding   as in λQ

where $\lambda \subseteq L$ and $Q \in D_L$ for sort L

This operator appends a behaviour expression Q to a label-set λ to create
a new expression.   The intended meaning of expression λQ is that it
describes the simultaneous occurrence of the actions denoted by the component
labels of λ with the behaviour evolving to that denoted by expression Q.
Should the λ label-set be a singleton label then only this action needs to

occur to permit the behaviour to evolve to Q.

Guarding contributes sequentiality to CIRCAL with events, which are
sets of simultaneous actions, following events.   The guarding label-set
represents how the device being modelled interacts with its environment.

choice   as in P + Q

where $P,Q \in D_L$ for sort L

This binary operator produces an expression which may perform different
events, either events belonging to expression P or to expression Q.
The environment will resolve the choice as to whether an event in P or in
Q occurs next.

For instance, in expression λ R + μ S the environment will choose
whether the λ or μ events (or neither) occur.

nondeterminism   as in P $\oplus$ Q

where $P,Q \in D_L$ for sort L

Here the environment has no control over which "state" the behaviour
is in, either subexpressions P or Q.   For instance, λ R $\oplus$ μ S denotes
the behaviour of a nondeterministic device which may wish to perform the
actions denoted by λ and evolve to behaviours R or maybe with to perform
μ and evolves to S.   Unlike the choice operator the other interacting
devices may not participate in making this decision, the non-deterministic
choice will somehow be made internally.

termination   as in Δ

where $\Delta \in D_L$ for sort L

This operator represents "no further action".

As an example an agent which wishes to perform the event denoted by λ
and then to terminate is represented by expression $\lambda \Delta$.

Termination may also arise in a less benign fashion when two or more
expressions wish to interact but each waits for the other to progress first.
This form of termination, called deadlock, is introduced by the composition
operator.

summation

Two auxiliary summation operators are defined using the basic CIRCAL operators.

$$\sum_{i=1,n} \lambda_i P_i \Leftarrow \lambda_1 P_1 + \lambda_2 P_2 + \dots + \lambda_n P_n$$

$$\sum_{i=1,n} P_i \Leftarrow P_1 \oplus P_2 \oplus \dots \oplus P_n$$

Auxiliary operators permit CIRCAL to be used with a flexibility similar to that of a programming language. They differ from the basic operators which give the CIRCAL calculus just those properties which allow it to be used as a realistic model of circuit behaviour. The introduction of expression identifiers and the auxiliary definition operator $\Leftarrow$ also allow recursive definition of the form

$$A \Leftarrow \lambda A$$

Δ is taken to be the identity of $+$. The empty sum $\sum_N \alpha_i P_i$ when predicate N is false also gives Δ since we require a "no action" behaviour. Note that Δ is not an identity of $\oplus$.

Some of the properties captured by these operators are given in the following list.

$X + X = X$	idempotent	$X \oplus X = X$
$X + Y = Y + X$	commutative	$X \oplus Y = Y \oplus X$
$X + (Y + Z) = X + Y + Z$	associative	$X \oplus (Y \oplus Z) = X \oplus Y \oplus Z$
$X + \Delta = X$	identity	
$X + (Y \oplus Z) = (X + Y) \oplus (X + Z)$	distributivity	$X \oplus (Y + Z) = (X \oplus Y) + (X \oplus Z)$
$\alpha X + \alpha Y = \alpha X \oplus \alpha Y$	indeterminacy	

concurrent composition   as in $P \cdot Q$

where $P \in D_L$, $Q \in D_M$

This operator captures the behaviour of two concurrently active devices interacting with each other and the environment.

A single device will wish to interact with other devices via the synchronisation of events. When composed with another device the two devices concur as to what actions can actually take place, giving the behaviour of the two device system.

Expressions P and Q are composed using the • operator which has type $D_L \times D_M \rightarrow D_{L \cup M}$. This basic CIRCAL operator is recursively defined in terms of guarding and choice.

<u>Definition</u>　　　For $A \Leftarrow \sum_i \lambda_i A_i$　　of sort L

$B \Leftarrow \sum_j \mu_j B_j$　　of sort M

then

$$A \cdot B \Leftarrow \sum_{\lambda_i \cap M = \emptyset} \lambda_i [A_i \cdot B]$$

$$+ \sum_{\mu_j \cap L = \emptyset} \mu_j [A \cdot B_j]$$

$$+ \sum_{(\lambda_i \cap M) = (\mu_j \cap L)} (\lambda_i \cup \mu_j) [A_i \cdot B_j]$$

Note that label-sets are obtained by listing labels within ( ) brackets. The usual set-theoretic properties hold for label-sets where α, β etc. are used to range over labels and λ, μ etc. to range over label-sets. A singleton label-set (α) may be written as α.

The synchronisation represented by the • operator may be explained as follows:

The first clause contributes to $A \cdot B$ those guards belonging to A whose labels do not intersect with M, the sort of B. Such guards appear independently of B and A can be thought of as advancing to A_i when λ_i occurs without the participation of B. The $\lambda_i [A_i \cdot B]$ guard results.

The second clause contributes to $A \bullet B$ those guards which are due to B and are independent of A, giving guard $\lambda_j [A \bullet B_j]$ in a similar manner.

The third clause contributes to $A \bullet B$ those guards formed by a synchronisation of guards from A and B.

To demonstrate the mechanics of CIRCAL synchronisation more clearly we can replace the third clause by the following equivalent, two-part clause.

$$\sum_{(\lambda_i \cap M) = (\mu_j \cap L) = \emptyset} (\lambda_i \cup \mu_j)[A_i \bullet B_j] + \sum_{(\lambda_i \cap M) = (\mu_j \cap L) \neq \emptyset} (\lambda_i \cup \mu_j)[A_i \bullet B_j]$$

The first sum introduces to $A \bullet B$ guards formed from the composition of independent labels; independent in that the label or labels λ_i in the label-set of a guard of A do not also occur in M, the sort of B. Also the label μ_j does not intersect with L, the sort of A. The events represented by λ_i and μ_j are then independent but they may occur simultaneously with A evolving to A_i and B to B_j giving the new guard $(\lambda_i \cup \mu_j)[A_i \bullet B_j]$.

The second clause introduces to $A \bullet B$ those guards which result from a synchronisation of at least some of the labels comprising a guard in A with some of the labels of a guard in B. The labels occurring in label-set λ_i and in M (the sort of B) must also occur as labels in μ_j and in L (the sort of A). Other labels may occur in λ_i that are not also in M but they are then independent and do not also need to occur in B. Similarly μ_j may contain labels which are independent of A.

The important feature is that the two label-sets $(\lambda_i \cap M)$ and $(\mu_j \cap L)$ are identical and A and B interact. This clause then contributes guards of the form $(\lambda_i \cup \mu_j)[A_i \bullet B_j]$ to $A \bullet B$.

A further definition completes the description of the composition operator.

<u>Definition</u> $X \bullet (Y \oplus Z) \Leftarrow (X \bullet Y) \oplus (X \bullet Z)$

that is $\bullet$ distributes over $\oplus$ and X running concurrently with Y <u>or</u> Z has the same behaviour as X running concurrently with Y <u>or</u> X concurrently with Z.

Useful properties of the $\bullet$ operator are given by the following axioms:-

$X \bullet X \qquad = X \qquad\qquad$ idempotent, where X is <u>deterministic</u>

$X \bullet Y \qquad = Y \bullet X \qquad$ commutative

$X \bullet (Y \bullet Z) \;\; = \;\; (X \bullet Y) \bullet Z \;\;$ associative

abstraction $\qquad\qquad$ as in $P - \alpha$
$\qquad\qquad\qquad$ where $P \in D_L$ and $\alpha \in L$

The abstraction operator causes ports to be hidden from the environment so preventing further devices from attaching themselves to the hidden port and so preventing further interaction via that port. The importance of this operation is that it allows a complex device to be modelled at different levels of detail, or levels of abstraction. The behavioural complexity of circuits makes abstraction crucial when producing tractable descriptions within the model.

This operation may be recursively defined in terms of the guarding, choice and nondeterminism.

<u>Definition</u>

$$[\sum_i \lambda_i P_i] - \alpha \Leftarrow \left[\sum_{\substack{\alpha \in \lambda_i \\ \alpha \neq \lambda_i}} \lambda_i - \alpha [P_i - \alpha] + M + \sum_{\substack{\alpha \notin \lambda_i \\ \alpha \neq \lambda_i}} \lambda_i [P_i - \alpha] \right] \oplus M$$

where $\qquad M \Leftarrow \sum_{\alpha = \lambda_i}^{\Sigma} [P_i - \alpha]$

That abstraction introduces non-determinism into descriptions of concurrent systems is an important feature of CIRCAL. This property is explained briefly in [1], and in greater depth in [2].

A further definition is required to complete the specification.

Definition $\qquad [\sum P_i] - \alpha \Leftarrow \sum [P_i - \alpha]$

and abstraction distributes over nondeterminism.

Abstraction is such that the order of hiding is not significant and

$$P - \alpha - \beta = P - \beta - \alpha$$

SOME SIMPLE CIRCAL EXAMPLES

a register cell

A binary register cell can be pictured by

```
in0 |       | out0
    |  RC   |
in1 |       | out1
```

with sort {in0, in1, out0, out1}. The in0 port may be used to input a zero, in1 to input a one, out0 to output a zero and out1 to output a 1.

The behaviour of a binary register where input and output may not occur simultaneously, is recursively defined by

```
RC  ⇐  in0 RC0 + in1 RC1
RC0 ⇐  out0 RC0 + in0 RC0 + in1 RC1
RC1 ⇐  out1 RC1 + in0 RC0 + in1 RC1
```

RC allows a zero or a one to be input from the environment giving expressions identified by RC0 and RC1 respectively. These expressions denote the ability of the register to input a zero or a one or to output the contents, the "stored" zero or one.

a simultaneous I/O register cell

The cell SRC has the same sort as RC but allows for the possibility
of input and output occurring simultaneously.

This register cell has behaviour defined by

SRC $\Leftarrow$ in0   SRC0   +   in1 SRC1

SRC0 $\Leftarrow$ out0   SRC0
         + in0   SRC0   +   (out0 in0) SRC0
         + in1   SRC1   +   (out0 in1) SRC1

SRC1 $\Leftarrow$ out1   SRC1
         + in0   SRC0 + (out1 in0) SRC0
         + in1   SRC1 + (out1 in1) SRC1

a delay cell

A delay component D may have sort $\{\alpha,\beta\}$ and be pictured by

$$\alpha \,\bullet\!\!\boxed{\ D\ }\!\!\bullet\, \beta$$

with behaviour given as

$$D \Leftarrow \alpha\ \beta\ D$$

Here a signal is input via the α port and output on the β port
following some unspecified delay period, with the behaviour then recursing.
Event β occurs after event α ;   they occur relative to each other and
are not governed by some absolute timescale.

a two-delay system

Another delay D' of sort $\{\beta,\gamma\}$ may be defined similarly:

$$D' \Leftarrow \beta\ \gamma\ D'$$

A relabelling operator may be introduced to produce specific device
descriptions from a generic description by consistently replacing a label by

another. For expression P of sort L with $\beta \in L$ and $\alpha \notin L$, P{α/β} has all occurrences of the β label replaced by α and has sort $L \cup \{\alpha\} - \{\beta\}$. Note the restriction on how labels can be replaced to preserve the distinction between them.

D' can therefore also be defined by

$$D' \Leftarrow D\{\gamma/\beta\}\{\beta/\alpha\}$$

Composing D and D' using the $\bullet$ operator gives the following picture

and the following behaviour expression

$$D \bullet D' \Leftarrow \alpha \beta [D \bullet \gamma D']$$

where

$$D' \bullet \gamma D' \Leftarrow \alpha \gamma \beta [D \bullet \gamma D']$$
$$+ \gamma \alpha \beta [D \bullet \gamma D']$$
$$+ (\alpha \gamma) \beta [D \bullet \gamma D']$$

Here signal input on α occurs before signal output on β and input on β before output on γ but the output on γ and a successive α input may occur in either order or even simultaneously.

Applying the abstraction operator to $D \bullet D'$ hides the β line

and gives the following expression

$$[D \bullet D'] - \beta \Leftarrow \alpha [D \bullet \gamma D'] - \beta$$

where

$$[D \bullet \gamma D'] - \beta \Leftarrow \alpha \gamma [D \bullet \gamma D'] - \beta$$
$$+ \gamma \alpha [D \bullet \gamma D'] - \beta$$
$$+ (\alpha \gamma) [D \bullet \gamma D'] - \beta$$

A two-delay device D2 of sort {α,γ} may be defined directly
and it is a trivial exercise to show that the constructed device meets
the specification.   We may then prove that

$$D2 = [D \cdot D'] - \beta$$

using induction on the depth of the recursive definitions.

The introduction of "time" in the next section allows the propagation
delays across devices and wires to be modelled and so allows the delays
belonging to a number of interlinked components to be related.

THE REPRESENTATION OF TIME

Universal time may be modelled by a sequence of instantaneously occurring timing signals or "ticks". When modelling a discrete signal the continuous time axis is then broken down into equidistant steps with the signal being sampled at each tick point. The two-valued interpretation of the preceding section gives the following signal and sample points.

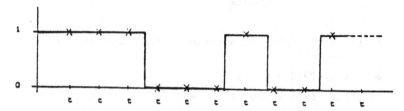

If this signal is produced on the port labelled α it has its behaviour represented by expression

$$t \ t \ t \ (\alpha 0 \ t) \ t \ t \ (\alpha 1 \ t)(\alpha 0 \ t) \ t \ (\alpha 1 \ t) A$$

The finer the grain of time, the closer the expression is to modelling the physical signal. If a multivalued logic is used an even closer approximation may be made to an analogue signal.

The universal timer has behaviour given by

$$T \Leftarrow t \ T \qquad \text{with sort} \qquad \{t\} \ .$$

This reflects time as an infinite sequence of pulses or ticks.

If we wish to model the actual occurrence of events on a wire we use five ports, four corresponding to the physical ends on the wire with the other being used for timing.

TW of sort $\{\alpha 0, \alpha 1, \beta 0, \beta 1, t\}$ may be pictured by

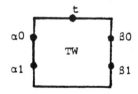

The behaviour of a timed wire is such that input and output only occurs when the timer ticks. The input signal change takes a predetermined number of ticks before it is output - the propagation delay.

No device should be capable of halting the timer since it models the passage of time. Our wire is then defined to accept ticks in the absence of input or output events.

A wire with a one unit propagation delay is defined by

$$TW00 \Leftarrow (\alpha1 \ t) \ TW10 + t \ TW00$$

$$TW10 \Leftarrow (\beta1 \ t) \ TW11 + (\alpha0 \ \beta1 \ t) \ TW01$$

$$TW11 \Leftarrow (\alpha0 \ t) \ TW01 + t \ TW11$$

$$TW01 \Leftarrow (\beta0 \ t) \ TW00 + (\alpha1 \ \beta0 \ t) \ TW10$$

DEVICE ANALYSIS

When a simple device has its behaviour denoted by a CIRCAL expression
the expression needs to be rich enough to capture the behaviour of the
device when it is used as a subcircuit in all possible circuits. For
instance the P and N type transistors described in [1] give rise to
extremely complex descriptions as a transistor behaves differently according
to the context in which it is used;   whether connected to power, to ground or to
other transistors.   Complex expressions also arise from the composition
of simpler expressions and the description of a large circuit may be such
that proof and analysis become intractable.   Use of the abstraction operator
allows internal details to be hidden so making descriptions simpler.   Two
other practical techniques are *restriction* and *constructive simulation*.

restriction

Two Nor gates may be composed to produce a flip-flop description which
models all possible interactions the device may perform with the environment.
However, many patterns of events may not be realistically generated by the
environment.   The set line of a flip-flop may have a fixed number of time
units between successive changes and this input timing property should be
captured and used to produce a simpler device description.   The allowable
behaviour of part of the environment can be defined as another CIRCAL expression
and then composed with the device description.

As an example consider a timed wire.   If the input is known to change
exactly three time units apart then we have the following restriction of
sort $\{\alpha 0, \alpha 1, t\}$

$$R1 \Leftarrow (\alpha 0 \ t) \ t \ t \ R0 + t \ R1$$
$$R0 \Leftarrow (\alpha 1 \ t) \ t \ t \ R1 + t \ R0$$

R1 • W(1,1,1) is the restricted behaviour of a two-delay wire with constant voltage one initially.   It may then be used in a less notationally complex proof when the restricted system is shown to satisfy some specification.

constructive simulation

Another approach to the problem of reasoning about complex devices is to examine their CIRCAL expressions experimentally.   This involves examining how a CIRCAL representation responds to a single pattern of events from the environment.   As with restriction this is effected by describing the event pattern as a CIRCAL expression and composing it with the device description.   The two techniques differ in that simulation allows us to examine a device under one pattern of events from the environment while restriction leaves an expression which can respond to many event patterns.

Simulation is the technique universally used to establish circuit "correctness".   Our notion of experimentation differs from the usual simulation in that we use our constructive technique for establishing device behaviour to produce a constructive simulation.   Rather than construc a monolithic description of a complex device and then simulate over it, we perform simulation on its much simpler components and compose the resulting expressions.   The associativity and idempotency of the • operator permits this in the following way:

For device D composed of sub-devices E and F, that is
D ⇐ E • F we may perform a simulation S on D , that is S • D,
by using the property that

$$
\begin{aligned}
S \cdot D &= S \cdot [E \cdot F] &&\text{by definition} \\
&= S \cdot E \cdot F &&\text{by associativity} \\
&= [S \cdot S] \cdot E \cdot F &&\text{by idempotency} \\
&= [S \cdot E] \cdot [S \cdot F] &&\text{by associativity and commutativity}
\end{aligned}
$$

The expressions being manipulated are much simpler and this procedure may be repeated, breaking E and F down and hierarchically simulating their components.

Simulations may also be constructed out of simpler simulations. If $S1 \cdot S2 = S$ then we can perform a simulation on device D — defined by $D \Leftarrow E \cdot F$ — by composing components E and F with simulations S1 and S2 respectively since

$$[S_1 \cdot E] \cdot [S_2 \cdot F] = [S1 \cdot S2] \cdot [E \cdot F] \quad \text{by associativity}$$

$$= S \cdot D \quad \text{by definition.}$$

An example of *constructive* simulation is given by the flip-flop analysis in [3] .

REFERENCES

[1] G. Milne, "CIRCAL: A Calculus for Circuit Description", INTEGRATION
     Vol.1, Nos.2 and 3, North-Holland, 1983.

[2] G. Milne, "Abstraction and Nondeterminism in Concurrent Systems",
     Proc. 3rd Int. Conf. on Distributed Systems, Florida, IEEE Computer
     Society Press, 1982.

[3] G. Milne, "A Model for Hardware Description and Verification",
     Proc. 21st Design Automation Conference, Albuquerque, N.M.
     (IEEE Computer Society Press) 1984.

[4] G. Milne, "CIRCAL and the Representation of Communication, Concurrency
     and Time", Report CSR-151-83, Dept. of Computer Science, University of
     Edinburgh, 1983.   (to appear in ACM TOPLAS).

PROBLEM 1   TWO-WAY CHANNEL

"Solution" using CIRCAL

Interpretation of Problem

A totally synchronous system with a clock generating ticks to the channel. On every tick input occurs on both ends simultaneously. The channel is constructed from two queues of similar length; if full output also occurs on each clock tick.

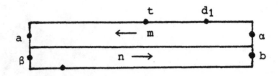

Definition   Channel $S : (V^i \times V^j) \longrightarrow$ CIRCAL

for value type V is such that $S(m,n)$ has sort $\{t,d1,d2\}\cup\bigcup_{x\in V}\{\alpha x, ax, \beta x$

with α,β input ports; a,b output ports; d1,d2 disconnect ports

and t the clock port.   This device is expressed by:-

$$S(\varepsilon,\varepsilon) \Leftarrow \sum_{x,y} (\alpha x \ \beta y \ t) \ S(<x>,<y>)$$

$$+ \sum_{y} (d1 \ \beta y \ t) \ T(\varepsilon, \ <y>)$$

$$+ \sum_{x} (d2 \ \alpha x \ t) \ R(<x>,\varepsilon)$$

for *empty* queues.

$$S(m,n) \Leftarrow \sum_{x,y} (\alpha x \ \beta y \ t) \ S(append(m,x),append(n,y))$$

$$+ \sum_{y} (d1 \ \beta y \ t) \ T(m'',n')$$

$$+ \sum_{x} (d2 \ \alpha x \ t) \ R(m',n'')$$

where queues m and n *are not full*

queues   new input   output

$$S(m,n) \Leftarrow \sum_{x,y} (\alpha x \ \beta y \ a(hd(m)) \ b(hd(n)) \ t) \ S(m',n')$$

$$+ \sum_{y} (d1 \ \beta y \ \ a(hd(m)) \ t) \ T(m'',n')$$

$$+ \sum_{x} (d2 \ \alpha x \ b(hd(n)) \ t) \ R(m',n'')$$

where queues m and n *are full*.

$$T(m,n) \Leftarrow \sum_{y} (\beta y \ \ a(hd(m)) \ t) \ T(m'',n')$$

for $m \neq \varepsilon$

$$T(\varepsilon,n) \Leftarrow \Delta$$

$R(m,n)$ and $R(m,\varepsilon)$ similarly by symmetry.

Note that m',n',m'' and n'' are defined using fairly standard queue manipulation functions:-

    m' = append (tl(m),x)   m" = tl(m)

    n' = append (tl(n),y)   n" = tl(n)

The above "solution" assumes that the disconnect signals also occur synchronously but that both disconnects do not occur simultaneously. "Solutions" which assume asynchronous input, asynchronous output or simultaneous disconnect or some combination of them can be produced in a similar way.

PROBLEM 8   SYNCHRONOUS AND ASYNCHRONOUS WAIT

"Solution" using CIRCAL

Interpretation of Problem

We assume that packets arrive on the α input on every clock tick.
Packets arriving at the asynchronous β input may occur "between" clock
ticks or even simultaneously with a clock tick.   We assume that the device
only holds a packet from the synchronous input for one time unit before
outputting it via the γ port.   The asynchronous inputs may be placed on
an infinite queue waiting for an empty packet.

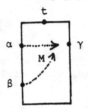

Definition   Device $M(p)$ has sort $\{t\} \cup \bigcup_{x \in P} \{\alpha x, \beta x, \gamma x\}$ for S of type

$P + (P \times P*) \longrightarrow$ CIRCAL for packet type P (which may be empty).
This "merger" is expressed by :-

$$M(\varepsilon) \Leftarrow \sum_{q,r} [(\alpha q \ t) \ M(q)$$
$$+ \ \beta r \quad M(\varepsilon, <r>)$$
$$+ \ (\alpha q \ \beta r \ t) \ M(q, <r>)]$$

> No stored packets.   Asynchronous, synchronous or both inputs
> may occur.

$$M(s) \Leftarrow \sum_{q,r} [(\alpha q \ \gamma s \ t) \ M(q)$$
$$+ \ \beta r \ M(s, <r>)$$
$$+ \ (\alpha q \ \gamma s \ \beta r \ t) \ M(q, <r>)]$$

> No queued asynchronous packets but a synchronous packet is waiting
> for a tick to enable its output.

$$M(s,R) \Leftarrow \sum_{q,r} [(\alpha q \ \gamma s \ t) \ M(q,R)$$
$$+ \ \beta r \ M(s, \text{append } (R,r))$$
$$+ \ (\alpha q \ \beta r \ \gamma s \ t) \ M(q, \text{append } (R,r))]$$

for s a non-empty, stored packet and R the queue of waiting, asynchronous packets.

$$M(\epsilon,R) \Leftarrow \sum_{q,r} [(\alpha q \ \gamma(\text{hd}(R)) \ t) \ M(q,\text{tl}(R))$$
$$+ \ \beta r \ M(\epsilon, \text{append } (R,r))$$
$$+ \ (\alpha q \ \beta r \ \gamma(\text{hd}(R)) \ t) \ M(q, \text{append } (\text{tl}(R),r))]$$

where the last synchronous packet was empty and a queue of asynchronous inputs is waiting. The head of this queue is then output on the next tick.

This example illustrates the ability of CIRCAL to represent both simultaneously occurring actions or actions occurring on their own. A sender, receiver and clock device may be composed with M as follows.

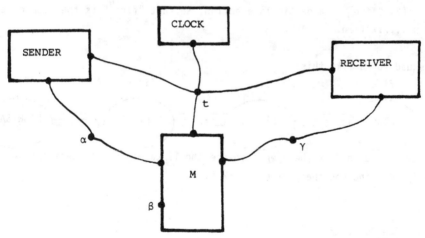

The sender and receiver interact with M synchronously and this synchrony is effected by the generation of a stream of ticks from the clock.

The clock device of sort {t} has behaviour defined by

$$\text{CLOCK} \Leftarrow t \quad \text{CLOCK}$$

and continuously changing time is broken down into discrete steps, as described in the CIRCAL preface.

FIRING SQUAD

R. Milner

University of Edinburgh

Solution in SCCS

1. Specification

We wish to define a <u>general</u> agent (call him LEFTGEN)

a <u>private</u> agent (call him LEFTPRIV)

a <u>sergeant</u> agent (call him RIGHTSARG)

so that a squad of size N (call it LEFTSQUAD(N)), defined by:

$$\text{LEFTSQUAD(N)} = \text{LEFTGEN} \otimes \overbrace{\text{LEFTPRIV} \otimes \ldots \text{LEFTPRIV}}^{N-2} \otimes \text{RIGHTSARG}$$

satisfies the equation, for some function f:

$$\boxed{\text{LEFTSQUAD(N)} = (1\!:\!)^{f(N)} \text{fire}^N \!:\! 0}$$

<u>Note</u>: (1) " $\otimes$ " is to be a restricted product in SCCS

(2) "fire" is a particulate action, so that "fire^N" is the atomic action fire x .....x fire.

The squad looks like this:

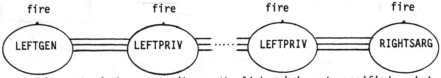

Of course, the sort of the agents (hence the linkage) is not specified - but clearly must include the particle "fire".

2. Outline Solution

We shall give a solution which works only for $N = 2^n$ ($n \geqslant 1$). We shall show that:

$$\text{LEFTSQUAD}(2^n) = (1\!:\!)^{3(2^n - 1)} \text{fire}^{2^n} \!:\! 0.$$

Actually we shall also show that:

$$\text{RIGHTSQUAD}(2^n) = (1\!:\!)^{3(2^n - 1)} \text{fire}^{2^n} \!:\! 0,$$

where RIGHTSQUAD is built as the mirror image of LEFTSQUAD.

The proof is by induction on n. The basic step is to show that:

$$\boxed{\text{LEFTSQUAD(2)} = \text{RIGHTSQUAD(2)} = (1\!:\!)^3 \text{fire}^2 \!:\! 0}$$

and the inductive step is to show that:

$$\boxed{\text{LEFTSQUAD}(2^{n+1}) \;=\; (1:)^{3 \cdot 2^n} \,(\text{RIGHTSQUAD}(2^n) \;\otimes\; \text{LEFTSQUAD}(2^n))}$$

- that is, after $3 \cdot 2^n$ time delay, it has split into two independent squads. Of course the mirror image proof will also show that:

$$\text{RIGHTSQUAD}(2^{n+1}) \;=\; (1:)^{3 \cdot 2^n} \,(\text{LEFTSQUAD}(2^n) \;\otimes\; \text{RIGHTSQUAD}(2^n))$$

and the inductive step is achieved by:

$$
\begin{aligned}
\text{LEFTSQUAD}(2^{n+1}) \;&=\; (1:)^{3 \cdot 2^n} \,((1:)^{3(2^n - 1)} \, fire^{2^n}{:}0 \\
&\qquad \otimes \; (1:)^{3(2^n - 1)} \, fire^{2^n} {:}0) \\
&=\; (1:)^{3 \cdot 2^n} \,((1:)^{3(2^n - 1)} fire^{2^{n+1}}{:}0) \\
&=\; (1:)^{3(2^{n+1} - 1)} \, fire^{2^{n+1}}{:}0,
\end{aligned}
$$

as required.

The definition of the agents, following the problem hint, is mainly a matter of getting the timing right.

3. The Agents

Let FIRE = fire:0 - an agent, who fires <u>now</u> and dies.

fire

(FIRE)

Recall the shape of LEFTSQUAD:

<u>Message flow -</u>

fire

along top links $\longrightarrow$

along bottom links $\longleftarrow$

The arrows show where each agent is waiting to interact; LEFTGEN is acting <u>now</u>. Recall the delay operator δ :

$$\delta P = P + 1{:}\delta P$$

fire

$\boxed{\text{LEFTGEN} = \text{sendr}{:}(\text{getr}{:}\text{sendr}{:}\text{FIRE} + 1{:}\text{sendr}{:}\text{LEFTEND})}$

sendr

LEFTGEN

getr

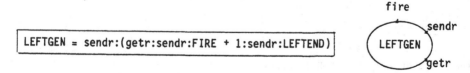

He sends a fast $\longrightarrow$ message; if he gets immediate response (getr) he acknowledges and fires; if not, he sends a slow message and becomes LEFTEND (of a smaller RIGHTSQUAD):

```
LEFTPRIV  = δ(getℓ:sendr:LEFTPRIV')
LEFTPRIV' = δ(getℓ:1:(getr:sendr:RIGHTGEN + 1:sendr:RIGHTPRIV)
            + getr:sendℓ:(getℓ:LEFTGEN + 1:LEFTPRIV))
```

He transmits a fast $\overrightarrow{\text{message}}$; if he gets a slow $\overrightarrow{\text{message}}$ then he either gets a fast $\overleftarrow{\text{message}}$ after 2 seconds, acknowledges, and becomes RIGHTGEN of a new RIGHTSQUAD, or transmits the slow message and becomes a member of the new RIGHTSQUAD. If he next gets a fast $\overleftarrow{\text{message}}$ he transmits it and similarly decides whether to become LEFTGEN or LEFTPRIV.

```
RIGHTSARG  = δ(getℓ:sendℓ:(getℓ:FIRE + 1: RIGHTSARG))
```

He reflects a fast $\overrightarrow{\text{message}}$; if it is immediately acknowledged, he fires.

Of course, the mirror images RIGHTGEN, RIGHTPRIV and LEFTEND are obtained by interchanging the agent prefixes RIGHT, LEFT and the action suffices r, ℓ.

4. The Combinator ⊗

To link the agents, we define
$$P \otimes Q = (P[\bar{\alpha}/\text{sendr}, \beta/\text{getr}] \times Q[\alpha/\text{getℓ}, \beta/\text{sendℓ}]\backslash\alpha\backslash\beta$$
Thus the linkage sendr ⟷ getℓ, getr ⟷ sendℓ is formed, and restricted. The algebraic laws easily show ⊗ to be associative, and an expansion theorem can be proved for composite agents:
$$P_1 \otimes \ldots\ldots \otimes P_k.$$
This expansion theorem is used implicitly in the following proofs; it just expresses the simple idea that "sendr" by P_i must synchronize with "getℓ" by P_{i+1} (producing 1), etc.

5. Some Proofs

The basis of the induction is easy:

$$
\begin{aligned}
\text{LEFTSQUAD(2)} &= \text{LEFTGEN} \otimes \text{RIGHTSARG} \\
&= 1:((\text{getr:sendr:FIRE} + 1:\text{sendr:LEFTSARG}) \\
&\quad \otimes (\text{sendℓ:(getℓ:FIRE} + 1:\text{RIGHTSARG}))) \\
&= 1:1:((\text{sendr:FIRE}) \otimes (\text{getℓ:FIRE} + 1:\text{RIGHTSARG})) \\
&= 1:1:1:(\text{FIRE} \otimes \text{FIRE}) \\
&= (1:)^3\text{fire}^2: 0, \quad \text{as required.}
\end{aligned}
$$

Leaving the general inductive step aside for a moment, let us compute

LEFTSQUAD(4) = LEFTGEN ⊗ LEFTPRIV ⊗ LEFTPRIV ⊗ RIGHTSARG

$$= 1:\{(\text{getr:sendr:FIRE} + 1:\text{sendr:LEFTSARG}) \otimes (\text{sendr:LEFTPRIV'})$$
$$\otimes \text{ LEFTPRIV } \otimes \text{ RIGHTSARG} \}$$

$$= 1:1:\{(\text{sendr:LEFTSARG}) \otimes \text{ LEFTPRIV' } \otimes (\text{sendr:LEFTPRIV}) \otimes \text{ RIGHTSARG}\}$$

$$= (1:)^3\{\text{LEFTSARG} \otimes (1:(\text{getr:sendr:RIGHTGEN} + 1:\text{sendr:RIGHTPRIV}))$$
$$\otimes \text{ LEFTPRIV' } \otimes (\text{sendl:}(\text{getl:FIRE} + 1:\text{RIGHTSARG}))\}$$

$$= (1:)^4\{\text{LEFTSARG} \otimes (\text{getr:sendr:RIGHTGEN} + 1:\text{sendr:RIGHTPRIV})$$
$$\otimes (\text{sendl:}(\text{getl:LEFTGEN} + 1:\text{LEFTPRIV}))$$
$$\otimes (\text{getl:FIRE} + 1:\text{RIGHTSARG})\}$$

$$= (1:)^5\{\text{LEFTSARG} \otimes (\text{sendr:RIGHTGEN}) \otimes (\text{get}\ell\text{:LEFTGEN} + 1:\text{LEFTPRIV})$$

$$\otimes \text{ RIGHTSARG}\}$$

$$= (1:)^6\{\text{LEFTSARG} \otimes \text{RIGHTGEN} \otimes \text{LEFTGEN} \otimes \text{RIGHTSARG}\}$$
$$= (1:)^6(\text{RIGHTSQUAD}(2) \otimes \text{LEFTSQUAD}(2))$$

which is what was required.

. . . .

Unfortunately, the use of dot...dot...dot is not enough to show that, since we
have proved what we want for n = 1 and n = 2, it follows for all n!

SCCS provides no magical way of shortening a general proof: eg. of the inductive
step here. What it does do is provide a way in which this proof could be formally
done, and in complex systems this provides formal (mechanical) proof-checking.
The full induction step, although I have not carried it out, is probably not
beyond handling with pencil and paper, because the only critical events before
squad-splitting are (a) initiation of messages; (b) reflection of fast message,
and (c) meeting of fast and slow messages at centre. What intervenes is very
regular.

Specification of a simplified Network Service in Z

(Problem 2)

Carroll Morgan

Programming Research Group
8-11 Keble Road
Oxford OX1 3QD

2 August 1983
revised October 1984

Abstract

The specification of a simplified Network Service is given using the Z specification technique.

1. Introduction

1.1 What is being specified

A simplified version of the ISO Network Service is specified by giving

- a model of its state
- descriptions of its events, in terms of their effects on that state

Most of the events described represent interactions between the service and its users; they are:

Service initiated	*User initiated*
ConInd	ConReq
ConCon	ConRes
DisInd	DisReq
DatInd	DatReq

Two further events are described which are not externally observable; from the users' point of view they simply represent possible non-determinism in the service. They are:

Disconnect	–	spontaneously release a connection
Drop	–	the final event for every connection (usually occurs after disconnection of both ends)

The advantage of treating these events explicitly is that precise meaning is given to terms (such as "spontaneous release") often used in informal descriptions of the service.

1.2 Structure of the specification

The specification is presented in stages

Endpoints	(EP)
Connections	(CON)
Network	(NET)
Service Access Points	(SAP)

which finally are integrated to give a specification of the service as a whole. Each specification stage is given a short name which may be used as a prefix when its material is used in other stages.

The state model and events are given in mathematical set theory, presented as *schemas* which introduce named observations and their relationships.

In the intermediate stages of specification, many more observations are described than will finally be visible; these observations are used to link the separate stages together. At the final stage, these observations are no longer necessary, and assume the role of "local variables".

1.3 Presentation

The specification itself is presented on every other page; on each facing page is a technical commentary, which describes features of the specification *technique*. In addition, an appendix provides a glossary of mathematical symbols.

2. Endpoints - EP

2.1 Endpoint state

With every connection supported by the service is associated two *endpoints*; at any endpoint one can observe the identity of the connection to which it belongs, and the data

Technical Commentary

o EP is a *schema* comprising the three components cid, sent, and rcvd. Each component represents an observation that can be made of the state of an endpoint.

o seq Data is the set of *sequences* of elements of the set Data.

o The schema newEP is constructed by adding the predicate

    sent = rcvd = <>

to the schema EP ; that is,

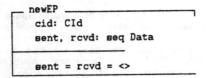

```
 ___ newEP _____
|  cid: CId
|  sent, rcvd: seq Data
|_____
|  sent = rcvd = <>
|_____
```

o <> is the empty sequence.

o The *decorated* schema EP' is the schema EP with its components similarly decorated:

```
 ___ EP' _____
|  cid': CId
|  sent', rcvd': seq Data
|_____
```

o ΔEP has the seven components: cid, sent, rcvd, cid', sent', rcvd', data.

o + is concatenation and <data> is the singleton sequence; therefore, sent' is formed by appending data to sent.

which has passed through it. Connection identifiers are drawn from a set CId; data is drawn from a set Data.

```
┌─ EP ─────────────────────┐
│   cid:          CId        │
│   sent, rcvd: seq Data    │
└──────────────────────────
```

When an endpoint is newly created, no data has passed through it.

```
┌─ newEP ──────────────────┐
│   EP                      │
│ ──────────────────────── │
│   sent = rcvd = <>        │
└──────────────────────────
```

2.2 Endpoint events

Events at an endpoint are described in terms of the state of the endpoint *before* the event

        EP

and *after* it

        EP'

and in terms of the data sent or received during the event

        data: Data

These observations are collected in the following schema, which also expresses the fact that an endpoint cannot move from one connection to another

```
┌─ ΔEP ────────────────────┐
│   EP                      │
│   EP'                     │
│   data: Data              │
│ ──────────────────────── │
│   cid' = cid              │
└──────────────────────────
```

The events DatReq and DatInd are defined in terms of ΔEP

```
┌─ DatReq ─────────────────┐
│   ΔEP                     │
│ ──────────────────────── │
│   sent' = sent + <data>   │
│   rcvd' = rcvd            │
└──────────────────────────
```

Technical Commentary

○ EP_1 is EP decorated with the subscript $_1$.

○ $\leq$ is the prefix relation over sequences: $rcvd_1$ is a prefix of $sent_2$.

```
 ┌─ DatInd ──────────────────────────────┐
 │   ΔEP                                  │
 │ ──────────────────                     │
 │   sent' = sent                         │
 │   rcvd' = rcvd + <data>                │
 └────────────────────────────────────────┘
```

2.3 Connection of endpoints

Two endpoints are *connected* if their connection identifiers agree, in which case each receives only what the other has sent, in the same order.

```
 ┌─ Connected ──────────────────┐
 │   EP₁                        │
 │   EP₂                        │
 │ ──────────────────           │
 │   cid₁  = cid₂               │
 │                              │
 │   rcvd₁ < sent₂              │
 │   rcvd₂ < sent₁              │
 └───────────────────────────────┘
```

This section has presented the essentials of endpoint events independently of any details of connection or disconnection — that is, that data is transferred in either direction between connected endpoints, without reordering.

Any specification of acknowledgements or flow-control would be given in this section also.

3. Connections – CON

3.1 Connection state

At every connection may be observed

- ○ the status of its endpoints
- ○ whether each endpoint is aware of the connection
- ○ whether the connection is to be dropped

The *status* of an endpoint is represented by the set

$$\text{Status} \triangleq \{\text{New, Req, Ind, Open}\}$$

New   indicates that the endpoint has not yet interacted with the connection.

Req   indicates that ConReq has occurred at the endpoint.

Ind   indicates that ConInd has occurred at the endpoint.

Open   indicates that either ConRes or ConCon, as appropriate, has occurred at the endpoint — that it has completed the connection establishment protocol.

Technical Commentary

o   EId ↠ Status is the set of partial functions from EId to Status.

o   P EId is the powerset of EId – the set of all its subsets.

o   Boolean is the set {True, False}.

o   #status is the number of elements in the set status. (Functions are sets of ordered pairs.)

o   dom status is the domain of the function status; that is, it is the set of elements eid of EId for which status(eid) is defined.

o   [src ↦ Req, dst ↦ New] is the function of type EId ↠ Status that takes src to Req and dst to New.

Each endpoint is uniquely identified by an endpoint identifier drawn from the set EId; the map status gives the status of either endpoint of a connection.

$$\text{status: EId} \nrightarrow \text{Status}$$

An endpoint is *aware* of a connection after its first interaction with it (ConReq, ConInd) until it has disconnected from it (DisReq, DisInd). The set aware contains the endpoint identifiers of the endpoints aware of the connection.

$$\text{aware: } \mathbb{P}\text{ EId}$$

The boolean drop indicates whether the connection is to be *dropped*. Being dropped is the ultimate fate of every connection; normally, a connection is dropped when both endpoints have disconnected.

$$\text{drop: Boolean}$$

Finally, each connection has exactly two endpoints, and only its own endpoints may be aware of it.

```
┌─ CON ──────────────────────────────┐
│   status: EId ⇸ Status             │
│   aware : ℙ EId                     │
│   drop  : Boolean                   │
├─────────────────────────────────────┤
│   #status = 2                       │
│   aware ⊆ dom status                │
└─────────────────────────────────────┘
```

3.2 Connection events

The event ConReq creates a connection between two new endpoints src and dst.

```
┌─ ConReq ───────────────────────────────┐
│   CON'                                  │
│   src, dst: EId                         │
├──────────────────────────────────────────┤
│   status' = [src ↦ Req, dst ↦ New]      │
│   aware'  = {src}                        │
│   drop'   = False                        │
└──────────────────────────────────────────┘
```

The event Drop destroys a connection; it can occur only when a connection is to be dropped, and neither of its endpoints is aware of it.

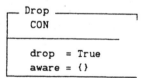

```
┌─ Drop ──────────────┐
│   CON               │
├──────────────────────┤
│   drop  = True       │
│   aware = {}         │
└──────────────────────┘
```

Technical Commentary

○   status ⊕ [dst ↦ Ind] is the function status overridden be the singleton
function [dst ↦ Ind].

status' (eid) =

if eid = dst then Ind
                     else status (eid)

The remaining connection events alter an existing connection - but the identities of its endpoints can never change.

```
┌─ ΔCON ─────────────────────────────┐
│   CON                              │
│   CON'                             │
│ ─────────────────────              │
│   dom status' = dom status         │
└────────────────────────────────────
```

ConInd makes the destination endpoint aware of the new connection.

```
┌─ ConInd ───────────────────────────┐
│   ΔCON                             │
│   src, dst: EId                    │
│ ─────────────────                  │
│   status (src) = Req               │
│   status (dst) = New               │
│   dst ∉ aware                      │
│                                    │
│   status' = status ⊕ [dst ↦ Ind]   │
│   aware'  = aware  ∪ {dst}         │
│   drop'   = drop                   │
└────────────────────────────────────
```

ConRes is a positive response by the destination endpoint, indicating that it will accept the connection.

```
┌─ ConRes ───────────────────────────┐
│   ΔCON                             │
│   src, dst: EId                    │
│ ─────────────────                  │
│   status (src) = Req               │
│   status (dst) = Ind               │
│   dst ∈ aware                      │
│                                    │
│   status' = status ⊕ [dst ↦ Open]  │
│   aware'  = aware                  │
│   drop'   = drop                   │
└────────────────────────────────────
```

Technical Commentary

ConCon is a positive response at the source endpoint, indicating that the destination has accepted the connection.

```
┌─ ConCon ─────────────────────────────────┐
│  ΔCON                                     │
│  src, dst: EId                            │
│ ─────────────────────                     │
│                                           │
│  status (src) = Req                       │
│  status (dst) = Open                      │
│  src ∈ aware                              │
│                                           │
│  status' = status ⊕ [src ↦ Open]          │
│  aware'  = aware                          │
│  drop'   = drop                           │
└───────────────────────────────────────────┘
```

DisReq at either endpoint makes that endpoint unaware of the connection, and indicates that the connection is to be dropped.

```
┌─ DisReq ──────────────────────────┐
│  ΔCON                             │
│  ep: EId                         │
│ ─────────────────                │
│                                  │
│  ep ∈ aware                      │
│                                  │
│  status' = status               │
│  aware'  = aware - {ep}          │
│  drop'   = True                  │
└──────────────────────────────────┘
```

DisInd at either endpoint occurs if the endpoint is notified that the connection is to be dropped.

```
┌─ DisInd ──────────────────────────┐
│  ΔCON                             │
│  ep: EId                         │
│ ─────────────────                │
│                                  │
│  ep   ∈ aware                    │
│  drop = True                     │
│                                  │
│  status' = status               │
│  aware'  = aware - {ep}          │
│  drop'   = drop                  │
└──────────────────────────────────┘
```

330

Technical Commentary

Finally, spontaneous release of a connection occurs when the service unilaterally decides
that the connection is to be dropped.

```
┌─ Disconnect ────────────────┐
│   ΔCON                       │
│  ───────────────────────     │
│                              │
│   status'  = status          │
│   aware'   = aware           │
│   drop'    = True            │
└──────────────────────────────┘
```

This section has presented the essentials of the connection/disconnection protocol
independently of any details of data transfer along a connection. The effects of any of
the following, for example, can be determined from the material here:

- ConReq then DisReq
- DisReq at both endpoints
- spontaneous release of the connection at any time

4. The network — NET

4.1 Network state

The two previous sections EP and CON can be used to construct the description of a
network of connected endpoints.

```
┌─ NET ───────────────────────┐
│   eps : EId ↠ EP             │
│   cons: CId ↠ CON            │
└──────────────────────────────┘
```

The map eps gives for any endpoint identifier the state of the endpoint it identifies;
cons does similarly for connections. The following predicates express the relationship
between the components of the network — firstly, that the maps eps and cons agree on
the association of endpoints and connections, and secondly that endpoints occur only in
connected pairs.

Technical Commentary

o
$$\exists EP = eps\ (e)|\ c = cid$$

is shorthand for

$$\exists EP|\ EP = eps(e) \land c = cid$$

which in turn is shorthand for

$$\exists cid:\ CId;\ sent,\ rcvd:\ seq\ Data|$$
$$(cid,\ sent,\ rcvd) = eps\ (e)$$
$$\land\ \ c = cid$$

o   This use of the schema EP.Connected as a predicate simply applies its predicate part

$$cid_1 = cid_2$$
$$rcvd_1 \leqslant sent_2$$
$$rcvd_2 \leqslant sent_1$$

o   From EP and CON (repeated here for convenience)

```
┌─ EP.newEP' ─────────────────────┐
│   cid': CId                     │
│   sent', rcvd': seq Data        │
├─────────────────────────────────┤
│   sent' = rcvd' = <>            │
└─────────────────────────────────┘
```

```
┌─ CON.ConReq ────────────────────┐
│   CON'                          │
│   src, dst: EId                 │
├─────────────────────────────────┤
│   status' = [src ↦ Req, dst ↦ New] │
│   aware'  = {src}               │
│   drop'   = False               │
└─────────────────────────────────┘
```

```
┌─ NET ──────────────────────────────────────────────┐
│   NET                                               │
│   ─────                                             │
│                                                     │
│   (∀e: EId; c: CId.                                 │
│                                                     │
│        (∃EP  = eps (e)| c = cid)                    │
│      ■ (∃CON = cons(c)| e ∈ dom status))            │
│                                                     │
│                                                     │
│   (∀(e₁, EP₁): eps.                                 │
│                                                     │
│      (∃(e₂, EP₂): eps| e₁ ≠ e₂.                     │
│                                                     │
│         EP.Connected))                              │
└─────────────────────────────────────────────────────┘
```

For all endpoint identifiers e and connection identifiers c, c is the connection of endpoint e iff e is an endpoint of connection c.

For every endpoint EP_1 there is some other endpoint EP_2 connected to it.

The NET events are constructed from events of EP and CON. The general event schema for NET is

```
┌─ ΔNET ──┐
│   NET   │
│   NET'  │
└─────────┘
```

ConReq chooses fresh endpoint identifiers src, dst and a connection identifier cid which then identify new endpoints (EP.newEP') and a new connection (CON' in CON.ConReq).

```
┌─ ConReq ────────────────────────────────────────────┐
│   ΔNET                                               │
│   EP.newEP'                                          │
│   CON.ConReq                                         │
│  ─────────────────────────────────                  │
│   src  ∉ dom eps                                     │
│   dst  ∉ dom eps                                     │
│   cid' ∉ dom cons                                    │
│                                                     │
│   eps' = eps ⊕ [src ↦ newEP', dst ↦ newEP']         │
│   cons' = cons ⊕ [cid' ↦ CON']                      │
└─────────────────────────────────────────────────────┘
```

○   From CON,

```
┌─ CON.Drop ──────────────┐
│  CON                    │
│  ─────────────────────  │
│                         │
│  drop  = True           │
│  aware = {}             │
└─────────────────────────┘
```

○   ΔCON occurs *twice* in ConInd — once in φCON, once in CON.ConInd. These *repeated* components merge, so that ConInd as defined here contains only one occurrence of each of the six components cid, sent, rcvd, cid', sent', rcvd'. This is the expansion of the definition:

```
┌─ ConInd ─────────────────────────────────────┐
│  ΔNET                                         │
│  ΔCON                                         │
│  cid: CId                                     │
│                                               │
│  src, dst: EId                                │
│  ───────────────────────────────────────────  │
│  CON = cons (cid)                             │
│                                               │
│  status (src) = Req                           │
│  status (dst) = New                           │
│  dst ∉ aware                                  │
│                                               │
│  status' = status ⊕ [dst ↦ Ind]              │
│  aware'  = aware  ∪ {dst}                     │
│  drop'   = drop                               │
│                                               │
│  cons' = cons ⊕ [cid ↦ CON']                 │
│                                               │
│  eps' = eps                                   │
└───────────────────────────────────────────────┘
```

Drop removes all trace of a connection (CON in CON.Drop) and its endpoints.

```
┌─ Drop ──────────────────────────┐
│  ΔNET                           │
│  CON.Drop                       │
│  cid: CId                       │
│ ─────────────────               │
│                                 │
│  CON = cons (cid)               │
│                                 │
│  eps' = eps  \ dom status       │
│  cons' = cons \ {cid}           │
└─────────────────────────────────┘
```

All of the remaining CON events update an existing connection, and do not affect endpoints.

```
┌─ φCON ──────────────────────────┐
│  ΔNET                           │
│  ΔCON                           │
│  cid: CId                       │
│ ─────────────────               │
│                                 │
│  CON  = cons (cid)              │
│  cons' = cons ⊕ [cid ↦ CON']    │
│                                 │
│  eps' = eps                     │
└─────────────────────────────────┘
```

ConInd may be defined

```
┌─ ConInd ──────────┐
│  φCON             │
│  CON.ConInd       │
└───────────────────┘
```

or more briefly,

$$ConInd \quad ≙ φCON ∧ CON.ConInd$$

and similarly

$$
\begin{aligned}
ConRes &≙ φCON ∧ CON.ConRes \\
ConCon &≙ φCON ∧ CON.ConCon \\
DisReq &≙ φCON ∧ CON.DisReq \\
DisInd &≙ φCON ∧ CON.DisInd \\
Disconnect &≙ φCON ∧ CON.Disconnect
\end{aligned}
$$

Technical Commentary

o   cid: CId, as well as occurring explicitly, is a component of EP, and hence of
      ΔEP.

o   This is the expansion of DatReq:

```
┌─ DatReq ──────────────────────────────────────────────┐
│  ΔNET                                                   │
│  ΔEP                                                    │
│  ep: EId                                                │
│                                                         │
│  CON                                                    │
│  cid: CId                                               │
├─────────────────────────────────────────────────────── │
│  EP   = eps  (ep)                                       │
│  CON  = cons (cid)                                      │
│                                                         │
│  status (ep) = Open                                     │
│  ep ∈ aware                                             │
│                                                         │
│  sent' = sent + <data>                                  │
│  rcvd' = rcvd                                           │
│                                                         │
│  eps'  = eps ⊕ [ep ↦ EP']                              │
│  cons' = cons                                           │
└─────────────────────────────────────────────────────── ┘
```

A similar approach may be used for the two endpoint events, which do not affect connections. They are additionally constrained, however, by the fact that they can occur only if the endpoint is Open (has completed the connection protocol) and aware (has not yet disconnected).

```
┌─ φEP ──────────────────────────────┐
│  ΔNET                               │
│  ΔEP                                │
│  ep: EId                            │
│                                     │
│  CON                                │
│  cid: CId                           │
├─────────────────────────────────────┤
│  EP    = eps (ep)                   │
│  eps'  = eps ⊕ [ep ↦ EP']           │
│                                     │
│  CON   = cons (cid)                 │
│  cons' = cons                       │
│                                     │
│  status (ep) = Open                 │
│  ep ∈ aware                         │
└─────────────────────────────────────┘
```

```
DatReq      ≙ φEP ∧ EP.DatReq
DatInd      ≙ φEP ∧ EP.DatInd
```

5. Service access points - SAP

A service access point is only a collection of endpoints. Each endpoint identifier in EId has two components, the first of which gives the service access point with which it is associated. Service access point identifiers are drawn from the set SId; the remainder of the endpoint identifier is drawn from the set Suffix.

```
┌─ EId ──────────┐
│  sid   : SId   │
│  suffix: Suffix│
└────────────────┘
```

The projection function

$$sid: EId \rightarrow SId$$

gives the service access point identifier for any endpoint identifier; in particular, the following schema does so for the endpoint identifiers used in previous sections.

Technical Commentary

```
┌─ Endpoints ─────────────────────────────┐
│   src,  dst, ep : EId                    │
│   from, to,  sap: SId                    │
│                                          │
├──────────────────────────────────────    │
│   from = sid (src)                       │
│   to   = sid (dst)                       │
│   sap  = sid (ep)                        │
└──────────────────────────────────────────┘
```

6. The service

6.1 Service state

This final stage of specification will integrate the sections NET and SAP to give a description of the service as a whole. The service state is simply a restriction of the network state - there may be no more than one endpoint known at any service access point.

```
┌─ SERVICE ───────────────────────────────────────┐
│   NET                                            │
│   ──────────────                                 │
│                                                  │
│     ∀s: SId.                                     │
│                                                  │
│        1 ≥ #{e: EId| ∃CON: ran cons.             │
│                                                  │
│                   s = sid (e)                    │
│                   e ∈ aware}                      │
│                                                  │
└──────────────────────────────────────────────────┘
```

6.2 Service events

In this section the externally observable parameters of each event will be distinguished by placing them in parentheses in the usual formal parameter position. The observations of state are in each case the observations in SERVICE and SERVICE'. All other observations now assume the role of "local variables" - they may take any values consistent with the predicates in which they appear.

```
┌─ ΔSERVICE ──────────┐
│   SERVICE           │
│   SERVICE'          │
│   SAP.Endpoints     │
└─────────────────────┘
```

ConReq (from, to: SId)   ≙ ΔSERVICE ∧ NET.ConReq
ConInd (from, to: SId)   ≙ ΔSERVICE ∧ NET.ConInd

ConRes (to : SId)   ≙ ΔSERVICE ∧ NET.ConRes
ConCon (from: SId)   ≙ ΔSERVICE ∧ NET.ConCon

Technical Commentary

o   The presentation of this specification in stages has the advantage that each
    stage can be studied on its own, since the method of combination of stages
    preserves properties of parts in the whole. Yet because of the occasionally
    almost magical connections between the parts, it's possible to lose context:
    "Where on earth did *that* component come from?".

    Mechanical assistance would help - it would be straightforward for a machine to
    answer the above question. More generally, it could recall, combine or expand
    schemas as required.

DisReq (sap: SId)   ≜ ΔSERVICE ∧ NET.DisReq
DisInd (sap: SId)   ≜ ΔSERVICE ∧ NET.DisInd

DatReq (sap: SId; data: Data)   ≜ ΔSERVICE ∧ NET.DatReq
DatInd (sap: SId; data: Data)   ≜ ΔSERVICE ∧ NET.DatInd

Disconnect (cid: CId)   ≜ ΔSERVICE ∧ NET.Disconnect
Drop   (cid: CId)   ≜ ΔSERVICE ∧ NET.Drop

7. Conclusion

This specification would not suffice as a contract between customer and supplier. Must the service *ever* perform a DatInd, for example? Could it spontaneously release *every* connection?

The first question is one of total correctness; one needs to know that a DatReq eventually *will* be followed by its corresponding DatInd, given the absence of events which specifically prevent it. But even this may not be sufficient - how long *is* eventually?

But the two questions above can also be seen as questions of *efficiency*; and this document, as the basis of a contract, supplies the terms in which such questions can be precisely answered. For most customers, "eventually" is not good enough - he may need more specific guarantees of performance. For example, it may be necessary to place a specific limit on the time between a DatReq and its corresponding DatInd, or on the frequency of spontaneous releases.

In the absence of guarantees of performance - eventual or otherwise - this specification is sufficient only to define what the service *can* do; the question of what it *must* do is not answered. Is this enough?

Appendix - Glossary of Mathematical Symbols

≙	"is defined to be"
∧	logical conjunction
∨	logical disjunction
⟶	logical implication
∀	universal quantification: "for all ..."
∃	existential quantification: "there exists ..."
N	the set of natural numbers (non-negative integers)
R	the set of real numbers (both positive and negative)
m..n	the set of natural numbers between m and n inclusive
max(m,n)	the greater of m and n
⊆	set inclusion
⊂	strict set inclusion
∪	set union
∩	set intersection
−	set difference
∈	set membership
{}	the empty set
{term| pred}	the set of term such that pred
(a,b)	the ordered pair a then b
#	the cardinality of a set
P	powerset: the set of all subsets

disjoint   pairwise disjoint:

$$\text{for } \underline{A}: \textbf{P P } A,$$

$$\text{disjoint } \underline{A} \triangleq$$

$$(\forall a, a': \underline{A}. ((a \cap a') \neq \{\}) \longrightarrow (a = a'))$$

A ⟶ B	the set of total functions from A to B
A ⇸ B	the set of (partial) functions from A to B
A ⟷ B	the set of relations from A to B
[a ↦ b]	the singleton function ("maplet") which maps a to b

λ   lambda abstraction

$$\lambda a{:}A.\ \text{term} \triangleq \{(a,\text{term})\mid a{:}\ A\}$$

f(x)	the function f applied to x
f x	the function f applied to x

dom   the domain of a relation (or function):

$$\text{for } R{:}\ A \leftrightarrow B$$

$$\text{dom } R \triangleq \{a{:}\ A\mid (\exists b{:}\ B.\ a\ R\ b)\}$$

ran   the range of a relation (or function)

$$\text{for } R{:}\ A \leftrightarrow B$$

$$\text{ran } R \triangleq \{b{:}\ B\mid (\exists a{:}\ A.\ a\ R\ b)\}$$

| ° | relational (or functional) compoosition |
| ; | forward relational (or functional) composition |

$$(f \; ; \; g) \; \triangleq \; (g \circ f)$$

f^k the relation (or function) f composed with itself k times:

$$f^0 = identity$$
$$f^1 = f$$
$$f^2 = f \circ f$$
$$f^3 = f \circ f \circ f$$

( )   image:

for R: A ↔ B; $\underline{A}$: ℙA

$$R(\underline{A}) \; \triangleq \; \{b: B| \; (\exists a: \underline{A}. \; a \; R \; b)\}$$

↾   domain restriction:

for f: A ↔ B; $\underline{A}$: ℙA

$$f \upharpoonright \underline{A} \; \triangleq \; \{(a,b): f| \; a \in \underline{A}\}$$

\   domain co-restriction

for f: A ↔ B; $\underline{A}$: ℙA

$$f \setminus \underline{A} \; \triangleq \; \{(a,b): f| \; a \notin \underline{A}\}$$

⊕   functional overriding

for f,g: A ↔ B

$$f \oplus g \; \triangleq \; (f \setminus dom \; g) \cup g$$

seq A   the set of sequences whose elements are drawn from A

$$seq \; A \; \triangleq \; \{s: \mathbb{N} \twoheadrightarrow A. \; (\exists n: \mathbb{N}. \; dom \; s = 1..n)\}$$

#s   the length of a sequence s

$$1..\#s = dom \; s$$

⟨⟩   the empty sequence {}

last   the final element of a sequence

for s: seq A

$$last(s) \; \triangleq \; s(\#s)$$

front   all but the last element of a sequence

for s: seq A

$$front(s) \; \triangleq \; s \upharpoonright 1..(\#s-1)$$

front is not defined for the empty sequence

∧	schema conjunction
∨	schema disjunction
∘	schema composition
⨾	schema forward composition
[name2\name1]	schema component renaming
↾	schema projection
\	schema component hiding
θ	the ordered tuple of the schemas component names

Specification of a simplified Network Service in CSP

(Problem 2)

Carroll Morgan
C.A.R. Hoare

Programming Research Group
8-11 Keble Road
Oxford OX1 3QD

5 November 1983
revised October 1984

Abstract

The specification of a simplified Network Service is given in CSP.

Because specifications of such services are notoriously difficult, it is especially pleasing that in this case the problem can be decomposed into several more easily achieved sub-specifications. This decomposition greatly improves the credibility of the overall specification.

1. Introduction

Problem 2 describes a simplified version of the ISO Network Service, and asks for a specification of it. The main simplifications are

Neither *resets* nor *expedited data* are described.

Each service access point (SAP) is limited to participation in only one connection at a time.

We discovered that the second simplification seemed to make the service harder rather than easier to specify; and so we chose instead to specify the simplified Network Service without that restriction. In fact, it was easiest to allow a SAP to participate in even an unbounded number of connections simultaneously.

We use CSP *[1]* as our specification language, and describe the allowable behaviour of the simplified network by constructing a process NETWORK whose traces are exactly the allowed sequences of network events.

1.1 Structure of the specification

We found it was possible to split the problem into three parts, which could be specified separately; by doing this, of course, the specification was made much less complex. The parts are:

Data transmission
SAP behaviour
Connection behaviour

Data transmission is the purpose of the network; all the complexities of connection establishment, for example, are just the means to that end. In this section we specify that all messages sent from one end of a connection arrive at the other end, in the order they were sent. We do in fact allow an unbounded number of messages to be in transit at any time (another simplifying assumption).

The specification of *SAP behaviour* covers the details of the way in which a SAP treats one end of a connection - *e.g.* that it must complete the connection protocol before sending or receiving data, and that it cannot send or receive data after it has (been) disconnected.

Finally, the specification of *Connection behaviour* covers the way in which events at one end of a connection relate to those at its other end - that a *ConReq* here appears eventually as a *ConInd* there, for example. (This really includes data transmission as a special case - so special, however, that we chose to describe it separately).

2. Data transmission

2.1 The alphabet of data events

The alphabet of data events is

DT = SAPname × {DatReq, DatInd} × Data

where **SAPname** is a set from which names of SAPs are drawn, and Data is some set of data elements that can be transmitted or received in a single request. We write

a.DatReq(d)

for a typical element of DT. a is the name of the SAP at which this event occurs, and d is the data transmitted.

For any particular a ∈ SAPname, we write a.DT for that subset of DT which is the set of data transmission events occurring only at a; that is,

$$a.DT = \{a\} \times \{DatReq, DatInd\} \times Data$$

2.2 The DATA process

For any two SAPs a and b, we construct a process DATA[a,b] which describes unboundedly-buffered bi-directional communication between them.

$$DATA[a,b] = \{t \in (a.DT \cup b.DT)^* \mid \forall s \leqslant t.$$

$$(s \downarrow a.DatReq \geqslant s \downarrow b.DatInd)$$

$$\wedge (s \downarrow b.DatReq \geqslant s \downarrow a.DatInd)\}$$

The alphabet of this process is a.DT ∪ b.DT.

The relation ≤ is the *prefix* relation over sequences; s ≤ t (t ≥ s) iff s is a prefix (initial subsequence) of t.

The standard operator *select* (↓) constructs the subsequence (not necessarily initial or contiguous) of its first argument which includes exactly those elements in the form given by its second argument. In this case, for example,

$$<> \downarrow a.DatReq \quad = <>$$

$$(s.<e>) \downarrow a.DatReq = (s \downarrow a.DatReq).<d> \quad \text{if } e = a.DatReq(d)$$
$$\text{for some } d \in Data,$$

$$= s \downarrow a.DatReq \quad \text{otherwise}$$

(. is sequence concatenation.)

Notice that in each element of the subsequence the selector "a.DatReq" is suppressed, leaving only the "d". Thus if

$$s = <a.DatReq(d_1), b.DatInd(d_1), a.DatReq(d_2)>$$

then

$$s \downarrow a.DatReq = <d_1, d_2>$$

We have given the process DATA[a,b] directly as a set of traces (rather than as a CSP *description* of a set of traces) only because in this particular case it is more convenient to do so.

3. SAP behaviour

3.1 More events

To describe SAP behaviour we must first introduce the remaining events of our alphabet.

They are of two kinds: connection establishment, and disconnection.

Connection establishment events are members of the set

$$CE = \quad SAPname \times \{ConReq, ConInd\} \times SAPname$$
$$U \quad SAPname \times \{ConRes, ConCon\}$$

We write

```
a.ConReq(b)
b.ConInd(a)
b.ConRes
a.ConCon
```

for typical elements of CE . As before, the first component gives the SAP at which the event occurs. ConRes and ConCon need no parameter since, by the time they are used, the identity of the "other" SAP is already known (from the preceding ConReq or ConInd). Naturally, this means that (so far) we can only talk about one connection at a or b at a time - we do this deliberately to simplify our presentation.

Disconnection events are members of the set

$$DC = SAPname \times \{DisReq, DisInd\}$$

We write

```
a.DisReq
```

for a typical element of DC . We can now define the set NET of all network events:

$$NET = DT \cup CE \cup DC$$

3.2 An example

Now we have introduced all the events, we can give an example of a typical exchange between SAPs a and b . The following trace should be read from left to right, top to bottom.

```
a.ConReq(b)
                          b.ConInd(a)
                          b.ConRes
a.ConCon
a.DatReq(d₁)
                          b.DatInd(d₁)
                          b.DatReq(d₂)
a.DatInd(d₂)
a.DisReq
                          b.DisInd
```

3.3 The SAP process

We first define the behaviour of a single SAP with name a. It engages in a number of cycles, in each of which it either initiates or responds to a connection with an arbitrary SAP named b. The following process describes *one* cycle only; its alphabet is a.NET (*c.f.* a.DT).

```
SAP[a] =

        U              (a.ConReq(b) →  ((a.ConCon) → a.DT*) until DIS[a])
    b ∈ SAPname

               ▯ (a.ConInd(b) →   ((a.ConRes) → a.DT*) until DIS[a])
```

where

```
        DIS[a] =   a.DisReq → STOP
                 ▯ a.DisInd → STOP
```

The binary operator until is defined as follows (. is sequence concatenation):

$$P \text{ until } Q = \{p.q|\ p \in P \land q \in Q\}$$

P until Q behaves like P *until* it stops behaving like P and starts behaving like Q. Recall that P is a prefix-closed set of traces, so this transition can occur at any time.

"until " is associative, with unit STOP .

4. Connection behaviour

We describe the connection process in three independent parts: *connection establishment*, *data transmission*, and *disconnection*.

4.1 Connection establishment

Here, in the process CON[a,b], we describe the protocol by which two SAPs establish a connection.

```
        CON[a,b] = a.ConReq(b) →
                   b.ConInd(a) →
                   b.ConRes    →
                   a.ConCon    → STOP
```

We are, of course, still describing only a *single* connection.

4.2 Data transmission

This is described by the process DATA[a,b] introduced in section 2.2.

4.3 Disconnection

We allow *any* interleaving of the disconnection events at each end:

```
        DIS[a,b] =

          (a.DisReq → STOP  ▯  a.DisInd → STOP)

       ‖ (b.DisReq → STOP  ▯  b.DisInd → STOP)
```

Of the eight possible behaviours this allows, some are certainly peculiar; for example, the following trace belongs to DIS[a,b] :

>   a.DisInd
>
>   b.DisReq

This and other similar behaviours are merely consequences of the network having *spontaneously* disconnected. In this example, it was a spontaneous disconnection which "caused" the event a.DisInd - but SAP b itself requested disconnection before the news reached it (in the form of b.DisInd).

We can characterise the behaviours involving spontaneous disconnection by noticing that they are exactly those in which a Dis*Ind* occurs first (rather than the more usual Dis*Req*).

4.4 The CONNECTION process

The process CONNECTION[a,b] is simply the combination of the three processes above: since each constrains the possible behaviour of a single connection, the connection must satisfy all three:

$$CONNECTION[a,b] = CON[a,b] \parallel DATA[a,b] \parallel DIS[a,b]$$

Although the CONNECTION process allows, for example, a.DisInd to precede a.ConReq, this is of no consequence; when the connection runs in parallel with the SAP processes, these will enforce correct behaviour of the connection endpoints.

5. Multiple connections; the network as a whole

5.1 Multiple connections

We now introduce *unique identifiers*, drawn from some set Id, to allow multiple connections at a SAP.

We extend the alphabet NET by annotating every event with a unique identifier; that is, the new alphabet is

>   Id × NET

in which typical events are written

>   i:a.ConReq(b)

Now we can allow an arbitrary number of simultaneous SAP processes by using unique identifiers to distinguish them; this is described by the process SAPS:

$$SAPS = \underset{a \in SAPname}{\parallel} \quad \underset{i \in Id}{\parallel} \quad i:SAP[a]$$

i:P is the process P with all its events annotated with i: .

We similarly allow any number of connections to proceed in parallel:

$$CONNECTIONS = \underset{i \in Id}{\parallel} \quad \underset{\substack{a,b \in SAPname \\ a \neq b}}{U} \quad i:CONNECTION[a,b]$$

Note that as we have specified it here, an identifier is used by at most one connection (because U was used in the definition of CONNECTIONS rather than ||), and hence at most once by any SAP. It is this simplification which allows us *in the specification at least* to ignore the problem of deciding when a connection has really terminated. There's no reason we need to know — new connections use new identifiers, and old identifiers are left lying around until no-one remembers them. In a potential implementation, however, it may be quite a problem to garbage collect these numbers for re-use.

5.2 The network as a whole

We finally construct our specification of the network by drawing together the two parts:

NETWORK = SAPS || CONNECTIONS

(Compare the dining philosophers: SAPs are *forks*, picked up by the connections. Each connection requires two!)

This magical use of the parallel combinator || conceals a great deal of tricky implementation detail: how, for example, do the two ends of a connection agree on a common identifier to use for it? How do we avoid the re-use of identifiers chosen at physically remote SAPs?

The point is, of course, that we don't have to say *how* it is done — we simply say that it *is* done. That is the power of specification.

5.3 A final example

Consider again the trace of section 3.2 (now suitably annotated with i:); in this example, a, b, and i are arbitrary but fixed:

```
i:a.ConReq(b)
                        i:b.ConInd(a)
                        i:b.ConRes
i:a.ConCon
i:a.DatReq(d₁)
                        i:b.DatInd(d₁)
                        i:b.DatReq(d₂)
i:a.DatInd(d₂)
i:a.DisReq
                        i:b.DisInd
```

Is this trace allowed by the process NETWORK? To answer this, we must ask if it is allowed by each of the *components* of NETWORK, and then by their components, and so on.

Since NETWORK = SAPS || CONNECTIONS (section 5.2), we must check whether the trace is allowed by both SAPS and CONNECTIONS. We consider SAPS first.

SAPS is a parallel composition of many independent subprocesses (section 5.1); among these are i:SAP[a] and i:SAP[b]. Now i:SAP[a] (section 3.3) constrains only those events in its alphabet i:a.NET; it makes no demands on the behaviour of events occurring, say, at SAP b. And i:SAP[a] allows

```
i:a.ConReq(b)
i:a.ConCon
i:a.DatReq(d₁)
i:a.DatInd(d₂)
i:a.DisReq
```

It in fact *requires* that ConCon follow (*i.e.* not precede) ConReq, that the Dat events follow the Con events, and that DisReq follow Conreq.

The process i:SAP[b] allows

> i:b.ConInd(a)
> i:b.ConRes
> i:b.DatInd(d₁)
> i:b.DatReq(d₂)
> i:b.DisInd

It has similar requirements.

To be allowed by CONNECTIONS (section 5.1), the trace must be allowed by i:CONNECTION[a,b] - and hence by each of the three processes i:CON[a,b], i:DATA[a,b], and i:DIS[a,b] (section 4.4).

i:CON[a,b] (section 4.1) allows (in fact, requires)

> i:a.ConReq(b)
>
> > i:b.ConInd(a)
> > i:b.ConRes
>
> i:a.ConCon

And i:Data[a,b] (section 2.2) allows

> i:a.DatReq(d₁)
>
> > i:b.DatInd(d₁)
> > i:b.DatReq(d₂)
>
> i:a.DatInd(d₂)

It requires only that each DatInd follow its corresponding DatReq .

And finally, i:DIS[a,b] (section 4.3) allows

> i:a.DisReq
>
> > i:b.DisInd

We see here that this disconnection was not spontaneous.

6. Conclusion - and a small problem

The interest of this specification example is much more in its structure than in its detail. We didn't expect such a lovely decomposition of the problem, particularly as protocols and services seem to be very difficult to deal with - to specify or to implement.

The success of CSP here is due in part to its very simple parallel combinator (indeed, in CSP, parallel composition is much simpler than sequential). One normally joins components of a specificaton with conjunction; in CSP, this simply means parallel composition.

The small problem is to do with the "spontaneous disconnect". Spontaneous disconnects occur (of course) whether the user wants them or not; they represent *internal nondeterminism* on the part of the service. We have allowed a user to ignore the possibility of spontaneous disconnection, if he wants to do so, while he continues with (say) data transfer. To that extent our specification is incorrect.

Internal nondeterminism can be introduced into a CSP process by *hiding* (see *[1]*), and that is what we would have to do to correct our specification. The hidden event would probably represent the moment at which the service decides that spontaneous disconnection is inevitable. The change would be confined to the description of connection behaviour.

It would not be overly difficult to extend this specification to deal with both expedited data and resets. Although the details might be fairly involved, we at least know that we can confine our extensions to section 2 (the DATA process), and leave the rest of the specification as it stands. This is of course an advantage of good structure.

Another advantage of good structure in a specification is that it gives us some chance of understanding it.

References

[1]   C.A.R.   Hoare; *Notes on Communicating Sequential Processes*; Programming Research Group Technical Monograph PRG-33; Oxford, August 1983

A Solution to Problem 7

- Parallel Combinator Reduction Machine -

Peter Mosses

Dept. of Computer Science

University of Edinburgh*

Abstract

A formal specification is given, allowing a wide class of parallel
implementations but excluding sequential implementations.   The
specification technique used is novel,and has not yet been shown to be
applicable to other problems.

The Problem

"To specify a machine which can reduce combinations

... by performing all possible reductions in parallel."

Taken literally, this informal statement of the problem has two rather
unfortunate consequences, which our "customer" presumably did not realise:-

(a)   Unbounded parallel processing:

Consider combinations of the form

   plus(times 1 1)(... plus(times n n)(0)...).

It is clearly possible to reduce each times i i --> i^2 ;

so a machine conforming to the specification would have to be able to
do n such reductions in parallel, for any n!

(b)   Eager reduction:

Combinations involving K, e.g.

   K 0 (plus 1 2), K 0(Y(plus 1))

may be independent of some sub-combinations, since K x y --> x.   But
machine conforming to the specification has to reduce these unnecessar
sub-combinations (in parallel).

Let us assume that our customer agrees to amend the informal statement of

---

* On leave (until January 1984) from:
  Computer Science Dept., Aarhus University,
  DK-8000 Aarhus C, Denmark.

the problem to avoid the above consequences.   Furthermore, we are to
produce only a functional specification for a reduction machine, rather
than a design specification.   In order to disallow sequential implementations,
we shall require that the interface to an implementation allows us to observe
partial results produced by reducing sub-combinations - such an interface
would be needed in practice if a machine was to be used for reducing
combinations corresponding to infinite lists (e.g. Y(P O)), etc.

The Modified Problem

Before we give an informal statement of the modified problem, let us introduce some terminology about combinations:

- A <u>redex</u> is an occurrence of the left-hand-side of a reduction rule.
- A redex x is <u>pertinent</u> in y iff
  - (i) $y = x x_1 \ldots x_n$, with $n \geq 0$;   or
  - (ii) $y = z x_1 \ldots x_n$, where z is a combinator and x is pertinent in some
    x_i, $1 \leq i \leq n$ (but $z x_1 \ldots x_m$ is not a redex for any $m \leq n$).

We may now state the modified problem as:

> "To write a specification that permits only those implementations
> that reduce combinations (correctly) and eventually eliminate all
> pertinent redexes that occur."

We shall not attempt to make this statement more precise, turning now to give
a specification that can be argued to solve the (modified) problem.

A Solution

For a machine to conform to our specification, we shall require that it has
an interface that allows us to observe the partial results produced after
discrete time intervals.   This amounts to a (mathematical) function

  imp: <u>Exp</u> -> (<u>Time</u> -> <u>Res</u>),

where <u>Exp</u> is the set of combinations (expressions),
  <u>Time</u> is $\{0,1,\ldots\}$,
  <u>Res</u> is the set of (partial) results, i.e. combinations with any
    redexes replaced by a place-holder "?".
For any $x \in$ <u>Exp</u>, imp(x) is a function from time to results.
We shall define a canonical interface function

  red: <u>Exp</u> -> (<u>Time</u> -> <u>Res</u>),

capturing the required (minimal and maximal) behaviour of conforming reduction

machines.   Now the (partial) results <u>Res</u> can be partially ordered, with
$x \sqsubseteq y$ iff (roughly) a reduction that produced x might produce y, later -
i.e. y contains (at least) all the "information" in x.   (Scott's Theory of
Domains makes much use of such partial orderings.)

We may then say that an implementation (characterised by) imp <u>conforms</u>
iff, for all $x \in$ <u>Exp</u>,

(i) imp(x) is a non-decreasing function:

  $imp(x)(i) \sqsubseteq imp(x)(i+1)$;

(ii) imp(x) eventually surpasses every value of red(x):

  $\forall i.\exists j.\ red(x)(i) \sqsubseteq imp(x)(j)$; and

(iii) imp(x) doesn't produce any arbitrary values:

  $\forall j.\exists i.\ imp(x)(j) \sqsubseteq red(x)(i)$.

These conditions ensure that imp(x) gives the same as red(x) in the limit
("at infinity"), but without restricting <u>how</u> imp(x) approaches the limit.

Auxiliary Definitions

It remains to define red and $\sqsubseteq$.   We shall only sketch their main features
- it would be straightforward to develop these towards a completely formal
definition.

We define red: <u>Exp</u> -> (<u>Time</u> -> <u>Res</u>) inductively, as follows.   For any
$x \in$ <u>Exp</u>, red x 0 = ? -- time has run out.   When there is time i+1 left,
we define red by cases according to the pattern (at the left) of its argument

  red((x)...)(i+1) = red(x...)i

  red(S f g x...)(i+1) = red(f x(g x)...)i

  red(K x y...)(i+1) = red(x...)i

  ...

  red(U f(P x y)...)(i+1) = red(f x y...)i

  red(P x y)(i+1) = P(red x i)(red y i)

  ...

  red(plus x y)(i+1) = m+n, if red x i = m, red y i = n;

        plus(red x i)(red y i), otherwise.

  ...

If no case matches, then there are too few (or too many!) arguments for
the leading combinator, so we take (for $n \geq 0$)

  $red(x_0 x_1 \ldots x_n)(i+1) = x_0(red\ x_1 i)\ldots(red\ x_n i)$

We define $\sqsubseteq$ to be the least relation on <u>Res</u> such that x $\sqsubseteq$ x, for all x

x $\sqsubseteq$ y, y $\sqsubseteq$ z implies x $\sqsubseteq$ z, for all x,y,z

f $\sqsubseteq$ g, x $\sqsubseteq$ y implies f(x) $\sqsubseteq$ g(y), for all f,g,x,y

? $\sqsubseteq$ x, for all x

plus x y $\sqsubseteq$ n, for all numbers n, for all x,y such that

      plus x y $\in$ <u>Res</u> (so that x or y must be partial)

etc.

It can be shown that $\sqsubseteq$ thus defined is a partial order, i.e. reflexive, transitive and anti-symmetric.

A version of the definition of red above has been written in the applicative language HOPE, and tested a little. In fact one may regard the HOPE program as an implementation conforming to the specification, computing red x i at time i - the interface function is red itself!

Conclusion

Let us conclude by considering whether the class of implementations that conform to our specification is an appropriate one.

It is easy to see that our specification rules out simple-minded sequential implementations, e.g. if the reduction of P x y proceeds by first reducing x then reducing y, this won't surpass the function red when x is Y I and y is reducible to "normal form" (a fully-reduced combination not containing "?"). Similarly for plus x y, etc.

However, it would be possible for a conforming implementation to try to decide whether x (in P x y) can be reduced to normal form, and if it can, then to go ahead and do that, before reducing y. But in general it is undecidable whether combinations have normal form, so there would still be some cases where a (purely) sequential implementation would not give the right results.

In fact, it seems that our specification characterises just the "fair" parallel implementations. In combinations such as P x y, the reduction of x and y must proceed fairly, which here means that the function imp(P x y) must include all the results {P x'y' | x' a result of imp x, y' a result of imp y}. Fairness is insensitive to finite delay (or advance) of processes, also to overall differences in their running speeds. Hence if x terminates (so that imp x becomes constant after some time), then one fair computation of P x y is to reduce x first.

Note that we have not ruled out "eager" implementations, that reduce (in parallel) non-pertinent combinations. Such implementations might indeed be quite efficient in practice, as non-pertinent combinations may become pertinent at a later stage in the reduction.

Finally, it should be stressed that the specification technique used here is not being advocated as a general method for use with concurrent systems. No attempt has (yet) been made to apply the technique to other problems. The technique was presented here only because it seemed to be the simplest way to approach the problem of specifying parallel combinator reduction machines.

Acknowledgement

This work was carried out whilst the author was supported by a Visiting Research Fellowship from the SERC.

A Temporal Analysis of Some Concurrent Systems

Ben Moszkowski

Computer Laboratory, University of Cambridge,
Corn Exchange Street, Cambridge CB2 3QG, England

Abstract

In previous work, we presented interval temporal logic (ITL), a formal logic for reasoning about time. It was shown that ITL provides a way to view programming constructs for assignment, repetition and parallelism as logical operators. This paper demonstrates the applicability of ITL to some problems given in the STL concurrency workshop. These include a bidirectional channel, a railway and a message-routing network.

Introduction

In the last few years, temporal logic [2,6] has been put forward as a useful tool for reasoning about concurrent programs and digital circuits. Our own work on interval temporal logic (ITL) [4,5] showed how to view features such as assignment and while loops as logical constructs, something that is not possible in classical predicate logic. We also gave ITL programs for lexical analysis, parallel in-place quicksorting and other tasks.

In this paper we will use ITL to express and reason about some of the concurrency problems discussed at a workshop arranged by Standard Telecommunication Laboratories [7]. The workshop's organizers freely acknowledged that the problems were vague and were to be viewed more as starting points than as fixed goals. With this in mind, we have selected five of the original exercises for presentation here. These partial solutions emphasis some of ITL's strengths. In general, we not only describe the systems but state useful properties as well. Ultimately, we hope to be able to directly execute such ITL descriptions.

Please note that the present exposition is *not* an introduction to ITL. The reader unfamiliar with ITL should consult either [1] or [3] for a detailed description of the logic's syntax and semantics.

Let us now briefly review some simple examples. The following ITL formula increases the variable I by 2 and the variable J by 3 in parallel:

$$(I \leftarrow I+2) \wedge (J \leftarrow J+3).$$

The property

$$\models \quad [(I \leftarrow I+2) \wedge (J \leftarrow J+3)] \supset [(I+J) \leftarrow (I+J+5)]$$

states that if we increment I by 2 and J by 3 then the combined sum $I+J$ is incremented by 5.

The ITL formula

$$while \ M \neq 0 \ do \ ([M \leftarrow M-1] \wedge [N \leftarrow 2N])$$

can be operationally viewed as repeatedly decrementing M by 1 and doubling N until M equals 0. The net result of this program is given by the semantically valid property

$$\models \quad while \ M \neq 0 \ do \ ([M \leftarrow M-1] \wedge [N \leftarrow 2N]) \quad \supset \quad N \leftarrow 2^M \cdot N$$

As these examples show, ITL can deal with imperative programs as well as their specifications.

Problem 1. Channel

This problem involves specifying a two-way channel which can be disconnected in either direction. Let us first look at a bidirectional system with endpoints A and

B connected by zero delay. The following temporal formula expresses this:

$$\boxed{a}\ (A=B).$$

This kind of behavior arises in many situations and we therefore abbreviate it as

$$A \approx B.$$

As the following property shows, zero-delay is symmetric:

$$\models\quad (A \approx B)\ \equiv\ (B \approx A).$$

The following variant of zero delay has a flag *Link* for indicating when the connection is known to be active:

$$\boxed{a}\ (Link\ \supset\ [A=B]).$$

Whenever *Link* is true, the endpoints A and B are equal. This form of dynamic behavior also occurs in descriptions of pass transistors. We abbreviate it as

$$Pass(A,B,Link).$$

If desired, an additional constraint can be added to the system so that once the *Link* flag becomes false, it remains so:

$$Pass(A,B,Link) \wedge \boxed{t}\ (\sim Link\ \supset\ stb\ Link).$$

Alternatively, we can terminate upon *Link* becoming *false*:

$$Pass(A,B,Link) \wedge halt\ (\sim Link).$$

The connection between A and B can also be modeled by means of unit delay:

$$A\ del\ B$$

Here the values of A are received by B one time unit later. We can make this bidirectional by having two pairs of signals:

$$(A\ del\ B) \wedge (B'\ del\ A').$$

Unit delay with a link parameter is also possible. Furthermore, this generalizes to n-unit delay.

Let us now consider a model involving *queue delay*. Before defining this, let us look at some suitable properties. At any instance, the input A equals the list of values to be sent and the output B equals the list of values received. We desire that messages be received in the order sent. A message is received iff it was previously sent; no loss or duplication of messages should occur. Here is an interval of behavior satisfying our intentions:

time	A (sent)	B (received)
0	<5,4>	<5>
1	<6,2,6>	<>
2	<>	<4,6,2>
3	<3>	<6,3>

For example, at time 0, two values 5 and 4 are sent, with the value 5 received immediately. At time 1, three values are sent and none is received.

We use a predicate $A\ qdel\ B$ and define it as follows:

$$A\ qdel\ B\ \equiv_{def}\ [Append(A)=Append(B)] \wedge \boxed{t}\ (prefix(Append(B),Append(A))).$$

Here $Append(A)$ is a temporal function that appends together A's values over time. It has the following property:

$$\models\quad Append(A) = A\ ||\ (\ if\ empty\ then\ <>\ else\ [\bigcirc Append(A)]),$$

where the binary operator $||$ appends its two list-arguments. For instance, in the example above, both $Append(A)$ and $Append(B)$ equal the list <5,4,6,2,6,3> on the interval from time 0 to 3. The predicate $prefix(l,l')$ is true iff the list l is a prefix of the list l'. The predicate $qdel$ can also be expressed in a more operational manner by means of an internal queue variable. We omit the details.

The input A can be disconnected by forcing it to equal <>. The following system uses this property to respond to a flag *Disconnect* becoming true:

$$(A \; qdel \; B) \wedge \boxed{t} \; (Disconnect \supset A \approx <>).$$

This specifies that once *Disconnect* is true, no further messages are sent from A. Messages already input are however eventually received. We can extend the system to be bidirectional by adding extra variables for the opposite direction:

$$(B' \; qdel \; A') \wedge \boxed{t} \; (Disconnect' \supset B' \approx <>).$$

It seems likely that *qdel* has utility in describing other concurrent systems. Consider some representative properties. All follow from the delay model's semantics.

$$\models \; (|A| \approx 1 \wedge |B| \approx 1) \supset [(A \; qdel \; B) \equiv A \approx B]$$

If a single message is always sent and received, then *qdel* is equivalent to zero-delay.

$$\models \; [(A \; qdel \; B) \wedge (B \; qdel \; C)] \supset A \; qdel \; C$$

Two connected queue delays form a queue delay between the endpoints.

$$\models \; A \; qdel \; A$$

Queue delay is reflexive.

Problem 4. Railway

The goal of this problem is to specify and reason about a railway. We represent the system by a vector $Track[0], \ldots, Track[n-1]$. Each element $Track[i]$ equals the train on track i. As trains move over time, the elements change in value. We also use a two-dimensional n-by-n array *Link*. If an element $Link[i,j]$ equals *true* then tracks i and j are connected to one another. Here is a possible configuration:

	Track[0]	Track[1]	Track[2]
Track[0]	~Link[0,0]	Link[0,1]	~Link[0,2]
Track[1]	~Link[1,0]	~Link[1,1]	Link[1,2]
Track[2]	~Link[2,0]	~Link[2,1]	Link[2,2]

In the problem statement each track has either 2 or 4 neighbors and connections are symmetric. These sorts of constraints can be readily incorporated. More dynamic aspects of behavior are also expressible in ITL. For example, the formula

$$stb \; Link$$

specifies that track connections do not change over time. The following ensures that the trains in the railway remain the same, i. e., trains do not enter or leave the system:

$$stb \; [bagval(Track)],$$

where the expression $bagval(Track)$ equals the unordered multiset of values in the list *Track*. The next formula ensures that at any instant of time, no train is on more than one track:

$$\boxed{a} \; \forall i,j < |Track| . (Track[i] = Track[j] \supset i = j).$$

Note that this still permits the trains to move around. The requirement that over every time unit each train moves to an adjacent track is expressible as follows:

$$\forall i < |Track| . \boxed{a} \; [skip \supset \exists j . (Link[i,j] \wedge Track[i] \to Track[j])].$$

If desired, we can introduce an extra vector *Train* whose elements give the track numbers trains are located on. Thus, $Train[3]$ always equals the track that train 3 occupies. Furthermore, the description might allow for the possibility that some tracks are unoccupied.

So far, ITL has been used to specify the railway's configuration and behavior. We can also use the logic as a command language for manipulating trains. For example, the statement

"Move the train on track 3 via track 6 to track 9"

might be expressed as the formula

$$(Track[3] \rightarrow Track[6]);(Track[6] \rightarrow Track[9]).$$

The following property shows that this ultimately transfers the train on track 3 to track 9:

$$\models \quad [(Track[3] \rightarrow Track[6]);(Track[6] \rightarrow Track[9])] \supset (Track[3] \rightarrow Track[9]).$$

We might request that trains on tracks 2 and 4 be switched:

$$Track[2] \leftrightarrow Track[4].$$

This does not mention what happens to the remaining tracks. The following formula on the other hand ensures that no other trains move:

$$Alter(Track,2,4).$$

Problem 5. Array Processor

This problem deals with specifying an array processor having a variety of instructions. Rather than describing the entire device, we investigate simpler processors involving many of the same issues. Consider the follow grid of nodes:

$A[0,0]$	$A[0,1]$	$A[0,2]$
$A[1,0]$	$A[1,1]$	$A[1,2]$
$A[2,0]$	$A[2,1]$	$A[2,2]$

Here is a description in which each cell $A[i,j]$ is initialized to the value $i+j$ and then continues to compute some function of itself and its neighbors:

$$\forall i,j<2.[A[i,j]=i+j \wedge f(A,i,j) \ del \ A[i,j]].$$

Over each unit of time, each cell $A[i,j]$ is assigned the previous value of $f(A,i,j)$. For example, we might compute the average of adjacent cells:

$$f(A,i,j)=(A[i-1 \ mod \ 2,j]+A[i+1 \ mod \ 2,j]+A[i,j-1 \ mod \ 2]+A[i,j+1 \ mod \ 2])\div 4.$$

An instruction input *Inst* might be added as follows:

$$g(A,i,j,Inst) \ del \ A[i,j],$$

where the function g can be defined according to the various desired instructions. We can also add an extra variable *Reg* that receives data in parallel:

$$[\forall i,j<2.(A[i,j]\cdots)] \wedge [h(A,Inst,Reg) \ del \ Reg]$$

We ultimately hope to execute such ITL descriptions within the framework of the programming language *Tempura*.

Problem 6. Packet Network with Rerouting

Let us now consider the behavior of a packet network. It turns out that the temporal assignment construct

$$A \rightarrow B$$

has utility in modeling and simulation of message-passing systems. Imagine that A and B are nodes. The above assigment is true if the message at A is successfully passed to B. The formula

$$(A="Hello") \wedge (A \rightarrow B)$$

sets A to the message string *"Hello"* and then passes this to B. We might pass the string directly to B using the construct

$$"Hello" \rightarrow B.$$

We can also swap the messages at nodes A and B in parallel:

$$(A \rightarrow B) \wedge (B \rightarrow A).$$

A node's message can be fed back to the node. For instance, the formula

$$[(I+1) \to I] \wedge (len \leq 50)$$

sends a numeric message from node I back to itself but with the message's value incremented by 1. In addition, the transmission takes no more than 50 time units. This shows how to incorporate timing into such descriptions.

We can indicate that a message transmission may terminate unsuccessfully if too much time is needed. The following formula tries to send A's message to B but can "time-out" if 100 time units elapse:

$$(A \to B) \vee (len \geq 100)$$

Message routing is indicated by specifying intermediate nodes. The formula

$$(A \to B);(B \to C)$$

sends a message from A via B to C. The fact that A's message arrives at C is shown by the following property:

$$\vDash \quad [(A \to B);(B \to C)] \supset (A \to C).$$

If we have a list of nodes $U[0], \ldots, U[9]$ then the formula

$$\exists i. \; [3 \leq i \leq 5 \wedge (U[2] \to U[i]);(U[i] \to U[9])]$$

indicates that a message is sent from $U[2]$ to $U[9]$ via one of the nodes $U[3], U[4]$ or $U[5]$. We can send a message from $U[0]$ to $U[1]$ to $\cdots$ to $U[9]$:

$$for \; 0 \leq i < 9 \; do \; (U[i] \to U[i+1]).$$

This is also accomplished by the following:

$$\exists J. \, [(J=0) \wedge halt \, (J=9) \wedge (J+1) \, del \, J \wedge stb \, U[J]].$$

The property

$$\vDash \quad [stb \, A \wedge halt \, (A=B)] \supset (A \to B)$$

says that if we hold A stable and terminate upon B equaling A, then we will have successfully sent A's message to B. This might be useful if, say, A and B have a noisy connection.

We can incorporate packets by representing a message as a list of values, each representing an individual packet. For example, the message

$$<"He" , "l" , "lo" >$$

has the three packets $"He"$, $"l"$ and $"lo"$. If U and V are list-valued variables, the following ITL formula specifies that U's packets are sent to V:

$$U \to V.$$

If both U and V have length n then the following achieves the same effect:

$$\forall i < n. \, (U[i] \to V[i]).$$

This indicates that the elements of U are simultaneously transmitted to the corresponding elements in V. We can also accomplish a message transfer by serially sending the packets. The next formula does this from one point A to another B using standard list operators:

$$halt \, (A=<>) \wedge rest \, (A) \, del \, A \wedge B=<> \wedge (B \, || \, <first \, (A)>) \, del \, B$$

Here the expression $rest \, (A)$ equals A's tail and $first \, (A)$ equals A's first element.

Problem 8. Mixing Synchronous and Asynchronous Input

Here we are to describe a system with three points: a synchronous input Syn, an asynchronous input $Asyn$ and a single output Out. Each is represented as a list of messages. The synchronous input Syn transmits to the output at regular intervals, say, every n units of time. Let us assume that the actual transfer takes zero time. This can be specified as

$$Pass \, (Syn, Out, Flag),$$

where the variable $Flag$ is true every n units of time. The following ITL formula achieves this:

$$\boxed{1}\ ([len=n]^* \to Flag).$$

Asynchronous transfers can occur at all other times:

$$Asyn\ qdel\ (if\ Flag\ then\ <>\ else\ Out).$$

Thus, the output *Out* can only receive messages from *Asyn* when *Flag* equals *false*. The entire system consists of the logical-and of the three formulas given above. A variant of the system might allow asynchronous transfers to take place when the synchronous input has nothing to send. Here is one way to do this:

$$Asyn\ qdel\ (if\ [Flag\ \land\ (Syn \neq <>)]\ then\ <>\ else\ Out).$$

What Do We Accomplish?

There is a great variety of specification tools available and the reader may indeed wonder about the merits of ITL. What after all is the purpose of an ITL specification? Well, for one thing, we feel that ITL provides a unified logical framework for describing and reasoning about parallel programs, timing-dependent digital circuits and other related dynamic systems. For example, the assignment operator $A \to B$ can be viewed as a programming language construct, a hardware register-transfer operator and as a message-passing primitive for communications systems. Thus, the simple property

$$\models\ [(A \to B);(B \to C)]\ \supset\ (A \to C)$$

is meaningful in a variety of contexts. Furthermore, we are currently developing the ITL-based programming language *Tempura* so that we will be able to execute ITL specifications. Other goals include computer-assisted verification of ITL properties and synthesis from ITL descriptions.

Conclusions

In earlier papers [4,5] we showed how to use interval temporal logic as a programming formalism. The present work applied ITL to a set of independently developed exercises and demonstrated how a channel, a railway and a message-passing network can all be modelled. Along the way, we gained insight into existing ITL operators such as " $\to$ ". A new operator *qdel* for queue delay was also discussed. In the future we plan to implement an interpreter for parallel algorithms and dynamic systems expressed in subsets of ITL. New temporal operators for stacks, parsing and other concepts will also be explored.

References

[1] J. Halpern, Z. Manna and B. Moszkowski. A hardware semantics based on temporal intervals. *Proceedings of the 10-th International Colloquium on Automata, Languages and Programming*, Barcelona, Spain, July, 1983.

[2] Z. Manna and A. Pnueli. Verification of concurrent programs: The temporal framework. In R. S. Boyer and J. S. Moore, editors, *The Correctness Problem in Computer Science*, pages 215-273, Academic Press, New York, 1981.

[3] B. Moszkowski. *Reasoning about Digital Circuits*. PhD Thesis, Department of Computer Science, Stanford University, 1983.

[4] B. Moszkowski and Z. Manna. Reasoning in interval temporal logic. Dept. of Computer Science, Stanford University, Technical Report STAN-CS-83-969.

[5] B. Moszkowski and Z. Manna. Temporal logic as a programming language. To appear in the proceedings of Parallel Computing 83, West Berlin, Sept., 1983

[6] N. Rescher and A. Urquart. *Temporal Logic*. Springer-Verlag, New York, 1971.

[7] Problem set for the concurrency workshop. In these proceedings.

SOLUTIONS TO PROBLEM NO. 2

Amir Pnueli

The Weizmann Institute of Science
Rehovot 76100, Israel

Introduction

The following notes were written *after* the workshop. Consequently I have had
the benefit of seeing first other people's solutions and being able to attempt to
improve upon them. On the other hand some of them exhausted my first choice for a
specification method (in particular those by W.P. DeRoever and L. Lamport) and forced me to look for additional variations.

The main theme of these notes is to try and combine an appropriate transition
system formalism, used to express safety properties, together with temporal logic,
that provides most of the liveness properties. The notes contain three such attempts
that all lie somewhere in the range delimited by Lamport's solution on one side and
DeRoever's solution on the other side.

The solution presented by DeRoever represents the pure temporal logic approach.
Typical to this approach is the need to give explicit guarantees that events may only
occur when a sufficient reason exists for them to occur. For example, that a message
does not arrive unless it was sent first. This is a somewhat artificial need and
never explicitly arises in specifications based on transition systems. In general,
many parts of the specification are more succinctly and intuitively represented by
transition diagrams. Transition diagrams, when properly designed, also provide some
aspects of modelling and decomposition of the specified system, that are most valuable
when we consider specification to be only the first step in the system design process.

All my approaches differ also from Lamport's solution. The first main difference
is that I based my transition system on CSP/CCS-like communication-based system of
processes. This seems to me a better choice than a global shared memory model. A
second difference is the identification of *live* states in the diagrams. These are
states that the system cannot stay in forever in a legal computation. By appropriate
choice of live states, we can represent most of the liveness properties in the diagrams
themselves, and do not need the additional temporal logic formulas for them.

First Attempt

In the first attempt we regard the complete network service as *one* process, and
each of its customers, called here endpoints, as a separate individual process. The
representation of each process is by means of a transition diagram. The edges in the
transition diagram are labelled by guards which are names of signals. In addition to
the signals (messages) mentioned in the problem formulation, we use here the signal:

FAIL.ind(a,b). It is similar to the signal DIS.ind(a,b) in that it *notifies* endpoint b which is assumed to be currently connected with endpoint a, of a disconnection of their mutual link. It does, however, identifies the reason of the disconnection as due to failure rather than to the decision of the other partner, endpoint a, to disconnect. This helps to ensure that the implementor of the service system cannot take the fact that spontaneous release due to failures is considered, as a liberty for initiating disconnections at will.

Formally, whenever a specification introduces events or signals that are not externally observable, or as in the case above splits a signal into two distinct signals which are not externally distinguishable, a homomorphism is implied. This means that the specification chooses to express itself in a richer alphabet of events and signals than was originally provided. It then defines the set of all behaviors over the richer alphabet that are admissible as correct behaviors of the specified system. Associated with the enrichment there is a homomorphism that maps some events, typically the internal events, to the empty event (not externally observable), and some other events to externally observable events. The set of admissible externally observable behaviors is then the homomorphic image under this homomorphism of the set of the specified behaviors over the enriched alphabet.

In our case this homomorphism maps each signal to itself except for FAIL.ind(a,b) which is mapped onto DIS.ind(a,b), being externally indistinguishable from it.

Signal names labelling transitions can appear either as input signals, such as CON.req(a,b)? or output signals, such as CON.ind(a,b)!. This helps to identify for each signal the processes that are responsible for its generation. The behaviors of a complete system specified as a collection of processes is operationally defined as follows:

At any point in the execution, each process is in one of its states represented by a node in the transition graph. We say that this node is the *active* node at that point. We may envisage a token placed on the active node in each of the processes. Each edge departing from a currently active node is said to be *enabled* at the present point in the execution. An enabled *transition* corresponding to a signal σ consists of a pair of enabled edges e_1 and e_2 one of which is labelled by $\sigma!$ and the other labelled by $\sigma?$. An execution step corresponding to a transition such as the above, consists of moving the tokens along e_1 and e_2. It is assumed that e_1 and e_2 belong to different processes.

The initial global state is defined by a set of initial nodes, one for each process. A sequence of steps, each corresponding to some enabled signal, beginning at the initial state is defined to be an *admissible* execution. The behavior of the specified system is defined to be the set of all admissible executions.

There is no need to point out the similarity between our transition diagrams and CSP processes. In many senses, our system can be viewed as a degenerate version of CSP.

An unimportant difference is that instead of naming processes in communication instructions, the signal name serves as a channel name in a style similar to CCS.

We begin our specification by specifying the assumed behavior of an endpoint. This specification corresponds to the *precondition* in a specification of a sequential program. That is, the implemented network is guaranteed to work properly only if the external environment, represented here by the customers-endpoints, behaves reasonably. This is not absolutely necessary. An alternative approach is to make no assumptions about the customers, but make sure that the system ignores requests that are made out of sequence or not according to the contract between customers and services. We prefer the first approach, and it provides us with a simpler first example of our notation.

Diagram 1: Transition Diagram for Endpoint a

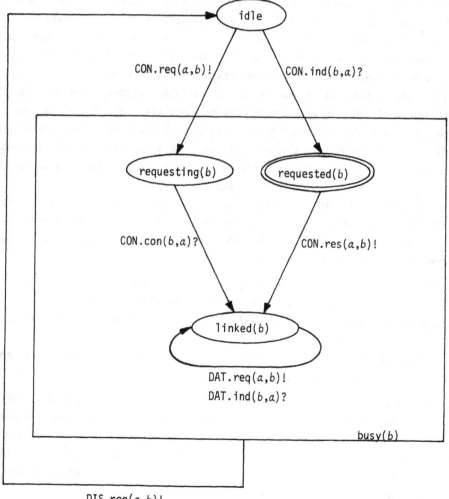

This diagram represents the part of the behavior of endpoint a that pertains to its relations with endpoint b. Similar parts correspond to each of the other endpoints in the net. That is, the full diagram for endpoint a appears as follows:

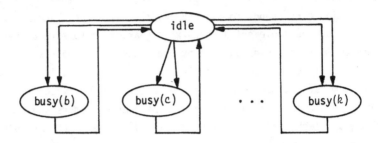

Endpoint a may exit to the busy(b) part either by initiating a CON.req(a,b) message and moving to 'requesting(b)' or by receiving a CON.ind(b,a) message and moving to 'requested(b)'. Out of the 'requesting(b)' situation it moves to 'linked(b)' on receiving an affirmation from b represented by the CON.con(b,a) signal. Being at the 'requested(b)' state, endpoint a is responsible for eventually issuing a CON.res(a,b) signal, expressing a positive response. At the 'linked(b)' state, endpoint a may issue DAT.req(a,b) signals (together with the corresponding data) and receive incoming data messages via DAT.ind(b,a) signals. We follow here and in the forthcoming diagrams, a convention due to David Harel ([H], of grouping several states into a super-state by using a box enclosing the grouped states. Any transition departing or arriving at the box boundaries is assumed to apply to each state belonging to the super-state.

Thus, in the diagram above, the super-state 'busy(b)' consists of the states: 'requesting(b)' , 'requested(b)' and 'linked(b)'. Out of each of the three states there is a transition (actually three of them) leading back to 'idle' that is possible under one of the following events:

DIS.req(a,b)! - Endpoint a deciding to break the connection. This also serves as a negative response out of the state 'requested(b)'.

DIS.ind(b,a)? - Endpoint a received a message that endpoint b decided to break connection.

FAIL.ind(b,a)? - Indication of failure of the $a \to b$ channel. This corresponds to the simultaneous release.

Another important concept appearing in this diagram is that of a *live state*. The state 'requested(b)' appears within a double ellipse. This defines the 'requested(b)' as a *live* state within the diagram. The meaning of a live state is that the execution cannot stay forever in that state and must eventually get out. Thus, being at state 'requested(b)' we expect endpoint a to eventually respond by either a CON.res(a,b) signal or a DIS.req(a,b)! signal.

Next, we present the diagram for the channel $a \to b$. There are two such diagr for each pair of SAP's (and hence endpoints), i.e. one for $a \to b$ and one for $b \to a$.

<u>Diagram 2</u>: Transition Diagram for the Channel $a \to b$

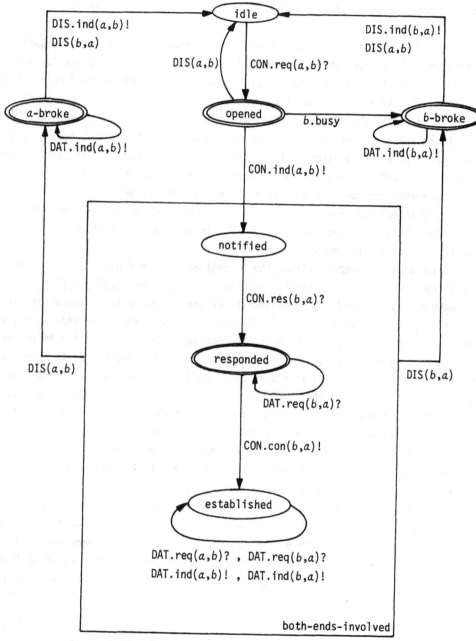

where $DIS(a,b)$: $DIS.req(a,b)?$ | $FAIL.ind(b,a)!$

In this diagram we follow the protocol for the connection from a to b until it is established, and then when it is broken. The development starts by receiving a CON.req(a,b) message at the SAP- a . Then, the channel examines the state of endpoint b . If endpoint b is currently busy, then the channel decides to break the connection by moving to the state 'b-broke'. From this state it proceeds to issue a DIS.ind(b,a) signal to the endpoint a . This signal is superceded if the channel hears beforehands that a decided to break the connection on its own. Endpoint b is considered to be busy if it is situated in the busy(c) super-state for some c . Note that c could equal a , the requesting node if precisely at that point b is trying to initiate a connection with a .

The possibility of the channel examining the internal state of endpoint b may seem objectionable on the grounds of the principle of locality of variables. We may remedy this deficiency by introducing a new signal: Refuse(b,a). For every endpoint c the signal Refuse(b,c)! may be generated by a self transition attached to any state different from the 'idle' state in the diagram for endpoint b . Correspondingly, the transition from 'opened' to 'b-broke' in the diagram for the channel may now be labelled by 'Refuse(b,a)?'. In this way, the examination of internal states is properly replaced by communication.

Being at the 'opened' state, the channel may find endpoint b at 'idle' and send it the CON.ind(a,b)! signal. It then waits at 'notified' until a CON.res(b,a) is received from endpoint b , or until a disconnect request or failure is received. On getting a CON.res(b,a) response, the channel proceeds to the state 'responded' where it waits to deliver the CON.con(b,a)! confirmation to endpoint a . Meanwhile endpoint b believes to the best of its knowledge that the connection has been established. It may therefore start delivering messages to the channel as soon as the channel enters the 'responded' state. Once the 'established' state is attained, data messages are received and delivered by the channel at both sides.

The connection may be broken at any point by either a or b . Noticing a request for disconnection (or a failure), the channel enters the state 'a-broke' or 'b-broke' waiting to notify the other endpoint of the broken connection. Meanwhile it may yet deliver some data messages intended for that endpoint.

The management of the data messages is not made explicit in this diagram. To represent the correct sequences of data messages we may introduce two data messages queues q_{ab} and q_{ba} for each pair of endpoints a and b . A more detailed diagram includes also actions associated with the transitions. These actions manipulate the queues. To obtain the detailed diagram we should extend each of the transitions as follows:

Each transition labelled by DIS(a,b)? (DIS(b,a)? respectively) should be labelled by:

$$DIS(a,b)? \rightarrow q_{ba} := \Lambda$$
$$(DIS(b,a)? \rightarrow q_{ab} := \Lambda \text{ respectively}).$$

This action clears the data message queue.

Each transition labelled by DAT.req(a,b)? should be labelled by:

DAT.req(a,b).m? → q_{ab} := q_{ab} * m

This action appends the message m to the end of the queue.

Each transition labelled by DAT.ind(a,b)! should be labelled by:

q_{ab} ≠ Λ ; DAT.ind(a,b).head(q_{ab})! → q_{ab} := tail(q_{ab}).

Thus, the transition is enabled only if the $a → b$ queue is nonempty. It then delivers the data at the head of the queue to endpoint b and proceeds to remove this message from the head of the queue.

Note that failure or simultaneous disconnect is initiated by the channel $a → b$ that may issue at any point a FAIL.ind(b,a) or a FAIL.ind(a,b) signal.

At first glance, this set of processes seems to be a satisfactory solution to the specification problem. However, when examined closer it appears to contain several deficiencies. The most serious one is that it is difficult and inefficient to implement in a world in which signals take nonzero time to travel between endpoints. For example, almost any implementation cannot escape having the following sequence as a prefix of an admissible behavior:

CON.req(a,b) , DIS.req(a,b) , CON.ind(a,b) , ··· .

This is because, having seen a CON.req(a,b), the network must decide to issue a CON.ind(a,b) at the b-SAP. If just before this message is issued the a endpoint decides to disconnect and issues a DIS.req(a,b), this information will not reach the b-SAP in time to stop the CON.ind signal under any reasonable implementation. However, our specification disallows such a sequence.

Another way of diagnosing that something is wrong is to observe that some states such as 'opened' are sensitive to signals occurring at remote ends of the channel. Any reasonable implementation can be immediately sensitive to close signals and sense remote signals only after some delay.

This raises a general question of a specification that is consistent, i.e. non contradictory, but may be difficult to implement in a distributed environment. We may want to impose a syntactic restriction that each transition or event may be restricted to test and modify only structures that are *localized* in some topological sense. To be precise, we cannot restrict *processes* to be localized, but we may require that each *state* in a process may be associated with some locality in the net. Different states may belong to different localities as may be observed by the following trivial process. This process receives a DIS.req message at a and delivers a DIS.ind message at b.

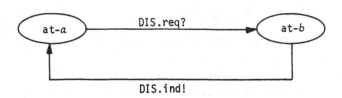

Thus, the criticism we have towards our $a \to b$ channel is that while some of the states are properly localized, i.e. 'idle' and 'b-broke' are a-localized and 'a-broke' is b-localized, all the other states mix signals local (close) to both a and b.

A proper implementation of a node that is attentive to signals at two remote locations must involve shuttling of control between two sites, each close to one of the sources of these signals. For example if we consider the 'notified' node in diagram 2, it is responsive to the signals CON.res(b,a) and DIS.req(b,a) both originating at b as well as to the signal DIS.req(a,b) originating at a. A proper implementation of it must be of the form:

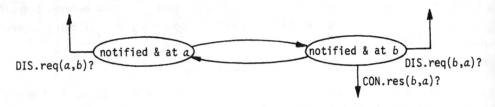

Quite possibly, the concrete implementation of this splitting involves sending contro messages back and forth between the two control sites. A *global* specification such a presented in diagram 2 hides the necessity for this internal communication. This may be acceptable as the proper level of abstraction at which a specification should be formulated. On the other hand it may enforce an implementation that is expensive and inefficient by imposing unnecessary constraints such as forbidding the sequence

$$\text{CON.req}(a,b) \ , \ \text{DIS.req}(a,b) \ , \ \text{CON.ind}(a,b) \ , \ \cdots$$

Second Attempt

In our second attempt we try to distinguish between local and remote signals. We assume that each signal incoming from an endpoint a, such as CON.req, CON.res, DIS.req and DAT.req is observed first at SAP-a and then propagated towards its target SAP where it arrives as an internal signal. We name the internal signals representing remote signals CON^.req, CON^.res, DIS^.req and DAT^.req respectively. For actually transferring these signals we may envisage a host of buffer processes of the form:

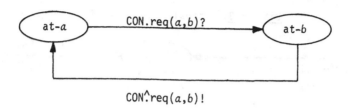

$$\text{CON}\hat{.}\text{req}(a,b)!$$

and similarly for the other incoming signals. With these conventions we may now draw a diagram for a typical SAP, SAP-a. Note that once we distribute a channel $a \to b$ into its a-side and b-side, we can combine the a-side of both the $a \to b$ channel and the $b \to a$ channel into one diagram - the diagram for SAP-a.

There are some minor differences between the specification presented in diagram 3 and the previous one.

First we have introduced an explicit Refuse(a,b) signal that is generated by SAP-a as a response to a request from SAP-b. Typically, this signal is generated by the SAP itself when it decides to refuse without bothering the endpoint with the request.

Another minor difference is the mechanism of failure or simultaneous disconnect. Here, failure may be generated by SAP-a. It is generated as a FAIL.req$(a,b)!$ signal that is propagated towards SAP-b, and then SAP-a proceeds to notify endpoint a of the disconnection by a regular DIS.ind(b,a) message. On the other hand, for symmetry sake, SAP-a is also attentive to accepting a remoted signal FAIL$\hat{.}$req(b,a) that may have been originated at SAP-b. Receiving this signal leads also to a DIS.ind(b,a) notification of endpoint a.

A major difference between the specification of the present section and the preceding one, is in the extended sensitivity to CON.res signals. As seems to be implied by the formulation of the problem, once SAP-a received a disconnect indication it should not accept any additional signals except for a new connect request. Consider however the following sequence of events where SIG denotes the origination of a signal and $\hat{\text{SIG}}$ denotes the arrival of that signal at the other end:

CON.req(a,b) , CON$\hat{.}$req(a,b) , Refuse (b,a), DIS.req(a,b) , DIS$\hat{.}$req(a,b) ,
CON.req(a,b) , Ref$\hat{\text{u}}$se (b,a) , DIS.ind(b,a), CON$\hat{.}$req(a,b) , CON.ind(a,b) ,
CON.res(b,a) , CON$\hat{.}$res(b,a) , $\cdots$.

In this case a requested connection and then changed its mind. However as a result of the request a refuse signal was sent from b to a. Endpoint a then decided to reestablish connection, but immediately after sending the request it received the previously sent refusal. Point a interprets this as a refusal to its most recent request and disgustedly signs off. Meanwhile its request reaches point that this time decides to respond positively. As a result we have endpoint a at idle, endpoint b believing it is responding to a valid connect request, and a positive CON.res message travelling towards a. In diagram 3 we have SAP-a intercept the message and respond by a refusal in state 'reject(c)'.

Diagram 3: Transition Diagram for SAP-*a*

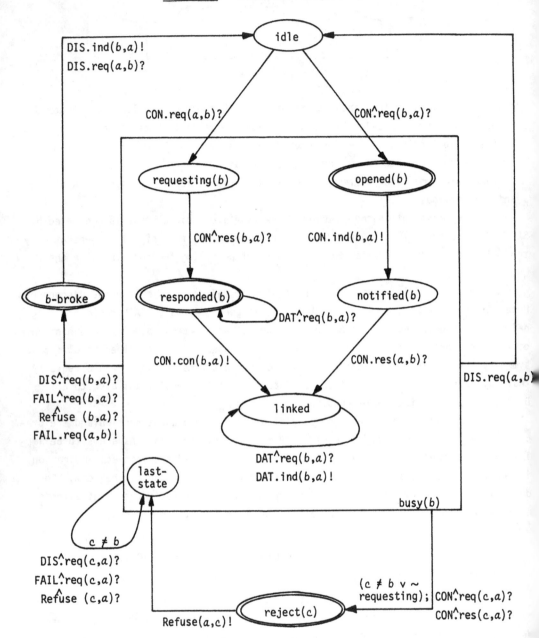

In fact, diagram 3 should be completed by the following additional transitions connecting to the 'idle' state. They are drawn here because of space limitations:

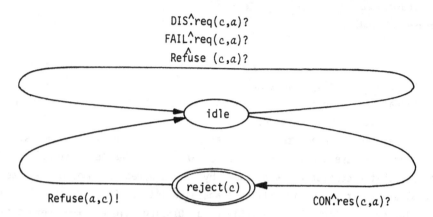

$$DIS\hat{.}req(c,a)?$$
$$FAIL\hat{.}req(c,a)?$$
$$Refuse\ (c,a)?$$

These transitions represent that in the 'idle' state SAP-a is ready to receive (without responding) the three signals DIS.req(c,a), FAIL.req(c,a) and Refuse(c,a). These may be due to signals that were generated while c and a were still connected. The SAP is also attentive to a CON.res(c,a) signal to which it responds by generating a Refuse(a,c) signal.

Third Approach

The third approach differs in two major aspects from the preceding attempts. The first point is that we extended our signals to include an additional field that is used as an identifier distinguishing between distinct signals of the same type. As a result each connection between two endpoints is also assigned a unique identifier. This turns out to be most useful in being able to distinguish between signals that are relevant to the current connection and those that are 'leftovers' from previous connections. The second point of difference is in the interpretation of the transition diagram representation that is used here. This will be discussed below.

The signals that we consider are:

CON.req(a,b,id)   DIS.req(a,b,id)
CON.ind(a,b,id)   DIS.ind(a,b,id)
CON.res(a,b,id)   DAT.req(a,b,m,id,j)
CON.con(a,b,id)   DAT.ind(a,b,m,id,j) .

This list includes all the signals that were mentioned in the formulation of the problem. Each of these signals has been extended by the addition of the identifier component. The data messages have been augmented with two identifiers, the first: "id" identifies the period of connection, and the second: "j", refers to a sequence number of messages within the same connection period. The data messages also explicitly refer to the data component as the field "m". Additional signals that we add to the description are:

   REJ.ind(a,b,id)
   FAIL.ind(a,b,id)
   Refuse (a,b,id) .

The message REJ.ind(a,b,id) signals to endpoint b that SAP-a has decided to reject
a recent connection request issued by endpoint b. The identifier component identifies which request is being rejected.

The signal FAIL.ind(a,b,id) notifies endpoint b of a failure or spontaneous
disconnect initiated by the network.

Both these signals are externally observable as DIS.ind(a,b) signals.

The signal Refuse(a,b,id) is issued by SAP-a in order to eventually notify
endpoint b that a connect request issued by b is hereby refused or rejected. When
this signal arrive at SAP-b, it will be translated into a REJ.ind(a,b,id) signal.
While the latter is externally observable as a DIS.ind signal, the Refuse signal
by itself is an internal signal and is not externally observable. Some additional
internal signals will be introduced later.

It is assumed throughout, that distinct signals of the same type, e.g. all
CON.ind signals, have distinct identifiers. On the other hand, signals of different
types may have the same identifier in order to indicate that one signal is a response
to the other.

The current formalism also makes use of transition diagrams that are associated
with processes. However, in contrast with the previous approaches, the transition
diagrams here serve as *recognizers* rather than *generators*. Each diagram consists of
states that can be parametrized and transitions that are labelled by signals. The
signals may also be parametrized by parameters such as the source and destination of
the signal, its unique identifier and additional components when they are relevant.

Some of the states are surrounded by a double circle, identifying them as *live*
states. The meaning of a live state is that the computation cannot leave a process
(a diagram) in a live state forever. It must eventually cause the process to get out
of the live state.

An appearance of a signal name σ on an edge, leading from a state s to a
state s' in a process P, implies that if the signal σ appears in a computation
when the process P is in state s it causes P to move to the state s'. We say
that process P performed a σ-transition. When a process P is in a state such
that a σ transition is possible from that state we say that P is σ-enabled.

With each process P we associate a list of signals *constrain*(P). For each
$\sigma \in$ *constrain*(P), we say that P *constrains* σ. The meaning of these constraints is
that a signal σ can only occur when *all* the processes P that constrain
σ are σ-enabled. In our specification no such explicit list is given for
any of the processes. The implicit understanding is that *constrain*(P) is the set
all signals that appear as label on some transition in P.

Diagram 4: Transition Diagram for SAP-a

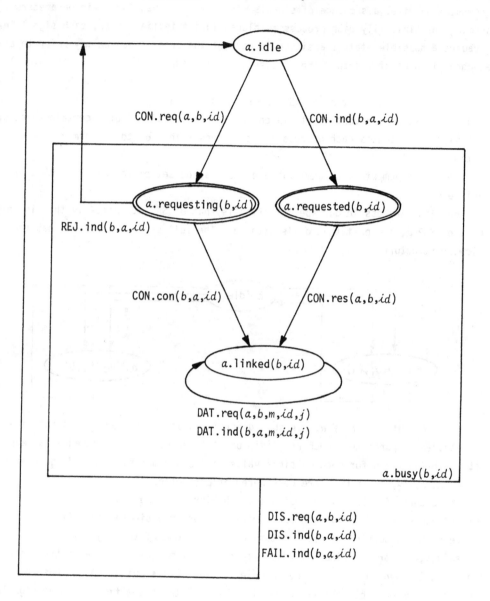

Let S be a specification consisting of a set of processes (diagrams) and ω
a computation, i.e. a sequence of signals with actual values for their parameters.
Assuming that initially each process is placed in its initial state, each signal in
ω causes a possible state transition in each of the processes. We may refer to a
sequence of joint states that the processes of S undergo when reading the signals
of ω as a *behavior* of S under ω. A computation ω is defined to be *admissible*
by S if there is a behavior of S under ω such that:
1. No process remains continually in one of its live states from a certain point on.
2. A signal σ causes each process P that constrains σ to perform a σ transition.

The set of computations admissible by S is the set of computations that S
specifies.

The first process in our specification is that of SAP-*a*. Actually this is only
a part of SAP-*a*, the part that deals with *b*. The full process for SAP-*a* has the
following structure:

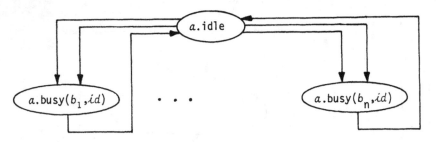

for each endpoint b_i, $b_i \neq a$. In such diagrams, states and transitions that are
parametrized by parameters such as '*id*' or '*j*', should be considered as a template
that is instantiated for each possible value of the parameter. Thus in the diagram
for SAP-*a*, *b*, *id*, *m* and *j* are considered as parameters.

The diagram for SAP-*a* constrains the behavior near the endpoints. It implies
that SAP-*a* may be busy only with one partner *b* under a single identifier '*id*'.
It enters the *a*.busy(*b*,*id*) super-state only under one of the signals
CON.req(*a*,*b*,*id*) or CON.ind(*b*,*a*,*id*). At the same time this constrains these signals
to occur only when SAP-*a* is at the *a*.idle state. Exits out of the *a*.busy(*b*,*id*)
super-state are possible only as a result of one of the connection breaking signals:
REJ.ind, DIS.req, DIS.ind and FAIL.ind that refer explicitly to *a*, *b* and the
current *id*. Other connection breaking signals are not allowed at this super-state.
This is because these signals appear in the other parts of the diagram for SAP-*a*, an
hence are constrained by the SAP-*a* process. Both the *requesting* and *requested* state
are designated as live states. Consequently if SAP-*a* is to stay within the
a.busy(*b*,*id*) super-state forever, it may only do so by eventually getting to the
a.linked(*b*,*id*) state.

Next, consider the diagram (diagram 5) for the CON(*a*,*b*,*id*) process that is

Diagram 5: Transition Diagram for CON(a,b,id)

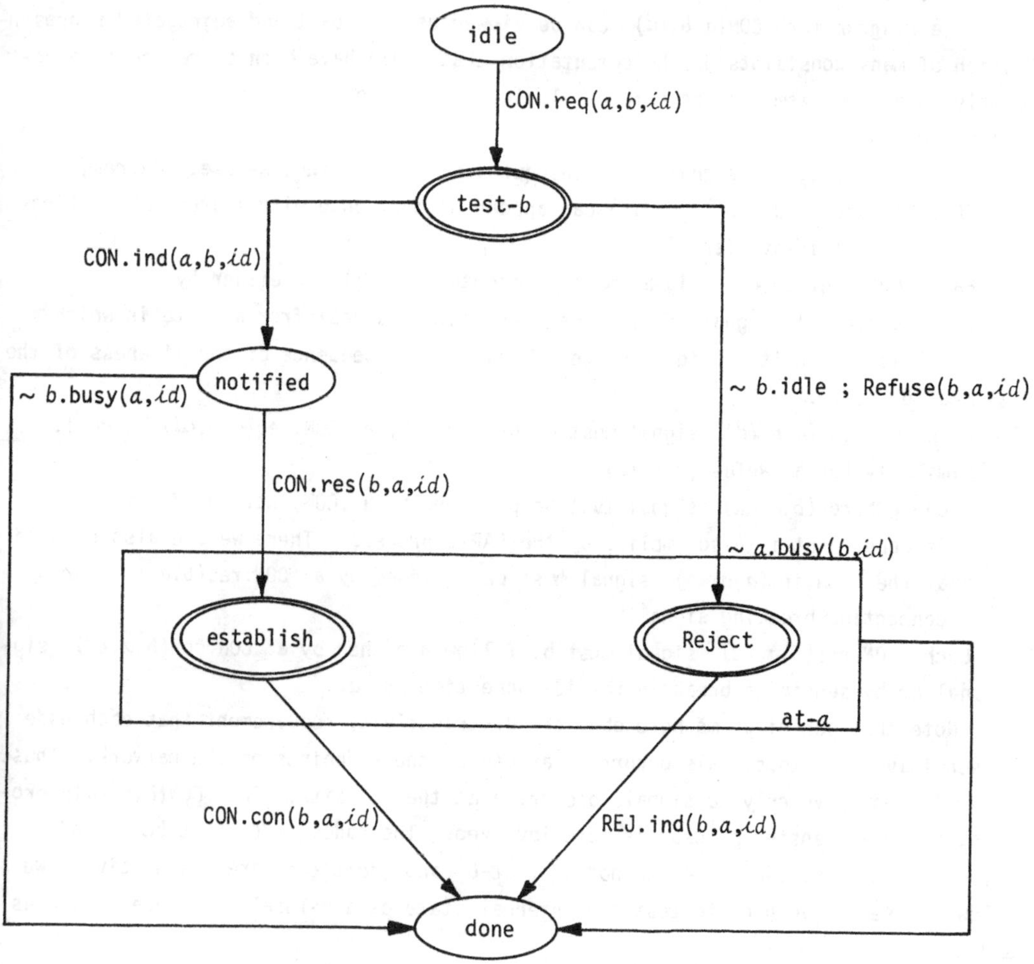

responsible for transmitting the connection signals between the SAP's. Essentially,
this process proceeds with the expected normal protocol of sensing a connection
request and then testing b. If b is idle then a CON.ind(a,b,id) signal is generated. In case b is sensed to be non idle a Refuse signal is generated. In the
first case the CON process may be depicted waiting at b until either a CON.res
response is obtained from a or b is sensed not to be busy with a under the identifier id. This sensing is a test on the state of the SAP-b process. It obviates
direct sensing of all the different connection breaking signals that could possibly
arrive at b, and relies on SAP-b being sensitive to all these signals and responding
to them by moving out of the b.busy(a,id) super-state. Note that while the 'Refuse'
signal is explicitly restricted to occur only when SAP-b is not in its $idle$ state no
such explicit restriction is required on the signal CON.ind(a,b,id). This is

because the diagram for SAP-b already constrains this signal to occur only from a b.idle state.

The diagram for CON(a,b,id) can be viewed as a compact and aggregated representation of many constaints on the computation that could have been expressed independently by a formalism such as temporal logic. It implies for example all the following requirements:

1. A CON.req(a,b,id) signal (and consequently the CON.ind, Refuse, CON.res, CON.con and REJ.ind signals) can appear at most once with source a, destination b and identifier id.

2. Each CON.req(a,b,id) signal must be eventually followed either by a CON.ind(a,b,id) signal or by a Refuse(b,a,id) signal from a state in which SAP-b is not in its b.idle state. This is a consequence of the liveness of the *test-b* state.

3. Each CON.ind(a,b,id) signal must be preceded by a CON.req(a,b,id) signal. Similarly for a Refuse(b,a,id).

4. Each CON.res(b,a,id) signal must be preceded by a CON.ind(a,b,id) signal. This constraint is also implied by the SAP-b process. There we are also ensured that the CON.ind(a,b,id) signal must be followed by a CON.res(b,a,id) or by a connection breaking signal.

5. Each CON.res(b,a,id) signal must be followed either by a CON.con(b,a,id) signal or by sensing a break in the id-connection at a.

Note that our diagrams here obey the distributivity requirement that each node be sensitive only to signals occurring at one of the endpoints of the network. Thus, SAP-a is sensitive only to signals occurring at the a site. The CON(a,b,id) process, being a transfer process is more involved. The nodes: *idle, establish* and *reject* are a-sensitive while the nodes *test-b* and *notified* are b-sensitive. We allow a b-sensitive node to test the internal state of a b-localized process such as SAP-b.

In diagram 6 we present the process DAT(a,b,m,id,j) that is responsible for routing the data messages across the network. It implies the following constraints:

1. The message identifier j is unique under the context of fixed a, b, m and id

2. Each DAT.req(a,b,m,id,j) is followed by a delivery of a DAT.ind(a,b,m,id,j) signal, or by delivery of the DAT.skip(a,b,id,j) from a state in which the id-connection is broken at b.

3. Each DAT.ind(a,b,m,id,j) must be preceded by a DAT.req(a,b,m,id,j) that by th SAP-a diagram must have been gene rated when SAP-a was in an a.linked(b,id) sta

A special signal DAT.skip(a,b,id,j) has been introduced in order to denote the act of decision to discard the data message. It is not externally observable and is needed only for the later statement of precedence between events.

In diagram 7 we control the failure process. The diagram implies that a FAIL.ind(b,a,id) must either be preceded by a FAIL.ind(a,b,id) signal, or followe by such a signal, or followed by a decision to discard the FAIL.ind(a,b,id) signal

Diagram 6: Transition Diagram for DAT(a,b,m,id,j)

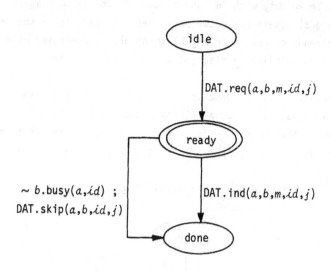

Diagram 7: The Process FAIL(a,b,id)

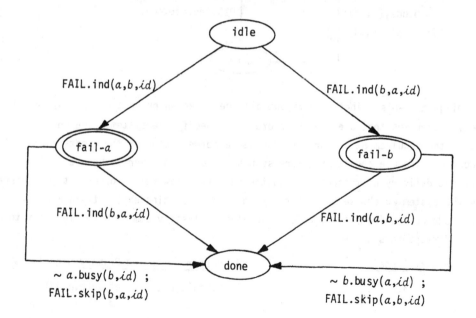

382

This decision is represented by a FAIL.skip(a,b,id) internal signal and is conditional on SAP-b not being busy with a under id. By the SAP-a diagram, the
FAIL.ind(b,a,id) signal itself may occur only when the SAP is in the a.busy(b,id)
super-state, i.e. already connected or establishing an id-connection with b.

Diagram 8, in a way similar to diagrams 6 and 7, controls the delivery of a disconnect signal from a to b under id. It ensures a response to each
DIS.req(a,b,id) signal. This response is either a delivery of a DIS.ind(a,b,id)
signal, or its deletion, signalled by a DIS.skip(a,b,id) signal that is possible
only when b is not id-busy with a. It also ensures, of course, that any such
response must be preceded by the proper DIS.req(a,b,id) request signal.

Diagram 8: The Process DIS(a,b,id)

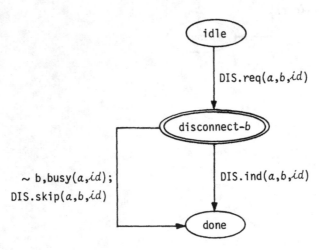

Diagrams 4-8 succinctly represent all the liveness properties and most of the
safety properties that are needed in order to specify the system. The only missing
part is the requirement of correct precedence between some of the events. We could
of course introduce a data structure such as a queue in order to ensure a first-in
first-out delivery of messages across the network. However in order not to overspe-
cify the system we choose the other alternative of stating explicitly a minimal set
of precedence requirement. The following table classify some of the signals into pr
mary and response signals:

Primary Signal	Responses to the Primary Signal
CON.req(a,b,id)	CON.ind(a,b,id) , Refuse(b,a,id)
DAT.req(a,b,m,id)	DAT.ind(a,b,id,j) , DAT.skip(a,b,id,j)
FAIL.ind(a,b,id)	FAIL.ind(b,a,id) , FAIL.skip(b,a,id)
DIS.req(a,b,id)	DIS.ind(a,b,id) , DIS.skip(a,b,id)

Note that in the case of FAIL signals, the DAT.ind signal is classified both as primary and as response signal (with different parameters). Furthermore for signals in this class not every primary signal is guaranteed a response.

We refer to the signals as belonging to one of the four classes: CON, DAT, FAIL and DIS, and then whether they are primary or response signals in that class. A general precedence statement is that signals of class c_1 *never overtake* signals of class c_2. The precise meaning of this statement is the following: Let p_1 and r_1 be a primary signal of class c_1 and its response, and let p_2 and r_2 be a primary signal of class c_2 and its response. Assume that p_2 happened *before* p_1, then if r_1 happens it can only happen after r_2. We can express this statement in temporal logic by the formula:

$$(\diamondsuit p_2 \wedge p_1) \supset (\sim r_1) \ U \ (r_2)$$

using the past operator $\diamondsuit$ and the *unless* operator U. The formula state, that being in a state in which p_1 just happens, and having p_2 happened in the past, r_1 will not happen unless r_2 happened first. Note that this implies that if r_2 never happens then so does r_1. An equivalent temporal logic formula is obtained by shifting the observation point to the occurrence if p_2:

$$p_2 \supset \Box[p_1 \supset (\sim r_1) \ U \ (r_2)] \ .$$

Using this basic notion of not overtaking, we complete the specification by the following precedence requirements:

1. No DAT signal may overtake another DAT signal.
2. No signal of the classes DAT, FAIL or DIS may overtake a CON signal.

Optionally we may also stipulate:

3. No CON signal may overtake another CON signal.

Requirement 1 is explicitly mentioned in the statement of the problem. Requirement 2 is needed in order to prevent the following anomaly:

CON.req(a,b,id),DIS.req(a,b,id),b.idle; DIS.skip(a,b,id),CON.ind(a,b,id),$\cdots$.

This behavior models the possibility that the DIS.req(a,b,id) signal arrived at SAP-b before the CON.req(a,b,id) did. It will find SAP-b at *idle* and hence decide to ignore the message, the decision being reflected by a DIS.skip(a,b,id) signal. Next, the CON.req signal arrives and SAP-b continue to establish the connection obvious to the fact that endpoint a is no longer interested in this connection.

This anomaly was resolved in the second approach by allowing point b to continue and send the CON.res signal and asking SAP-a to be sensitive to this signal and respond by a refusal. Here it is feasible to not let the situation develop as a result of the fact that all the signals carry a unique identification.

[H] Harel D. - Statecharts: A Visual Tool for the Design and Specification of Complex Systems - Weizmann Institute, Nov. 1983.

A CSP solution to the "trains" problem

A.W. Roscoe
Programming Research Group, University of Oxford

The problem as stated leaves one in doubt as to what one must do. Is one meant to abstractly specify the safety and liveness properties one desires of the network? Is one meant to provide some plausible "implementation" which gaurantees the basic principle that two trains must not be simultaneously on the same piece of track? Perhaps we are even meant to enter the realm of inventing scheduling algorithms for the flow of trains. Of course any complete solution to the problem must, in some sense, address all of these issues. The scheduling problem seems, however, to be outside the scope of the workshop.

The solution presented here is a CSP program which addresses the second question above. It can be proved to satisfy certain abstract conditions, and can of course be used as a base (guaranteeing safety) upon which to build any scheduling programs. It is by no means the simplest program which guarantees safety: instead it shows how CSP can be used to create a control structure more realistic than if, say, the actual events of a train entering or leaving a piece of track were "negociable".

The only approach we make towards scheduling is to allow trains to book line sections one step ahead, and to seek an alternative line if the first one they try to book is in use. The element of external control left in the network is in the hands of (notional) train drivers. It would of course be expected that the drivers be controlled and regulated by some signalling system; this higher level of detail is omitted.

Of course the particular control structure chosen here is only one of many which have the desired safety properties. No special merit is claimed for the particular solution given, and the reader is invited to devise his own program to model his own ideas on how the network should be regulated and controlled. The main purpose of this solution is to illustrate the power of CSP in precisely specifying parallel interaction.

As in all CSP programs, communication is achieved by the synchronisation of *events*, or *actions*, of the elements of the network. Each process has its own *alphabet* of events; in the operation of the network, an event can only occur if all the processes in whose alphabets it are willing to communicate it. This situation is easiest to imagine when no event is shared by more than two processes, since we then avoid the situation where three (or more) processes have to agree on some communication. This convention has therefore been followed in the present solution.

The following solution can be applied to any network of the form described in the problem, except that one simplifying assumption has been made. This is that all lines consist of only one section: of course, this restriction is not serious, as the old section boundaries can be transformed into (rather simple) extra crossing points. There are three types of process in the network: LINE, TRAIN, and CP (crossing point).

Each line has a unique name (typically λ), and two end (crossing-) points (typically α, β) which we assume distinct. In use, a line has a direction and becomes an ordered triple (λ, α, β) (the line with name λ, being used to travel from α to β). We will use the notation l and $\bar{l}$ to denote the two senses of any line, and follow the convention that $\bar{\bar{l}} = l$. If l is any (directed) line, $N(l)$. $S(l)$ and $E(l)$ will denote its name, starting point, and end point respectively.

For each line λ, there will be a process LINE(λ) in our network. It acts as a resource which, when not in use, is prepared to be acquired by either of its end points. When it is in use it tells anyone wishing to use it that it is unavailable. Whichever end it is acquired by, it is willing to be released by either (since a train might have travelled from one end to the other).

Thus, for each line λ, whose endpoints are α, β , we define

$$
\begin{aligned}
\text{LINE}(\lambda) \quad = \quad &\text{get}.\lambda.\alpha \rightarrow \text{con}.\lambda.\alpha \rightarrow \text{BUSY}(\lambda) \\
&[] \;\; \text{get}.\lambda.\beta \rightarrow \text{con}.\lambda.\beta \rightarrow \text{BUSY}(\lambda)
\end{aligned}
$$

$$
\begin{aligned}
\text{BUSY}(\lambda) \quad = \quad &\text{get}.\lambda.\alpha \rightarrow \text{dis}.\lambda.\alpha \rightarrow \text{BUSY}(\lambda) \\
&[] \;\; \text{get}.\lambda.\beta \rightarrow \text{dis}.\lambda.\beta \rightarrow \text{BUSY}(\lambda) \\
&[] \;\; \text{rel}.\lambda.\alpha \rightarrow \text{LINE}(\lambda) \\
&[] \;\; \text{rel}.\lambda.\beta \rightarrow \text{LINE}(\lambda)
\end{aligned}
$$

The alphabet of the processes LINE(λ), BUSY(λ) are defined to be the set of symbols which they can possibly use. Note that the alphabets of distinct LINEs are disjoint.

Each train has a unique name (typically t). The train runs around the network, controlled by its driver. Before it can reach a crossing point it must have a line booked on which to leave the crossing point (it is assumed for simplicity that trains always leave a crossing point on a different line to the one on which they enter it). When a train has no line booked it is prepared either to negotiate with its next crossing point to book one, or to reverse its direction of travel. When a train has a line booked it is allowed either to enter the new line (via the crossing point) or to reverse (which releases its booked line). We denote the set of all train names by T.

The process TRAIN(t,l) represents train t running along the directed line l, with no other line booked. The process TRAIN(t,l,l') (where E(1) = S(l')) represents train t running along line l with line l' booked at E(l).

Thus, when β = E(l), E(l) = S(l')   we define

$$\text{TRAIN}(t,l) \;=\; \text{reverse.t} \;\rightarrow\; \text{TRAIN}(t,\overline{l})$$
$$\square \; (\;\square_{S(m) \neq \beta} \; \text{book.t.m} \;\rightarrow\; \text{req.t.m} \;\rightarrow\; (\text{con.t.m} \;\rightarrow\; \text{booked.t.m} \;\rightarrow\; \text{TRAIN}(t,l,m)$$
$$\square \; \text{ref.t.m} \;\rightarrow\; \text{refused.t.m} \;\rightarrow\; \text{TRAIN}(t,l)))$$

$$\text{TRAIN}(t,l,l') \;=\; \text{reverse.t} \;\rightarrow\; \text{rel.t.l'} \;\rightarrow\; \text{TRAIN}(t,\overline{l})$$
$$\square \; (\text{goto.t.}\beta \;\rightarrow\; \text{arrive.t.l} \;\rightarrow\; \text{enter.t.l'} \;\rightarrow\; \text{leave.t.l} \;\rightarrow$$
$$\text{rel.t.l} \;\rightarrow\; \text{TRAIN}(t,l') \;)$$

Once again, the alphabets of TRAIN(t,l) and TRAIN(t,l,l') are the set of all events which they can possibly ever use. Communication with the driver has one of the forms "reverse", "book", "booked", "refused", "goto". All other events are communications with a crossing point. The alphabets of distinct trains are disjoint, and the alphabets of TRAINs are disjoint from those of LINEs.

Crossing points also have unique names (typically α, β). They have two roles. Firstly they act as intermediaries between TRAINs and LINEs. Secondly they control the timings of transitions from one line to another - specifically they only allow one train to be using them at any time (to avoid crashes). The solution given here treats these two aspects of their behaviour as independent; a more sophisticated solution might include a third parallel process representing a "register of bookings" to prevent "rogue" trains from entering, and perhaps to assist in the changing of points. (The solution here is good enough for the well-behaved TRAINs defined above.)

$$\text{CP}(\alpha) \;=\; \text{CP1}(\alpha) \;\|\; \text{CP2}(\alpha) \;, \quad \text{where}$$

$$\text{CP1}(\alpha) \;=\; \square_{\substack{S(1)=\alpha \\ t \in T}} \; \text{req.t.l} \;\rightarrow\; \text{get.}(N(1)).\alpha \;\rightarrow\; (\text{con.}(N(1))..\alpha \;\rightarrow\; \text{con.t.l} \;\rightarrow\; \text{CP1}(\alpha)$$
$$\square \; \text{dis.}(N(1)).\alpha \;\rightarrow\; \text{ref.t.l} \;\rightarrow\; \text{CP1}(\alpha) \;)$$

$$\square \; (\;\square_{\substack{S(1) \neq \alpha \\ t \in T}} \; \text{rel.t.l} \;\rightarrow\; \text{rel.N(1).}\alpha \;\rightarrow\; \text{CP1}(\alpha) \;)$$

$$\text{CP2}(\alpha) \;=\; \square_{\substack{E(1)=\alpha \\ t \in T}} \; \text{arrive.t.l} \;\rightarrow\; (\;\square_{S(m) \neq \alpha} \; \text{enter.t.m} \;\rightarrow\; \text{leave.t.l} \;\rightarrow\; \text{CP2}(\alpha) \;)$$

The alphabets of CP(α), CP1(α) and CP2(α) again consist of precisely the symbols which could ever be used by them. Note that the alphabets of CP1(α) and CP2(α) are disjoint, as are the alphabets of distinct CPs. Note further that with the exception of the "train-driver" commands described above, every symbol in the alphabet of a LINE or TRAIN is in the alphabet of some CP, and that every symbol in the alphabet of each CP is contained in the alphabet of some LINE or TRAIN.

The solution to the problem is thus

TRAINS || CPS || LINES

where TRAINS, CPS and LINES are respectively the parallel composition of all TRAINs, CPs and LINEs, correctly initalised to reflect their starting position.

The system as it stands has two levels of "user". Firstly, the TRAINs can be thought of as using the "network" which consists of the CPs and LINEs. To these users the communications between CPs and LINEs are irrelevant and should be hidden from them. We should thus form the process

NETWORK = (CPS || LINES)/L,

where L is the union of the alphabets of the LINEs. NETWORK is a process which interacts correctly with TRAINs without unnecessary communication. The second level of user is provided by the train drivers. To these users the "booking" communications between TRAINs and CPs are irrelevant and should be hidden. (The remaining communications are interesting since they reveal the train's position.) Thus to the drivers the system appears as

SYSTEM = (TRAINS || NETWORK)/B,

where B is the set of all symbols of the form req.t.m, con.t.m, ref.t.m or rel.t.m.

We thus see that CSP allows us to construct systems in a structured fashion, progressively hiding internal communication.

CSP also allows us to analyse our programs by abstract methods. We can, for example, specify and prove correctness properties of programs by using mathematical models such as "traces" and "refusal-sets". The traces model [H] lets us prove partial correctness properties of processes, by studying their possible sequences of communications (traces). Such a property one could prove of our present process SYSTEM is (for each line l)

$s \in traces(SYSTEM) \Rightarrow length(s|\{leave.t.l, leave.t.\overline{l} : t \in T\})$

$\geqslant length(s|\{enter.t.l, enter.t.\overline{l} : t \in T\}) - C,$

where C is 0 or 1 depending on whether there is or is not a train initially on l (or $\overline{l}$). (This property simply says that at no time can there be more than one train on any line.)

The slightly more complex refusal-sets model ([HBR], improved in [BR], [B] [R]) allows us to specify total correctness properties, for we study not only the traces of processes, but also the sets of communications which a process can refuse at each point in its history. A typical (and weak) property one could prove of SYSTEM is "freedom from deadlock" (i.e. at all times there is at least something SYSTEM can do.   This model would allow one to precisely analyse the causes of local deadlock and related conditions in SYSTEM.   In either model it is easy to show that the structured hiding used to construct SYSTEM has no effect on the external behaviour of the system: all hiding can be moved to the outside.

$$\text{SYSTEM} = (\text{TRAINS} \parallel \text{CPS} \parallel \text{LINES})/(L \cup B)$$

References

[B] S.D. Brookes, A Model for Communicating Sequential Processes, Oxford D.Phil Thesis (1983) (available as a Carnegie-Mellon Tech. Report).

[BR] S.D. Brookes and A.W. Roscoe, An Improved Failure-set Model for Communicating Processes, To appear.

[H] C.A.R. Hoare, A Model for Communicating Sequential Processes, Tech. Report PRG-22, Oxford University Programming Research Group.

[HBR] C.A.R. Hoare, S.D. Brookes and A.W. Roscoe, A Theory of Communicating Sequential Processes, Tech. Report PRG-16, Oxford University Programming Research Group. (To appear in an extended form in JACM, also presently available as a CMU Tech. Report.)

[R] A.W. Roscoe, A Mathematical Theory of Communicating Processes, Oxford D. Phil Thesis (1982).

The Train Set Problem

M. W. Shields

Electronics Laboratories
University of Kent at Canterbury

The layout is considered as being composed of a set *Sect* of sections. A section may contain cross-overs or points, but we shall not explicitly model these. Instead, we assume that:

(1) To each section S, there is a set X_S of entry points. We assume $X_S \neq \emptyset$.

(2) There exists a set of point settings P_S. At any time, a section will have its points set in such a way that precisely one train may enter the section at some entry point and leave it either at that point (by reversing) or at another determined by the points setting. A setting may thus be described by a partial injective function $\pi : X_S \to X_S$ satisfying $p \in dom(\pi) <=> p \in range(\pi)$ and $\pi(\pi(p)) = p$. P_S is a set of such functions.

(3) An entry point is a place where two lines of track, one from each section, are linked. We therefore require that each entry point p belongs to exactly two distinct sections.

With each section, we associate a control ("signal box") from which points may be reset and the movement of trains controlled. Each section will be considered independently powered, so that the "signalman" has complete control over the movement of trains on his section.

1. A CCS Description - Hack #1

We may represent a section by an agent written in CCS as follows:

$$Empty\_Sect_S(\pi) <= \sum_{p \,\in\, dom(\pi)} \alpha_p(tr).Sect_S(tr,\pi,p)$$

$$+ \; \beta_S(\pi').Empty\_Sect_S(\pi')$$

This equation may be read "Section S, if empty and with setting π, may either receive a train *tr* from one of its entry points p which is such that the points setting will allow it to exit the section in one piece, after which it is transformed into a section containing a train *tr* which has arrived from entry point p and which has points setting π - OR - it may receive a control signal from the signal box to change its points setting to π'.

The equation to describe a section which has a train in it is given below.

$$Sect_S(tr,\pi,p) <= \bar{\alpha}_{\pi(p)}(tr).Empty\_Sect_S(\pi)$$

$$+ \; \gamma_S \bar{\alpha}_p(tr).Empty\_Sect_S(\pi')$$

This equation is to be read as follows: a section containing a train *tr* which has arrived from entry point p and which has points setting π may either allow the train to leave the section from the other entry point determined by the points setting - OR - it may receive a control signal from the signal box to change the direction of the train, so that it reverses back through p.

Note that an agent $Sect_S$ may not receive an α signal, nor may an agent $Empty\_Sect$ transmit an $\bar{\alpha}$ signal. Informally, we may see from this that at most *one* train may be in a section at any one time and that no trains may come magically into existence at an entry point of an empty section.

The entire layout could thus be described by an expression:

$$Layout <= \underset{S \in Sect}{\prod} Empty\_Sect_S(\pi_S)) \backslash A$$

where A is the set of all ports α_p and π_S is some initial points setting of the section S. Intuitively, trains are passed from section to section through matching α ports. The restriction ensures that trains cannot be removed from or placed onto the layout from the environment...

2. A CCS Description - Hack #2

$\cdots$ which poses a slight problem. How do the trains get onto the layout in the first place ? Of course, we could modify the definition of the agent *Layout* so that it is a parallel combination of a mixture of *Sect*s and *Empty_Sect*s, but this is a rather boring way of going about things. Instead, we shall introduce a set of Engine Sheds, in which trains may be thought initially to reside. A shed D has a set of entry points X_D, which enable it to be linked to the rest of the layout. We modify constraint (3) above to:

(3') An entry point is a place where two lines of track, one from each section, or shed are linked. We therefore require that each entry point p belongs to exactly two distinct sections or sheds.

The equation for a shed is as follows:

$$Depot_D(T,p) <= \underset{tr \in T}{\Sigma} \bar{\alpha}_p(tr).Depot_D(T - \{tr\},p)$$

$$+ \alpha_p(tr).Depot_D(T \cup \{tr\},p)$$

$$+ \beta_D(p').Depot_D(T,p')$$

The may be read as follows: A shed D containing trains constituting a set T and with an entry point p set may either allow one of the trains to leave, via p, OR may allow a train to enter, via p OR may receive a control signal from the shed supervisor to change the free entry point to p'. If we add the engine sheds to the system we have:

$$Trains <= \underset{D \in Sheds}{(\prod} Depot_D(T_D,p_D) \underset{S \in Sect}{\mid (\prod} Empty\_Sect_S(\pi_S)) \backslash A$$

for appropriate values of the initial parameters.

It may now be argued that, trains being available, they will be passed from section to section without any undue creation, deletion or collision. However, the avid train-spotters among you may have noticed something - or rather not noticed something. Signals are passed from section to section, all right, but we can't *see* them. *Trains* is equivalent to an object which receives input but delivers no output. If we were less ambitious and did not include the control signals, but allowed the system to run in a non-deterministic manner, we would have the rather depressing equation *Trains* $\approx NIL$. (*NIL* is the agent that does nothing - a good description of a British Rail porter, but as for the system as a whole - let's be fair).

We may easily get round this by causing the *signalman* to output a signal $\bar{\delta}_S(tr)$ every time a train enter his section of track. The amended description of the track section would be:

$$Empty\_Sect'_S(\pi) <= \underset{p \in dom(\pi)}{\Sigma} \alpha_p(tr).\delta_S(tr).Sect'_S(tr,\pi,p)$$

$$+ \beta_S(\pi').Empty\_Sect'_S(\pi')$$

and for a section containing a train:

$$Sect'_S(tr,\pi,p) <= \bar{\alpha}_{\pi(p)}(tr).Empty\_Sect'_S(\pi)$$

$$+ \gamma_S \bar{\alpha}_p(tr).Empty\_Sect'_S(\pi')$$

while the equation for the whole layout would be:

$$Trains <= \underset{D \in Sheds}{(\prod} Depot_D (T_D, p_D) | \underset{S \in Sect}{(\prod} Empty\_Sect'_S(\pi_S)) \setminus A$$

3. A Note on Correctness

This section is only a sketch and requires a little familiarity with the more formal side of CCS. On the other hand, it is not technically very deep.

Intuitively, at any instant in time, the layout will be in a certain global state, which may defined by a vector V with coordinates corresponding to trains and sections. $V(tr)$, with have a value which describes whereabouts on the layout tr will actually be (some section or depot). $V(S)$ will give the current point setting and if necessary last entry point used. $V(D)$ will give the current free entry point.

We may use V to describe what we feel ought to be the behaviour of the layout, using it as a parameter to an expression $Trainsset(V)$. The body of this would be an enormous if statement, giving conditions under which various inputs or outputs could occur and the new value of the parameters of V which should hold afterwards. If V_o is the vector describing the initial values of the parameters to $Trains$, then in order to prove correctness, we would need to establish that:

$$Trains \approx Trainset(V_o)$$

The proof of this would involve case analysis, using the *expansion theorem*.

5. CONCLUSIONS

5.1 LANGUAGES AND THEORIES

The various notations or methods have been generally described as "theories" of concurrency. However there is a distinction between a *language* for describing objects such as behaviours and a *theory* of the same objects, behaviours, etc.. A *language* is adequate if it permits the articulation of the necessary basic concepts. A *theory* is adequate only insofar as it describes or contains those concepts: that is it says what kinds of thing constitute objects within the theory and what are the properties of such objects. Thus we may have an adequate language for, say, differential calculus without a theory of it. In such a case we could talk about an object without knowing what is sensible to say. A *scientific* as opposed to a mathematical theory, is yet a further step. One expects there to be some process of arbitration which can corroborate or refute a class of statements which are phrased in "empirical" (as opposed to theoretical) terms. There must therefore be a definition of real world phenomena for concurrent systems which constitute the empirical domain of the theory. Without this one has pieces of axiomatic mathematics without any scientific theory.

Are formalisms for concurrency such as were presented at this workshop languages or theories (mathematical or scientific), in the above sense? The participants in the workshop did not concern themselves with explicitly making claims that their theories were valid in this "scientific" sense, that is that they were valid models of "reality", and rightly so. There is not a unique empirical domain for theories of concurrency. Rather the implicit claims are of the form: "There are certain restricted empirical domains, applicable to certain useful classes of engineering endeavour, of which this language and this associated theory are a valid model." Such a restricted empirical domain could for example be the environment provided to processes by an operating system, and could include a much simplified model of time with no simultaneity. This puts a restricted, somewhat utilitarian, interpretation on "scientific theories". Rather than claiming "reality behaves like this model", the claim is "there is a useful range of engineering applications in which the empirical domain is restricted enough to conform to this model". Within this utilitarian interpretation, we would say that the formalisms comprised "languages" together with "theories".

5.2 THE NEED FOR A THEORY OF CONCURRENCY

Scientific Theories consist of schemes for constructing abstract models of the phenomena of some area of experience. In the case of concurrent systems the area is that of concurrent, communicating sequential processes of some kind. For a theory to be satisfactory it should fulfil a number of criteria. It should be explanatory, that is it should improve one's understanding of the phenomena and provide some simplification and generalisation of their behaviour. It should be predictive, that is the theory should be such that inferences can be drawn from abstract constructs expressed in the notation of the theory which can be interpreted as referring to observable phenomenological behaviour. Thirdly, and strongly associated with predictability, the theory should be testable; behavioural properties which are capable of being refuted by experiment should be predictable within the theory.

A number of questions now naturally arise. The "area of experience" is not a naturally occurring phenomenon such as the solar system; it is usually one or more artifacts (computer systems for example). Do we then still have the need for "scientific theories"? If so do the same criteria for the properties of a satisfactory theory apply? Since we are interested in constructing designs for concurrent systems and in constructing the systems themselves, what is the role of theories in the "engineering" process (of artifact design and construction)?

Traditional engineering disciplines are certainly related to scientific theories. Civil engineering design principles rely on theories such as Newtonian mechanics, and electrical engineering techniques are based upon electro-magnetic theory, for example. The theory enables the prediction of the behaviour of artifacts from their designs so that it is possible to propose a design and consider and discuss its behaviour before it is built. This is clearly beneficial since there is an opportunity to establish the suitability of a design before investing in its construction.

The process of developing an engineered artifact includes the following activities: analysing requirements in the application area and determining a need for a putative artifact; producing a specification which fulfils the requirement; developing a design which meets that specification. It is helpful if the engineer can be assured of the self-consistency of specifications and designs and that the designs satisfy their specifications. Also, less obviously, the act of formulating a specification expressed in a language whose semantics is derived from the abstractions of the theory can greatly assist in understanding the nature of the putative artifact itself and its application.

From these considerations we can discern some of the roles played by a theory in the engineering process. A theory which is predictive can be used as a semantics of design, since clearly it can predict the behaviour of designs. If the semantics derived from the theory is "constructive", that is if the semantics of a composite artifact is determinable entirely from the semantics of its parts, then the systematic construction of designs is facilitated. Insofar as a theory provides a means of expressing an abstract model of an artifact, such expressions can be used in the role of specifications. Less certain, but suggested by the foregoing discussion, is the possibility that the property of a theory being explanatory can assist the conceptual understanding of the artifact and its application.

This much is generally agreed and understood. The availability of several theories of concurrency and the fact that they have limitations results in a quandary. The majority of software engineering practice is emerging from a craft industry into some kind of engineering discipline. Ad hoc, craft techniques are slowly being replaced by methods based on a scientific theory. The choice of theory is still mostly being made in an ad hoc manner, usually by the person or group with most influence in a particular sociological aggregate choosing the formalism which most comfortably conforms with its cognitive models. Some more objective criterion is desirable.

The difficulty in choosing a theory is that different theories capture different views of an object. Certain kinds of property may simply not be expressible within the formalism of a given theory. We have not yet found a useful, objective, determinable and comprehensive way of categorising the concurrent systems which we wish to construct. As a result, matching the descriptive power of a given theory to a particular type of problem is not yet within our grasp.

5.3 CURRENT KNOWLEDGE

There are at present several groups of theories of the behaviour of concurrent systems: Net Theory, Temporal Logics, Algebraic schemes for describing behaviours such as CCS, Path Expressions, Event Systems and Vector Firing Sequences, Program-language-like schemes such as CSP, to name but some. These theories do not compete. That is to say they do not provide conflicting explanations of the same phenomena; they do not offer the possibility of contrary predictions of the behaviour of the same object, artifact, or system. Hence, in general, we cannot choose between these theories by the classical scientific approach of searching their fields of application for counterexamples to any individual one of them.

The differences between these theories lies in the views they provide of their objects of description. Some can describe aspects of behaviour which others cannot, and more often than not this relationship is symmetric. Some theories can describe particular facets more succinctly, in a way more easily related to human cognitive models of concurrent processes, more manipulably, or more mathematically tractably than others. It is possible to see how certain theories can be related to others, in that a behaviour described in the terms of one theory may be demonstrated to conform to that described in another.

Most of these differences are qualitative and some are somewhat subjective. There is at present no formulated framework within which theories of concurrency can be placed and related to each other. The result is that any choice of one theory over another, for whatever purpose, is most likely to be made for qualitative and subjective reasons.

5.4 PROGRESS TO DATE AND QUESTS FOR THE FUTURE

A major aim of the workshop was to try to find a "unifying framework" of theories of concurrency, so that choices of theory for the purposes of the engineering process can be made objectively. It was not to treat the set of problems as a benchmark and make comparisons between the presented theories based on it. This would have been premature. As is usual with workshops of this kind, the aim was unrealistically ambitious. This is to be expected, since workshops in general are structured in order to explore a problem area and its ramifications.

What progress has been made, then, towards reaching the aim? We believe we understand better the nature of the "need for a theory" in an engineering context. The problem of how to compare and relate theories of concurrency was recognised and discussed. The format of the workshop, namely that of posing a number of problems as a central theme, seemed to encourage useful discussion and comparison. In an attempt to crystallise this, a final session was held in which impromptu talks on the subject of "A Unifying Framework for Theories of Concurrency" were solicited. L. Lamport put forward the point of view that there was no unifying framework. Rather, let those concerned with the engineering process state what questions they wish to be answered, and then the proponents of the theories may be able to indicate which theories can answer particular types of question.

In order to determine what we need to know about different kinds of concurrent system, we need to be able to distinguish classes of system in a well defined manner; that is the distinctions between the classes needs to be determinable and precise. For this we need an understanding of the nature of concurrent systems which, as argued at the end of 5.2, at present escapes us.

Another talk in the final session of the workshop was given by M. Shields. He discussed the minimal properties one would assume about behaviours of non-sequential systems. These include an absence of "time-travel" and a partial ordering of atomic events. The behaviours of systems are then modelled as labelled sets of posets, and various notions of behaviour such as sub-behaviours and event consistency are modelled by order-theoretic properties. Using this approach, which is reported more fully in M. Shields: Non-sequential Behaviour 1 and 2 (Edinburgh University Department of Computer Science CSR-120-82, CSR-144-83), he adduces a relationship between different concurrency theories, namely order-theoretic event systems, certain nets, behaviour systems, CCS, trace vectors and modal logics.

A third talk was given by A. Pnueli. He categorised the approaches into two kinds, branching structures and sets of linear sequences. He showed that different kinds of properties could be inferred from different kinds of approach. Systems described in terms of sequences of behaviours can be demonstrated to be safe or otherwise. Descriptions permitting the statement of liveness properties can be composed and refined. Temporal logic can be grafted on to other formalisms.

The fourth talk in the final session was given by H. Genrich. He presented Net Theory as a unifying description with its own framework for concurrency. Processes are represented by particular net structures and the relationships between processes and systems are represented by mappings between nets. In this way nets and the morphisms between them form a category. He contended that the conceptual beginning of net theory is the study of the properties of concurrency, concurrency being a binary relation between "real phenomena", the co-existence of two events or two state occurrences. The nature of linear processes is such that they display the continuity phenomenon of linear orders and possess the properties of Dedekind continuity. He argued that net theory provides a general setting for the study of system theory.

5.5 SUMMARY

Any attempt to formulate a concept in a written language helps one's clarification and understanding. Expressing the concept in a formal language which constitutes a theory in the scientific sense assists yet further by providing a model which can simplify and generalise. It seems to the writer of these conclusions that a formalisation of general event systems may well constitute a theory with the attributes necessary to assist the understanding of concurrent systems, in the way which we require. It captures in a formal manner those minimal properties of time in the context of concurrent systems, and should therefore enable us to define special cases which separate concerns, for example to specialise by formalising properties of specific kinds of system (with, say, specific communication properties). At the same time such a formalism as presented by Shields in this workshop is sufficiently general that it would seem neither to prejudice the choice of formal language with which to express a design, nor to be a design language itself. On the other hand it does seem to provide a formal framework within which concurrent design languages might be classified. Shields develops and builds on substantial previous work of G. Winskel, P.Starke, J. Winkowski, and A. Mazurkiewicz, and in this writer's view the work of these researchers indicates a line of enquiry which is well worth pursuing.

In this discussion we have been trying to relate the search for a unifying theory of concurrency to the engineering development of concurrent systems. It may be worth emphasising further the relationship between the processes of engineering and phenomenological theories which are intrinsically mathematical in nature. The engineering process is one of discovery; that is the process of discovering the desired artifact. It is accepted that software artifacts or programs, whether comprising concurrent processes or not, are mathematical objects. (In fact one could well argue that the artifacts which are the result of any proper engineering discipline based upon a scientific theory are mathematical objects, for the theory comprises a mathematical model purporting to describe and capture the attributes of objects within that engineering domain. Therefore any artifact belonging to that domain will be describable, and have properties definable in the formalism of that mathematics.)

The engineering process is therefore one of mathematical discovery. There will be certain constraints, of course, imposed by the phenomenology of the application area. If the theory is adequate, however, one would expect such constraints to be expressible within its formalisms. We should therefore anticipate that the processes of engineering development will contain the same activities as those of mathematics: the activities of conjecture, proof, theory formulation, search for counter-examples, etc.

In conclusion we may summarise as follows. Whilst no philosophers' stone has been found, some progress has been made. We should feel more confident if we choose a particular theory (CCS, CSP, Path Expressions or whatever) as a basis for a method: we have at least the beginnings of a way of relating it to other theories; we should be able to identify its probable strengths and weaknesses in terms of abstraction, manipulability, support for provable inferences, and support for decomposition, structure and refinement; and we should have a reasonable idea of its role in our current favourite view of the engineering life-cycle (whatever that may be!).

Appendix: List of Participants

Academic Participants:

E.Abramsky	Queen Mary College, University of London, now at Imperial College, University of London
J.R.Abrial	
E.Astesiano	University of Genoa
H.Barringer	University of Manchester
M.Broy	University of Passau
R.M.Gallimore	UMIST
H.Genrich	GMD Bonn
A.Kaldewaij	University of Technology, Eindhoven
J.R.Kennaway	University of East Anglia
R.Kuiper	University of Manchester
L.Lamport	SRI International
P.E.Lauer	University of Newcastle-upon-Tyne
T.S.E.Maibaum	Imperial College, University of London
G.Milne	University of Edinburgh
R.E.Milne	STL
A.J.R.G.Milner	University of Edinburgh
U.Montanari	University of Pisa
C.Morgan	University of Oxford
B.Moszkowski	University of Cambridge
P.Mosses	University of Edinburgh, now at University of Aarhus
V.Pratt	Stanford University
A.Pnueli	Weizmann Institute of Science
W.P.de Roever	University of Utrecht / University of Nijmegen, now at University of Technology, Eindhoven
A.W.Roscoe	University of Oxford
J.Sifakis	University of Grenoble
P.S.Thiagarajan	GMD Bonn, now at University of Aarhus

Organising Committee:

B.Cohen	STL, now at University of Surrey
B.T.Denvir	STL
W.T.Harwood	STL, now at Imperial Software Technology
M.I.Jackson	STL
P.M.Taylor	STL, now at Brighton Polytechnic
M.J.Wray	STL, now at Imperial Software Technology

The following industrial participants assisted the organising committee by acting as session chairmen and rapporteurs:

T.R.Arnold	British Telecom
J.Cameron	Michael Jackson Systems Ltd.
J.Cartmell	Software Sciences Ltd.
A.Hill	CEGB
K.Jackson	Systems Designers Ltd.
P.Scharbach	GEC
R.C.Shaw	STC-IDEC
K.Turner	ICL

Workshop Secretary:

M.P.Eden	STL

Lecture Notes in Computer Science